In Celebration of Cricket

IN CELEBRATION OF CRICKET

KENNETH GREGORY

THE PAVILION LIBRARY

First published in Great Britain 1978

First published in the Pavilion Library in 1987 by
Pavilion Books Limited
196 Shaftesbury Avenue, London WC2H 8JL
in association with Michael Joseph Limited
27 Wrights Lane, Kensington, London W8 5TZ

Consulting Editor: Steve Dobell

British Library Cataloguing in Publication Data
In celebration of cricket.
1. Cricket—History
I. Gregory, Kenneth
796.35′8′09   GV913

ISBN 1-85145-144-7
ISBN 1-85145-116-1 Pbk

Printed and bound in Great Britain by
Billing & Sons Limited, Worcester

IN CELEBRATION OF CRICKET

Compiled and Introduced by Kenneth Gregory

Foreword by Sir Leonard Hutton

To K. H. S.

Foreword

by Sir Leonard Hutton

I have always found it most interesting to read of those cricketers who played before I was born, and of the period so often referred to as the Golden Age. I feel a great gratitude to the players of the 1870s and 1880s and of the years before the First World War. It was they who blazed the trail and played such an important part in the development of the game both in England and overseas. Having travelled the length and breadth of England in search of cricket, in South Africa, and across the vast continent of Australia, I can fully appreciate what those early players endured and how well they sowed the seeds of the game we know today.

I always regret I was unable to see W. G. Grace, Arthur Shrewsbury, Ranji, Sir Stanley Jackson, Spofforth and Tom Richardson, or – coming nearer to my own time – Ted Macdonald, the first Australian to play for Lancashire as a professional. I almost saw him when I was ten, but when I arrived at Park Avenue, Bradford, for my first Lancashire and Yorkshire match, the gates were closed. My first view of the men who wear the red rose was delayed until I played against them for Yorkshire.

I well remember playing against S. F. Barnes and Wilfred Rhodes, and the first ball I received from Harold Larwood. I was very frightened on all three occasions, but managed to overcome this fear. However I did retain this feeling of fear throughout my cricketing life when facing a bowler for the first time. Very often, when he ceased to be a mystery, I would become slightly bored. I hasten to add I did not become bored when facing the Australians Bill O'Reilly, Ray Lindwall and Keith Miller, who never gave me a moment's peace.

As a boy I often gazed at the pictures of old cricketers. They looked grim and tough with their moustaches and the odd beard here and there. The cricketers of the Golden Age certainly looked forbidding, but one of them played a most important part in my early career. His name was George Hirst – George Herbert, as he was known to his friends – the man who once made 2,000 runs and took 200 wickets in a season. I was with him when he was asked if he thought this record would ever be broken. George replied, 'I don't know. But whoever does it will be damned tired.' George Hirst was most kind to me. I first met him as a schoolboy, and in the years of my teens came to know him very well indeed. After a session at the Headingley nets, I would often carry his bag to the tram, and we would talk on the journey to City Square, Leeds. On one occasion – I would be fifteen or sixteen years old at the time – he placed his hand on my arm and said, 'Whatever you do, don't get like Victor Trumper.' This remark rather stunned me. After a long pause I asked him why. 'Victor Trumper was so superstitious that he made his life a misery. The trousers he wore for batting were renovated so much they bore only a slight resemblance to the original.' I tried not to be superstitious, but could not resist putting on my left pad first, and the breaking of a good bat that had brought me success was like losing a close relative.

I came to know Wilfred Rhodes very well in his later years. He was not an easy talker, but when he spoke he was well worth listening to. In a reflective mood, he once said to me, 'I bowled against some good 'uns, but the best was Bradman.' Wilfred played his last game against the Australians at Scarborough in 1930; Bradman made 96 but, as Wilfred said to me, 'I would have had him before he'd scored if I'd had a good mid-off.' Once, in my early days with Yorkshire, I saw Wilfred in the dressing-room during a match at Sheffield. I asked him if he could come round to the nets and bowl a few at me. For twenty minutes Wilfred bowled in his braces. It was a revelation: never before or since has a bowler made me misjudge the length of a ball as Rhodes did.

During the 1950–51 tour of Australia, a little old lady came to see me in my hotel at Sydney. She produced a cricket ball from the shopping bag she was carrying. 'Over forty years ago Mr Rhodes gave me this ball.' I looked at the ball: inscribed on it was one of Wilfred's greatest bowling feats in Australia. She went on, 'I thought perhaps Mr Rhodes would like his grandchildren to have this.' I brought the ball back to England and handed it to Wilfred at my earliest opportunity. He looked at the ball. I sensed that for a few brief moments the memories came back to him of that perfect Sydney wicket when he had dismissed the best batsmen in Australia. A nice smile came across his fine face; he turned to me and said, 'Thank you very much. How was she?'

Herbert Sutcliffe was a great hero of mine. I was fortunate to open the innings with him for Yorkshire. I found him most kind and helpful in every way. He was the finest player of the hook stroke I have ever seen, a fine judge of the short single, and no one could play fast bowling better. Herbert enjoyed Test cricket, particularly against Australia, which brought out his great Yorkshire fighting qualities. His association with Jack Hobbs was the best opening partnership cricket has seen. It was entertainment at its best, on good wickets or bad they were superb.

As a schoolboy I saw Donald Bradman make 309 runs in one day against England at Headingley. Open cricket was played in those days; containment had not been invented, and in the last hour of play England still bowled with two slips and a gully and no extra cover. Bradman moved his small feet quicker than any other batsman before or since; he played off both with a preference for the back foot, and his ability to find the gaps in the field was uncanny. He never used his energy to hit the ball straight to a fielder. Bradman and Hammond were the two batting giants in Australia and England at this period. Hammond's driving off the front foot was without equal; Bradman's pull stroke to mid-wicket was absolute perfection.

I think Walter Hammond was the finest cricketer I played with or against. He made batting so easy, graceful and effortless. His double century in the Lord's Test of 1938 was one of the finest innings I have seen. Batting with Walter was sheer delight; I never felt there was any possibility of a run-out or misunderstanding. He had a mental picture of the field before each ball was bowled. He could hit the ball like a horse. On one occasion in South Africa when I was batting with him, he hit a half-volley so hard in my direction that I could only turn and take a nasty crack between the shoulder-blades. I can still feel the blow. As a slip fielder, he was second to none – no diving to left or right, collecting green marks on his immaculate flannels. It was not necessary for Walter to spread himself on the ground as with normal slip fielders. His bowling action was just as graceful as all his cricket, the perfect sideways-on delivery which any aspiring bowler should copy. In his youth, I believe he could bowl very fast indeed. Walter was the complete cricketer, and I never tired of watching him. His walk to the wicket indicated that a master would soon take strike.

During the past thirty years we have seen cricketers who can be compared with the greatest in the history of the game. Sobers, Worrell and Weekes from the West Indies, Graeme Pollock, Barry Richards and Mike Proctor from South Africa, and Alec Bedser the great-hearted Surrey fast-medium bowler who came to Trent Bridge for the first Test against Australia early in June 1953 having already that year bowled something in the region of 500 overs. No captain of England had a greater trier than Bedser; he gave everything he had to cricket, on and off the field, and can be compared with the giants of the Golden Age. Colin Cowdrey and Peter May, with their sophisticated techniques, were both great players of the modern game and it is hard to imagine anyone better. Young cricketers of the future will be able to watch them on film, also the contrasting styles of two great entertainers with bat and ball, Miller and Sobers.

There are few good players in Australia; you are either a champion or a no-hoper. Keith Miller was a champion, he didn't believe in being second best. He was loaded with natural cricketing ability, and was a very strong man to go with it. No man played the game straighter than Miller. He would not appeal unless he thought you were out. He would be genuinely sorry if a batsman was given out to a bad umpiring decision. He would have made a fine captain. With the ball in his hand he could change the direction of a game in four or five overs. Keith was a positive cricketer who could not be defensive. I had some classic Tests with him and his friend Mr Lindwall.

Keith would open the bowling at three-quarter pace. I knew if I hit him for four all hell would break loose. He disliked being hit for four, ones and two's didn't upset him. On one occasion at Sydney I hit him for four; the ball hit the pavilion pickets with a crack. Miller applauded the stroke, but I wished I'd never played it. The next three deliveries were loaded with atomic energy. I survived, but more by luck than management.

Garfield Sobers played in his first Test against England at Sabina Park, Jamaica, in 1954. I was told I was going to see a young man who was going to be a very great cricketer. He did not make a great start to his Test career. He bowled slow left arm, and batted well down the order. He was slim and moved like a cat; he gave me the impression of being a nice, cheerful young player. He was orthodox, except for the odd flash outside the off-stump. Like Bradman, he had learned his cricket on the finest pitches in the world, pitches on which you could play strokes; sadly the young cricketers of England rarely do. As with all great players, Sobers saw the ball early. He had time, lots of time, to turn quick bowlers into medium-pacers. His feet moved as on skates; sometimes he would produce a stroke that really was unbelievable. He was one of the overseas players I would have liked in my team – Keith Miller was the other.

We are fortunate to have a fund of information on the great cricketers of the past, and for this we must thank our cricket writers, who have contributed so much to a hundred years or more of cricket. Their contribution has been immense; they have spread the gospel of cricket far and wide in many lands, bringing joy and warmth to many a cold, dark, winter's night.

The Masters

Token appearances by the above – Fry for Surrey and Richardson for Somerset have been ignored.

The periods during which the Masters flourished may be summarized as follows:

BEFORE 1914

Barnes, Faulkner, Fry, Grace, Hill, Jackson, Jessop, Lohmann, MacLaren, Noble, Ranjitsinhji, Richardson, Shrewsbury, Spofforth, Trumble, Trumper, Vogler.

BEFORE AND AFTER 1914–1918

Gunn, Hobbs, Macartney, Rhodes, Taylor, Woolley.

INTER-WAR YEARS

Constantine, Grimmett, Hammond, Headley, Larwood, McCabe, Mailey, Oldfield, O'Reilly, Ponsford, Smith, H. Sutcliffe, Tate.

BEFORE AND AFTER 1939–1945

Bradman, Compton, Donnelly, Hutton.

AFTER 1945

Bedser, Evans, Laker, Lindwall, Miller, Pollock, Richards, Sobers, B. Sutcliffe, Trueman, Worrell.

Those seeking a link between past and present may care to be reminded that Rhodes bowled at both Grace and Bradman, that Bradman faced Bedser who later played in the same Surrey side as J. H. Edrich – who scored his 100th first-class century in 1977.

Introduction

by Kenneth Gregory

One afternoon in the late 1960s, I watched a twelve-year-old attempt a sweep. As his games master snorted, I murmured something about Compton.

'He hit the ball,' retorted the aggrieved one. 'I remember seeing him ...'

A diminutive spectator in front of us turned, mouth open.

'Down at Hastings in ... Never heard of him, have you, boy?' The weight of forty summers seemed oppressive. 'Never heard of Compton. When I was your age ...' Inspiration came:

'Cowdrey, boy!'

The diminutive one's face lightened, his interrogator sighed at having made contact.

'He's a jolly good bat, sir.'

'I'm glad you think so.'

'Our Colts played against him last week.'

Age grabbed at its tottering senses.

'His father's quite good, too. Plays for England.' Pause. 'Or used to.'

In Celebration of Cricket seeks to remind the connoisseur of players and moments he has long cherished but perhaps has not thought of for a while, and small boys of whatever age that there were giants before they were born. Its form was suggested by the memory of an article in *The Cricketer* when that periodical celebrated its golden jubilee in 1971. The then editorial director, E. W. Swanton, asked G. O. Allen, L. E. G. Ames, J. H. Fingleton and W. J. O'Reilly to name the twenty greatest players of the half-century 1921–71. Not unnaturally, they disagreed in their selections but were unanimous (or would have been had not O'Reilly modestly omitted himself) concerning the top ten – five Englishmen, three Australians and two West Indians: D. C. S. Compton, W. R. Hammond, J. B. Hobbs, L. Hutton, M. W. Tate; D. G. Bradman, R. R. Lindwall, W. J. O'Reilly; G. A. Headley, G. S. Sobers.

Figuring on all lists but that of Ames were A. V. Bedser, C. V. Grimmett, H. Larwood and S. J. McCabe. Ames preferred F. S. Trueman to Larwood, and was alone in voting for K. S. Duleepsinhji, A. P. Freeman, H. Sutcliffe and F. E. Woolley.

And what of the half-century preceding the Great War? The year 1865 had witnessed the arrival in first-class cricket of W. G. Grace, who must obviously head the list, together with F. R. Spofforth, K. S. Ranjitsinhji* and S. F. Barnes, Arthur Shrewsbury (perhaps the founder of modern batting) and George Lohmann, Tom Richardson and Victor Trumper. Here problems begin to present themselves: should we prefer an exponent of the classic art of left-arm spin, Rhodes, or of a recently discovered skill, the South African googly bowler, A. E. Vogler?

Should H. W. Taylor, who during one Test series repeatedly confounded Barnes, be omitted? Should G. A. Faulkner, whose all-round skill rivalled that of Sobers? Happily, I have to discard none of these players, merely confess an inability to select the ten greatest masters of the earlier half-century. Homage is paid, sometimes in studies, often in eye-witness accounts of the giants in action. The occasional scorecard is added because, after all, a card is what puts even the most evocative prose into perspective. And since no reader can be expected to live continually on the heights, I have augmented glimpses of Mephistopheles (certainly Spofforth) and Hamlet (probably C. B. Fry) with one of that incomparable Gravedigger, C. I. J. Smith. Most of the masters are viewed in the context of Test cricket, the greatest artist being he who is greatest in the highest reaches of his art. Besides, many of cricket's most notable non-Test achievements went unnoticed until the following day, when sports editors realised they had sent correspondents to the wrong matches. As I turned over the pages of the 1921 *Manchester Guardian* to see what Neville Cardus had written of Armstrong's Australians, I was amazed to discover he had passed most of the summer watching Lancashire and likening that county's batting to the plays of Ibsen in sombre mood – which did not prevent Cardus, years later, from describing the Australian games in detail.

Those to whom statistics mean a rise in blood pressure will note their discreet usage, not to prove anything but to illustrate. For instance, the English, South African and West Indies Test bowlers who felt uplifted on dismissing Woodfull, Ponsford, Jackson, Brown or Fingleton without undue effort were premature in their elation, Bradman's

*I am indebted to Mr P. G. H. Fender for the memory of how, batting at Hove against S. E. Gregory's Australians in 1912, Ranji (by now H.H. the Jam Sahib – almost forty and overweight) regarded the bowling of C. E. Kelleway, W. J. Whitty, S. H. Emery, T. J. Matthews and C. G. Macartney with amused detachment. 'Would you like me', he asked his partner, 'to nominate my stroke before the ball is delivered?' Ranji made 125, and young Fender was impressed.

average on the fiteen occasions when he entered with the score less than ten being 106·23. So much for the terrors of a new ball. Bemused by the example of a cricketer who really should be referred to in these pages as HE or HIM – and to placate those who hate the sight of figures – I am encouraged to provide what is perhaps the ultimate in statistical application. Suppose the ten masters of 1921–71 (with T. G. Evans as wicketkeeper) had played as a team and contributed their highest Test scores – all, save O'Reilly, being capable of centuries. Such an ensemble merits the most determined opposition: I suggest the *Awful to Watch XI*, once outlined by Bernard Hollowood in a chapter of unbridled passion. For brevity's sake, and without permission, it will be referred to as Hollowood's XI. The location Lord's, and the duration five days, the hourly scoring rate of each innings (in brackets) has been strictly adhered to.

MASTERS' XI

J. B. Hobbs (46) bowled by full toss	211
L. Hutton (27) not out	285
D. G. Bradman (53) run out	334
Wides (Bailey attacking the leg stump)	27
Total (two wickets, declared)	857

Hobbs was dismissed a few minutes after five on the first afternoon at 326, the declaration being made at 5.19 pm on the second day. The remaining batsmen passed the time advantageously: Hammond (scratch) playing four rounds at Rye, Sobers at Sandown Park, Headley sleeping, and Compton at home – the last named having forgotten to turn up.

Hollowood's side thereupon decided to repeat their slowest hourly rate in Tests, and agreed that Boycott should be held back in the event of a collapse. At 11.58 am on the final day, after thirteen hours and twenty-nine minutes batting, the score was as follows:

HOLLOWOOD'S XI

P. E. Richardson (13) handled the ball	117
T. E. Bailey (9) retired hoarse	68
K. D. Mackay (7) hit ball twice*	31
K. F. Barrington (16) not out	82
G. Boycott (11) not out	17
No balls (O'Reilly's temper lost)	37
Total (two wickets)	352

* That is, in the same over. In 1956 Arthur Mailey reported with awe of having watched Mackay for half an hour at the nets, 'practising his letting-the-ball-go-outside-the-off-stump stroke'.

Two incidents related to this innings must be mentioned: on the fourth afternoon Mr Swanton entered the Long Room and turned the chairs so that sleeping members faced the wall, and at 11.58 am on the final day two groups of spectators, armed with pickaxes and shovels, invaded the arena and began to dig holes in the wicket. When interviewed on television, they denied any political motives – they were representatives of Wapping Young Conservatives and the City of London Socialist Workers' Party, adding they expected to be paid out of public funds. The match was accordingly abandoned. Fair-minded readers will not question the likelihood of the above events taking place, only the enormity of the Masters' score. They shall be reminded of 1 March, 1958 (that most dreadful of days for fielding sides), when Pakistan regretted the dismissal of E. D. Weekes for, with the Kingston scoreboard reading 602 for three – C. C. Hunte run out 260, Sobers not out 270, the incoming batsman was C. L. Walcott.

We must now consider the deterioration of cricket over the years. First, however, a confession which may substantiate or invalidate the opinions which follow. I have long believed that the years 1926–39 represented a second golden age in the art of batting, if not in depth, at the top. Consider how two Test sides might have batted had not the tragically early death of A. A. Jackson and the retirement through ill health of Duleepsinhji ordained otherwise; Jackson was an opening batsman, but as I admired the classical style of W. A. Brown, he shall go in later.

Australia, 1934: Ponsford, Brown, Bradman, Jackson, McCabe, Kippax, Woodfull ... As Grimmett and O'Reilly did most of the bowling, this order would have been possible.

England, 1938: Hutton, Barnett, Duleepsinhji, Hammond, Paynter or Leyland, Compton, Ames ...

But it was in 1938 that Woolley marked his retirement with an article in *Wisden:* 'I do not think there are so many good players in the game now as before the war', i.e. 1914. This was a view held by many with long memories; more debatable was Woolley's contention that before 1914 'there were something like thirty players up to his [Hammond's] standard and he would have been in the England team only if at the top of his form'.

Here two facts must be considered: the golden age blossomed during the years 1895–1905, and Woolley's career began in 1906. He was therefore comparing the Hammond of 1938 with players at the fag end of the golden age. Now could this proliferation of batsmen as good as Hammond have resulted from a paucity of outstanding bowlers? Again we must consider contrasting opinions. During the inter-war years, only

Tate and Larwood were generally regarded as being in the same class as their predecessors before 1914, yet during the century's first decade Ranjitsinhji had become increasingly critical of bowling standards. But if we suppose he was taking 1902 as a peak year (Hirst, Rhodes, Lockwood, Braund, Barnes and F. S. Jackson bowled for England in that year), we must also recall Jessop's view of that apparent peak – 'a dearth of good bowlers'.

Perhaps the golden age has been over-rated, perhaps that fine Australian batsman of the 1890s, F. A. Iredale, was right when he stated there was no one to take the places of Grace, Shrewsbury, William Gunn and Lohmann. Apparently not. Alfred Lubbock, a centurion for the Gentlemen in 1867, summed up the golden age *and* the years preceding it with grim finality; having first put W. G. in his place – 'always played carefully and never took risks' – the demolition continued with a swipe at the publication of averages, the reluctance to play in rain and darkness, the need for a tea interval, and the disappearance of fine hitting to leg – 'far more ornamental than Ranji's glances. From an onlooker's point of view I do not think the game (unless Jessop is in and scoring) quite so attractive or interesting as it was in the 1860s.' In short, cricket has been deteriorating ever since those distant years BC when, as Andrew Lang suggested, the Irish demi-god Cuchulainn played one hundred and fifty Colts of Ulster:

Colts b Cuchulainn	0
Cuchulainn not out	1

Probably the only season when a bowler took 1,000 wickets in May.

Cricket has appeared to deteriorate because, reflecting the times, it has changed. Most men, being conservative, do not like change unless it benefits themselves. With cricket now reflecting the uniformity of the welfare state, not to mention the vulgarity of the consumer society, it is not surprising that some middle-aged or elderly spectators long for a return to the cricket of the 1930s or (as they imagine it to have been) of the Edwardian age when the amateur presumably enjoyed £600 a year and a room of his own. I emphasise the role of the amateur because during the four home series against Australia, 1895–1905, exactly twice as many amateurs as professionals were chosen for England as specialist batsmen. And it is batting, either by its magnificence or drabness, which colours an age. We are apt to take for granted Trumble's bowling in 1902, although day after day it was as remarkable as Trumper's batting; 1930 will always be associated with Bradman but, as Woodfull was quick to point out, the Australians could have got by without him – whereas had Grimmett been injured, his loss must have been fatal.

Oddly, the revolution in cricket was legislated for in 1935, although its beneficiaries did not realise their power until 1950 or thereabouts when, as Sir Leonard Hutton wrote, 'I suddenly became aware that bowlers were no longer trying to get me out but to contain me.' In short, the serfs, aware of the weapon handed them, refused any longer to indulge the whims of the batting *seigneurs*. Understandable from the bowlers' point of view, it changed cricket as a spectacle and influenced the attitude of prospective viewers.*

As O'Reilly once confided, 'No one ever came to see me bowl, they came to see that so-and-so (meaning HIM) try to make hundreds off me.' Honours in that Titanic conflict were more or less even.

In 1935 the lbw law had been altered so that a batsman could be given out to a ball pitching outside the line of the off-stump, but only if the interception took place in the line of wicket to wicket. Batsmen had long used pad play as a legitimate part of defence, although they scored quite fast in spite of it. The 1935 lbw (New) ruling, as victims were classified in the scorebook, had been tried experimentally by the 'Second Class' or Minor Counties in 1902 but did not meet with the approval of the captains (one reason being that it might cause trouble in country areas with inexperienced umpires) and so was dropped. The intention of the administrators in 1935 was to help all types of bowlers and increase off-side play. One of the very few to advocate a reversal of the law after one year was the then England captain, R. E. S. Wyatt: 'My reasons are that it encourages bowlers to bowl off-breaks and in-swingers resulting in *less* off-side play.' Forty-one years later, in his farewell report as treasurer of MCC, G. O. Allen described the change in the laws as the most disastrous piece of cricket legislation in his lifetime, reducing off-side play, producing a race of front-foot batsmen, and contributing more than anything else to the demise of the leg-spinner and slow left-hander. To illustrate Mr Allen's final point, we should note the differing triumphs of two great wicketkeepers: in 1932 L. E. G. Ames of Kent claimed 100 dismissals (64 stumpings), in 1960 J. T. Murray of Middlesex 102 (7 stumpings).

In retrospect it seems clear that if any one season influenced the legislators, it was 1928 when, after a wet May, the little rain that fell was on the north of England. Half a century later, it seems idyllic and innocent. Roused by an earlier advertisement – 'Ponsford made over 400 with our cheapest bat', a rival firm let it be known that their bats would

* Myth has it that the two million who watched first-class cricket in 1947 did so because, lacking cars, they had nothing else to do. I prefer to recall the *great* stroke players on show: Hutton, Gimblett, Washbrook, Compton, Barnett, Emmett, W. J. Edrich, Cox, Hardstaff, Ames, Robertson and others, using their feet against battalions of spinners.

last for at least a season. *Wisden* wrote of Ames, one of its Five Cricketers, that he had not yet had any practice in standing back. Match after match produced a glut of runs (72 more than 1,000), 37 totals exceeding 500; 19 batsmen topped 2,000 (five 3,000), there were 414 centuries and 13 opening partnerships of more than 200. Freeman, who sometimes opened the Kent bowling with another leg-spinner, C. S. Marriott, reached 200 wickets on 27 July, and 300 on 15 September. Larwood bowled faster than any Englishman since N. A. Knox, and a strangely unholy communion was celebrated at Old Trafford on August Bank Holiday when 35,000 sat enthralled as Watson and Makepeace plundered 40 overs from Rhodes for 42 runs. Unhappily, the final day was rained out when it was possible that Lancashire (or Yorkshire) might have gained first innings points by late afternoon. It was a year when Somerset set out to awe their opponents with the handsomely hyphenated trio of H. S. R. Critchley-Salmonson, J. Madden-Gaskell and R. C. Robertson-Glasgow, when the West Indies played Wales and were soundly thrashed for their temerity. A fifty-five-year-old non-Welshman, S. F. Barnes, suffered from countless missed catches but finished with 48–14–118–12; Constantine defeated Middlesex almost single-handed at Lord's; Hammond performed incredible all-round deeds for Gloucestershire; serenely dominating the season however was Hobbs, his encounter with E. A. Macdonald in the Champion County (Lancashire) v The Rest game suggesting gentlemanly farce. The Master reached his century in an hour and three-quarters, followed by a further 50 in half an hour: Macdonald 30–3–183–2. As a result of these strange happenings, wise men at Lord's demanded larger stumps, a new lbw law to prevent pad play (presumably Hobbs had wasted much time playing Macdonald with his pads), and pitches on which batting would become difficult. As the argument continued, England's mature touring side – nine of the seventeen members were aged thirty-four or over – trounced Australia.

Those who wanted an end to 'batting' wickets had their prayers answered by the 1950s. One reason, I suspect, was the battering our bowlers, Test and county, received from touring sides after the Second World War. True, we beat South Africa in the Tests of 1947, the power of Melville and Nourse being offset by the superior brilliance of Compton and W. J. Edrich; after that, the deluge was supplied by Bradman's Australians, by Sutcliffe and Donnelly in 1949, and finally by Worrell, Weekes and Walcott. So bowlers began to act defensively on pitches which grew slower as the years went by. Eventually, the New Zealander J. R. Reid could say that whereas in 1949 there were perfect batting wickets everywhere in England, by 1965 there were only two. Meanwhile the appeal of first-class cricket diminished, partly because 'seamers' controlled events with over rates beyond belief. Naturally Test players took the hint, over rates which were tardy in the 1950s dwindling to 80 or so in a six-hour day by 1976. The official explanation was a surfeit of fast and medium-paced bowlers, no one recalling the inter-war years when gamesmanship was practised in more subtle fashion. On 26 June, 1926, while Australia scored 338 for six, England bowled 140 overs – three-quarters of them by Larwood, Tate and Root. A fortnight later at Leeds, Macartney scored a century before lunch which so disturbed the bowlers' rhythm that they managed only 132 in a day. Even at Leeds in 1948, when Lindwall, Miller, W. A. Johnston, Loxton, Bedser and Pollard (none of them slow) were in charge, the daily average was 112 overs.

The cynic may account for the difference between over rates in 1926 and 1976 by quoting Parkinson's Law: 'Work expands so as to fill the time available for its completion.' If a three-day Test (and they were generally the norm until 1947) could be expected to total 360 overs or so, then the daily overs bowled in a five-day Test must naturally be $\frac{360}{5}$, i.e. the 72 overs India and England obliged with in 1976–77. Those with a chaste passion for simple arithmetic have by now deduced that when Test matches are extended from three to five days, the hours available are increased by 57 per cent, but the overs bowled daily decreased by 36 per cent. Whether batsmen are facing fast bowlers with long runs or slow bowlers with short runs is irrelevant, it is now a captain's duty to guarantee the fewest possible overs by any means short of commanding his side to sit down and conduct them in a sing-song. Had a modern captain been in charge of England on 11 July, 1930, HE would not have scored 309 not out. Although a posse of 'seamers' – and today Larwood, Tate, Geary and Hammond would doubtless be so described – did most of the bowling, they were permitted or encouraged by their captain, A. P. F. Chapman, to send down more than 130 overs in just under six hours. A captain of the 1970s would have used his intelligence.

(*Bradman has pulled a ball from Larwood to the boundary, Tyldesley at mid-wicket growing even redder at the thought of retrieving it. England's captain walks across to Larwood*)

CAPTAIN: Have to pitch 'em up, Harold.
LARWOOD: Last time I pitched one up, he drove me past mid-on.
CAPTAIN: How about your bootlaces?
LARWOOD: What's wrong with 'em?

CAPTAIN: May be coming undone, better tighten them. Where's Maurice?

TATE: Hello, skipper. (*Confidentially*) That's Bradman batting.

CAPTAIN: Maurice, you've got the biggest feet in the side, scuff up Harold's foot-holds. He's bowling down wind, you might accidentally get some dust in Bradman's eye.

TYLDESLEY: (*Staggering back from boundary*) Ball, skip!

CAPTAIN: Dick, I think you'd better change places with Maurice Leyland.

TYLDESLEY: Ee! all way t' third man?

CAPTAIN: Just for a couple of balls, then change back again.

(*Tyldesley and Leyland slowly change places; Bradman is now only just visible through clouds of dust*)

TATE: Think that'll do, skipper.

CAPTAIN: (*Reflecting bitterly*) If only Harold would wear his hair long, we could send for a headband from my boutique. (*Cheerily*) Right! Good luck, Harold. Oh, hadn't you better take your sweater off?

LARWOOD: I'm not wearing sweater.

CAPTAIN: Nor you are. Put it on in case you get cold. (*Thinks*) Why doesn't he scratch his bottom? (*In voice of authority*) Come on, chaps. Bradman hasn't scored for five minutes.

(*Larwood bowls a ball to the off-side which Bradman cuts for four. Duckworth throws down his gloves and turns to Hammond*)

DUCKWORTH: Maurice and his ruddy great feet! I've got dust in mi eye.

(*Hammond borrows and unfolds the cleanest handkerchief on the field from Sutcliffe but fails to remove dust. England's captain signals to the pavilion; there is a long delay, followed by the emergence of a physiotherapist*)

LARWOOD: Can't bowl more, skip. Maurice's dug a hole a foot deep.

(*The captain signals to the groundsman. An early lunch or tea is taken*)

The only ploy a modern captain would not have used at Leeds in 1930 was the insult-from-silly-point one: 'Yah! why don't you try to score?' All the same, 80 overs in a day instead of 130* must surely have found Bradman a mere 200 not out at the close.

We are unlikely to see a batsman score 300 in a day against Test bowling again, just as the feat of D. W. Carr will remain in splendid

* It is possible to be too enthusiastic. At Fenner's in 1934, J. G. W. Davies dismissed Woodfull for 21 and Bradman for 0 – the latter with an off-break which did not turn. McCabe followed at 71, and the Cambridge bowlers queued up for the kill. At the close the Australians were 481 for five, Ponsford not out 229; in six and a quarter hours, and not all the bowlers could have been as slow as J. M. Barrie, the university got through 171 overs.

isolation, in cricket's theatre of the absurd. Consider the background: CARR, Douglas Ward, born 1872, played very little cricket at Oxford; bowled hopefully for the Mote Park and the Band of Brothers; aged thirty-two, begins to practise the googly – the following year discovers he has lost the leg-break; at thirty-six does quite well in club cricket, at thirty-seven makes his debut for Kent (against Oxford University) before returning to Mote Park. Would he care to play for the Gentlemen in their two matches against the Players? Be only too glad – takes 15 wickets. Would he care to play for Kent in the championship? Anything to oblige – 51 wickets in seven matches. Would he care to play for England against Australia? Well, if the selectors really want him to. Odd happenings at the Oval: perfect pitch, MacLaren insists on omitting his fast bowler – Carr opens attack with Barnes, bowls S. E. Gregory for 1. With the score at 9, MacLaren banishes Barnes to mid-off (where the bowler contemplates the height of his dudgeon), replacing him with Sharp whose tally of wickets for the season will total 26. Carr dismisses Noble and Armstrong lbw, and is then bowled into the ground. Match drawn, tactical genius of MacLaren in doubt. Lord Londesborough invites Carr to play for his side against the Australians at Scarborough: eight wickets for 105, including Bardsley, Armstrong and Macartney. Carr reacts modestly: 'In a short time everyone will be able to distinguish between the two breaks.'

We are unlikely to witness again the sartorial eccentricity which formerly delighted the eye. One of my favourite cricket photographs shows Chapman leading England out at Old Trafford in 1930. The captain wears his usual Quidnuncs cap, a young man at his elbow (I. A. R. Peebles) an Oxford sweater. In the context of the 1970s, such dress would be condemned as socially divisive, the matter referred to a government board; it would, had not a hugely beaming Tate – in his twenty-seventh Test and therefore presumably the owner of an England sweater, been sporting Sussex Martlets. It may be, of course, that the Sussex committee were acting as Tate's sponsors and paying him to advertise the county of his origins. (In 1977 an England player was driving an American-style automobile with his name on the side and the vital intelligence that his sponsors were . . .) The moral of this story is that, having flaunted his sweater, Peebles then proceeded to tie HIM in all kinds of knots, nearly bowling him first ball, having him missed by Hammond, and then caught by Duleepsinhji for 14.

We are unlikely to witness again a triumph of the ancients as the inter-war years did. Learie Constantine once pointed out that the leading English batsmen of the period reached their peak at thirty-five and, such consummate technicians were they by this age, maintained it for another seven years. But for the war, Hammond would certainly have supported this theory. At the start of the 1928 season, the quartet of Hobbs, Mead, Woolley and Hendren, whose combined ages totalled 162 years, were to make a further 247 centuries in first-class cricket. So with the slow bowlers. On 17 May, 1928, Freeman celebrated his fortieth birthday: during the next eight English seasons he was to take 2,090 wickets at 17·85. In Australia another balding gnome, Grimmett, was to reach his peak in his thirty-ninth year, after which he took a further 169 Test wickets before being unaccountably dropped for the 1938 tour of England. Needless to say, in the Australian seasons of 1938–39 and 1939–40 he was the most successful bowler – 100 victims in fourteen matches, and perfecting his 'wrong wrong 'un', a ball delivered like a googly that broke from the leg side.

We are unlikely to see any change from the current five-day (thirty-hour) Test matches, gate money and television fees being of primary importance. Until 1930 all Tests in England lasted three days – unless the final one in a series was played to a finish, against sides other than Australia until 1947. The argument that it is better to have a finished five-day Test than an unfinished three- or four-day one is irrefutable in theory, except that in practice a five-day Test is just as likely to be drawn. And after the Durban marathon of 1938–39 none will support the idea of timeless Tests as used to be the norm in Australia. Yet it must be said in their favour that neither side could play for a draw, in fact the only series between the wars to make spectators question the essence of timelessness was in 1928–29 when, after the breakdown of J. M. Gregory, the Australians were reduced to using Grimmett, among others, with the new ball, England's batsmen progressing slowly and irrevocably. (Whether Hammond scoring at 25 runs an hour could be boring is a matter of opinion.) In sum, however, five series between the wars saw the average match concluded half-way through the sixth (five-hour) day, the rains of Melbourne and Brisbane sometimes assisting. Timeless Tests promise purgatory, but comparing the four drawn matches of 1970–71 with the twenty-five finished ones of 1920–37, we find that the latter required only an additional 58 balls to produce a result. However, Australian wickets have changed, the shine is kept on the ball, field placings have become so scientific that scoring is almost impossible – so we are told – the implication being that O'Reilly and Verity permitted their fieldsmen to wander aimlessly around, that a modern timeless Test would last a fortnight.

What we are likely to see for the remainder of time are the garish advertisements now disfiguring cricket grounds. Doubtless if I had been brought up to watch Hammond, Barnett, Wellard and other west-country heroes against a background of rarely helpful advice, I should take the signs for granted. And most certainly I shall be reminded that concerts and opera performances are now sponsored; fortunately, when Rodolfo sings to Mimi that her tiny hand is frozen, my eye is not distracted by a large sign above the soprano's head – MYNN'S MITTENS. But in cricket, as in all else, progress is inevitable; perhaps advertisers should be encouraged to display moderation, the sense of compromise and simple adjustment we find in the utterances of that aristocratic cleric, the Reverend Lord Frederick Beauclerk, DD, who insisted that cricket was 'unalloyed by love of lucre and mean jealousies', before admitting it was worth 600 guineas a year to him. How much it is worth to the businessmen who skitted throughout the summer of 1977 brandishing cheque books, few can say. Certainly their generosity paled beside that of a German who offered £1·75 million to finance a chess match between Korchnoi and Fischer – a sort of single-wicket contest familiar to Beauclerk.

In Celebration of Cricket concerns cricketers I have watched with admiration, affection and awe – or would like to have seen – days when inspiration seemed to be governing events, and what can only be called odd occasions. My batsmen were all capable of destroying an attack (perhaps not Shrewsbury, but we know what W. G. thought of him), my bowlers supreme masters of their craft. If I *must* explain the inclusion of C. I. J. Smith, I shall do so thus: suppose Ranji, Bradman and Hammond were challenged to bat and employ only one stroke – say, glance, pull and cover drive. A Barnes or O'Reilly would know how to contain them. But allow Smith only one stroke and, as Mr Peebles tells us, it would have no effect on his batting. Besides, Smith brings back memories of provincial music halls, of whelks, and pints of old and mild. mild.

Other memories shall be less ribald. I remember the first county game I attended. Because the refreshment tent was close at hand, I sat at mid-wicket. I watched a slightly built man measure out his run; I noted that the wicketkeeper had decided to go for a walk. Not exactly, he suddenly stopped, then turned and squatted on his haunches. Sundry slips promised their undivided attention. The bowler ran up and, as the wicketkeeper took the ball shoulder-high, the batsman went through the motions of a forward stroke. This happened several times; few runs were scored, wickets fell, and I concluded the bowler was too fast. Which is all that need be said of Larwood.

A few weeks later I watched J. C. White, whose pace was slow to stationary, bowling at Hammond who, from time to time, thumped the ball into the covers while men in coloured caps went in token pursuit. I still think Hammond the most majestic sight I have seen on a cricket field. Once the Gloucestershire wicketkeeper received a blow in the face and Hammond stood behind the stumps to the sharp spin of Parker and Goddard. I wonder to this day why wicketkeepers bother to wear pads.

In due course I learned to hate. If this sounds an exaggerated way of describing a boy's reactions, let me remind readers that in the 1930s Yorkshire not only made a habit of winning the county championship but also of winning their matches with a day to spare. At least they did whenever I saw them. Granted Sutcliffe batted as one who, in his spare time, ruled some distant colony, there was certainly grim humour in Arthur Mitchell's defence, and Leyland, I heard, was a lovable character but his bat was broader than laid down in regulations. Occasionally, three of Bowes, Smailes, Verity and Robinson would find the opposition obdurate, the fourth one rarely did. It was too much. Yet Yorkshire cricket had its uses, especially when the Australians were touring. Then I expected the selectors to pick half the Yorkshire side for England – Australia might lose a Test, and a weakened Yorkshire its county game. Such was my reasoning. There must have been a flaw in it because Yorkshire would promote someone from the second eleven (he was generally called Smurthwaite) who proved to be better than Bowes. Later I grew more tolerant of Yorkshire perhaps because they possessed the perfect batsman. Once, soon after the last war, a large crowd had assembled in the Parks at Oxford to savour the greatness of the Master, by then Hutton having succeeded to Hobbs's title. An hour's serene play, caressing the ball with an eye on eternity, terminated by (I must confess) an unworthy stroke. As the Master departed, a very pretty girl passed me.

'What's the matter?' I asked.

'If Hutton's out,' she replied, 'I must go back to *Paradise Lost*.'

I think I can imagine how each of the supreme cricketers in this book played, all save one. Trumper, I am sure, was merely Hammond, McCabe, Barry Richards and a few more combined in one, Barnes was probably erect as Laker at the moment of delivery, and O'Reilly thereafter. I may be wrong in my conjectures but they make some sort of sense. What I cannot imagine is an innings by Jessop – a supreme cutter and a devastating driver, yes, but a man who would regard a good-length ball outside the off-stump with interest and then hit it over the square-leg boundary, him I cannot imagine. The nature of Jessop's logic escapes me. Not so memories of the greatest of batsmen (I glimpsed Hobbs but briefly in his old age), whom I would dearly love to see countering one of today's scientifically placed fields. Still I must own I saw Bradman on only four occasions: two centuries, a double century and one failure – out in the 80s. I was not surprised when he advocated an extension of the lbw law so that a batsman could be given out to a ball pitching outside the line of the leg stump. It would have meant as much to him as an extra stump or two, a smaller ball or a shorter pitch.

How anyone played O'Reilly when the ball was turning I cannot imagine. I wish I had seen Macdonald bowling at Hobbs, and Mailey at anyone, C. E. Pellew skirting the boundary in 1921. My favourite bowler for the desert island of my mind is Grimmett, the two cricketers I would bequeath to schoolboys yet unborn, Compton and Keith Miller. The sun was afraid not to shine when they strolled on to a cricket field. And if I must declare my own interest, the answer is simple – or would have been ten years ago. Today I must report that I have seen Woolley *and* Barry Richards.

Martha Grace, née Pocock

by Kenneth Gregory

Towards the end of 1859, as Lord Palmerston was settling into the prime ministership for the last time, Dr Henry Mills Grace was a worried man. Not that the recently published *Origin of Species* happened to be on his reading list, nor had he been disturbed by the sight of Landseer's lions in Trafalgar Square – and if the French wished to fight the Austrians, that was their affair. But could he, as captain, continue to include his fourth son in the West Gloucestershire Cricket Club side when other more experienced players were available? Two years previously, on the day after the boy's ninth birthday, he had watched him score 3 not out; after this effort, the boy lost form in spite of much practice in the orchard where even the stablelads bowled, while Don and Ponto, two pointers, and Noble the retriever performed wonders in the field. Dr Grace considered the outcome of the years 1857–59 and shook his head: Innings 19–Times not out 4–Runs 20–Highest score 5–Average 1·33. So very unlike his talented son, Edward, who played everything with a cross bat and scored freely. Ponto, who stood at mid-off, thought little of Edward. A dog with classical instincts, he watched a ball pitch outside the off-stump and immediately moved towards extra-cover in anticipation of a proper stroke. However, everyone else regarded Edward as a splendid batsman.

But if Dr Grace was worried, his wife was not. Less parochial in her outlook, and more concerned with fundamentals, she soon felt she should lend a hand in selecting the England XI. Accordingly she wrote a letter:

Downend,
near Bristol.

To Mr George Parr.

Dear Sir,

I am writing to ask you to consider the inclusion of my son, E. M. Grace – a splendid hitter and most excellent catch – in your England XI. I am sure he would play very well and do the team much credit. It may interest you to learn that I have a younger son, now twelve years of age, who will in time be a much better player than his brother because his back stroke is sounder, and he always plays with a straight bat. His name is W. G. Grace.

I am, Sir,
Your obedient servant,
Martha Grace.

She had presided over the progress of W. G. with dedication. Given a bat at an age when most boys were still busy with rocking-horse and bricks, he did nothing for several years but learn to stop the ball. Runs were of small account, thought Mrs Grace, unless a batsman was technically well-founded. A half-century against Clifton in 1860 may have been a great achievement for a boy of twelve, but Mrs Grace was not unduly elated, just as she was not unduly depressed by a succession of failures during the next two years. W. G.'s bat was straight, and he whose bat is straight will have all other things added unto him.

In due course, that is, for in the early months of 1863 W. G. suffered a serious attack of pneumonia. His father prescribed, his mother succoured, and W. G. rose from his bed inches taller than any of his brothers, though no less diminished in strength. Back to the orchard for practice and maternal advice, and then he began the season with a score of over eighty. No longer was he content to stop the ball; in his own words, 'I decided to put bat to ball.'

Not that it was always gratifying to have Mrs Grace in attendance. When W. G. played for the Gentlemen of England against Oxford University in May 1866, he contrived to get himself caught at short-leg off a half-cock stroke (one he was very soon to master), and departed downcast. As well he might, for a few moments later spectators heard some terrible words uttered: 'Willie, Willie, haven't I told you over and over again how to play that ball?' A pause, an apologetic 'Yes, mama'. Then, and 'Go out and practise it at once.' Doubtless Mrs Grace added a few words concerning the correct placement of the front foot for the forward square-cut. As the years passed, the sons grew more devoted to their mother, and she to them and her grandchildren. If she was unable to attend an important match, the score sheet would be posted to her night by night – not infrequently telegrams arrived at Downend with vital intelligence:

GILBERT DUCK TODAY BAD STROKE ME FORTY-TWO STOP EDWARD

to be followed, more likely than not, by

SECOND INNINGS ME TWO HUNDRED NOT OUT EDWARD WAITING STOP GILBERT

All details relating to W. G.'s prowess were cut from newspapers and magazines by Mrs Grace and pasted into scrapbooks for perusal and analysis during the winter evenings. Yet her interests extended far. During important matches at Clifton, she would sit in the centre of the grandstand and receive the leading players of the age on the completion of their innings, commending virtue and dismissing incompetence with unpleasing comment. As she disliked left-handed batsmen as a matter of principle, and was aghast when fielders jerked in the ball underhand, offenders tended to avoid the grandstand. Mrs Grace reigned supreme, her son the most discussed man in England and certainly setting a better example than did Mr Gladstone. *His* bat, it might be owned, was taken up straight but came down with marked indications of casuistry – not that this word was used at Downend.

In the summer of 1844, when Gloucestershire were playing Lancashire at Old Trafford, Martha Grace died suddenly aged seventy-two. Flags were lowered, the game abandoned, and E. M. and W. G. hurried home. But if the mother of the Graces had gone, cricket remained. So it is fitting that today the Births and Deaths columns of *Wisden* enshrine the memory of only one woman:

> Grace, Mrs H. M. (Mother of W. G., E. M., G. F.), b July 18, 1812, d July 25, 1884

She must enjoy the discomfort felt by the shade of E. M., for her cricketer sons are referred to neither alphabetically nor in order of birth. Still, Willie took her advice and made sure his bat was straight.

*

Now, of course, there are fashions in heroes. It is a fascinating topic which has unfortunately not fascinated the biographers who might have written perceptively about it. I imagine that in the great age of Greece, which is assuredly not today, a hero who was not manly enough to weep in public would never have been acceptable to the mass of the people. In the glory of Rome, a hero had to have an air of triumphant brutality, a kind of brazen humour, to take the fancy of the mob. In Victorian times, a hero was a good deal more complicated. He had to imply that sport was no joke, that life was real and earnest, that he could take the rough with the smooth, and also reveal a streak of artfulness and stubborn eccentricity, before people could see him as one of themselves, only larger than life. Such a man was Dr W. G. Grace, the superhuman cricketer of all time, but characterful enough to accept with courage the death of a son and a daughter, human enough to have had a pretty rough time earning his medical degree. *Alistair Cooke*

W. G. Grace

The young Grace dominated the game as no one else before or since. During the years 1867–76 he played 280 completed innings with an average of 57, the next best figure of 36 being obtained by combining the ten most productive seasons of *seven* other men. Grace also took 840 wickets.

However at this time a cricketer was judged by his success in the Gentlemen v Players matches; if the Players won twenty-two of twenty-four games from 1850 to 1864, and the Gentlemen seventeen of twenty-five from 1867 to 1876, the change-about was due primarily to the presence of a single man. To have taken 128 wickets at an average of 14 was an achievement but, considering the change in the preparation of pitches over fifty years, it is incredible that Grace could equal the deeds of the other supreme batsman in Gentlemen and Players matches:

1867–76	Grace	Innings 41	Runs 2540	Average 65
1919–28	Hobbs	Innings 34	Runs 2281	Average 71

These were decades, incidentally, when both batsmen scored eleven centuries. Bradman, inevitably, had two even more devastating spells in Test cricket – eleven hundreds in twenty innings (March 1929–February 1932) and in twenty-two innings (January 1936–January 1948).

But after Hobbs and Bradman had made each of eleven centuries, they spent days either watching other members of their sides do the same or fielding to centuries by their opponents:

1936–48	Bradman	11 centuries, other batsmen 31
1919–28	Hobbs	11 centuries, other batsmen 27
1929–32	Bradman	11 centuries, other batsmen 18

However, when Grace made his eleven hundreds, the others totalled *four* – not least, of course, because W. G. proceeded to bowl out the opposition.

The *Daily Telegraph* summed up the situation in 1869: 'Not merely is Mr Gilbert Grace the best batsman in England; it is the old story of the race: "Eclipse first, the rest nowhere".'

Grace's Style

by the Hon. R. H. Lyttelton

A batsman with style in the sense of L. C. H. Palairet Grace is not, nor ever was. His strokes went to the ropes, but they seemed to do so as the result of perfect timing, coupled with arm, shoulder and body work, not wrist. If I had to describe in a word the secret of Grace's miraculous success, I should say it was his power of correct timing. He got the full weight of bat, arms, shoulders and body on to the ball at the very right second; and if a player does this, though his muscular development may be very small, still it is surprising how hard the ball will be hit. Grace, however, is a man of enormous stature, muscle and weight; and when these gifts are added to perfect timing the result is complete, not to say brutal, effectiveness. When dealing with a ball outside the off-stump, Grace seems to fall over it and absorb it with his terrific weight; the full power of his shoulders and his gigantic frame make the ball look a very feeble thing, merely to be directed wherever he pleases, but of elegance and absence of effort there is none. In the case of Palairet, Druce, or H. K. Foster, there would be a graceful movement, a hit like a flash of lightning, apparent absence of effort, the ball among the spectators and cover-point looking at it with his arms akimbo. It was the same with his on drive, or leg hit. With Grace every muscle of his body seems to go into the stroke; it gives the spectator a sense of effort and ponderous weight; but all in combination with absolutely perfect timing, the eye watching the ball like a hawk.

Fast bowlers against Grace in his prime knocked him about when they got a rough wicket to bowl on, which they frequently did, but Grace stood knocking about because, comparatively speaking, he got far less of it than other bats. Grace's power of placing fast bowling is a gift that belongs to him, and to him alone. He does not hit at it in the sense of slogging; neither does he appear to play either forward or back; but no matter what the length he is on the ball, and hitting it absolutely at the right moment. He appears to push it past the fields, and to have an instinct within him which tells the exact position of every field, and the power to put the ball out of reach. A beautiful fast leg-stump ball, Grace somehow or other shoves past short-leg for two runs, while an ordinary player would be perfectly content if he had only stopped it. I remember one occasion when Tom Emmett, in those days a very fast bowler, made a ball get up and hit Grace a tremendous crack on the funny-bone, a most painful blow as all of us know, but after a little interval Grace went on batting, and the very next ball he hit tremendously hard on the on-side for six. To slow bowling, however, Grace always appeared to me to bat with less confidence. He did not often leave his ground, though I remember that in one match on a difficult wicket, when Bates and Peate were making the ball perform extraordinary antics, Grace was the only man on the side who smothered the ball on the blind spot by stepping out and driving it. The other bats were conscious that the bowler was having a good time, and this fact made them play in a cramped way, standing fast to their ground. Consequently the bowlers pitched the ball up and the batsmen played back, thus being unable to smother the ball before the twist could work. Grace, therefore, was the only man who compelled the bowler to bowl rather short, and a twist is no good in the case of a short ball. But on hard wickets, to slow bowling, Grace did not leave his ground half so frequently as W. L. Murdoch or A. G. Steel. The consequence was that slow bowlers pitched the ball up to him with less fear of being driven. Still, notwithstanding all this he scored gigantically against all bowling, and in his prime a side was comparatively happy when it got Grace out for under 60 runs an innings.

It has always been to me a matter of regret that the Australians, with their new methods, and splendid variety of bowling, never met Grace when in the very tip-top of his play. It is true that he had not long passed his prime when they came over here in 1878, and it is also true that he scored very largely against them, though he probably found Spofforth, Boyle and Turner three of his hardest nuts to crack. My belief in his superlative skill is so great that I believe he would have made havoc of even their bowling if he had happened to have met them in his prime, and no greater praise can be given a player than this. [*1900*]

Gentlemen v Players

PLAYED AT LORD'S, 29 AND 30 JUNE 1868– GRACE AGED NINETEEN

Had I been a wicketkeeper or a batsman at Lord's during this match, I should have liked (*plus* my gloves and pads) to have worn a single-stick mask, a Life Guardsman's cuirass and a tin stomach-warmer. The wicket reminded me of a middle-aged gentleman's head of hair, when the middle-aged gentleman, to conceal the baldness of his crown, applies a pair of wet brushes to some favourite long locks and brushes them across the top of his head. So with the wicket. The place where the ball pitched was covered with wet grass wetted and rolled down. It never had been, and never could be, good turf. I send a specimen or two for your inspection.

I have no hesitation in saying that in nine cricket-grounds out of ten within twenty miles of London, whether village green or county club grounds, a local club could find a better wicket, in spite of drought and in spite of their poverty, than a Marylebone Club supplied to the Players of England.

Frederick Gale

The Gentlemen won by eight wickets.

THE GENTLEMEN

First innings		*Second innings*	
E. M. Grace run out	1	not out	22
B. B. Cooper b Willsher	28	not out	0
W. G. Grace not out	134		
C. F. Buller b Grundy	4	b Wootton	0
R. A. H. Mitchell b Willsher	1		
H. A. Richardson b Grundy	8		
W. F. Maitland b Lillywhite	2		
V. E. Walker c Pooley b Lillywhite	5		
C. A. Absolom b Lillywhite	3	c Grundy, b Lillywhite	8
J. Round b Lillywhite	0		
R. Lipscomb run out	7		
B 5, lb 3	8	B	1
Total	201	Total (two wkts)	31

First innings	O	R	W	*Second innings*	O	R	W
Wootton	16.3	39	0	Wootton	7.1	15	1
Silcock	18	26	0				
Willsher	16	34	2				
Grundy	25	63	2				
Lillywhite	14	31	4	Lillywhite	7	15	1

THE PLAYERS

First innings		*Second innings*	
H. Jupp c Absolom, b W. G. Grace	4	run out	14
G. Summers b Lipscomb	5	c and b Absolom	4
J. Ricketts c Mitchell b W. G. Grace	1	b Lipscomb	13
James Lillywhite junior c Maitland b W. G. Grace	0	b Absolom	0
W. Mortlock b W. G. Grace	9	lbw b E. M. Grace	19
E. Pooley b Lipscomb	21	c Buller b Lipscomb	4
F. Silcock run out	0	b W. G. Grace	26
T. A. Mantle c E. M. Grace b W. G. Grace	12	b W. G. Grace	4
G. Wootton b W. G. Grace	8	c Richardson b W. G. Grace	18
J. Grundy not out	29	c E. M. Grace b W. G. Grace	8
E. Willsher c Round b Absolom	22	not out	3
B 1, lb 3	4	Lb 2, w 1	3
Total	115	Total	116

First innings	O	R	W	*Second innings*	O	R	W
W. G. Grace	32	50	6	W. G. Grace	20.1	31	4
Lipscomb	29	52	2	Lipscomb	29	27	2
E. M. Grace	8	8	0	E. M. Grace	17	23	1
Absolom	5.1	1	1	Absolom	26	32	2

Umpires: T. Hearne and H. Royston

1885

At Scarborough the Gentlemen v Players match was played on a treacherous pitch, the Players' bowlers including Peate ('it is the opinion of those who have watched Yorkshire cricket most closely and longest, that of the great trinity of slow left-handers, Peate, Peel and Rhodes, the first was also the greatest' – H. S. Altham), W. Barnes, W. Attewell, W. Flowers and G. Ulyett.

THE GENTLEMEN

W. G. Grace c Emmett b Attewell	174
C. W. Wright c Scotton b Barnes	4
F. M. Lucas b Attewell	7
T. C. O'Brien c Hunter b Ulyett	21
F. Townsend b Ulyett	2
H. W. Bainbridge b Attewell	14
K. J. Key lbw b Attewell	4
H. V. Page b Flowers	1
A. H. Evans lbw b Ulyett	14
S. Christopherson not out	9
E. W. Bastard c and b Attewell	7
B 5, lb 1	6
Total	263

THE PLAYERS 59 (Christopherson seven for 24) and 179 (W. Gunn 82; Evans five for 20)

1876

On 3 July, at Lord's, W. G. scored 169 for the Gentlemen, hitting Tom Emmett for a six and a seven in the same over – to the chestnut trees, all run out. In due course he arrived at Canterbury where, appearing for Kent and Gloucestershire, he caught out five of the England side before making 91. Then began a remarkable August week:

THURSDAY, 10TH: Kent total 473, Lord Harris 'cutting Grace again and again in his polished Eton way'.

FRIDAY, 11TH: Grace fails, MCC collapsing for 144 and obliged to follow on. Deciding he might as well travel home to Bristol that evening, W. G. announces that he will hit out. He does so. At the close of play is 133 made in an hour and fifty minutes, out of 217 for four.

SATURDAY, 12TH: Grace continues to bat and impresses *The Times:*

No one attempted to forecast the result, and few, if any, dreamt that Mr Grace would rub out the debt of arrears himself. But he did. This feat puts into the shade that of Mr Ward in 1820, whose score of 278 has till now been regarded as the most wonderful of its kind on record. The enormous total of 344 completed by Mr Grace on Saturday occupied six hours and a quarter, thus giving an average of 57 runs per hour. He had to contend against all the Kent bowlers save one. Three of them went on three times and three twice. In one instance Mr Yardley bowled from the right arm and then from the left. Never was a more striking exhibition of endurance against exhaustion manifested. To explain the progress it may be well to say that play began at 12 o'clock on Saturday, and in 90 minutes the overnight total of 217 advanced to 323, and ten minutes later the arrears were pulled off. At 4.35 Mr Grace had scored just 300, and at 5 o'clock the figures 500 appeared on the telegraph, of which total Mr Crutchley claimed no ordinary share. Mr Turner, after resisting several changes of bowling, fell to the first ball delivered by Lord Harris. Six wickets 506. Now came the close of Mr Grace's career – caught at mid-off, and great was the joy thereat.* His score of 344 contained 51 fours, 8 threes, 20 twos and 76 singles ...'

* *The Times* omitted to mention that in mid-afternoon W. G. adjourned to the officers' tent and, while the fielders lay prostrate, knocked back much champagne and seltzer. This revived him.

SUNDAY, 13TH: Travels home in heat wave.
MONDAY, 14TH: At Clifton against the powerful Nottinghamshire side, W. G. makes 177 out of 262 in just over three hours. 'The sun was hot and great the punishment.'
TUESDAY AND WEDNESDAY, 15TH AND 16TH: Heat wave continues, Richard Daft and Oscroft open with partnership of 150 for Notts. However, in the second innings W. G. takes eight for 69, Gloucestershire winning by ten wickets. As the defeated crawled home, they encountered the Yorkshire team on a railway platform and were mocked for their vain endeavours.
THURSDAY, 17TH:* Gloucestershire bat first against Yorkshire at Cheltenham – close of play 353 for four, Grace 216 not out. 'Lockwood, who was captain of Yorkshire, found it difficult to get anyone to bowl. A pathetic appeal to Allen Hill to "have another shy at the big 'un," was declined. Tom Emmett said: "Why don't you make him, you're captain?" "Why don't you bowl yourself," retorted Hill, "you're frightened." "Give me the ball," answered Emmett – and sent down three consecutive wides.' After the first evening, Tom observed: 'Dang it all, it's Grace before meat, Grace afterwards and Grace all day, and I expect we shall have more Grace tomorrow.'
FRIDAY, 18TH: Emmett's fears justified. W. G. carries his score to 318 not out. Grace's 839 in a week, made out of 1,336 while he was at the wicket, occupied seventeen and a half hours, and included 2 sevens, 4 sixes, 4 fives and 103 fours. In the three matches he also took 15 wickets for 20 runs apiece.

It was in 1876 that a United South of England side travelled north to play XXII of Grimsby. One Canon Tatham later recalled that everyone thought W. G. was lbw when he had made 6; a stern look at the umpire decided the matter – 'Not out'. All twenty-two of Grimsby fielded and fifteen bowled, Grace carrying his bat for 400 out of 681. 'It was subsequently stated that his score was 399, not 400, one being added' – presumably to avoid friction.

Awed by the above, and other happenings, the *Saturday Review* (now best remembered for Bernard Shaw's theatre notices in the 1890s) paid tribute:

Modern cricket has produced the greatest cricketer the world has ever seen, or probably ever will see. Mr W. G. Grace's two brothers are far above the ordinary run of players, but Mr W. G. Grace stands by

*A remarkable day, the first performance of *Götterdämmerung* being given in Bayreuth.

himself far beyond the reach of rivalry. The public will go any distance to see Mr Grace, and the public are very much dissatisfied if they cannot see him almost every day in the season. But there is no use in having Mr Grace on one side unless there be three or four crack bowlers on the other. Mr Grace and his brothers are men of exceptional physique, and can travel all night and play cricket all day without fatigue or discomfort. The champion, as he is called, is wholly indifferent to atmospheric influences. The hotter the weather the better he plays. Nor do he and his brothers confine themselves to batting only. When their turn comes to take the field they do the ordinary work of an eleven. It is a blazing July noon, and the Players of England have just taken the field. They have already had three long and fatiguing days against the Gentlemen at the Oval, and now their task is going to begin over again. The thermometer in the sun stands at about 110°, and there is no shade at Lord's. There is a goodly ring of spectators, and the Pavilion is well filled. The scorers have ensconced themselves in the retirement of their box, in company with what, on closer inspection, turns out to be a jug of goodly proportions. The umpires have adjusted the wickets and fixed the bails, and are now standing in that attitude of contemplation of nothing in particular by which the umpires are usually distinguished. Here comes the champion, as cool and collected as ever, and ready for the fray. As he walks to the wicket, a shudder passes through the fieldsmen at the thought of the hot and weary hours that must elapse before that tall figure executes its return march to the Pavilion. Long-leg retreats to a far-distant corner, wondering how many hundred yards of ground he is expected to cover. Cover-point wakes himself up to meet the hits that will come straight at him with the velocity of lightning. A sturdy Yorkshireman, bare-armed to the elbow, takes up the ball. There is a moment of hushed expectation, and even the umpire, for the very love of dear life, feels it necessary to keep both eyes open, and to watch the game. The champion stands in his well-known position – he has described it himself for our benefit – and so he will be standing two hours hence. He begins cautiously – few really great men are rash – the bowling against him is the best England can produce, and for a few overs he feels his way. But the hitting soon begins, and, what is still more aggravating to the opponents, the scientific placing of the ball which frustrates all attempts to get the field in the right position. The bowling is changed, this and that expedient is tried, but without avail. At length the heat of the weather begins to produce its effect. The deliveries of the fast bowlers are less deadly, cover-point and long-leg do not run so briskly as they did, and the batsman takes advantage of the opportunity to launch out with increased vigour and freedom.

The umpire, while taking a furtive glance at his watch to ascertain the distance of time that divides him from his dinner, is very nearly cut in two by a vicious hit to square-leg, and one of the scorers is observed to disappear suddenly from sight amid a crash as of broken crockery. After the interval matters mend, but little from the outside. Hour after hour passes, and there is the champion in his old position. The field becomes demoralised, the bowlers are utterly exhausted, even the boys at the telegraph can hardly summon up strength to put up the numbers that are so perpetually increasing. At last, some desperate appeal is made for leg before wicket, and an umpire, long since unconscious of what was going on around him, decides against the batsman. Immediately, eleven men prostrate themselves on the ground in a state of collapse, and the champion marches indignantly to the Pavilion, inveighing against the stupidity of umpires, deploring his ill-luck in being given out just when he was so well set, and explaining to all who listen to him how impossible it is that, with his system of placing the feet, he could ever be leg before wicket. The match of which this is a sketch is but an example of dozens of other matches of which Mr Grace is the hero. Modern cricket, in fact, seems to have resolved itself into a match between Mr Grace on one side and the bowling strength of England on the other. Will the former succeed in knocking the latter out of time, or will the latter be ultimately able to restrain the former within some reasonable bounds? At present, Mr Grace has clearly the mastery over his opponents. His powers, so far from showing signs of diminution, are showing signs of increase. No longer content with his hundreds and two hundreds, he has gone in this season for scores of three hundred and upwards, and there seems no reason why, if he can find anyone to stop in with him, and run his runs with him, he should not next season make five hundred off his own bat. How can a few bowlers of eminence hope to cope with such a man, who can go on all day, and every day in the week, and who, to all appearances, will be as good ten years hence as he is now? [*1876*]

Ten years hence? Nineteen years later, when aged forty-six, W. G. accomplished one of his greatest feats. Said *The Times*:

At Lord's yesterday,* the scene of so many of Dr Grace's great cricket triumphs, the most wonderful player of our time achieved another feat marked by all his old excellence. From noon until nearly half-past six he was at the wicket, and then, being a little wearied by his hard work

*The previous week, when making 257 and 73 not out against Kent, W. G. had been obliged to share the headlines, Oscar Wilde being sentenced to two years' imprisonment.

under a hot sun, in a declining light, he was beaten by a ball from Dr Thornton, which kept low and which he played outside. It must be something of a record even for Dr Grace to make over a thousand runs in the first month of the season. By his 169 yesterday his aggregate for the ten innings played by him in a little over three weeks reaches 1,016. The champion seems to have taken a fresh lease of his cricket life. He seemed determined to make a big effort yesterday to get the thousand runs, and this and the fine bowling and fielding caused an unwonted steadiness in his play. Before luncheon he batted beautifully; but afterwards he was a little slow in getting back his game – in fact, for a few overs he played Mr Nepean's slows very badly, and once or twice put the ball up dangerously towards the fieldsman. Still, the exercise of more care and his anxiety to reach the four figures did not make his cricket less attractive. There was all the old power in the drive and the cut, while few balls to leg escaped unpunished. Dr Grace has played many a quicker innings; but the bowling and fielding were very good, and Hearne and Rawlin were especially difficult to score from. He made some bad strokes and narrowly escaped being run out midway through the innings. He was batting altogether for a little over five hours, and was ninth out at 362. An idea of his rate of scoring will be gathered from the fact that he made 50 out of 108 in an hour and a half; his 100 was scored out of 198 in three hours, and his last 69 occupied two hours and a half. He hit 21 fours, 5 threes and 11 twos. At the different landmarks, so to speak, of the innings the crowd of 7,000 who had come up to Lord's were very enthusiastic, and when at last it was over the champion had a wonderful reception, the members in the pavilion rising to applaud him. [*31 May, 1895*]

*

At Lord's the same season, on a very fast and fiery pitch, W. G. made 118 for the Gentlemen against the bowling of Tom Richardson and Mold. In 1902, when a few days short of his fifty-fourth birthday, he made 82 at the Oval, playing S. F. Barnes with 'ease and agility'.

F. R. Spofforth

Spofforth struck me as being a very remarkable man possessed of rare mental ability and of other assisting personal qualities which enabled him to bring to a successful conclusion almost anything he took in hand. He started as a fast bowler and then studied medium-pace and slow bowling, his objective being a completely disguised combination of the three paces; and those who saw him bowling at his best will remember to what perfection he attained in this direction. His action on delivery was exactly the same for all of the three paces, and it was in his magnificent concealment of change in the pace of his bowling that he stood out from all other bowlers of all time.

J. W. Trumble, writing in 'The Times', 26 July, 1928

What a sight it was to see Spofforth bowling when the game had to be pulled like a brand from the burning! He looked the Demon every inch of him, and I verily believe he has frightened more batsmen out than many bowlers have fairly and squarely beaten. *George Giffen*

ENGLAND v AUSTRALIA, 1882

by H. S. Altham

Few people regarded the approaching Test Match at the Oval with anything more disturbing than eager interest. The England Eleven was selected by Lord Harris, Mr Burbidge, and Messrs V. E. and I. D. Walker, and the names when published must have read well enough to reassure all but the most determined Jeremiahs. The batting seemed overwhelmingly strong; with the exception of Peate, 24 was the lowest average of any member of the side, and the batting order was so insoluble a problem that No. 10 on the list had perforce to be, in the first innings, A. N. Hornby and in the second C. T. Studd. In bowling, Peate and Barlow could both show remarkable figures up to date, whilst Ulyett in the last Australian match with Yorkshire had taken seven of their wickets for 89, and Steel and Studd had both met with considerable success with the ball in the games with Cambridge Past and Present and Middlesex respectively.

Most important of all, perhaps, was the fact that Palmer, who had bowled with splendid consistency all the tour, was at this time *hors de combat*. Surely, then, as the crowds streamed into the ground on the morning of Monday, 28 August, all the omens must have seemed favourable, and few of them can have dreamt that before sunset on Tuesday they would have seen, 'the first flight of the winged victory from the White Cliffs of Albion to the long wash of Australian seas'.

When the Australians came down to breakfast in their familiar quarters in the Tavistock Hotel, Covent Garden, the anxieties uppermost in their minds must surely have concerned the weather and the toss. Autumn was hard upon the heels of spring. There had been heavy rain in London on the Saturday, and more again in the early hours of Monday, and it was morally certain that the Oval wicket could not improve. It must then have been no small relief to them when Murdoch beat Hornby, the English captain, with the toss, and at ten minutes past noon, on a ground already packed thick with eager spectators, Massie and Bannerman went down the pavilion steps to face the bowling of Peate and Ulyett. The morning's play brought to Australia nothing but disaster; at one time six wickets were down for 30 runs, and though Garrett and Blackham then made a plucky stand, only 18 more had been added when the teams left the field for luncheon.

Punctually at a quarter to three the game was resumed, and in the first over young Maurice Read delighted his Oval friends by catching Garrett beautifully at long-off; twenty minutes later the innings was over, and that for 64 runs, the lowest score that the tourists had made in all their thirty matches to date. Certainly the English bowling had been steadiness personified – fourteen consecutive maidens at one period – and Barlow's figures of five wickets for 19 runs in 36 overs were splendid; but the Australian batting was in several cases nerveless and unworthy of them, and they must have taken the field a sadly chagrined team.

When Spofforth yorked the Champion for a paltry 4, and got Barlow caught at forward point with the total no more than 18, their spirits leapt up again; but then Ulyett, after an agonising first over, hit well, Lucas defended with a cool head and a classically straight bat, and the score crept up to within seven of the Tourists' total, when the Yorkshireman, with something of the light-heartedness that had given him the name and the nature of 'Happy Jack', danced out to Spofforth, missed him, and was bowled. From that moment the tide turned; two runs later Lucas was caught at the wicket, and with Studd clean bowled and Alfred Lyttelton also captured by Blackham off his gloves, six wickets were down and the scores were but equal. Barnes failed, a plucky stand by Steel and Maurice Read then added 26 precious runs, but Hornby only just managed to hoist the hundred before falling to one of the 'Demon's' deadliest breakbacks. Peate gave no trouble, and the Australians left the field 38 runs down, but comforted in the knowledge that after their batting collapse of the morning they might easily have had to face twice as big a deficit.

The clouds that were gathering as they drove home afterwards in their hansoms to an anxious meal and an early bed broke during the night, and a heavy downpour, as they were setting out again next morning, made play impossible until ten minutes past twelve. Barlow, in his interesting book of reminiscences, has recorded his opinion that the conditions were at that time unfit for cricket; the ball was like soap, and the mud in the bowlers' holes so bad that the groundsmen had to remove it with a spade before they could be filled with sawdust. It was Australia's great chance, and splendidly did Massie and Bannerman take it; the latter defended grimly, while Massie took his life in his hands and went for the bowling. Runs came fast in spite of bowling changes, the arrears were cleared off and W. G. Grace was seen to be pulling anxiously at his beard. At last Steel induced him to hit across a straight half-volley, and Massie's great innings was over – 55 runs in as many minutes out of a total of 66. Clever bowling changes by Hornby soon got rid of Bonnor and Horan, and with Bannerman and Giffen also gone, England began to breathe again, but a little shower eased the wicket a trifle once more, and Murdoch played a captain's innings, only terminated by a brilliant piece of combined work in the field by Hornby, Studd and Lyttelton, and when the last wicket, Boyle's, fell, Australia was 84 runs on.

George Giffen has told us how in the breathless ten minutes that divided the innings the Australians desperately debated their chance, how Spofforth declared that 'this thing can be done', and how they filed down the pavilion steps ready to do or die. A general cheer greeted them, followed by a deeper one still when it was seen that Hornby had elected to open the last innings himself with Grace. Spofforth, at the Vauxhall end, and Garrett began the bowling, and with the score at 15 the 'Demon' beat and bowled the English captain. Barlow followed, only to meet with the same fate his very first ball. The crowd was silent, grimly intent, but the next half-hour saw their enthusiasm and confidence revive, for in that time Grace and Ulyett added 36 priceless runs. Thirty-four only wanted, and eight great batsmen to get them. Surely the bitterness of defeat was past. But at 51 Spofforth, who had crossed over to the pavilion end, whips down his extra fast one at Ulyett, the Yorkshireman plays for the break-back which is not there, just snicks it – Blackham does the rest. Two runs later Grace tries to drive Boyle, just fails to reach the pitch of the ball, and is well caught at mid-off – 52–4–32. Lucas is joined by Lyttelton, who hits a splendid four and the score creeps up to 60.

Now comes the real battle. Boyle and Spofforth set their teeth and bowl as they have never bowled before; maiden follows maiden, four of them, eight of them, twelve of them in succession. Then Spofforth whispers to Murdoch and Bannerman, the latter purposely misfields a hit of Lyttelton's, and he is down at the far end facing the 'Demon', with the dark background of the pavilion behind the deadly arm. Four more maidens and a devastating break-back shatters his stumps; the last act of the drama has begun. Steel can do nothing, and at 70 is sucked out by Spofforth's slow ball and caught and bowled. Maurice Read, who had done so well in his first Test Match innings, is entirely beaten by his second ball and seven wickets are down with 15 runs still wanted. But Lucas is still there, cramped, it is true, by the wonderful bowling, but meeting it with indomitable nerve and resource; surely he and Barnes and Studd can pull us through together? Barnes, one of the most brilliant professionals of the day, and Studd, who has already twice topped the century against these self-same terrors. Five runs are added, precariously enough, and then a gasp goes up all round the ground – Lucas has played on. 75–8–5.

Whether Studd was really as nervous as 'Buns' Thornton subsequently declared – 'walking round the pavilion with a blanket round him' – can never be proved, for the tragic fact is that he never got a ball. Lucas had fallen to the last ball of Spofforth's over, and the first of the next from Boyle jumped up quickly and Barnes was caught at point off his glove. Peate – *spes ultima Troiae* – was a poor, but not a negligible, batsman. He had made 20 in his last innings against the Australians for Yorkshire, and now it only needed one fair hit from his bat and another from Studd's to land England home the winner. Peate, it is evident, means to settle the thing out of hand. He hits his first ball dangerously to leg for two, is all but bowled by his second, plies his bat like a flail at his third and knows that it has been his last.

That accomplished writer, Horan, has told us something of the desperate intensity of that last half-hour, how one spectator dropped down dead, and another with his teeth gnawed out pieces from his umbrella handle; how one English batsman's lips were ashen grey and his throat so parched that he could hardly speak as he passed the writer in the field on the way to the wicket; how the scorer's hand trembled so that he wrote Peate's name like 'Geese'. Giffen relates how, when Peate's wicket fell, the crowd sat for a moment voiceless and stunned, and then broke over the ground in one wild rush to cheer the men who had won the fight.

Spofforth was carried shoulder-high into the pavilion, and if ever a man made cricket history it was he that day. Fourteen wickets for 90 runs was his share of the spoil, and at the final crisis he had bowled his last eleven overs for two runs and four wickets.

Punch paid him tribute in the following lines:

Well done, Cornstalks, whipt us
  Fair and square.
Was it lucked that tripped us?
  Was it scare?
Kangaroo land's 'Demon', or our own
  Want of devil, coolness, nerve, backbone?

At the end of the week the *Sporting Times* published the now historic obituary notice which started the saga of 'The Ashes'.

In Affectionate Remembrance
of
ENGLISH CRICKET
which died at The Oval
on
29th August, 1882.
Deeply lamented by a large circle of
Sorrowing Friends and Acquaintances
R.I.P.
N.B. – The body will be cremated and
the Ashes taken to Australia.

[*1926*]

AUSTRALIA

First innings		*Second innings*	
A. C. Bannerman c Grace b Peate	9	c Studd b Barnes	13
H. H. Massie b Ulyett	1	b Steel	55
W. L. Murdoch b Peate	13	run out	29
G. J. Bonnor b Barlow	1	b Ulyett	2
T. Horan b Barlow	3	c Grace b Peate	2
G. Giffen b Peate	2	c Grace b Peate	0
J. McC. Blackham c Grace b Barlow	17	c Lyttelton b Peate	7
T. W. Garrett c Read b Peate	10	not out	2
H. F. Boyle b Barlow	2	b Steel	0
S. P. Jones c Barnes b Barlow	0	run out	6
F. R. Spofforth not out	4	b Peate	0
B 1	1	B 6	6
Total	63		122

First innings	O	M	R	W	*Second innings* O	M	R	W
Peate	38	24	31	4	21	9	40	4
Ulyett	9	5	11	1	6	2	10	1
Barlow	31	22	19	5	13	5	27	0
Steel	2	1	1	0	7	0	15	2
Barnes					11	5	15	1
Studd					4	1	9	0

Fall of wickets: 1–6, 2–21, 3–22, 4–26, 5–30, 6–30, 7–48, 8–50, 9–59, 10–63

1–66, 2–70, 3–70, 4–79, 5–79, 6–99, 7–114, 8–117, 9–122, 10–122

ENGLAND

First innings		*Second innings*	
R. G. Barlow c Bannerman b Spofforth	11	b Spofforth	2
W. G. Grace b Spofforth	4	c Bannerman b Boyle	31
G. Ulyett st Blackham b Spofforth	26	c Blackham b Spofforth	15
A. P. Lucas c Blackham b Boyle	9	b Spofforth	2
Hon. A. Lyttelton c Blackham b Spofforth	2	b Spofforth	10
C. T. Studd b Spofforth	0	not out	0
J. M. Read not out	19	b Spofforth	0
W. Barnes b Boyle	5	c Murdoch b Boyle	2
A. G. Steel b Garrett	14	c and b Spofforth	0
A. N. Hornby b Spofforth	2	b Spofforth	9
E. Peate c Boyle b Spofforth	0	b Boyle	2
B 6, lb 2, nb 1	9	B 3, nb 1	4
Total	101		77

First innings	O	M	R	W	*Second innings* O	M	R	W
Spofforth	36.3	18	46	7	28	15	44	7
Garrett	16	7	22	1	7	2	10	0
Boyle	19	7	24	2	20	11	19	3

Fall of wickets: 1–13, 2–18, 3–56, 4–59, 5–60, 6–63, 7–70, 8–96, 9–101, 10–101

1–15, 2–15, 3–51, 4–53, 5–66, 6–70, 7–70, 8–75, 9–75, 10–77

Umpires: R. Thoms and L. Greenwood

G. A. Lohmann

by C. B. Fry

He made his own style of bowling, and a beautiful style it was – so beautiful that none but a decent cricketer could fully appreciate it. He had a high right-over action, which was naturally easy and free-swinging, but, in his seeking after variations of pace, he introduced into it just a suspicion – a mere suspicion – of laboriousness. Most people, I believe, considered his action to have been perfect. To the eye it was rhythmical and polished, but it cost him, probably, more effort than it appeared to do. His normal pace was medium; he took a run of moderate length, poised himself with a slight uplifting of his high square shoulders, and delivered the ball just before his hand reached the top of its circular swing, and, in the act of delivery, he seemed first to urge forward the upper part of his body in sympathy with his arm, and then allow it to follow through after the ball. Owing to his naturally high delivery, the ball described a pronounced curve, and dropped rather sooner than the batsman expected. This natural peculiarity he developed assiduously into a very deceptive ball which he appeared to bowl the same pace as the rest, but which he really, as it were, held back, causing the unwary and often the wary to play too soon. He was a perfect master of the whole art of varying his pace without betraying the variation to the batsman. He ran up and delivered the ball, to all appearances, exactly similarly each time; but one found now that the ball was hanging in the air, now that it was on to one surprisingly soon. He had complete control of his length, and very, very rarely – unless intentionally – dropped a ball too short or too far up. He had a curious power of making one feel a half-volley was on its way; but the end was usually a perfect length ball or a yorker. He had that subtle finger power which makes the ball spin, and consequently he could both make the ball break on a biting wicket and make it 'nip along quick' on a true one. He made a practice of using both sides of the wicket on sticky pitches. If he found he was breaking too much, he would change from over to round the wicket, and on fast pitches he soon had a go round the wicket at a batsman who appeared comfortable at the other sort. But he was full of artifices and subtleties, and he kept on trying them all day, each as persistently as the others, one after another. With all his skill, he would never have achieved his great feats but for his insistence of purpose. He was what I call a very hostile bowler; he made one feel he was one's deadly enemy, and he used to put many batsmen off their strokes by his masterful and confident manner with the ball. He was by far the most difficult medium-pace bowler I ever played on a good wicket. [*1900*]

EGO (i)

Those who perpetually assert that pre-1914 war cricket was infinitely better than the between-the-wars cricket, and those who say that the days when W. G. wore his beard were the greatest days of all, do much unfairness to our own times, but it is true that character was more in evidence than it is now. The reason is to be found in the pattern and texture of the Victorian age. It was an age of richness in individual character. Dickens is often dismissed as a caricaturist who distorted men and women out of their natural size and habits, but it is nearer the truth to say that he was an inspired reporter who found his material lying prodigally heaped round him. He was fortunate in that he was born into an age which possessed a super-abundance of energy, did everything with all its might and had Herbert Spencer as its prophet. 'I am not by nature adapted to a relation in which perpetual compromise and great forbearance are needful,' he said, and in the words is summed up the aggressive individualism which was the distinguishing mark of the Victorian era. Dons, divines, schoolmasters, sportsmen, all of them far from shying nervously from eccentricity, embraced it, gloried in it, played up to exaggerated ideas of their own ages. 'You can't do that, you can't do that,' bellowed W. G. in that high piping voice of his, leaning out of a window of the pavilion, hirsute, domineering, welcoming a scene rather than shrinking from it, defying the Australians to bowl the same bowler two overs running, a portrait, framed in ivy, red brick and black beard, of the age he represented. But the point has been made often enough before, and the social historian who generalises at his peril and sometimes lives to see his arguments confuted, is at least safe in asserting that our age cannot rival that of our grandfathers in the aggressiveness with which they asserted their independence, their right to be, however eccentrically, themselves. *Dudley Carew, 1946*

A. Shrewsbury

by H. S. Altham

I remember very well Mr H. D. G. Leveson-Gower telling me of a conversation he once had with W. G. one night during the opening months of the war at the latter's home in Eltham. The Champion had been asked to name the greatest batsman with whom he had been associated in the fifty years of his unique cricketing life. With a stroke of his silvery beard and an inimitable twinkle of those bright eyes from behind their bushy brows, he had, with little persuasion, agreed that he himself should be considered *hors concours*, but as regards the *proxime accessit* his answer came quick and decided, 'Give me Arthur!' No more convincing evidence can surely be imagined.

Modelling himself as a boy on the classic style of Richard Daft, Shrewsbury from his very first appearance at Lord's in 1873, at the age of seventeen, for the Colts of England against the MCC, left no room for doubt as to his class. Two years later he won a regular place in the County eleven, and never afterwards looked back. Blessed with anything but a robust constitution, he had something of a struggle to keep fit, and throughout the whole of his career he would make any sacrifice that would enable him to sleep in his own bed at home, away from which he rarely got a full night's rest. But a winter in Australia in 1881–82 did great things for him physically, and on his return his success steadily increased, until in 1887, with an average of 78 for an aggregate of 1,652 runs, his supremacy defied comparison.

A great player on all wickets, it was on difficult pitches that he was seen at his very best; his mastery of the back-stroke, which he played with a good deal of wrist action rather than in the now popular dead-bat method; his capacity for watching the ball right on to the bat; his inexhaustible patience – these combined to make him probably the greatest batsman on sticky wickets that has ever lived. For, indeed, some of the best contemporary judges are agreed that some of his innings under these conditions could have been played by no other batsman, not even the Champion himself. Of these the most notable were perhaps his 164 in the second Test Match of 1886, his 81 not out (batting throughout the innings) for the Players against the Gentlemen in 1891, and his 106 and 81 in the first Test Match of 1893. All three were played at Lord's, where he was always at his best, and all three under the greatest possible difficulties. The first of these innings has been described by both Lord Harris and Barlow as positively the finest they ever saw. It lasted seven hours, was played on three different types of wicket – fiery, slow and sticky – and against Spofforth at his very best. In his 81 against the Gentlemen he was batting on each of the three days on a rain-ruined wicket, and the next highest score was Abel's 18; whilst the great double in 1893 was accomplished against the redoubtable C. T. B. Turner, the 'Terror', on a wicket that always gave that great bowler considerable help.

In the whole of his career Shrewsbury made fifty-nine scores of over a hundred in first-class matches, and of these ten passed the 200 mark. In 1892, Mr Ashley-Cooper tells us, he was engaged at the beginning of the season to coach the Warwickshire players, and every day would bat against them in the nets for half an hour. To encourage the bowlers he would place half a sovereign on the stumps, but never once in all the months he was there did he lose his money! A good many years later – and this for a sceptical generation – he met Sydney Barnes at his best in a private match, and on a desperately difficult wicket, but carried his bat through the innings, playing, we are told, as confidently and well as though the wicket were good and easy.

It is an old story how in the days before the tea interval Shrewsbury, if not out at luncheon, would generally remark to Kirk, the Trent Bridge attendant, as he went in to bat, 'A cup of tea at half-past four, please,' and how often Kirk had to carry the cup out to him. In every sort of representative game he was consistently successful, and his form in Australia was as fine as at home. Mr Warner, in his *Cricket Reminiscences*, tells us that Tom Wass first attracted attention at Trent Bridge by bowling Arthur Shrewsbury out at the nets, a thing that had not been done for years! Of a naturally serious turn of mind and a reserved disposition, he enjoyed the respect and admiration of everyone associated with him, and when in the spring of 1903, believing himself to be suffering from an incurable malady, he took his own life, the world of cricket recognised in universal tribute that one of the greatest figures in the game's history had passed on. [*1926*]

*

It is pleasant to record that Shrewsbury, the first master of pad play as a second means of defence, had admirable judgement. In eighty-two completed innings against Australia and the Gentlemen, he was lbw on only four occasions.

The use of pads, or perhaps placement of the feet, is well indictated by the manner in which three supreme batsmen were dismissed during their careers. Grace, Hobbs and Bradman were all either bowled or lbw once in every 2·8 innings, but whereas Hobbs was lbw once in 9·6 innings, and Bradman once in 10, Grace succumbed thus only once in 25 innings.

*

In 1881–82 a team organised and managed by Shrewsbury, Alfred Shaw and James Lillywhite toured Australia, having first visited America where the conditions were most primitive and the critics ignorant. A match against New South Wales (20,000 attending on the Saturday) was remarkable for a curious arrangement that the pitch could be changed after each innings.

After the game with Victoria, Shrewsbury described the events in a letter:

Adelaide,
December 22nd, 1881.

Dear Father,

Just a few lines to inform you how I am getting on and also to give you a short account of the match we have just finished playing against Eleven of Victoria [16, 17, 19 and 20 December]. Alfred has been very fortunate in winning nearly all the choice of innings until this match when unfortunately he lost it and the Victorians went in to bat on as perfect a wicket as you would wish to see; in fact the slightest touch registered four runs. At the call of time they had obtained 249 for eight wickets. During the night we had a large quantity of rain which completely upset all our calculations and rendered the wicket up to the luncheon time next morning almost unplayable, the consequence being that the two remaining wickets were disposed of next morning for two runs, making a total of 251. On our side going to bat we were soon made aware of the altered state of the wicket and at luncheon time we had lost four good wickets for 48 runs, myself and Bates being not out. The betting about this time was 20 to 1 against us and anyone could have readily obtained it. After luncheon the wicket played much better and we ran up a total of 146. I was given out caught at wicket soon after we commenced, the ball hitting my leg-guard and Blackham, the wicketkeeper, before he could distinguish whether the ball hit my guard or bat, appealed and the umpire gave me out. Only the wicket-keeper appealed and he expressed his sorrow afterwards to me for having done so. It is just possible but for this mishap we might have saved the follow on. As it was we were 105 behind. We fared much better in our second venture, scoring 198, leaving the Victorians 94 runs to obtain to win. I should have mentioned that we only intended playing three days, and the game on the Monday night stood as follows: Victoria 251, England 146; England, seven wickets down 161, myself and A. Shaw being in. The boat in which we had to leave for Adelaide set sail next day at 1 o'clock pm, so we had every reason for not playing the match out. However, the Victorians informed us that they should certainly expect us to play the match out as it was their rule and we should get to Adelaide early enough and that they would delay the steamer, instead of sailing next day at 1 o'clock midday, until 7.30 at night. Under these circumstances we agreed to stop. One of the opposite players remarked that many of his friends had money on the match and they had a right to have a show for it.

Next morning we ran the score up to 198, leaving Victoria 94 to obtain to win, which they had not the slightest doubt of doing. The wicket was rolled and swept and they commenced their innings. The bookmakers were betting 6 to 1 against us. MacDonnell and Groube were the first pair of batsmen and from the first ball delivered to the former Pilling neatly stumped him. Horan filled the vacancy and I ran in from point and caught him from the second. Blackham succeeded and played the remainder of the over. Bates bowled a maiden to Groube and Peate responded ditto to Blackham. I may say that the wicket was playing very bad and treacherous and runs were difficult to obtain. Groube obtained a single from Bates next over and in the following one of Peate's I had the pleasure of disposing of him at point. Bonner followed and amidst great cheering and excitement Peate bowled him the following ball. Matters now began to look anything but flourishing for the Victorians, especially when Pilling very neatly stumped Blackham off Bates. Edwards succeeded and after receiving a few balls off Bates, played one on to his wicket. It would be impossible to describe the astonishment that prevailed among the onlookers; they appeared to be in a state of trance and not to fully realise what was going on. There were six of their best wickets down for 7 runs, and of these Peate had obtained four for no runs. Boyle during this time was playing confidently and well and every credit is due to him for the very plucky manner in which he played an uphill game amidst a number of disasters. Boyle and McShane made a slight stand until the latter played one into my hands at point. It was when Palmer came in that the stand of the match was made, a stand which appeared to bring the onlookers to their senses again and cause them to applaud every hit, whether great or small. When Palmer was caught by Alfred at slip and Boyle caught at forward short-leg it was pretty evident which side would win, and when Barlow bowled Allen I shall never forget the excitement that prevailed and the hearty cheers that welcomed us to the pavilion. The termination of the match was worth seeing, and for myself I heartily thank those members of the Melbourne Cricket Club who insisted on us playing the match out. On returning to our hotel each member of the team met with quite an ovation from the large crowd that had assembled there, and at the station the same thing occurred and three cheers were given us at the latter place. No doubt they would like to have won very much indeed, but I must say they took their unexpected beating with a very good grace. They are very strong teams both at Melbourne and Sydney and it will require a first-class team to beat them. Boyle was caught before he had obtained 30 runs, at the wicket by Pilling and was given in by Lillywhite, a mistake which at the then state of the game might have lost us the match. We have met with a splendid reception today at Adelaide, the Mayor of Port Adelaide, also the Mayor of Adelaide meeting us and driving us to the Town Hall and there giving us a formal welcome to South Australia, the Corporation and Civil Officers being present. You must please excuse the hurried way in which this letter is put together as I have at the time of writing a number of friends waiting to show me round. I almost require a Secretary.

Your affectionate Son,
ARTHUR SHREWSBURY.

*

A report that two members of the English side had contracted to 'sell' the last innings of this match – some easy chances were missed – disturbed Shaw who tried to obtain definite proof but was unable to do so.

THE ENGLISH

I am writing, not to inform the public of the manner to play cricket, but to offer them my regrets that some people, sensible, polished and well-raised, can find a pleasure to take in a labour so dangerous. To stand upright during so many hours of an extreme heat; to take a violent exercise without any need; to run deliberately a grave danger not less than that which one is obliged to encounter on a field of battle – all this is folly of the most profound. I cannot believe that there is really some pleasure at all in it. You English are eccentric; and the verity of it is that you play cricket because in playing it you show yourselves different from all the rest of the world. *Anatole Gonjon, 1884*

The English Professional

by the Hon. R. H. Lyttelton

When W. G. Grace scored his 1,000 runs in May, 1895, a national shilling testimonial promoted by the *Daily Telegraph* amounted to £5,281 9s 1d, a Grace Fund collected by *The Sportsman* realised £2,377 2s 6d (less £21 8s 10d expenses) and a Gloucestershire county local fund £1,436 3s 8d – total £9,073 6s 5d. The value of the pound was approximately twenty times greater than in 1977.

*

We would not say one word against the personal character of the English professional cricketer, for the great majority of this class are honest, hard-working and sober men. We only say that it is not in the interests of cricket that any branch of the game should be left entirely in their hands. Your professional, as a rule, is the son of a small tradesman, or person in that rank of life, and has been born in a neighbourhood where the greatest interest is taken in sport of all kinds, cricket during the summer months being sedulously played. These neighbourhoods are far more frequent in the northern than the southern counties, the sporting tendencies of the people of Lancashire, Yorkshire and Nottingham being developed to a much greater extent than in the more southern shires. These three counties, and especially Notts, turn out large quantities of young professionals yearly.

A boy who has been born in one of these cricketing districts is sure to devote a fair share of his time to watching the victories and defeats of his village club, and consequently to imbibing that feeling of 'pleasing madness' connected with the game which attacks every cricket enthusiast. The height of his ambition is to bowl a ball or two to the village champion batsman, and when the opportunity arises to gratify his wish you will see him, hardly higher than the stumps, bowling with an action exactly similar to the crack village bowler, and scorning to encroach so much as an inch over the line of the bowling stump. And oh! what sleepless nights ensue from the anticipation of actually seeing with his own eyes on the following Saturday one of the real cracks of England – one who has positively played in Gentlemen v Players, or represented England against Australia! No wonder the boy becomes imbued with keenness for the game, when everyone in the village, from the parson to the old lady who keeps the sweetshop, is continually talking about cricket. As the boy grows older he begins to make his mark in the village club, and when he is eighteen or nineteen, to the delight of his father, mother, sisters and himself, he is selected to make one of the twenty-two colts of his county that are chosen to play against the county team. After having played in public, and perhaps tasted the pleasures of success, the father finds that his son is restless and disturbed in his trade, and wishes to give it up and become a professional cricketer. So it happens that his name is sent up to the county secretary as wanting a situation, and the young fellow finds himself launched into the world on his own account as a cricket professional.

With regard to the young man's prospect of success on starting in his new life, we are bound to say that, assuming he has only the average cricket ability of the ordinary professional, his chances of even making a livelihood are not particularly bright. He may, and no doubt will, earn as much as £2 a week, or even more, during the summer months; but at the end of August or beginning of September he will find himself with very little money in his pocket, and seven of the coldest and worst months of the year to face. He *may* get employment in the winter months – many professionals do, either as colliers or as porters, or some other work. We have known them to do clerk's work for railways in the winter; but all work for men only willing to stick to it for a few months is extremely uncertain, and there can be no doubt that many cricket professionals have a bad time in the winter.

On the whole, professionals who have an assured place in their county eleven have, for men of their social position, a very good time. They only get nominally £5 a match, but this often means a minimum wage of £10 a week, and besides this they are well known and consequently well advertised, and this means a good deal. Many have shops for sale of cricket goods and golf clubs, footballs and archery, *cum multis aliis*. A great many become publicans, which, though many of us think a loathsome profession, is at any rate a livelihood, and they become publicans because they are well known and popular, and brewers like such men to manage their public houses. Even if they keep no shop, they are constantly selling bats and balls, and a fair proportion of them, the picked men of the profession, get permanent posts in public schools. When there is no county match on a great many, especially in the North, get engagements in the detestable modern one-day league match. Leaving publicans out of the question, at the present day, from our own knowledge, the following old and young professionals keep cricket shops: Daft, Shaw and Shrewsbury, Gunn, Watson, Briggs, Sugg, Nichols, Abel, the two Quaifes, Walter Wright, Baldwin, Peate,

Ward, Tunnicliffe, and George Hearn, and there are no doubt many more; while the following have permanent engagements as coaches at schools, often with a shop also: Wright of Nottingham, Louis Hall, Woof, Emmett, F. Ward, Wootton and Painter.

In addition to all this, in some counties there has arisen, in the last year or so, a system of winter wages, or a bonus paid about Christmas, and when all things are considered, we cannot help thinking that a professional of ability who is steady has a better time of it than any other working man; and even if not a publican or shopkeeper, many have trades to which they can turn their hands in the winter.

The first-class professional cricketer is usually a well-made, strong-looking man, ranging from two or three and twenty to thirty-five, with agreeable, quiet manners. He is a great favourite with the crowd, and when his side is in may be seen walking round the ground surrounded by a body of admirers, any one of whom is ready and willing at any moment to treat his ideal hero to a glass of anything he may wish for. It is greatly to the player's credit that in the face of this temptation to insobriety he is such a sober, temperate man. I have never seen on a cricket field a first-class professional player the worse for drink, and I have only on one occasion heard the slightest whisper against the sobriety of such a man during the progress of a match. I believe that, as a class, and considering the thirsty nature of their occupation and the opportunities that offer themselves for drinking, there is no more sober body of men than cricket professionals.

At present cricket is perhaps the most popular of all our national recreations; it is certainly the most popular *game*, though football has lately made great strides in popular opinion, and it is rightly considered to be the manliest and the freest from all mischievous influences. What these latter are, and what a pernicious and enervating influence they exercise on other branches of our national sports, is known to everyone. I allude to the betting and bookmaking element, which from the earliest days has been the curse of sport. What is the worst feature about horse racing? To what do English lovers of true sport owe the fact that every racecourse is the rendezvous of the biggest blackguards and knaves in the kingdom? Is it not betting, and the pecuniary inducement it offers to every kind of dirty, shabby practice? The sullying influence has spread to the running-path, and even, if report says true, to the river and football field. Happily there is never the slightest whisper of suspicion against the straightness of our cricket players, and this is entirely owing to the absence of the betting element in connection with the game. It is an unfortunate fact that the tendency of first-class cricket nowadays is to swamp the amateur by the professional. Some of our best county teams are almost wholly composed of the latter class. The time taken up in big matches is so great, owing to their being drawn out by a late start and early finish each day, that the amateur is beginning to realise his inability to give up from his business or profession so much of this valuable commodity. What has happened in consequence? Cricket – i.e. first-class cricket – is becoming a regular monetary speculation. Thousands upon thousands troop almost daily to see the big matches, flooding the coffers of the county or club, which does its very best to spin out the match for the sake of the money. If this continues, our best matches will become nothing better than gate money contests, to the detriment of the true interests of the game and its lovers. [*1898*]

*

R. H. Lyttelton died in 1939 aged eighty-five. His family is well represented in *Wisden* with a dozen or so entries – viscounts, privy councillors, bishops, a general and sundry clerics. The Rt Hon. Alfred Lyttleton, who played for England in the 1880s, died prematurely in 1913, and received a noble eulogy from the prime minister, H. H. Asquith.

Another Lyttelton (Oliver, Lord Chandos) turned up in Vincent Square, SW1, in 1961 for the National Book League v The Authors match. Several scribes who feature in this book – Bernard Hollowood, Ian Peebles, Alan Ross and E. W. Swanton – performed with marked dignity for The Authors; another, Edmund Blunden, observed how relieved they seemed not to be appearing for the opposition, the Authors' opening bowlers being R. R. Lindwall and K. R. Miller. While the luncheon guests wondered whether the hat worn by Dame Peggy Ashcroft really was as wide as a popping crease. Lord Chandos rose to utter an indecent story. He had once heard from his wicketkeeping uncle Alfred that hours of standing behind W.G. had convinced him the Doctor did not wash behind his ears. This heresy is now only rivalled by the alleged appearance of a betting shop at Lord's.

Pounds and Pence

We have noted from R. H. Lyttelton that in the 1880s and 1890s a professional cricketer could earn £10 a week; in the 1970s he naturally earns more. It may be of interest to compare expenses; the best equipment has been selected.

EQUIPMENT

1900 £ p				1977 £ p
1 50		Cricket bag, one		23 25
80	@ 40p pr	Pads, two prs	@ £23·40 pr	46 80
1 26	@ 42p each	Sweaters, three	@ £7·25 each	21 75
2 70	@ 90p each	Bats, three	@ £29·95 each	89 85
1 20	@ 40p pr	Gloves, three prs	@ £10·60 pr	31 80
1 44	@ 24p each	Shirts, six	@ £6·75 each	40 50
3 00	@ 75p pr	Trousers, four	@ £9·95 pr	39 80
3 30	@£1·10 pr	Boots, three prs	@£18·25 pr	54 75
15 20				348 50

HOTEL ACCOMMODATION

29p	Bed and breakfast, plus dinner (provincial)	£12 50
67p	First-class hotel for princes, lords, etc.	(not applicable)

TRAVEL

GWR		BR
80p	London–Bristol return	£10 15
	NB. Most cricketers now travel by road, often in sponsored cars	

COMFORTS

25p	Spiritual: one bottle of best Scotch whisky	£4 30
5p	Intellectual: weekly cost of *The Times*	90p
1½p	*Daily Mail*	48p
5p	Of the weed: three ounces of best tobacco	£2 50
5p	Travelling Bible: one copy of *Wisden**	£3 85

* *Wisden* contained 590 pages in 1900, 1,120 in 1977.

Australian Amateurism

by A. G. Moyes

The first Test [of 1884–85, another of Alfred Shaw's sides led by Shrewsbury] was played at Adelaide, the first ever played on that ground. Unfortunately the game and the season were marred by unpleasantness caused by demands from the players who had just returned from the 1884 tour of England that they should be given half the proceeds of the matches played at Adelaide and Melbourne. It was an extraordinary request, particularly from men who reckoned they were amateurs, and the English managers rightly rejected it. The team – Murdoch's team, who were to represent Australia – were offered 30 per cent of the takings and when this was refused, Shaw himself made a personal offer of 20 per cent. Very naturally, public opinion was against these mercenary gentlemen and on discovering this, they offered to play for 40 per cent of the profits, to pay their own expenses out of it, and give the rest to charity. This was also rejected, and finally the South Australian Association took over financial responsibility and paid each team £450, greatly to the disgust of the Englishmen. It was a most discreditable attitude for the players to take, but it is fair to say that they were not all involved, Spofforth for one being against it. To add to the troubles, Murdoch declined to agree to Lillywhite, one of the team managers, acting as umpire, and since it was not possible to obtain experienced men from Melbourne or Sydney, two local men* acted. According to report, some of the decisions were not entirely satisfactory.

[*1959*]

*The two local men called upon to umpire were I. Fisher and J. Travers; England won the match by eight wickets.

T. Richardson

by Ralph Barker

Richardson, 'Honest Tom' or 'Long Tom', as he was known, was a massive fellow of well over six feet, slim but muscular, with dark, curly hair, heavy black moustache, rather low forehead, bushy eyebrows and black, penetrating eyes. He looked as though, born elsewhere, he might have slipped naturally into the role of bandit or brigand; in fact he was the kindliest, most sensitive of men. A giant of inexhaustible energy and unfailing good humour, he enjoyed wonderful health and was hardly ever incapacitated or below his best. His stamina was almost more remarkable than his skill, and he was said to bowl as fast at the end of a hard day's bowling as at the start. Of no other bowler of his time, or perhaps of any other time, could this be said.

Fast bowling came naturally to Richardson, even as a boy, and his exploits on Mitcham Common, where he earned the nickname of 'Curly', were legendary before he ever went to the Oval. In those early days he had no real knowledge of bowling as an art, and he had never studied the methods of others, which accounts for the doubtfulness of his action at the beginning. But he quickly adapted himself in those early matches for Surrey. Great as was Richardson's pace – and with Kortright, Kotze, Knox, Freeman, Lockwood, Jones, Larwood and Tyson he was among the nine or ten fastest bowlers of all time – his contemporaries attributed his deadliness to his abrupt, startling off-break, which seemed to bite only occasionally, so that the batsman was never ready for it. He could make a ball bite on a billiard-table wicket on which slow and medium-pacers were unable to turn the ball at all. His break seems to have been absolutely natural – he had no idea how he did it, and sometimes, when he consciously attempted it, the ball went the other way. The break must have come from the spin caused by the sweep of his fingers across the ball as it left his hand, the sweep being accentuated by a turn of the wrist. He swung the ball, too, from off to leg, though this was entirely due to body action and had nothing to do with seam or spin. He took a long run, leapt into the air in his last stride but one, and delivered the ball with a long and powerful swing. He arched his back in that final stride, and the whole of his body from the hips upward was employed in the swing, though it was said that he could have bowled fast with the swing of the arm alone.

Coupled with the pronounced break or swing from off to leg, which varied from ball to ball, and his stamina and pace, Richardson's strength lay in his phenomenal accuracy. His length was fuller than that of most fast bowlers, which he could afford because of his break and body-swing; no doubt this is why he hit the stumps so often. Hour after hour, match after match, season after season, he maintained his great pace and yet scarcely ever bowled a bad ball. It has been held that he was an unimaginative bowler, that he simply ran up and thumped them down, paying no attention to variation of length or pace, and it is certainly true that he was a natural bowler who did not rely to any great extent on deception. But the impression of him as wholly lacking in subtlety is false. He kept the ball up to the batsman because he found it was more effective than bowling short. He bowled at the wicket because he found, on Mitcham Common or at the Oval, that it paid him best. He only bowled off the wicket occasionally, to allow for the ball to come back. He deliberately varied his pace and length – he did not bowl every ball as a carbon copy of the previous one, as he is sometimes said to have done. It may have looked like that from the ring, or even to the batsman, but Richardson himself knew best about this. One of his most effective deliveries was the yorker, deliberately aimed.

Batsmen quickly learned to employ the leg glance, off either the front or the back foot, against Richardson, as the ball was nearly always coming in to the bat. 'Why don't you have a man down there, Tom?' he was asked again and again. He rarely allowed it, at any rate in county cricket. This was through no rigidity of mind, but because he wanted to leave that shot open. Sometimes batsmen took runs off him, but the danger of missing and being lbw was always there. This shows Richardson as a man with a readiness to trade runs for wickets. It was not a matter of a narrow outlook that could not think in terms of adjusting the field, but of a continual trap for greedy batsmen. Somewhere here, perhaps, lies a part of the explanation for his great harvest of wickets.

As a man it might seem that Richardson lacked the temper for a great fast bowler. His disposition was mild, he does not seem to have regarded batsmen with the hostility of a Spofforth, a Barnes or an O'Reilly. He never pitched the ball short deliberately, and the more fiery the wicket, or the more apprehensive the batsman, the fuller his length. In his anxiety not to hurt batsmen he would even reduce his pace. If a man had been hit, or had failed to score, perhaps, in the first innings, he could be sure of sympathetic treatment from Richardson. Next time Richardson bowled to him he would moderate his pace and keep the ball outside the off-stump. This mildness and consideration was not weakness of character, as Herbert Strudwick found years later when he first played for Surrey. When one of the senior professionals bullied him, and ordered him to a lower dressing-room, the man who stood up for him – quietly, but openly and effectively, in the face of the oppressor – was Tom Richardson.

When A. A. Lilley, the Warwickshire and England wicketkeeper, first played with Richardson, he stood up close, as was his habit with fast bowlers. Almost immediately he was hit very painfully in the chest. In the next over, when Lilley essayed to stand up to Richardson again, Richardson simply reduced his pace. On being asked by Lilley whether he preferred the wicketkeeper to stand up close or to stand back, he grinned. 'You just stand where you like,' he said, 'I shan't hurt you.' Grace, who was captaining the side, had to intervene, ordering Lilley to stand back. 'He won't bowl full out,' Grace told him, 'until you do.'

Tom Richardson bowled for the love of bowling. He must have had a taste for getting wickets, too, but if wickets didn't come he scorned to frighten people out. He just went on bowling. [*1967*]

Bradman's Birthplace

The 1886–87 team to Australia played against twenty-two of Cootamundra. The mayor of the place stood as one of the umpires. One of the local batsmen hit the ball to Johnny Briggs at cover-point, and he, whipping it back with his usual deftness and accuracy to Sherwin, the other batsman who had thrown in his bat was easily run out. But he made no effort to go, though Sherwin said, 'Out, my dear fellow, out.' No one had dreamed of appealing to the umpire, but at last we did so. All the answer that could be got from his worship was, 'Damned good bit of fielding that, wasn't it?' This novel reply produced a convulsion of merriment, and the batsmen had another innings.

R. G. Barlow, 1908

*

> Had such umpiring been in vogue half a century later when Cootamundra's favourite son was batting, the convulsions might have split the Empire.

CAPTAINCY

Captaining an eleven is nothing more nor less than leading men in a particular sphere – the cricket-field. And to be a good captain, a man must first of all have the natural gift for leadership – which is probably an inborn quality synonymous with force of character – and then be able to apply this gift to the requirements of cricket.

Jubilee Book of Cricket, 1897 (probably C. B. Fry)

H. Trumble

*A. G. Moyes**

On 8 March, 1904, Hughie Trumble at Melbourne took seven wickets for 28 runs – including the hat-trick – for Australia against England, and then retired from international cricket. No artist in any walk of life has made a more impressive farewell.

Trumble was born to be a bowler. Nature endowed him with a tremendous frame – he stood 6 feet 5 inches – a shrewd brain, strong fingers and an extraordinarily equable temperament. Nothing could ruffle Hughie, not even a decision that he knew was incorrect. His rise to fame wasn't a matter of days or weeks, but of years; in fact, his selection for his third tour in 1896 didn't please some of the critics, for they reckoned his promise had never shown fulfilment. Then, like the diligent schoolboy who has been baffled over a mathematical problem, he suddenly got the right answer. It was in a Test Match at the Oval. Hughie took six for 59 and six for 30. The 'tall Victorian', as writers of that day described him, was a popular hero.

Possibly one of the reasons why he took so long to achieve fame was the presence of Turner and Ferris, two men who kept alight the flame that Spofforth had lit. They did such tremendous things that other bowlers were mere appendages. Even George Giffen was among the reserves, called upon only when the attackers-in-chief failed. In 1896 there was no Turner, neither was there a Ferris. It was Trumble's chance. Until he retired he was in the forefront of the battle, and he built up a record that, mathematically, at any rate, has never been equalled. He took 141 wickets† in Anglo-Australian Tests, and he did the hat-trick twice. No one else can claim so many wickets or two hat-tricks.

Trumble used every inch of his height to achieve a peculiar trajectory that helped to confuse the batsman. He bowled many balls that from

* Now best remembered as one of Australia's leading writers on cricket, he had been included in the side to visit South Africa in 1914–15 (a tour cancelled owing to the outbreak of the Great War) under the captaincy of W. W. Armstrong. Among others disappointed were T. J. E. Andrews, W. Bardsley, C. E. Kelleway, C. G. Macartney, J. S. Ryder and W. J. Whitty.

† 141 wickets at 20·88, balls per wicket 56. His victims included T. Hayward (14 times), A. C. MacLaren (13), G. L. Jessop (7), L. C. Braund (6), F. S. Jackson (6), J. T. Tyldesley (6), W. G. Grace (3) and C. B. Fry (3).

the pavilion looked like half-volleys, but on closer inspection they were not what they seemed. The ball dropped shorter than expected. The angle at which it descended was calculated to deceive. And on a wet wicket the ball rose again sharply and cut all manner of capers. He was, as one contemporary batsman put it, 'almost unplayable'. Added to this, Trumble was tireless. His easy action allowed him to bowl for long periods, he had perfect control and a shrewd understanding, and he knew that his peculiarity of flight helped him to attack strength where most bowlers attack weakness. So he would feed the batsman on his pet shot, seeking to lure him into an indiscretion.

Trumble could spin the ball. Here, again, his clever brain told him that a little turn is a dangerous thing. He pitched the ball on the stumps, and the batsman had to play at it with his bat, not his pads. He tried to turn only enough to beat the bat and hit the pads or the stumps. He gave nothing away, allowed the batsman no mental rest, kept at him ball after ball, purposeful, cunning, relentless. His stock of variations of length and flight was unending. He could be played but never battered, never collared and he never bowled a ball just to get rid of it. There was an unhurried certainty about his control, and he never lost variety, and so gathered more wickets than any other bowler in the series between England and Australia.

Apart from his two hat-tricks, Trumble's finest efforts were twenty-eight wickets in the 1901–2 series, twenty-six wickets in England in 1902, including six for 53 and four for 75 at Manchester when Australia won by 3 runs, and eight for 65 at the Oval, his victims being MacLaren, Palairet, Tyldesley, Braund, Hayward, Jessop, Hirst and Lilley. He and Noble carried the Australian attack during those seasons. They were as a combination the legitimate successors of Turner and Ferris, though, of course, neither was a left-hander.

In the field Trumble excelled at slip, where his tremendous reach gave him an effective area far greater than usual. In batting he was useful, his partnership of 165 with Clem Hill at Melbourne in 1897–98 being even now the seventh-wicket record for Australia against England.

Many of our generation remember Trumble the secretary of the Melbourne Cricket Club, rather than Trumble the cricketer. They saw him in the flesh at the Melbourne Cricket Ground, where he controlled the affairs of the famous club with charming courtesy. His tall figure, crowned by a hat* with a very broad brim, stood out in any crowd. There he would be surrounded by those who loved to listen to his talk,

* Shortly before his death in 1977, the 10th Viscount Cobham (as the Hon. C. J. Lyttelton, Worcestershire's captain in the late 1930s) presented one of the Trumble hats to the MCC.

hearing him click his fingers as he forecast how the wicket would play.

Trumble the official was a personality, just as Trumble the bowler had been, a man who gave unstintingly to the game and who played it according to its finest traditions. [*1950*]

*

Trumble toured England with Australian sides on five occasions between 1890 and 1902, his tally of wickets being as follows: 1890 – 53 at 21·47 (balls per wicket 47); 1893 – 123 at 16·39 (39); 1896 – 148 at 15·81 (39); 1899 – 142 at 18·43 (45); 1902 – 140 at 14·27 (40). In 1899 he also accomplished the 'double'.

ARMOUR

When the West Indian Martindale was hurling down bumpers in 1933, Patsy Hendren persuaded his wife to fit protective side-pieces to his cap – the outcome being Sherlock Holmes looking in three directions. More recently, J. M. Brearley has taken to wearing a crash helmet underneath his cap, a precaution also taken by B. A. Richards.

It would be interesting to know who was the last Test batsman to scorn wearing a glove on his top hand. Certainly Trumper and Hill wore only one glove – Grace, Fry, Ranji and Jessop being less daring. In 1926 Bardsley and Woodfull were photographed walking out together, each with one unprotected hand, to face Larwood and Tate. When the Australians played Middlesex the same year, J. M. Gregory batted without any gloves at all against the not inconsiderable pace of G. O. Allen.

When asked about this habit, Bardsley replied, 'But I don't get hit on the top hand.'

V. T. Trumper

by M. A. Noble

Victor Trumper, unlike most other batsmen, never played himself in before trying to score. If he considered his first ball should be hit for four he hit it. On rare occasions he failed to time it properly and thus brought about his early downfall. It was then that people said: 'What a pity he does not leave them alone and play Scotch for a few overs.' Had he done so he would not have been Trumper. Nevertheless, this was the only weakness in his batting, because it sometimes helped the element of chance to bring about his early dismissal. Before he had accustomed himself to the light, or the pace and height of the pitch, and being unaware of the characteristics of the bowler, he might attempt a back-cut, easy enough later on but difficult at the moment. The ball, perhaps doing something unexpected, would be edged into the slips or behind the wickets. Again, in a fast bowler's first over he might make a pull shot off a straight ball just short of a good length, a ball which, making pace and lifting quickly and high off the pitch, would be mistimed and edged, giving a catch close in on the on-side.

One of his maxims used to be: 'Spoil a bowler's length and you've got him.' And a very sound maxim it is, for no kind of bowling is any use unless it is of good length. Invariably he put his precept into practice. Sometimes, however, he did meet a bowler who kept his length despite Victor's onslaught. This did not stop him, though it made it harder for him to make his wonder strokes, and perhaps slowed down his rate of scoring. It was when he was 'up against it' that he revealed his genius. The marvellous thing about him was that, when other batsmen, of international or any other calibre, were in sore distress with the bowling on a bad, a fiery or a crumbling wicket, he always appeared to be most at ease. Most of his best efforts were made on such wickets, and against bowlers able to extract the last ounce of assistance from them.

The reason for this, I think, was to be found in his attention to and concentration on the bowler's fingers just prior to the delivery of the ball. He could invariably spot the overspin from a left-hander, and, instead of shaping for a leg-break, was ready for the straight one which skidded through, and, of course, he at once walked in front of the wicket and banged it to the on-side where the fieldsmen were few. Dealing with a good length ball just outside the off-stump, breaking away, he would sometimes let it go, but not often; and the way he could follow the course of that break and late-cut it for four was a sight for the batsman at the other end to marvel at. You had to be in with him to realise his ability to the full. The most difficult and dangerous strokes were made with consummate ease. His action was so free, in fact, that onlookers were often deceived into the belief that he was facing the easiest of bowling.

His success against left-handers on bad wickets* was due to the fact that he never allowed the bowlers to make him play at the blind spot, to be beaten by the break off the pitch. He would go down the pitch, turning the ball into a harmless and scorable half-volley. He played left-handers on a bad wicket in a measure similar to his treatment of slow leg-break bowlers on good wickets. When facing a ball just short of a good length on the off-stump, breaking away to the slips, he would step right across to the off-side and, meeting it as it broke, would pull it away from the numerous fieldsmen on the off, right across the wicket to the on-side. The bowler, believing his length to be short, quite naturally pitched the next time a little farther up. Instantly Victor would jump into it and make a forcing shot into the country. To left-hand swervers he did not use his legs to cover up nearly as much as most batsmen do. That is to say, his legs were not used for that special purpose. They were in this position, certainly, but only as a means of enabling him to make the stroke with certainty, and not with the object of defending the wicket.

Victor always acted on the principle that it is a fatal error to allow a slow bowler to make you play forward to him – what is commonly called 'scratching'. His anticipation of the pitch of the ball was uncanny, and his decision to use any particular stroke was made so early in the ball's flight that, being also quick-footed, he was yards down the pitch before another less gifted batsman would have decided upon the stroke to be made. That was the reason of his success in making full tosses and half-volleys of balls which might easily have been fatal had they been allowed to hit the pitch and take the dangerous leg-break. This method of attack had the effect of making the bowler drop them shorter, when, by stepping back and getting into proper position, he could hit them just where he pleased. This is how he knocked the bowler off his length.

Sometimes, however, when he had jumped out, the ball would drop shorter than anticipated, and, being unable to make a full-toss of it

* At Melbourne in 1903–4, Rhodes caught Australia on a sticky wicket. The batsmen scored as follows, Trumper batting first: 74, 10, 5, 0, 1, 18, 2, 1, 8, 0, 2 not out.

or a half-volley, he would change the direction of the stroke. Following the course of the break, he would pick it up, as it were, and make a long, low hit over the covers and between the outfields, and, if necessary, would lift it right over the off-side fence; but he used this stroke only when he found it impossible to place the ball correctly. If this also was deemed to be too risky, he frequently changed his mind, and, while the ball was in its flight, would come right back and use the cut to great purpose.

His method of dealing with 'Bosie' bowling was simple. He did not bother trying to detect the finger action. If he could get out to it, the wrong 'un did not matter, and if it were bowled short there was plenty of time to detect and deal with it after it had left the pitch. His ability to score quickly off medium-pace bowling was amazing. Instead of playing forward in the orthodox way, he would surprise the bowler by getting across the wicket and, with a straight bat, would hit a good-length ball on the rise from the pitch outside the off-stump with great force and along the ground between mid-on and square-leg. This stroke was made possible because of his perfect timing and his exceptionally strong wrists. If mid-on were moved to a wider and more forward position to block this stroke, he would at once make a far easier one between the bowler and mid-on. If mid-on were brought back and square-leg brought forward to fill the gap, he would wait for the good-length ball pitched on the wicket, not outside the off-stump, and would hit it past the square-leg umpire like a flash. In this manner he was always beating the fieldsmen.

The marvel of his placing was such that I do not remember his ever being caught close in on the on-side, though hundreds of times the ball was in the air when passing the fieldsmen. Seeing ball after ball hit in this way, the bowler was apt to conclude that he was pitching them on the short side and so would pitch them up a little more. Then Victor would sprint down the pitch and drive them anywhere he pleased. His remarkable on-side play obviated the necessity of his using the cut, which always possesses an element of danger. This was not because Victor could not cut, for none could make that particular stroke better than he, but because nearly all the fieldsmen were on the off. I know of no stroke in cricket of which Trumper was not absolute master. That is a big claim to make for anyone, but I make it unreservedly, because I have seen nearly all the great batsmen of the last forty years, from Grace downwards, and have seen none to equal him.

Every cricketer knows how difficult it is to score freely off leg-theory, when so many fieldsmen are placed on the on-side. Your play becomes cramped and you find it dangerous to utilise the strokes which you would use normally and without penalty. Victor employed a method known to all, yet seldom employed by other than the most fleet-footed and versatile players. To any ball tossed a shade higher, and within comfortable reach, he would run down the pitch, at the same time drawing away to the on-side, and drive it straight or to the off. If it was a short-pitched ball, he would back quickly in the direction of square-leg and square- or late-cut it across the wicket to the off-side, where, probably, only one fieldsman would be stationed. The wrist power behind these late-cuts made from an awkward position, and the pace at which the ball travelled to the boundary, were astonishing.

The outstanding feature of his batting was not so much that he made so many varied and beautiful strokes, but that he had the ability to get into the proper position which made those strokes possible. Fast bowlers more than any others had a chance of dismissing him early in his innings. They are more difficult to time, and he treated them with the same scant respect meted out to all others. When he really got going it was difficult to know where to pitch the ball. Anything short of a good length would be banged to the leg boundary. If off-theory were attempted his numerous square- and late-cuts were brought into play, and his strong wrists and forearms, together with perfect timing, enabled him to straight drive anything overtossed. When a yorker on the leg-stump was pitched up to him he would pivot on the left leg and, raising the right foot, would glance it to fine-leg. The fact that the bat was substituted for the foot at the last moment was not always readily discerned by the bowler, who, momentarily imagining that the ball was certain to hit the foot, would appeal for lbw, only to find immediately afterwards, much to his surprise, that he had been hit for four.

Victor's best, most effective and most beautiful stroke, was one made off a fast ball well up on the middle stump. The bat would meet the ball at half-volley, and, with a flick of the wrist at the moment of contact, it would be forced along the ground at great pace forward of short-leg into the country. No assistance was given here by the pace of the ball from the bowler as there is in making the leg glance; it was pure wrist-work and wonderful timing.

It was often said that no one could place a field for Trumper, and that was literally true, for when he received balls which most batsmen would hit on the off, where most of the fieldsmen were, he would upset all calculations by banging them to the other side where the country was practically open. That, together with his ability to hit into three separate parts of the field nearly any ball bowled to him, illustrates the difficulties of a captain in effectively placing a field for his batting.

Since his day Australia has produced several good batsmen – C. Gregory, J. R. M. Mackay, C. G. Macartney, J. M. Taylor and A. Kippax, for instance – each of whom, in turn, has been described as 'the coming Trumper', but none of them has approached the master in all-round ability, yet the fact that all comparison on a high scale in Australia is made with Trumper shows in what estimation his genius was held. And there are many in England, too, who will readily acknowledge that even the Mother of Cricket produced no greater son. [*1926*]

*

The dismal English summer of 1902 saw cricketers treading in bogs, but Trumper scored 2,570 runs and 11 centuries – the highest 128. Once he had reached three figures, Trumper felt it was someone else's turn.

A few months later at Redfern Oval, Sydney, Trumper played a remarkable innings for Paddington in a grade match. At this time, a hit over the fence counted five instead of six, the player making the stroke being obliged to walk to the non-striker's end. In spite of this, Trumper scored 335 in 165 minutes, with 22 fives and 39 fours. One drive broke a window in a shoe factory 150 yards away.

Opponents had no doubt of Trumper's genius. C. B. Fry described him as having no style but being all style; the South African C. B. Llewellyn preferred bowling at him on perfect wickets – 'He tries hard on a "sticky",' Sir Pelham Warner said simply; 'He was like no one and no one was like him. He was as modest as he was magnificent.'

Trumper's widow outlived him by almost half a century. Shortly before her death in 1963, she said to a friend: 'I wish the present-day batsmen would use their feet more and jump down the pitch.' Sarah Trumper had been fortunate.

Cricket Prospects for 1902

> 'First-class cricket, properly organised and run as an attractive variety show, would be a fine paying concern.' AN AMERICAN FINANCIER TO AN INTERVIEWER

The Anglo-American 'Willow-and-Leather' Syndicate (President: Mr Pierpont Morgan; capital, ten million dollars) beg to intimate that their season will open at Lord's on the first of April. They have obtained an exclusive lease of this well-known ground, and their list of star artists fairly licks creation.

Turnstiles open at 7 am. No free passes. One continuous round of amusement from 9 am to 6 pm. Program for each day of the opening week:

9 am – Prince RANJI and Lord HAWKE will take center. These aristocratic willow-wielders will then demonstrate on slow half-volleys, putting on 200 runs in the hour. Positively no disappointment. However often they are bowled or caught, they will continue to whack the sphere until the hour be expired. The Prince and the Peer every morning from nine to ten!

10–11 – Grand exhibition of bowling and fielding by the United Yorkshire troupe. (Specially and exclusively engaged.) RHODES, HAIGH and HIRST will perform the celebrated Hat Trick. There are no spots on the Yorkshire bowlers!

11–11.30 – Comic interlude, entitled 'No-Ball; or, The Doubtful Deliverer and the Umbraged Umpire'. Messrs MOLD and JAMES PHILIPS have been booked at fabulous cost to give this screamingly-funny performance each day of the opening week.

11.30–12.30 – CHARLES B. FRY will lecture on 'The Use and Abuse of the Leg-Glance'. The glory of C. B. as the champion cricketing word-spinner needs no polish to increase its glitter. Wise words from a brave batsman daily at 11.30! (Schools admitted to this turn at reduced fees.)

12.30–2.0 – The Champion Midgets! Splendid show by Messrs ABEL and QUAIFE. Skill *versus* size. The little wonders will smack the pilule to the boundary every time. Followed by ABEL's celebrated turn: 'How I walk back to the Pavilion.' Howls of delighted applause!

From 2 to 3 – The entire troupe will be fed in the Pavilion, and the public will be admitted to view the fascinating scene. But the practice of offering the performers buns and lumps of sugar is very dangerous and cannot be permitted.

At 3 precisely – Dr W. G. GRACE will lead the way into the field, and will give his world-renowned performance, including the Deep-Square-Leg Trick, the Scratching-the-ground-with-a-Bail Trick, etc., etc. At the conclusion of his turn he will be umpired out 'lbw' to a leg-break, and will then speak a stirring monologue. (Copyright strictly reserved.)

4–5 – The Oxford and Cambridge elevens will play tip-and-run. The scene on the ground will be a careful reproduction of the famous 'Varsity match. Beauty and brightness will be seated on real drags; Peers (warranted hall-marked), Cabinet Ministers and Judges will watch the proceedings from the pavilion. Real triple-distilled essence of British Aristocracy will pervade this turn. Huge attraction for visitors from the States.

5–6 – America *versus* England. Magnificent International Match. America will be represented by (among others) FRY, HAYWARD, JESSOP, PALAIRET, HEARNE, etc. (all of whom conclusively can show American descent. Their pedigrees have been made specially for the Syndicate, and are unquestionably genuine). England will number among its foremost champions Messrs TIMSON, SNOOKS, STUBBS, etc., of the Lower Pottlebury Cricket Club. America will win! The Supremacy of the Eagle over the Decrepit Lion will be established daily! Unique scene!

The whole of the troupe will join in singing 'The Star-Spangled Banner' (solo verses by S. M. J. WOODS, G. J. V. WEIGALL and S. M. CROSFIELD), at the conclusion of which stumps will be drawn for the day.

A.C.D.

*

The above appeared in *Punch* on 14 August, 1901, a year after the writer had secured his proudest entry in *Wisden*:

W. G. Grace c Storer b Doyle 110,

and the year before he became Sir Arthur Conan Doyle.

The no-balling of Mold by Philips at Trent Bridge on 25 June 1900 became a *cause célèbre*; A. C. MacLaren defended Mold in the *Manchester Evening News*, possibly on the grounds that he had been throwing for over ten years. However, things were not as bad as they had been in the mid-1880s when, in a Gentlemen v Players match at Lord's, three throwers were on view.

K. S. Ranjitsinhji

by C. B. Fry

The brightest figure in the cricket world is Kumar Shri Ranjitsinhji, whom we all love for his supple wrist, silk shirt and genial ways. A volume might be written about him, for he contains much besides runs. Viewed as a cricketer, he is decidedly a subject for appreciation – except to bowlers. He makes enormous scores with the consistency so dear to the British heart, and makes them by such original methods. There is little of the old school about Ranji. But then he is a genius, and none the worse for it. There is that in his strokes which baffles the most confident analyst. One feels inclined to say with a certain profane cricketer, 'Come, Ranji, this isn't cricket, it's infernal juggling!' But fortunately it is cricket, and the very best. No one ever wants him to stop getting runs. It is so exciting to wonder what is coming next, and there is no waiting. Even bowlers find a sneaking pleasure in seeing him spoil their analyses. They want to discover how he does it. Fielders do not mind scouting-out, as W. G. calls it, for hours when Ranji is in. He provides fun and new sensations. As for the man in the crowd, he has come many miles for this, and is proportionately pleased. From the average batman's point of view Ranji is a marvel and a despair. 'Yes, he can play,' said someone once, 'but he must have a lot of Satan in him.' Certainly one would not be surprised sometimes to see a brown curve burnt in the grass where one of his cuts has travelled, or blue flame shiver round his bat in the making of one of those leg-strokes. Yet there is nothing satanic about Ranji except his skill. He is mellow and kind and single-hearted, and has no spark of jealousy in his composition. No one has a keener eye for what is good in other people; the better they play the more he likes it. He is a cricketer to the tips of his slim fingers, an artist with an artist's eye for the game. With the stroke that scores four to leg when the ball was meant to go over the bowler's head he has no sympathy. He is very amusing on the subject of what he calls 'cuts-to-leg'. Apart from their value to his side, Ranji's big innings please him in proportion as each stroke approaches perfection. He tries to make every stroke a thing of beauty in itself, and he does mean so well by the ball while he is in. His great success is partly due to this attitude of mind; but there are other reasons why he is, on all but the stickiest of wickets, the best bat now playing. He starts with one or two enormous advantages, which he has pressed home. He has a wonderful power of sight which enables him to judge the flight of a ball in the air an appreciable fraction of a second sooner than any other batsman, and probably a trifle more accurately. He can therefore decide in better time what stroke is wanted, and can make sure of getting into the right position to make it. So he is rarely caught, as most of us are, doing two things at once – moving into an attitude and playing at the ball simultaneously. Even in cases where body movement is part of the stroke he is the gainer, for besides quickness of judgement he has an extraordinary quickness of execution. Practically he has no personal error. His desire to act and his action seem to coincide. This enables him to make safely strokes that for others to dream of attempting would be folly. But with far less natural quickness Ranji would have been a great cricketer for the simple reason that he is a great observer, with the faculty for digesting observations and acting upon them. He takes nothing on trust. He sees a thing, makes it his own and develops it. Many of his innumerable strokes were originally learnt from other players, but in the process of being thought out and practised, have improved past recognition. This is due partly to his natural powers – eye, quickness and elasticity – and partly to his hatred of leaving anything he takes up before bringing it to the highest pitch of which he is capable. Ranji has made a science of taking liberties. One may fairly suspect him of regarding Tom Richardson's ball as bowled in the interest of cutting and driving rather than with a view to hitting the sticks. Not that he ever despises bowling, however cavalierly he may seem to treat it. While at the wickets he takes it entirely under his own management. It is a musical instrument upon which he plays, often improvising; a block of stone which he carves into shape to his taste, not with vague, smashing blows, but with swift, firm, skilful strokes. His work has a fine finish; there is nothing crude or amateurish about it. And such a touch! It may be of interest to know that Ranji has worked very hard indeed at cricket. Some of his strokes have cost months of careful net practice. He does nothing blindly. He thinks about the game, starts a theory and proceeds to find out what use it is. Some of his strokes again were discovered by accident. For instance, his inimitable leg-play began thus: when a boy he started with the usual fault of running away from every fast ball that threatened to hit him. But instead of edging off towards square-leg, as most boys do, he used, with characteristic originality, to slip across the wicket towards point. Suddenly he found out that by moving the left leg across towards the off, keeping his bat on the leg side of it and facing the ball quite squarely with his body, he could watch the ball on the bat and play it away to leg with a twist of the wrist. Nowadays he can place to leg within a foot of where he wishes almost any ball that pitches between wicket and wicket. His back play is as safe as a castle, and he scores with it repeatedly. His idea is that to be a good bat a mastery of both back and forward play is necessary, but that of the two the former is the more important. He has a slight prejudice against forward play for forcing strokes. There is a moment in a forward stroke when the ball is out of sight and the stroke is being played on faith, so that if the ball does anything unexpected, or the judgement is at all at fault, it is mere chance whether the stroke be good or bad. This opinion is amply borne out by the fact that players who depend entirely upon forward strokes cannot make runs consistently except on true wickets. Why does he ever get out? Perhaps he knows himself. There may be reasons, but they are not apparent. [*1900*]

by Philip Trevor

I shall never forget the day when I first saw 'Ranji' bat. I cannot from memory fix the year exactly, though obviously I could easily do so by referring to records, and in that way I could, of course, acquaint myself with every detail of the match in question. I prefer, however, not to do so, for I want to jot down my original impressions and feelings without titivating them up. It was in the month of August, I know, or possibly in early September. I was on short leave, and staying at Hastings at the time, when the placards told me that at Bexhill a grand cricket match was to be played. An effort was then being made to exploit Bexhill as a kind of second Brighton. Freeman Thomas, I remember, captained the home side, and the visiting side were the Sussex eleven, which included Kumar Shri Ranjitsinhji. Freeman Thomas had a very strong eleven, which included, among others, the fast bowler Woodcock, and the famous wicketkeeper, Dick Lilley. Among the Sussex eleven were W. L. Murdoch, C. B. Fry and 'Ranji'. It may seem surprising that these six names are the only six fixed in my memory. Personally I am surprised the other way. It was so essentially 'Ranji's' day that I can be pardoned for forgetting nearly everything about everyone else.

Sussex batted first, and I think I may say without fear of exaggeration that the wicket was the worst and most dangerous on which I have seen a first-class match played. Woodcock was bowling his fastest, and those who have played with and against Woodcock know, or knew, that for a few overs he could make a new ball travel about as fast as it is wanted to travel. I remember that it struck me at the time that Lilley was standing nearer the bowling screen than the wicket. Probably that is an exaggeration. At any rate, I have never seen a wicket-keeper stand farther back. And well he might, for Woodcock's fast balls were coming from the pitch like rocketing pheasants. One of the batsmen, when he had returned safely to the pavilion, so I was told, said that he was glad that the wicket was as bad as it was and not a little better. As things were, Woodcock's good-length ball, pitched just clear of the leg-stump, went over his head. On a slightly better wicket it would have got him in the eye. To the best of my recollection Sussex scored 71, of which Ranji got 49. Most men and women of my generation have, I imagine, seen Cinquevalli juggle with knives and finish his wonderful performance uncut by them. Ranji's performance that day put Cinquevalli's feats in the shade, for the ball never touched anything but the middle of his bat. He smiled quietly when it went too far over his head for him to touch at all, and when it was a shade more pitched up he did one of two things. He sprang in like a cat and drove it hard, or he whipped round and scored fours off his face. I was so amazed and enthralled that I could hardly applaud, and members of my family thought I was little short of cracked when I said: 'This is the greatest ever.' [*1921*]

Morale Boosters

Francis Thompson's 'At Lord's' – the most famous of cricket poems – paid tribute to the run-stealers flickering to and fro, 'O my Hornby and my Barlow long ago'.

But the two famous Lancastrians inspired more than a great lament. During the siege of Ladysmith (1899–1900), John Stuart of the *Morning Post* referred to the Manchester Regiment thus: 'It is a great thing to make a regiment that will charge any place on earth; it is a greater thing to have made a regiment that will sit tight like the Manchester under heavy fire, cracking "pawky" little north-country jokes that somehow recall the brave days of Hornby and Barlow.'

Doubtless the Manchester Regiment recalled the great occasion at Trent Bridge in 1882 when Barlow opened for Lancashire. The innings lasted two and a half hours and totalled 69. Barlow carried his bat for 5.

ENTRY

Bright Phoebus Apollo (occasionally known as the sun) swung high in the bending blue, imparting a full flood of mellow warmth and shedding a stream of golden glory over the level green as W. G. Grace swung out of the tent with his bat under his arm, resembling nothing so much as an Assyrian monarch on the frieze of an ancient entablature.

London newspaper, 1888

The Back Glide

Perhaps the simplest way to play the shot is to step a little towards the wicket with your right foot and then quickly draw your left foot up to it, at the same time turning to face the ball full; you can then play the ball just in front of your legs with a little half push, half turn of the bat.

The way I play the stroke myself is different. I step across the wicket a little with my left foot, put my bat in front of my right leg behind my left calf and then just as the ball comes to the bat I pivot round on the toe of my right foot, turning the other part of my body towards the on-side. But I would not recommend this method to anyone to whom it does not come naturally. *K. S. Ranjitsinhji, 1902*

A. C. MacLaren

by C. B. Fry

There is no more definite personality among cricketers than Archie MacLaren. Were he less remarkable a batsman, his strong individuality and wise, deliberate ways would suffice for distinction. Naturally his traits call less for criticism than for appreciation. For has he not won a pre-eminent position in the sunny world of cricket? Of course he started with advantages. A clean eye, a strong wrist, a minimum of personal error – and you have a potential champion. But equally he owes his success to serious thought, patient application and a sound, hopeful heart. There are problems to solve, difficulties to conquer and grey days to live through before an assured reputation can be won with all its pleasant sunshine. He is a genius, but not of the kind that finds fulfilment without hard trying. They say those who learn easily forget soon. Archie always strikes me as one who, having found just a little difficulty in learning, has mastered his lesson all the better; who, perhaps, had to take his points one by one and elaborate them severally till he established his present robust, versatile game, and stood forth a well-nigh perfect batsman. Whatever the process of development, there are no two ways about the result. That is not only solid and strong, but brilliant. Archie goes in to bat armed at all points, able and ready to meet any bowling upon any wicket. No one was ever less a fair-weather batsman. Never is he more likely to come to the front than when runs are badly wanted or difficult to get. Who makes a century against Australia in the fourth innings of the match? Who makes 32 for Lancashire against Surrey on a bird-lime wicket, with 70 to win and no one else looking like getting 2? Why, Archie, and no other. And so one has confidence in him, expects big scores to his name and understands how they are put together. The keynote of his style is fixity of purpose. He knows exactly what he means to do and does it. This applies not only to his innings as a whole, but also to each particular ball as played. He declines to be puzzled or nonplussed. If it pleases him to start with free cricket, he does so. Should he fancy to play himself in rather carefully, this too happens. On the whole he is a careful player. Even when he is scoring most severely there is nothing rash or ill-considered in his strokes. As a matter of fact no great bats, however dashing and brilliant their game, really play carelessly. They may give a contrary impression, but their attention is closely concentrated and their strokes quite deliberate. Ranjitsinhji appears scarcely to look at the ball or take any trouble. His electric flashes seem almost as insolently careless as they are brilliantly successful. Actually he watches the ball with feline insistence every time. Francis Ford looks like six-feet-six of 'don't care'. His bat acts like an irresponsible flail; but he knows, he knows. Archie MacLaren's concentration is more easily perceived. That is the difference. Sometimes – not often – he lets himself go. Poising his bat well back and rather high, he swings it at the good-length ball with a strong swooping motion that has glorious results. As a rule he plays well within his strength.

All his strokes are good, and few batsmen have more. His off-drive is as effective, if not quite as graceful as Lionel Palairet's. His hitting is as clean and sound as Stanley Jackson's. His cutting and hooking are second only to Ranji's. But in none of these strokes is he as frequent as the above three players respectively. He has two specialities. His back play is magnificent; it is not only extremely safe, but has that latent scoring power, so rare and so telling. His method is uncommon. Stepping back decidedly with his right foot, his bat held rather high, he comes down plumb on the ball with a distinct though nicely modulated swing. The bat meets the ball with no compromise. Then again, he is very skilful at forcing good-length balls away to the on-side; this he effects with a swinging flick of the wrist helped out by a slight following turn of the whole body. Most of his runs come from this stroke.

Archie is very determined and always in earnest. Does he lack humour? Well, he has a Scotch name. He is very thorough. Even when he is clean bowled, there is no mistake about it, no half-and-half measures, no being caught in two minds; he has tried a definite, full-fledged stroke and failed, and he goes away leaving that impression and a great sense of belief behind him. We know him well; rarely does he 'Stand ready to strike *once* and strike no more.' [*1902*]

Fielding in the Golden Age

*by Digby Loder Armroid Jephson**

Much has been written with regard to the batting of the past season [1900], and much has been written with regard to the bowling; much praise, and rightly too has been bestowed on the one, and on the other a modicum of commendation. To write in the same congratulatory vein of the fielding necessitates the pen of a ready writer, the pen of a Defoe. As these are not numbered among my possessions, it is a difficult task. To write well of the fielding in 1900 is but to forge a romance that exists nowhere, save in the writer's brain.

Taken as a whole the fielding has been bad, thoroughly bad. Men stand in the field today like so many 'little mounds of earth', or waxen figures in a third-rate tailor's shop. The energy, the life, the ever-watchfulness of ten years ago is gone, and in their place are lethargy, laziness and a wonderful yearning for rest. Today a ball is driven through two so-called fieldsmen, and instead of a simultaneous rush to gather it, to hurl it to one end or the other, the two 'little mounds of earth' stand facing each other with a lingering hope in their eyes that they will not be compelled to fetch it. There are, unfortunately, but a few counties, regarded as sides, to which the above censure does not apply.

The two northern counties, the two best elevens of the year fielded well, perhaps as well as any teams it has been my pleasure to play against, but the majority of the rest are absolutely outclassed by many a local club throughout the country. Naturally on every county side there are exceptions to this general sloth, men who believe that the game does not wholly consist in the making of a hundred runs, or the taking of five wickets; men who delight in chasing the ball with the possible chance of saving a run, and who never 'slack' however long their outing may have been. These are the members of a team that help to win your matches, the fieldsmen whose energy, pluck and endurance go far to remedy your deficiencies in other parts of the game.

The success of Yorkshire is due, in a very large degree, to their field-

* In 1899 Jephson had achieved immortality of sorts against the Players at Lord's, the occasion of W. G.'s last appearance for the Gentlemen at headquarters – some thirty-four years after his first. The Players' bowling was tremendous: Lockwood, Hirst, Rhodes, Walter Mead and Albert Trott, their batting (with Hirst at nine) impressive. But the Gentlemen won by an innings and 59 runs – a great century by Fry, 78 from Grace (whose partner then called him for a short single), and Jephson's bowling: 18.4–7–21–6. This havoc was accomplished with lobs.

ing. There are many fine fields on the side, and an article of this description would be void of all interest if mention were not made of Hirst and Denton, perhaps the finest mid-off and the finest outfield of the year. The one is in front of you, and you may as well attempt to drive through a brick wall as pass those hands of iron; and the other, hovering on the edge of the green circle, has made you run many a three when you were crediting yourself with a four. They are cat-like in their activity; before the bat has struck the ball, by some strange intuition, they divine the direction it will take, and move, whilst the so-called fieldsman – the little mound of earth – stands open-mouthed, watching the ball go by. All through the season their catching has been good and their ground work perhaps better; their fielding has been full of life, full of vigour. And of Lancashire the same may be said. Here there are many good fields, and again two stand out above their fellows – A. C. MacLaren, the captain, and Tyldesley. A. C. MacLaren is ubiquitous, his presence is felt everywhere and it is a daring youth that shirks when he is in command of a team. He is full of nerves, he can scarcely stand still as the ball leaves the bowler's hand and it is only on the fall of the coveted wicket that the stern features relax and he rests for a moment. In all positions in the field is he good, exceptionally good; and so marvellously keen is he for the downfall of the unfortunate batsman that on occasion he has been known to bowl, but rarely, I am sorry to say, with marked success. At the present time he, G. L. Jessop and A. O. Jones, are in all probability the three players that can fill more places in the field, and fill them splendidly, than any other first-class cricketers. Tyldesley, like Denton, is always to be found in the outfield, and there is little to choose between them. Both have the same untiring energy, both go for catches, however seemingly impossible they may appear, preferring to miss rather than to stop the ball first bound, as is the method adopted by the so-called fieldsman – the 'little mound of earth'. Again, both throw well, with a low quick return that invariably reaches the wicketkeeper or the bowler after pitching but once. Not with the terrible inaccuracy, the inaccuracy of length and direction that characterises the efforts of a very large majority of the players of today.

Mention must be made of the good fielding of Gloucestershire and of Kent. Both are young sides and both are strangely aware of the importance of this branch of the game, that in so many teams is regarded as an aggravated nuisance, knowing well that many a game has been won, not by brilliant batting, or sensational bowling, but by unflagging exertion in the field. G. L. Jessop, besides having saved dozens of runs, runs that the restful field would willingly have given to the other side, has thrown out thirty or so batsmen. Readers of this will perhaps remark to themselves – 'It is all very well, but how many runs has he lost shooting at the stumps?' Yes, very likely many have been lost, but think a moment. What is a four or many fours on a good wicket compared to the dismissal of Ranjitsinhji, Fry, Abel or Hayward. Again, rare instances occur of a ball being thrown in well so that the wicket can be broken by the bowler or the stumper, arriving the fraction of a second too late. The batsman is in, whereas had the wicket been hit he would have walked slowly, miserably, probably discontentedly, to a seat in the pavilion. I am not advocating indiscriminate throwing, but if there did not exist this terrible inaccuracy of length and direction in the returns of the majority of the fieldsmen of today, many a wicket would have fallen that stood for hours piling up tedious fours.

Looking back calmly and dispassionately on the past season, there is another feature that strikes the interested spectator, namely, the growing inclination on the part of certain fieldsmen to remove themselves as far as possible from the *dangerous* ball that travels at *too great a speed.* Discretion has ever been considered the better part of valour, and perhaps this is the right view for the great batsmen and the great bowlers of a side to take, but it is emphatically not the plan of campaign for the privates of an eleven. For fieldsmen numbered among these last, I should strongly recommend a study of the fielding of Albert Trott, one of the finest fields at slip or in near proximity to the wicket that I have ever seen. There is no funk here, the big strong hands flash out, they give with the ball, it is held and many a fine batsman has walked disconsolately away, who would have stayed to all eternity had he but selected a fieldsman of discretionary valour.

Another feature that presents itself is that the lethargy, the laziness, the wonderful yearning for rest, are more noticeable in our great batsmen than in our great bowlers. A great batsman having produced a colossal score seems content with his performance, he loafs in the field, and when not loafing he peacefully slumbers. Sometimes, fortunately for the side on which he plays, he drifts into the slips and sustains a rude awakening when the rising ball is faintly touched and he receives it on the wrist or on the ankle, as the case may be. Naturally for a while, so long as the pain is acute, he is awake, and perhaps during this lucid interval he makes a catch or two, but then again the yearning for rest is felt, and peacefully he dozes. It were a good thing for cricket if many a great batsman could be confined to the slips, for there there is always this chance of a sudden shock, a sudden realisation that he is in the field to do some work.

The same idea of rest, of *dolce far niente* pervades many of the great bowlers of today, but not, I think, to so great an extent. This is probably due to the fact that they know and feel keenly the disappointment of a missed chance, a chance that they have been bowling over after over to obtain. Feeling this they do not sleep, they do their best to help their fellow workers in the field. We have all felt it, this clinging desire for rest. It may be that we are tired, that we play too much cricket; it may be the subtle influence of a bright June day, or the soothing light from the soft green turf; but from whatever cause it springs it has been with us in a more pronounced form this season than ever before in my experience of the game. We nearly all do it, we cricketers who are not included in the category of great batsmen or great bowlers, and its effect on matches is prodigious. [*1901*]

A RUINED BAT

In 1897 G. L. Jessop scored 101 in forty minutes against Yorkshire at Harrogate. Part of the credit for this feat belonged, it would seem, to his bat.

Somerset Villa,
Cheltenham.
March 24, 1898.

Stuart Surridge & Co.,
London, S.E.

Dear Sir,

You will be pleased to hear that one of your bats that I purchased at the Oval was used in all my matches, both first and second class last season. I should in all probability have been using it next season had not the damp got hold of it whilst crossing over to America.

Sincerely yours,
GILBERT L. JESSOP

The Philadelphian newspaper which described Jessop as 'the human catapult who wrecks the roofs of distant towns when set in his assault' might have used more extravagant language had not the Atlantic waves ruined the Harrogate bat.

M. A. Noble

by A. E. Knight

In some respects Noble is a greater and stronger personality, as he is a much sounder batsman, than Trumper. Bowling on his day a medium-paced ball of perfect length, swerving away slightly in the air and breaking back after pitching, varied with an occasional faster one which goes with the arm, he has been deemed by many competent judges among the very greatest of medium-paced bowlers. Ranjitsinhji has been said to have regarded him as the best medium-paced bowler he ever played against. In his bowling equally with his batting, there is a note of superb determination, of patient, restrained and deliberate effort. The same impassively inflexible energy marks him whether ten runs are needed to win with every wicket to fall, or whether facing an inevitable defeat. He never takes a risk, never scrambles for the run or for the bowling, whether first or last at the wicket.

On the sticky wickets of Australia his batting seemed to me of a greater skill than that of Trumper, if not as great as that of the little Englishman, Tyldesley. Noble and Tyldesley never deliberately chanced their arm upon these impossible situations. They played as upon perfect pitches, watching the ball the more keenly in its hurried rise or turn. Trumper played as though more conscious of the supreme difficulty; he overcame it, so to speak, by ignoring it or directly eliminating it, by jumping to the pitch and hitting with all the power at his command. 'You cannot watch the ball here,' he seemed to say, and every one of those two elevens of 1903–4 save Noble and Tyldesley would agree with him. The haste of Noble is never otherwise than solemn and silent. After Trumper and Duff have stormed the castle or whirled onward in some Balaclava charge, the studious strategy of a von Moltke such as Noble, evinces the limitations of the Sydney crowd.

Noble, however, throws no sops to the democratic Cerberus, howl he never so greatly. There is a rare combination in him of prudence with enthusiasm; rare at all times and places is such a blend. Noble has often been compared with Yorkshire's great left-hander George Hirst. He is, I think, quite as clever in all-round technical skill as Hirst, but greater in his grasp, in his more facultative energy, in organising capacity. Like Hirst, Noble is a very solid player, but after a different fashion, more yoked to the car of a deliberate intelligence, or purely intellectual purpose. Neither the one nor the other ever quite rise to the creative capacity as of a pure artist like Trumper. Noble's qualities are in a sense acquired, not the gift of the blind gods alone. He is a quaint blend of deliberateness and of the ease born of natural facility and swing. A great captain, devoid of gesticulation and fuss, his accurate information, his unbounded labour and wide range of knowledge, give to him a statesman-like grasp and the actions of a mind accustomed to rule.

The power and influence of this great cricketer will be best understood by his action at times of crisis. When in the First Test Match of 1903 at Sydney, an umpire's decision, adverse to Hill, had created an incredible outbreak which threatened to overwhelm the game and the ground, Noble quietly led the English captain by the arm away from the spectators whom he appeared about to address, and alleviated the excitement by continuing the play under conditions most unseemly and inappropriate. The very highest traditions of the game were fed by action at once so statesman-like and yet dictated by the finest feeling of courtesy. The conduct of cricket in Australia particularly owed much to him. In the Fourth Test Match, when Australia's hope of the rubber was seen to be an impossible one, the crowd amused themselves or vented their cynicism by derisively calling to Rhodes as he bowled. They marked each of his deliberately regulated steps by shouting 'One', 'Two', 'Three', following on with a sepulchral grunt as the ball was delivered. No despondency characterised the play of Noble, the great captain who remained to stem the unfortunate tide which overwhelmed his colleagues one by one. None on either side played as he did in that prolonged struggle.

The noisy absurdities become more deafening, and derisive jeers greet the failures of the Commonwealth. There is no danger now of the ground being rushed, nor could any howling derision affect this iron nerve, but Noble is intensely serious, as becomes the captain in a game receptive of so much international attention. Hence, when antiphonic chants arise from all sides, and the derisions are too offensive in their absurdity, Noble feels that such are not in keeping with the game. He sits upon his bat, and leaves the crowd to choose between their fun and the cricket. The shouting ceases, he resumes play; the shouting is renewed again, he lies down to await the pleasure of the cynics. His persistency triumphs, and with amusing but truly admirable inconsistency the crowd reward him with a cheer, and the game continues until England's victory. Too great to be a sycophant, this man, unable 'to suffer fools gladly', wrings from the crowd a far-off respect. So completely Bohemian themselves, their yesterdays as cheerful as their tomorrows are confident, the mind which realises difficulties and the patient execution which defies fate with its persistency suffer much at their lips. Generous cheers greeted the victors, while this man, greatest of them all, passed to his room almost unhonoured. [*1906*]

*

Monty Noble, in particular, captivated Barnes. Here was an off-spinner of the old and original school (very similar to the latter-day Jim Laker) who possessed all the variations of the art. Noble would gain tricks of flight by delivering the ball at various heights – gaining this by dipping or straightening his right leg at the moment of release – and he had an out-curve as distinct from the ordinary off-break. If a breeze came in from fine-leg, Noble was in his element as he curved, floated and dropped the ball with sidespin and overspin. He brought to the cricket field much of the technique of the baseball pitcher. *Jack Fingleton*

*

In 39 Tests against England, Noble scored 1,905 runs average 31, and took 115 wickets at 24 each.

7 for 2½

'Old Lady Whortleberry's always been nervous since she lost her first husband. He died quite abruptly while watching a county cricket match; two and a half inches of rain had fallen for seven runs, and it was supposed that the excitement killed him.'

'Reginald's Drama', *Saki*

C. B. Fry

Max Beerbohm calls at Wadham College, Oxford, 1895

'Where,' I asked of the porter, 'are Mr Fry's rooms?'

'Fry,' he said slowly, 'which Fry do you mean? What initials?'

Was there then more than one Fry? T.H.E. were the only initials I had ever supposed the great athlete to possess, but it appeared he was known officially as Mr C. B. Fry.

by R. C. Robertson-Glasgow

For combined excellence of mind and body Alfred Lyttelton might come up for comparison with Fry, but even he must surely retire before the Commander's overwhelming versatility.

In ancient Athens, perhaps in the Ideal Republic, Fry would have been raised by natural acclamation to eminence. In modern England he was thrice baulked at the first hurdle of the political race. He was born for the highest work with men of the highest ability; as a young man, he was rated as at least the equal of such as Lord Birkenhead and Lord Simon. But, by the very diffuseness of his genius, he became, as it were parcelled, or watered down. He had ambitions rather than ambition. He was too various for the single aim; he lacked the ruthlessness that is ever present, however deftly disguised, in the careerist.

He was a continual shock to the mere traditionalists. 'I was not,' he has said, 'popular at Lord's, being regarded in the light of a rebel.'

Lord Birkenhead, standing with him one summer day in the rose gardens of the training ship *Mercury*, said: 'This is a lovely place and a fine show, C. B. But for you it has been a backwater'; and Fry replied: 'The question remains whether it is better to be successful or happy.' Not quite as the world judges, Fry has been both.

He has admitted of himself: 'I am d——d lazy, with a huge fund of energy; and I'm no use till I am cornered.' He was 'cornered' very early in life. Money was short. In 1891, he went from Repton to Oxford with thirty shillings to spend and an eighty pounds p.a. scholarship on the books of the Bursar of Wadham. He had been meant for the Indian Civil Service, but side-stepped it, for want of mathematics. He was first on the Wadham list of scholars, one F. E. Smith being fourth, 'with a Lancashire accent that would rival Gracie Fields'.

Fry began with a Blue for association football, soon to make a famous partnership at back with W. J. Oakley. In athletics he was first string against Cambridge in the hundred yards and the long jump, but, Fry-esquely, fancied himself most as a high hurdler. It was on the Iffley Road track at Oxford that he set up the world's record long jump of 23 ft 6½ in, a performance that his classical tutor had been invited to witness, but had dismissed with: 'I am afraid that would not interest me.' In cricket he played four times against Cambridge, scoring 100 not out in 1894, his year of captaincy. His fastish bowling is almost forgotten; but he took six wickets in an innings against Cambridge in 1895, and twice did the 'hat-trick' against the MCC, his victims including A. E. Stoddart and T. C. O'Brien.

After Oxford he drifted, briefly and for the only time, and the stream carried him to teaching at Charterhouse. There he decided that journalism would give him three times the income for a tenth of the time expended. In various magazines sketches of famous cricketers appeared under his name at a time when it was thought vaguely improper for an amateur to make money out of his knowledge of games. His connection with the *Manchester Evening News* ended when he telegraphed 1,200 words from the Outer Hebridges at the ordinary postal rates. He transferred his pen to Sir George Newnes's new venture, *The Captain*, and in 1904 Newnes made him, in preference to the vegetarian Eustace Miles, editor of *C. B. Fry's Magazine*.

It was in the early years of this century that his talent as a batsman blossomed into genius and he became one of the greatest, and surely the most scientific, players in the history of the game. Together, K. S. Ranjitsinhji and he* became an almost insoluble problem to those who bowled against Sussex. In 1901 Fry scored six consecutive centuries. Numerically, Don Bradman equalled this feat during the Australian season of 1938–39, but, in quality, Fry's six centuries must be held the greater, as his opponents included Yorkshire (twice), Middlesex, Surrey and Kent, at an age very rich in bowling. In 1902 he played at back in the association football cup-final for Southampton against Sheffield United.

So far he had won fame as an athlete and a living as a writer. But he had used only a fraction of C. B. Fry. In 1908 he cast the whole of himself into the work of the training ship *Mercury* at Hamble, on the Southampton Water. He is there still, in spite of offering himself as a coal-miner at the age of seventy.

Fry denies that he was in any sense 'called'; he was simply annoyed

* During the six seasons, 1899–1904, Fry and Ranji scored (in all first-class matches) 28,769 runs, average 62.

at the sheer stupidity of allowing such a work to die with its founder, Charles Hoare, the banker. But he found both interest and funds lacking. His own and his wife's enthusiasm supplied the first need, his ingenuity and power of appealing, the second. From the start he combated the notion that a training ship was a form of reformatory and he persuaded *Punch* to publish a cartoon with a lad looking at Winston Churchill, then Home Secretary, and asking him whether he couldn't be trained for the sea without first robbing a till. Fry gave to the *Mercury* its distinctive spirit of service and self-reliance, and the *Mercury* gave to the Royal Navy and the Merchant Service those who have shown that Britain does not rule the waves merely in the words of a song.

In 1912, Fry took time off from his now established *Mercury* to captain England in the Triangular Test tournament against Australia and South Africa. At first, the Selection Committee had invited him as captain for the first match only; Fry, typically and rightly, said: 'All or none.' He led England to victory, playing a great defensive innings of 79 in the Oval Test against Australia.

Soon after the first European war, he went to Geneva as an associate with Ranjitsinhji on the Indian delegation, and worked most industriously on the Finance Committee. He was also a strong candidate for the vacant throne of Albania, whose head delegate, a bearded bishop, was looking for 'an English Country Gentleman with £10,000 a year'. But 'Ranji', perhaps unwilling to part with £10,000 and a valued friend simultaneously, did not encourage the project.

Returning home, Fry was again offered, in his fiftieth year, the cricket captaincy of England against Australia. For Hampshire, he scored 59 and 37 against the formidable Australian bowling; but an injured finger settled the question. There followed years of routine work, one serious illness, and silence.

Then, one May morning of 1934, at Lord's there stood on the steps outside the pavilion, a man with a monocle, writing; gaily and fluently writing. He appeared to be something between a retired admiral and an unusually athletic Oxford don. He wore marine gaiters and one of those waistcoats that are born to put the whole race of pullovers to shame. No cricket had started; so I presumed to ask him whence came the facile stream. C. B. Fry said: 'My dear fellow, I am describing my idea of how the game should go, if it were going.' The *Evening Standard* was at work. He had been given an assistant to handle his 'copy'; and this worthy technician, meaning so very well, said to the master: 'Why, Commander, you might be a journalist yourself, instead of just an amateur.' And C. B. Fry said . . . [*1943*]

FRY, 1895

He often cramped the limited number of strokes he possessed by over-caution and perhaps by diffidence. Further, he handicapped himself by assuming all kinds of impossible attitudes to make them.

K. S. Ranjitsinhji

RANJITSINHJI, 1902

Although I have never been able to play in the least like him, I have certainly made more runs from the time I began to study the way he used his bat. *C. B. Fry*

FRY, 1905

We find in him a batsman of the highest class, free and easy in his methods, pleasing to the eye in his play, and executing all the strokes that are possible in batting with masterly confidence. A superb back play renders his defence perfect. The bat comes straight and true, retards the further progress of the ball, and sends it with lightning velocity through the fieldsmen to the boundary. The working of the legs is beyond reproach; the attitude and poise of the body and the swing of the bat are quite majestic. His driving is terrific, being low and beautifully timed. Sometimes the bowler – and quite as often the batsman opposite – has great difficulty in avoiding the ball driven back. It is safer not to back up if you are batting with him. He is not a puller like 'W. G.' But he can do it. Safety and the exigencies of his side demand the not frequent use of this particular stroke. But then he hooks with the precision of a master hand. Balls the slightest bit short, fast or slow, go past the square-leg umpire with rare speed, keeping the umpire up to the mark if inclined to be sleepy (for umpires do get sleepy sometimes). What shall I say, then, as to his leg play, his glances and his glides? Well, no one executes them better or so surely. He makes them with any amount of wrist-work, too. *K. S. Ranjitsinhji*

*

In 1902 the *Daily Express* engaged Fry to write on the Test Matches against Australia, no one objecting in spite of the fact that the batsman was an automatic choice for England. As it turned out, the triumphant failures of Fry and Ranji (they totalled 24 runs in eight innings and were then dropped) made things easy. However it would appear that the credit for Ranji's most famous 'invention' was appropriated by his Sussex colleague. Describing the start of the England innings at Lord's,

A. C. MacLaren not out	0
C. B. Fry c Hill b Hopkins	0
K. S. Ranjitsinhji b Hopkins	0

the *Daily Express* explained part of it thus: 'Hopkins's second ball, which pitched on my legs, about four inches clear of the wicket, I was able, with a stroke I do not reckon in my repertoire, to cock up into the hands of short-leg. That comes of playing the new-fangled leg-glance instead of the old-fashioned leg hit. I hope to forget how to play the stroke I invented for that ball.'

Perhaps it was as well the following year that Fry was not called upon to contribute a morning-after account of the Gentlemen v Players match at Lord's, for the amateurs' second innings score ran

C. B. Fry not out	232
P. F. Warner c Hunter b Hargreave	27
K. S. Ranjitsinhji c Hunter b Gunn	60
A. C. MacLaren not out	168
B 8, lb 2, nb 3	13
Total (two wkts, dec.)	500

On the other hand, the *Daily Express* correspondent would have had ample time to compose his article in Latin and translate that into Greek as he batted, before dictating the finished English piece on his return to the pavilion.

ST. REV.

Somerset have always been predominantly an amateur side, and clerical wicketkeepers vied with one another in excellence at excommunicating the batsmen of the 1890s. *Dudley Carew*

The Honourable F. S. Jackson

by C. B. Fry

The name of F. S. Jackson connotes all that is best in the best cricket. He is captain of the England eleven, a more than first-class batsman and a first-rate bowler. There, for most people, F. S. Jackson begins and ends. He is a great cricketer.

Does, then, that high, broad forehead think only of cricket problems? Do those firm lips tighten only for an effort to compass an extra inch or two of off-break? – those keen, shrewd, blue eyes stay wide open only the better to see a fast yorker? By no means. The same imperturbable decision, the same wholesome alertness, the same direct common sense as are familiar in 'Jacker' to comrades and opponents in Test Matches are recognised in 'Mr Stanley' by clerks, foremen and hands of the big business in Leeds. Recognised, too, no doubt, and appreciated, in the boardroom of the *Yorkshire Post*, and of other important companies. But does a single spectator at Lord's know that the batsman whose cutting and driving stir his enthusiastic applause is a director of the Yorkshire Post, Limited?

On the whole – though we say it who should not – there is some foundation for the recent outcry against the exaggerated importance attaching to success in games. But it should be clearly understood that this faulty perspective is not the fault of the men who achieve distinction in popular forms of athletics. If ever there was a standing, living, breathing contradiction of the 'flannelled fool' fallacy it is a man like Stanley Jackson. Did you not know him as a great cricketer you would entirely fail to discover him as such in the ordinary relations of life. Such men as he regard cricket, even of the most important kind, as mere interesting by-play. His conversation is not of 'strokes' and 'form', but of social, political and broadly general interest. He has succeeded in cricket because, given the physical attributes demanded by the game, he has brought to it the same sterling qualities of intellect and character which ensure success in any undertaking – broad-minded, shrewd common sense, the power of seeing facts as they are, of being equal to the occasion, the only kind of equality worth consideration between man and man, or men and things.

Surely here is a fine type of Englishman; shrewd, level-headed, fit for success in politics or commerce, yet without a touch of the kind of cleverness which rather should be called cunning; pleasant, tactful and polished; full of wide interests, but careful of detail; a fine man of business, a fine officer, and a fine cricketer. The whole man, were he less natural and positive a personality, might be regarded as a strange mixture – this almost a dandy, save for the unmistakable manliness – this product of Harrow, Cambridge, militia-regimental life, business life in a big provincial town, social life in London, field sports, and cricket. The difficulty is to recognise how small a part is cricket in the whole, when the product is known chiefly as a cricketer. A leading cricketer is almost condemned to cricket – even on the terribly serious playground of a great war. When serving with his regiment in South Africa he was going his usual round of the sentries one dark night. A voice from the darkness, a Yorkshire voice, forgot the rigidly prescribed, 'Halt! Who goes there?' and inquired instead, 'Beg pardon, sir, but it ain't true that Somerset have beaten Yorkshire, is it? I have betted 'arf a crown that it ain't true, and I know as *you* can tell me, sir.' The officer was astounded and shocked at the breach of discipline, but sympathised with a Yorkshireman interested in the fate of his county. 'It went to my heart,' says Mr Jackson, 'as much that he should lose his "'arf-crown" as that we should lose the match. But I happened to have seen the sad news in a cablegram from home, so I had to tell him the truth. Then I severely reprimanded him.'

There is no doubt that before answering the question at all, or inflicting the reprimand, the officer twirled up the ends of his neat yellow moustache, first one end, then the other, and thus considered the matter for a brief but decisive ten seconds, just as he would had it been a matter of changing the bowler, or taking a man from the slips. And there is no doubt that both information and reprimand were conveyed in a modulated, quiet, but distinctly audible voice, as of a minister giving instructions to his private secretary.

It has always been understood that Mr F. S. Jackson will sooner or later devote himself to a political career. Whether there is proper foundation for this expectation is not quite certain. He has always taken a close interest in politics, he is a good speaker, and he has behind him the distinguished and successful career of his father, Lord Allerton, who is best known for his administrative work when, as the Right Hon. W. L. Jackson, he acted, first as Financial Secretary to the Treasury, and afterwards as Chief Secretary for Ireland. Time and the propitious hour will show. Stanley Jackson is the kind of man the country needs at Westminster; but he might, to judge by the current course of Parliamentary life, find the atmosphere of the House not altogether congenial.

As a cricketer he has won a great reputation, not only for mastery of the art of batsmanship, but for nerve, confidence and ability to produce his best effort at a crisis in an important match. 'Jacker's' confidence is quite proverbial. But it is pardonable to suggest that a considerably larger number of first-class batsmen equal him in nerve and confidence than approach him in actual skill.

He is recognised as one of the best all-round cricketers in the history of the game. Leaving W. G. Grace out of the comparison, he ranks with A. G. Steel, George Giffen, and M. A. Noble in point of success, both as a batsman and as a bowler, in England v Australia matches. He is a fine fast-medium right-hand bowler, with a beautifully easy action, a natural knack of spin, and – brains. But his title to be reckoned a great all-round cricketer might rest on his batting alone. He is a great all-round batsman, who has no rival whatever in the present generation of cricketers in the matter of versatility; he has an extraordinary ability of adapting his play to all kinds of the very best bowling, on all kinds of pitches, fast or slow, crumbling or sticky, true or treacherous, easy or difficult; and this without altering his style. There are several batsmen who are first-rate on every kind of pitch, but all of them, in some degree, alter their style to suit the occasion. Stanley Jackson adapts his style to the occasion with a nicety of judgement that almost hides the skill. In his manner of playing he does not admit difficulties. Be the wicket dead or fiery, he is uncramped, and master of his own free, natural, generous style. He has been a great run-getter in Test Matches, because the best bowling on these exacting occasions has never got the upper hand of him, even if now and then it has got him out.

Stanley Jackson is a living example, as a batsman, of the power of unconscious auto-suggestion. He tells himself unconsciously that determined concentration has nothing to fear from any bowling; and he does what he tells himself to do. It is called 'confidence'.

[*1905*]

*

In 1905 Jackson (later Sir Stanley, PC, MP) headed the England batting and bowling averages against Australia, and won the toss five times.

At Harrow his fag had been Winston Churchill.

G. L. Jessop

In 1900 a West Indian side, captained by R. S. A. Warner (a brother of P. F.) and including Learie Constantine's father, Lebrun, visited England and enjoyed themselves immensely. However at Bristol on 28 June, their undisciplined behaviour in the field interfered with a batsman's progress. As Jessop hit numerous deliveries over the pavilion, down the road and in the general direction of the Bristol Channel, the West Indians fell to the ground, where they lay shrieking with laughter. But for this, Jessop's 157 in an hour would have been scored somewhat faster.

*

by Gerald Brodribb

Many cricket watchers tend to reckon the pleasure of their watching according to the batsman's rate of scoring. In previous days any side whose rate fell below a run a minute was regarded as loitering, and this would make an individual's average rate work out at 30 runs an hour. Among the really great batsmen, Woolley and Trumper stand near the top at 55 runs an hour, C. G. Macartney, K. S. Ranjitsinhji, K. S. Duleepsinhji and R. E. Foster at about 50; Bradman, Weekes, A. C. MacLaren and Compton somewhere between 45 and 50. These figures are based on evidence spread over a whole career. Though he was not as prolific a run-getter as these I have mentioned, Jessop was a very consistent scorer, who averaged 32 runs in the course of his career of over 800 innings; he scored over 50 hundreds, including five double centuries, and four times scored two centuries in a match – always a rare feat. That in itself is a fine record, but the supreme feature about it is that Jessop's runs were scored at an average rate of *80* runs an hour.

One of his most sustained hitting feats was at Bradford in 1900. In Gloucester's first innings of 269, Jessop scored 104 in seventy minutes, which included 1 six over the football stand off Rhodes. He also hit 16 fours (2 of which were hits into the crowd off Hirst). It was a lucky innings, but in the second innings, when Gloucester went in wanting 328 to win, Jessop nearly won the match with an astonishing innings of 139 out of 182 in ninety-five minutes, 'quite ten of which were spent in recovering the ball' after he had hit it out of the ground. He reached 50 in twenty-five minutes and 100 in fifty-nine, without at that point having given a single chance, though he gave one soon afterwards. 1900 was a year in which Wilfred Rhodes was carrying all before him, and he took as many as 261 wickets in the season, but in this innings Jessop belaboured him unmercifully. Rhodes was bowling all the time from the football stand end, and, as already stated, Jessop in the first innings had once hit him over the stand on to the football pitch for six. It is no special feat to hit a ball to the roof of the stand, but one right over is a different matter, and at that time six runs were awarded only if the ball cleared the stand completely. In the course of this remarkable innings, Jessop hit Rhodes no less than six times right over the top of the stand on to the football pitch, and registered his 7th six of the innings – again off Rhodes – when he pulled a ball right over the side wall and out of the ground in the direction of wide mid-on. Early in the innings he took 18 runs off an over from Rhodes (0, 6, 0, 6, 2, 4) and the innings became more and more hectic as time went on. The last over Rhodes bowled to him went this way:

1st ball: a cut for four.
2nd ball: a hit for six over the clock on to the football pitch.
3rd ball: not played.
4th ball: a hit deep into the spectators on the off-side, one of whom caught the ball, but four runs only.
5th ball: a hit for six over the football stand.
6th ball: Jessop brilliantly caught on the edge of the long-off boundary by Tunnicliffe.

So Jessop was out, and Gloucester lost by 40 runs. His innings reads: 1, 1, 6, 6, 2, 4, 1, 4, 3, 2, 4, 4, 4, 4, 4, 2, 2, 3, 6, 1, 1, 6, 4, 6, 2, 2, 1, 4, 2, 2, 4, 1, 1, 1, 1, 1, 1, 2, 2, 1, 4, 4, 2, 4, 6, 4, 6. In the course of the two innings of 104 and 139, Jessop had recorded 8 sixes – all off Rhodes – and the news report also mentions several big hits for which only four runs were given; they include two off Hirst into the crowd in the first innings, and two more over the boundary in the second innings, one on to the roof of the football stand off Haigh and the other off Rhodes, already mentioned, which was caught by a spectator. That makes at least twelve hits over the boundary of which we have definite evidence, and no doubt several others cleared it too. Jessop was always reluctant to talk of his own feats, but he once told me that during the match he hit Rhodes over the boundary line 'some fifteen or sixteen times'. Among the other bowlers were Hirst and Haigh, both formidable enough, but Jessop frequently hit the good Yorkshire bowling with special success, and in 1911, when scoring 122 not out in the first Test Trial at Sheffield, he twice on-drove Hirst right over the covered stand and into Bramall Lane, which runs alongside it.

*

On 3 September, 1907, Jessop was playing for Gentlemen of the South against Players of the South at Hastings, the former having secured a first innings lead of 102 in spite of Jessop being bowled Fairservice 0.

*

Jessop's [second] innings began soon after lunch on the second day with the Gentlemen's score at 25 for three. C. P. McGahey was already batting, and the two batsmen put on 108 for the fourth wicket in the next thirty-five minutes; Jessop scored 87 of these runs, having reached his 50 in twenty-four minutes. McGahey was out with the score at 133 for four; but Jessop went on to reach his 100 in forty-two minutes, his 150 in sixty-three minutes, and at the interval his score, according to F. E. Woolley, was 184. Soon after tea Jessop was out – caught (between his knees) by H. R. Butt at deep mid-off off Woolley's bowling. He had scored 191, and not long afterwards the innings closed for a total of 313. Jessop had hit the ball right out of the ground five times to record 5 sixes, and he also hit 30 fours, 2 threes and 10 twos. Despite the extreme pace, his batting was almost faultless, the only possible chance being with his score at 158, when he lofted a hit to square-leg and Woolley, running a long way from third-man, made a fine effort to reach and hold the ball, but just failed to do so.

Frank Woolley says what he most remembers is how Relf, when Jessop was getting started, mentioned to his captain H. R. Butt that he 'could get rid of the bloke'. Butt thereupon put him on to bowl, and 26 runs came off Relf's first over, amid general hilarity. Woolley also says he can still see the way Jessop's fingers were constantly 'working' round the handle of the bat as he came up to bowl to him. Everything about Jessop was quite unorthodox: he crouched down low with bent knees, his bat was abnormally heavy (about 2 lb 9 oz), his peculiar grip made it impossible for him to cover-drive in the normal way, and his famous square-cut was a sort of backhand, in which he was never over the ball. Woolley also says that Jessop never 'hooked' but 'lapped' the ball away to leg, that he constantly hit fast bowlers on the rise over cover's head, and not infrequently slashed them over the ropes. I have heard it said that Jessop was exceedingly double-jointed, and this might account for his flexibility and the way he hit like a spring suddenly uncoiling.

I have tried to pin-point the 5 out-of-the-ground sixes. There are various legends of Jessop hits at Hastings, which may or may not concern this particular innings, since Jessop frequently made runs there. These legends tell of a hit that landed in Queen's Road over the entrance gate and smashed a shop window where now is a shop called 'Colliers'; of one which sent the ball through a first-floor window of a house in Station Road which is directly opposite the entrance to the Bus Station, a carry of at least 130 yards; and whenever Jessop is mentioned at Hastings, someone talks of how he used to break the windows of the Free Christian Church in South Terrace. [*1960*]

*

Mechanically, if not automatically, do Mr Jessop's hands shift up and down the bat in proportion to the length, pace and direction of the ball delivered.

For the mighty straight, or all but straight, drive which lifts the ball out of the ground, Mr Jessop, at the moment of striking, holds the bat at the extreme end of the handle.

For the forcing stroke, which sends the ball humming like a top between cover-point and extra mid-off, the handle is gripped as near as possible in the middle. Whilst, to execute (crouching like a beast of prey about to spring) that manœuvre peculiar to himself which results in a good-length straight ball being despatched to cause trouble amongst the crowd on the square-leg boundary, Mr Jessop slips his right hand downwards till it touches the blade of the bat.

Philip Trevor, 1901

*

In 1901, as in 1900, Yorkshire won the championship and played the Rest of England at Lord's where Jessop took a fancy to St John's Wood Road, his 200 coming in two and a quarter hours. Being a properly disciplined side, Yorkshire never once lay on the ground and shrieked with laughter.

C. Hill

by A. G. Moyes

When a batsman has made 96, 99, 98, 97 and 98 in Test Matches against England, three of them in successive innings, it's a fair assumption that he is both skilful and unfortunate. When you learn that he has made four centuries as well you know that he is something out of the ordinary. Such a man was Clement Hill, the greatest left-handed batsman we have ever seen.

Cricket was in the Hill family. Father John made the first century on the Adelaide Oval in the year in which Clem was born. Clem's brothers, Roy and Solly, both played for the state with distinction, while Frank and Peter had more than a passing acquaintance with the batting art.

As a youngster Clem made 360 for Prince Alfred College against St Peter's College, breaking the record that Joe Darling had held. He was an infant prodigy, but, unlike some of them, he didn't fade out. He was in the South Australian side at the age of seventeen, gaining his place because one of those chosen originally could not get away from business. That man's name is forgotten. It shouldn't be, for he helped to give a chance to a future champion.

Hill had a great season, but it was merely the first of many. He finished it by scoring 150 not out and 56 for the state against Stoddart's side, playing Richardson better than anyone else. He made the 150 on 28 March, which had been popularly supposed to be his birthday. Later it was discovered that he was actually born on 18 March. That didn't matter much, but the fact that an eighteen-year-old youngster could play so superbly against an English team meant much to those who were vitally interested in Australian cricket. But not to all, for when the side to tour England in 1896 was chosen Clem Hill was omitted. He forced his way into it by playing a magnificent innings of 206 not out against New South Wales. It was a dazzling effort, since he got 154 out of the last 197 runs scored.

In England, however, Clem wasn't a success in the Tests. His time had not yet come. In the series which followed he was to establish himself for all time. In the first three matches he did moderately well, and then came the Fourth Test at Melbourne. Australia had lost six for 58 to Richardson and Hearne when Hugh Trumble joined Hill. They added 165 runs for the seventh wicket, an Australian record to this day.

Hill, who was only twenty years of age, had batted No. 3, a position he was to make famous, and in which he was to be followed by Macartney and Bradman. The faster Richardson bowled the more merciless was this youngster. His bat was a flail. Nothing could stand before him. It was one of Test cricket's greatest innings, and it is remembered to this day. In the second innings Hill was out for 0!

And the rest of his career – is it not written in the books designed for that purpose? After all, the man himself is our memory, the cricketer and his methods, his impact on the game.

Clem was my hero when I was a lad in Adelaide. I never dreamt that one day I would play under his leadership: it was enough to stand afar off and admire. We had heard all about Trumper and the great English players, but Hill was there on view. To us he was the whole game of cricket. The others were more or less phantoms, legendary figures. I may as well confess that I never quite lost that hero worship, even when playing with Clem in the South Australian side. By that time I knew that Trumper was a superior player: Clem never left you in any doubts about that. But I also knew that there were few Clem Hills. He may not have been a great tactician, but he was a marvellous chap to play with, always cheerful, always encouraging, even when he tersely told you what should happen to you for some shocking stroke you might have perpetrated.

One night in Sydney he came into the room where Don Steele and I were sleeping. We had both made ducks that day, Don being 'yorked' by Tibby Cotter, and I ... well, forget it. 'Hard luck, son,' he said to Don. Then he turned to me ... The lights went out ... But when the second innings came there was a cheery word of advice that helped a lot. Clem was like that: he loved to see the younger ones get runs.

When Clem took his stance at the wicket purpose and aggression were evident. He wasn't very tall, but he was sturdy, with powerful forearms. He gripped the handle lower than any other top-notcher I have seen, with the attitude of a man who is determined to hit the ball hard. When he moved out to drive it was a perfect advance, one foot behind the other and right to the pitch of the ball. He could slide back with uncanny speed either to glance or to force the ball to the on-side. He loved this forcing shot, and played it with certainty. He could drive straight or past cover with rare speed. When he hit the fast bowler past point it was like the crack of a whip. I have never seen a batsman who could hit the fast bowler with greater fury than Hill. So-called 'bumpers' would have made him dance, but with glee. He could hook with the best of them.

I remember Clem as a fighter always. He could be dour when necessary, but he loved to attack. There were no strokes he could not play, and, being so quick on his feet and so powerful and determined, he was always dangerous, even on a bad wicket. He declined to be subservient to any bowler. He loved to talk cricket. Who could forget that mannerism of his – the flick of the fingers that showed how quickly the bowler sent the ball through? And then he would vary it by turning his hand as he flicked, to indicate the manner in which the bowler turned one back. And sometimes he would gesture with that curved-stem pipe that was his inseparable companion. He was a man born to lead, but by direct methods rather than by finesse. He attacked frontally, never sought the flank. He would go straight through a difficulty. No situation was too difficult to face or to solve. [*1950*]

*

Sir Pelham Warner thought Hill almost a left-handed Trumper, something of a combination of Bardsley and Woolley.

W. Rhodes

by A. A. Thomson

His achievements in cricket resemble those of the high-minded heroes of Samuel Smiles. Not even the most industrious of apprentices who eventually married the alderman's daughter ever achieved the equivalent of starting as England's slow bowler at No. 11, rising to be England's opening batsman at No. 2 and then, twenty-seven years after his first cap, coming back and helping his country to victory in a match-winning bowling performance. If figures are a guide, then he was the greatest of all-rounders, for he made his 1,000 runs twenty times and took his 100 wickets twenty-three times. The years in which these feats coincided were sixteen in number, a record anywhere any time. He is the only cricketer who has scored over 30,000 runs and taken over 4,000 wickets, who has scored over 1,000 runs and taken 100 wickets against Australia and scored over 2,000 runs and taken over 100 wickets in all Test Matches.

It is almost embarrassing to look up the accounts of his triumphs. Figures do not tell everything, but they tell a good deal, just as a map may tell an imaginative person more than a picture.

Consider his seven for 17 at Birmingham in 1902, when he and Hirst flung the Australians out for 36 on a wicket that M. A. Noble described as a perfectly good one; his memorable fifteen for 124 at Melbourne in 1904, which has never been approached, except by Verity's fifteen for 104 at Lord's, thirty years later;* above all, his five for 94 at Sydney in the second innings of the First Test of the 1903–4 series, in which he bowled 40 overs on a perfect batsman's wicket with all Australia's might against him. Trumper at his blazing best made 185 not out, but he did not make many of them off Rhodes. Though he took more wickets in his career than any bowler who ever lived, he was no mere potter of rabbits, any more than Hirst was. He preferred getting the best batsmen out. Year after year in England, he caused a holocaust among the batsmen on flypaper pitches, but in dry seasons, when wickets were easy and batsmen were comfortable, he performed some of his most remarkable feats. His accuracy reached and kept perfection during extremely long spells of bowling and he never, on a good wicket,

* And, of course, Laker's nineteen for 90 at Old Trafford in 1956.

descended to being a mere closer of one end. His scheming brain was ever at work and he would have scorned purely defensive bowling. No Mountie was ever more relentless in getting his man. When he was called back at the age of forty-nine for the unforgettable Oval match of 1926 and was asked if he could still pitch his old immaculate length, he replied: 'Oh, well, I can keep 'em there or thereabouts.' He took a wicket with his first ball in Australia and with his last ball in first-class cricket. He never relaxed. He never took his eye off the ball. He had a record Test career of thirty-one years.

In talking of batsmen, he unhesitatingly named Bradman as the greatest he had known. I gathered that he thought Hobbs the next best and Trumper perhaps the third. Rhodes's admiration of Bradman was easily understandable, for there is in him some affinity with the Australian's steel core. It has been said that if the superhuman power of concentration which Sir Donald Bradman devoted to his batting had been given to any other calling, he might well have succeeded in any career and climbed to the top of any tree. I would myself have said the same of Rhodes's matchless concentration on bowling. That concentration might have taken him anywhere. But where else could it have taken him more satisfyingly?

He spoke of Jessop's match at the Oval and his controlled voice conveyed the responsibility rather than the excitement of that immortal last wicket stand.

'I might have been out twice. Off my glove, the ball went down. It might just as easily have gone up. When I made the winning hit, I just ran and went on running. George was at the other end, and they caught *him* . . . And, mind you,' he added thoughtfully, 'if George Hirst hadn't saved the follow-on in the first innings, neither Jessop nor anybody else could have saved the match.'

Of grounds he said: 'There's only one Lord's, but Old Trafford is a lovely ground . . .'

Of the classic tension of a Yorkshire v Lancashire match he said: 'Oh well, *they* were always a bit keen, but we didn't bother all that . . .'

He said it with a perfectly straight face. A Yorkshireman has his own happy conception of irony.

His bowling action was polished, easy and handsome. To call it mechanical is a compliment in the sense that it had the tireless precision of a well-tuned aircraft engine that would never let its pilot down. On the 1903–4 tour the Australian crowds would barrack his short run up: "One-two-three-*four*, one-two-three-*four* . . ." But he never faltered. Every ball looked exactly alike. Every ball was different. On a bad wicket he must have been a nightmare; a batsman would feel like a hero of an Edgar Allan Poe story. The ball, which without warning would leap, pop or shoot, was more like a jumping cracker than an ordinary cricket ball. On an innocuous wicket his persistently good length was a joy for everyone but the batsman to see, and every delivery differed from the last just by that hair's breadth that could deceive. His modesty prevented him from making extravagant claims for his own accuracy. ('There or thereabouts.') Indeed he might well have said with his predecessor (or spiritual grandfather) Ted Peate: 'This talk of pitching on a spot is tommy-rot, if you will forgive the expression. If you can pitch 'em on a newspaper you're not doing too badly . . .'

With Rhodes, as with Peate, there would be a difference in the pitch of all deliveries, though every one of them would be of perfect length. It was in the elevation that the subtle difference occurred. Rhodes deceived them all . . . Alas, regardless of their doom the little victims played forward or back, as they had done before, and the subtly varied flight of the delivery made the ball do something different, not enormously so, but just enough to make the difference between being in and being out. He must have known every batsman of note in thirty-odd years and, one time or another, he got them all out.

All this thirty-odd playing years he was learning something; the foibles of batsmen are like the frailties of the larger human race. Some we have in common and some are all our own. Wilfred Rhodes knew them all and profited by them 4,184 times. 'There's more in bowling than in just turning your arm over,' he said to me. 'There's such a thing as observation.'

Rhodes was a realist and a perfectionist. He knew exactly how each ball should be bowled and how each stroke should be played, and he was perhaps, as a man of his supreme talents might well be, a little scornful of any effort less than the best.

Late in life Rhodes has been visited with a sad affliction; his magnificent eyesight, which must have been about the best the game has ever known, has progressively worsened until now he is almost blind. Nothing, however, could be further than he from the sentimental conception of an afflicted person. He remains upright as a dart, still the straight, fresh-faced country lad who came from Kirkheaton, well over half a century ago. When I called on him he opened the front door and led me into his sitting-room; when I left, he showed me out and told me he had been tidying up his garden.

'It's no trouble,' he said, pointing downwards. 'I can see those two big white stones.'

That valiance of character, that tenacity of purpose would conquer any difficulty in the world. [*1953*]

*

In his forty-ninth year, Rhodes performed the 'double'; during the eleven years, 1919–29 (at the end of which he was fifty-one), Rhodes's seasonal average was 1,100 runs at 32, and 118 wickets at 15.

WORLD XI

When Cardus gave a broadcast talk in 1950 on his World XI of the twentieth century, he chose Hobbs, Trumper, Bradman, Macartney, F. S. Jackson (captain), Faulkner, Miller, Rhodes, Oldfield, Larwood and Barnes.

This side would, of course, play three-day matches.

Dramatic Finish at the Oval, 1902

by C. B. Fry

Thanks chiefly to the magnificent play of G. L. Jessop, F. S. Jackson and George Hirst, England scored the 263 required to win for nine wickets, and thus won the match by a wicket. Needless to say, the closing stages of the game were dramatic beyond description. It is no exaggeration to say that a finer batting performance has never been achieved. To appreciate the value of it, it is necessary to know that the wicket was all through in favour – most distinctly in favour – of the bowlers. Although no rain fell overnight the pitch yesterday morning, owing to a very heavy dew, was wetter than at close of play on the second day, and it remained a damp-affected pitch to the end.

The Australian bowlers gave it as their opinion that the wicket played more difficult up to lunch than at any time on the previous day. They could make the ball break as much as they liked, and that rather quickly – decidedly more quickly than on the second day. It was not an absolutely sticky wicket, but it was beyond doubt a difficult one. A score of 150 would not have been a bad one under the circumstances; 200 a very good one; 262 was a triumph, against such bowling as the Australians possess.

None but a great batting side could have won the game as played. Not only did the ball break, but it came along at different paces and heights, and several times kicked up nastily, chest-high. It was not impossible to get runs, but to do so demanded the very best brand of play.

The Australian innings was finished off by Lockwood for an addition of seven runs. He clean bowled Armstrong with a trimming fast off-break, and got Kelly lbw to a well-pitched-up straight ball.

At the start of the England innings it was obvious that the batsmen had a difficult task. Trumble and Saunders made the ball talk at once. MacLaren played on to Saunders. He began to run in to drive the ball, and stopped his stroke and blocked the ball. It went off the inside of his bat at an abrupt angle into the wicket. Tyldesley was clean bowled by a fine ball, which pitched on the leg-stump and hit the off. He shaped to play to leg, and failed to alter his stroke in time. Palairet was bowled by identically the same ball, which beat his bat as he played forward. The ball, unfortunately, hit Kelly between the eyes and knocked him out for some minutes. Three wickets for 10.

F. S. Jackson shaped admirably directly he joined Hayward, but the latter was not at all comfortable, and was badly missed at forward short-leg off Trumble. The score was raised to 28; then a drizzling shower fell, and play was stopped for thirty-five minutes. In Saunders's first over after the resumption of the game, Hayward was caught at the wicket in playing forward at the go-away off ball. Kelly also appealed for a stump. Four for 31. It transpired subsequently that Hayward was caught, not stumped.

With Braund in, Jackson continued to play in masterly style. Thanks to his good strokes, the score was raised to 40, when Braund was rather unluckily caught at the wicket off a quick-rising off-break from Trumble, which passed between his gloves. So half the side were out for only 48. The bowling had been excellent on a difficult wicket, and the batting had failed for this and no other reason.

Then began the great partnership between Jackson and Jessop, which turned the fortunes of the day, and made victory possible. They kept in till lunch, taking the score to 87, being respectively 39 and 29 not out. Jackson played superbly. He watched the bowling most carefully, judged the length of the ball every time, played back like a book and lost no chance of scoring. Jessop set about the bowling at once in his usual style, and licked it all over the place. He was more severe upon Saunders than on Trumble, who seemed to keep him rather quiet for him. He picked his balls well, and made no mis-hit or chancy stroke.

At 28 Jessop gave a very difficult chance off Saunders to Trumper at long-off. It was a terrific skimming hit, and the ball swerved away from Trumper to the right as he ran in full tilt. The fielder did well to get to the ball at all. It would have been a most remarkable catch.

During the interval the pitch dried somewhat, and seemed after lunch to play rather plainer. But it was still queer. Jessop did not rush the bowling to start with as much as before, but he scored at a great rate, and soon passed Jackson who, seeing the run of things, restrained himself chiefly to defensive play. Gradually Jessop seemed to take the measure of the bowling all out, and hit terrifically.

The score mounted rapidly to 157, when Jackson returned a slower ball, fairly well pitched up, to Trumble. Had he not been waiting on Jessop and restraining himself, he would probably have hit the ball harder and clear. His 49 was a superb piece of cricket. He proved himself what he is – a great player on a sticky pitch. His back play was an object lesson. He scored by hard off-drives from Saunders's overpitched balls, and also turned him cleverly to the on-side with well-timed flicks. He made one lucky shot between Kelly and short-slip at 41, and also cut a full facer very hard at Armstrong's stomach at wide short-slip off Trumble. But it is absurd to call two such difficult chances in criticising his scientific and judgematic play. Taking everything into consideration, it was as fine an innings as he has ever played. He and his slashing partner had added 109 to the score.

Jessop was 83 when Jackson left. Saunders had been taken off and Armstrong put on at 145 – the first change of bowling. Jessop had quilted the left-hander most unmercifully. By punishing Trumble into the pavilion and elsewhere, he soon ran his score up to 96. The hit which put him at 96 landed high up above the balcony, and he completed his century by a hard late-cut off Armstrong. He then drove the same bowler finely to square-leg where Hopkins nearly got to the catch. This stroke got him out, for soon after he got the same ball, but, hesitating to make the full square-leg drive, cocked the ball round with a quarter-stroke to Noble at short-leg behind the wicket rather deep.

So closed an altogether magnificent innings. The best the great hitter has ever played. He drove, pulled and slashed in his own best style. He scored to every part of the field; from first to last he made not a single mis-hit, save the one that got him out, and picked his balls with the finest judgement. Not the least skilful part of his play was his clever dealing with the difficulty Trumble sometimes caused him. Finer hitting has never been seen. On such a wicket the sureness of the drives was astonishing. It is impossible to do justice in prose to this superb innings, which put victory within the sphere of the possible. He made all the bowling, except Trumble's, appear trash, which it was not.

When Jessop was out 66 runs were wanted, with three wickets to fall, and the hope of winning looked gloomy. But Hirst played a great innings. He began by hitting Armstrong grandly to long-leg, and played back to Trumble in excellent style. Saunders resumed after Jessop left, but Hirst was severe upon him too. With Lockwood he raised the score to 214; then the fast bowler was lbw to Trumble bowling round the wicket – 49 to win.

Then Hirst and Lilley played excellently together. Both hit well. Lilley scored 16 by good driving; an on-drive high was a beauty. He was out unluckily rather to a great catch overhead, off a skimming low drive, by Darling at mid-off some yards deep – 248 for nine; 15 to win. The excitement was intense.

Rhodes showed perfect nerve, and played like the good batsman he is. Noble was on instead of Saunders. A single by Hirst off Trumble made it a tie; then Rhodes drove the same bowler past mid-off, and the game was won.

Hirst's innings was perfect. He showed the most complete nerve at the crisis, and he played brilliant cricket into the bargain. He crowned the good work of Jessop and Jackson. His pulling and driving were splendid, and he placed his strokes well. He tackled Trumble's fine length off-breaks and various tricks with consummate skill. It was a gem of an effort, his 58 not out. Had he failed, of course, the game would have been lost.

Rhodes gave a difficult low chance in the slips off Trumble, but the odds were on the ball. His not out 6 and the way he made it was worth more than most centuries.

Trumble bowled grandly all through the innings unchanged. Saunders was very difficult while he kept his length, but he was now and then loose. Jessop knocked him off his bowling. What a victory!

*

Jessop's century in an hour and a quarter (the second fifty came in fifteen minutes) is the fastest scored in England–Australia Tests.

This was an extraordinary day: when the match was over, the Australians produced an autograph book and politely asked if members of the Press Box would sign.

*

AUSTRALIA

First innings		*Second innings*	
V. T. Trumper b Hirst	42	run out	2
R. A. Duff c Lilley b Hirst	23	b Lockwood	6
C. Hill b Hirst	11	c MacLaren b Hirst	34
J. Darling (captain) c Lilley b Hirst	3	c MacLaren b Lockwood	15
M. A. Noble c and b Jackson	52	b Braund	13
S. E. Gregory b Hirst	23	b Braund	9
W. W. Armstrong b Jackson	17	b Lockwood	21
A. J. Hopkins c MacLaren b Lockwood	40	c Lilley b Lockwood	3
H. Trumble not out	64	not out	7
J. J. Kelly c Rhodes b Braund	39	lbw, b Lockwood	0
J. V. Saunders lbw, b Braund	0	c Tyldesley b Rhodes	2
B 5, lb 3, nb 2	10	B 7, lb 2	9
Total	324	Total	121

	First innings				*Second innings*			
	O	M	R	W	O	M	R	W
Lockwood	24	2	85	1	20	6	45	5
Rhodes	28	9	46	0	22	7	38	1
Hirst	29	5	77	5	5	1	7	1
Braund	16.5	5	29	2	9	1	15	2
Jackson	20	4	66	2	4	3	7	0
Jessop	6	2	11	0				

Fall of wickets: 1–47, 2–63, 3–82, 4–82, 5–126, 6–174, 7–175, 8–256, 9–324, 10–324.

1–6, 2–9, 3–31, 4–71, 5–75, 6–91, 7–95, 8–114, 9–115, 10–121

ENGLAND

First innings		*Second innings*	
A. C. MacLaren (captain) c Armstrong b Trumble	10	b Saunders	2
L. C. H. Palairet b Trumble	20	b Saunders	6
J. T. Tyldesley b Trumble	33	b Saunders	0
T. Hayward b Trumble	0	c Kelly b Saunders	7
F. S. Jackson c Armstrong b Saunders	2	c and b Trumble	49
L. C. Braund c Hill b Trumble	22	c Kelly b Trumble	2
G. L. Jessop b Trumble	13	c Noble b Armstrong	104
G. H. Hirst c and b Trumble	43	not out	58
W. H. Lockwood c Noble b Saunders	25	lbw, b Trumble	2
A. A. Lilley c Trumper b Trumble	0	c Darling b Trumble	16
W. Rhodes not out	0	not out	6
B 13, lb 2	15	B 5, lb 6	11
Total	183	Total (nine wickets)	263

	First innings				*Second innings*			
	O	M	R	W	O	M	R	W
Trumble	31	13	65	8	33.5	4	108	4
Saunders	23	7	79	2	24	3	105	4
Noble	7	3	24	0	5	0	11	0
Armstrong					4	0	28	1

Fall of wickets: 1–31, 2–36, 3–63, 4–67, 5–67, 6–83, 7–137, 8–179, 9–183, 10–183

Second innings: 1–5, 2–5, 3–10, 4–31, 5–48, 6–157, 7–187, 8–214, 9–248

Umpires: C. E. Richardson and A. White

The Great Bat Auction

On 15 September, 1902, forty-four bats were auctioned in aid of the Cricketers' Benevolent Fund Society; the sum realised was £242 3s 6d (about £4,000 by today's standards). Sixteen were bought by A. Farrants of Ye Olde Spotted Horse, Putney, other purchasers giving their addresses as London, Monmouth, Trowbridge, Colwyn Bay, Ostend and Johannesburg. Several members of the victorious Australian touring side donated bats, the public's response affording some indication of how such masters as Clem Hill and M. A. Noble were regarded.

	£	s	d
Major W. C. Hedley (three of whose four innings for Devon in 1902 had totalled 1 run)	1	15	0
W. Barnes (who once scored a century at Lord's when drunk)	1	15	0
W. H. Scotton (the bat of the supreme stone-waller and therefore presumably unsullied)	2	0	0
S. M. J. Woods	2	5	0
M. A. Noble	2	5	0
S. E. Gregory	2	10	0
A. A. Lilley	2	12	6
L. C. Braund	2	15	0
P. F. Warner (this bat was destined for Ostend)	3	0	0
J. T. Tyldesley	3	0	0
Clem Hill	3	0	0
L. C. H. Palairet (even those who lived to watch R. H. Spooner, F. E. Woolley and A. F. Kippax, regarded Palairet as the greatest stylist)	3	10	0
W. L. Murdoch (the first Australian to score a Test 100 in England)	3	10	0
J. Darling (captain of the 1902 Australians)	3	10	0
W. Gunn (this bat went to Johannesburg)	3	12	6
T. Hayward	4	0	0
A. C. MacLaren	5	5	0
C. B. Fry	5	5	0
Fuller Pilch (on a fiery Lord's pitch in 1837, Pilch was out 'hat knocked on wicket')	5	10	0
R. Abel	6	0	0

	£	s	d
A. Shrewsbury	8	0	0
G. L. Jessop	8	0	0
K. S. Ranjitsinhji	13	13	0
Victor Trumper	42	0	0

But if Trumper's bat had become hallowed in 1902, a darker and more battered piece of wood remained, its handle so thick that only the mightiest paws could grasp it. Gradually, throughout the day, the bids for this bat mounted – '£20', '£25', '£30'. A telegram arrived offering 30 guineas, the telephone rang – '£40'. Shortly before 10 o'clock the honour of England was preserved:

W. G. Grace	£50	0	0

INFLATION

The modern cricketer will do a lot for money. He will hawk autographed miniature bats in Calcutta, one of the world's most impoverished cities, to children in the crowd at £15 a time.

John Woodcock, The Times, 10 May, 1977

The South African Googly Masters, 1907

*by R. E. Foster**

The season will always be remembered by two distinct features. 1 – The extremely bad weather. 2 – The South Africans' bowling. The less said about the former the better, though the rain and the consequent soft wickets did raise a very interesting question; namely, would the South Africans have fared better in a good dry season? Now, looking at their performances against the counties, it seems difficult to conceive how they could have improved on their magnificent record, however good and fast the wickets might have been. Before their arrival in this country we were told that they must have hard wickets to really suit their particular kind of bowling, but the way they bowled, not only in representative games, but against the counties on sticky wickets, was a revelation to many a good judge of cricket. The feature of their bowling on these wickets was the extraordinary pace the ball came off the pitch. This was to be expected on fast wickets, but no one had foreseen that the same thing would happen on really slow ones. Truly, as one old hand said in the Test Match at Leeds, it was like playing Briggs through the air and Tom Richardson off the pitch. Now, the opinion of English cricketers who went to South Africa with the MCC team in 1905 is, that there is all the difference in the world between our fast good wickets and the South African matting wickets, and this lies in the varying height in the bound of the ball. On the matting the ball nearly always has to be played about chest high, a fact enormously increasing the difficulty of dealing with such bowling. On our fast wickets the ball may turn very quickly and go either one of two ways, but it nearly always comes the same height; and I maintain that the English team would have got any amount of runs under such conditions, and more than that, the South Africans would not have done so well in a dry season. Had the Test Matches been played on matting it quite possibly might have been another matter, though it is open to question (their batting being rather a weak point) if the bowling could have carried them to victory in representative games. The South African bowlers

* In 1900 Foster (1878–1914) scored a century for Oxford in the university match; ten days later, also at Lord's, he made 102 not out and 136 against the Players. His 287 at Sydney in December 1903 remained the highest individual Anglo-Australian Test score until Bradman's 334 at Leeds in 1930. He was captain of England in 1907.

could be hit on a good wicket, and it is possible that a little more enterprise might have spelt success. Jessop showed they could be hit, in a magnificent display in the First Test Match, on a good wicket; but he also showed, at Leeds and the Oval, that they could not be hit on a bad wicket, for not only did the ball turn too quickly, but it came a different height and pace. The result of a comparison of the dangers presented by the South African attack on fast and slow wickets seems to point to a preference for the latter, and I know this to be the opinion of most of the players who represented England against them.

Now let us turn to a detailed description of the bowling. The interest in the attack of the South Africans is centred round four men – Schwarz, Vogler, Faulkner and White. These men all bowled with a leg-break action, and could make the ball come in from the off. Though England can claim the 'proud originator' of this style of bowling in Bosanquet, it has been left to South Africa to improve it – I will not say perfect – as I am convinced that this style is capable of still further improvement, which in time will be brought nearly to perfection. Bosanquet taught Schwarz, and Schwarz taught the others and the others are better than their mentors, as Bosanquet has practically given up bowling in this way, and Schwarz, possibly because he finds he can get as many people out as he wishes, only breaks the ball from the off, but always with a leg-break action. His has been a great achievement this year, of which he and the South Africans may justly be proud, for he is top of the bowling averages, having taken 143 wickets with an average of 11·51 apiece, a performance that speaks for itself. It is rather hard to explain his great success, as, though his bowling is the most difficult to hit of the four bowlers mentioned, it is much the easiest to play, because he only breaks one way, and the batsmen have never got to think of the possibility of the ball breaking the other way. The ball comes very slow through the air, and having hit the ground goes off at the most extraordinary pace. There is nothing very deceptive in the flight, but the break varies from 6 inches to 18 inches, and on sticky wickets he is quite capable of breaking a yard. Now, a bowler of this description, you will say, must bowl many loose balls; certainly he does, but the pace the ball comes from the wickets imparted by the spin, makes it very difficult indeed for the batsman to place it accurately between the fielders, six of whom are placed in various parts of the on-side, and hitting at random at such bowling courts disaster, and I am sure is one of the causes of his success this year. In addition to this reason, Schwarz is extraordinarily deadly to the last four or five batsmen, and the man who goes in for his county side in rather a humble position seems to have no notion how to play such bowling. He is a great bowler, but I am convinced he gets many more wickets than he should. Play him with your legs – old pavilion critics forgive, but we have to deal with bowling you never had to trouble about – don't hit at him, place him for ones and twos, and wait for the real bad one which you will occasionally get and can score off. Very often a bowler of Schwarz's description will suffer at the umpire's hands, but it must be well-nigh impossible to tell if the batsman is out when a ball comes so quickly off the pitch, and knowing how much the bowler is capable of making the ball break; finally, I cannot help thinking that Schwarz would prove more deadly could he control his break – i.e., break nothing to a foot, and I believe that he would get many good batsmen out with the ball that does not break at all.

A. E. Vogler

by R. E. Foster

A. E. Vogler was undoubtedly the finest bowler of a very good lot, indeed many good judges consider him the best bowler in the English cricket season of 1907. He has rather a hesitating run up to the wicket, but in the last few steps never gets out of his stride. The ball is well concealed from the batsman before delivery, and the flight and variation of pace are very deceptive indeed. With a new ball, Vogler makes the ball swing quite a lot and often starts bowling fast-medium off-break, with a swerve. He then will have two slips and a short leg, and perhaps no man out in the country. With the newness worn off the ball he will settle down to his ordinary slow-mediums, in which case his field will be, with the exception of three men, disposed of on the on-side of the wicket. Vogler, like Schwarz and other bowlers who have cultivated this particular type of bowling, imparts that spin to the ball which enables it to leave the pitch at such a wonderful pace. His usual ball is the leg-break, but once in two overs perhaps he will bowl what the South Africans have designated 'the wrong 'un'. Now it is almost impossible to see this ball coming; it seems to the batsman that the ball is delivered in identically the same manner and yet it comes the other way, i.e., from the off. After very careful watching the only difference one can detect, and this is possibly fancy, is that the hand seems to be turned rather more over in the action of delivery. The ball seems to come more out of the back of the hand, and the batsman may be able to see almost the palm of the bowler's hand. But it is almost impossible to notice any difference, and I was told Sherwell had said that Vogler was the bowler he found most difficult in detecting. Vogler's ordinary leg-break will turn from 2 or 3 inches up to 18 inches, but the other one coming from the off rarely breaks more than 3 or 4 inches and frequently comes perfectly straight through, and in this case will come even faster off the pitch than the balls that turn. This possibly is due to the bowler intending to bowl the off-break, and, through not quite turning the hand or fingers sufficiently, imparts a top spin. This makes the ball come straight through very quickly and is one of the most difficult balls to deal with – lbw so often resulting. Vogler bowls a slow yorker or well-pitched-up ball that is very deceptive in the flight and seems more to quiver than swing in the air. He clean bowled C. B. Fry with this ball both at Leeds and at the Oval in the Test Matches. As will be seen then, Vogler is a bowler of infinite variation, unbounded resource, and what is better than all, of great natural ability. He can bowl for a long time and does not seem to tire or lose his length. His performances at Lord's this year against a very strong MCC eleven and again in the First Test Match were as good as anything seen at headquarters for years. Vogler's average for the season works out at 133 wickets for 15 apiece, and in Test Matches he was, taken all through, much the best and most consistent bowler on the South African side, though actual figures bring Faulkner out above him, due mainly to a great performance in England's first innings at Leeds. Schwarz does not come out so well, a third of his total number of wickets being obtained in the last innings at the Oval when the English side were risking wickets in order to obtain runs quickly, another instance of the argument that Schwarz cannot be hit recklessly. In Vogler the South Africans possess undoubtedly a bowler of the highest class, and in the writer's humble opinion the greatest bowler playing cricket in either hemisphere at the present time, and we may dismiss him with many congratulations on his great performances, and many thanks for the great interest and pleasure his bowling has afforded this summer to all lovers of cricket.

*

Faulkner and White in the ordinary way deliver much the same ball as the English batsman is accustomed to expect and receive from a leg-break bowler of the Braund–Vine type with two notable differences – (*a*) the ball comes from the pitch at a far greater pace; (*b*) the terrible 'wrong 'un'. In the first case, as has been said above, this characteristic is evident in each of the four bowlers under consideration, and the reason for it is very difficult to explain. A possible cause may be found in the fact that ordinary leg-break bowlers deliver the ball chiefly by the swing of the arm and allowing the ball to come from the back of the hand, whereas the South Africans seem to deliver the ball with a flick, relying entirely on finger and wrist for spin. In the second case both bowlers can effectively bowl the ball that comes from the off with a leg-break action, but again in a measure differ. Faulkner makes the ball break quite a lot from the off and practically always makes it break; White on the other hand makes the ball break comparatively little and very often comes straight through, therefore Faulkner is more likely to clean bowl a batsman and White to get him lbw. Neither has a deceptive flight, and it is possible to see the off-break coming in both cases occasionally. Indeed I venture to think that with more practice against such bowling, batsmen would soon find far less difficulty in seeing the break and possibly might never be at fault. In Vogler's case and in future artists of his class that may arise (as this type of bowling and the art of concealing a break will greatly improve), I doubt if the batsmen will ever be impossible to deceive.

I believe this new type of bowling will deteriorate batting from the spectator's point of view, for it is a very great invention, and it is possible it may completely alter cricket, and no one who has not played against it can realise the difference it makes to a batsman and his shots. It must again be reiterated that this type of bowling is practically in its infancy, and if persevered with – as it surely will be – must improve and become more difficult to deal with.* Now a batsman when he goes in may receive a ball which either breaks from the off, perhaps from the leg, or again may come straight through very quickly. If he survives half-a-dozen overs he ought to be getting set, but such bowling never allows a batsman to get really set, because he can never make or go for his accustomed shots.

*

The effect of the googly in 1907 may be deduced from the South African bowling averages: Schwarz 137 wickets at 11·79, White 56 at 14·73, Vogler 119 at 15·62 and Faulkner 64 at 15·82. Schwarz required 31 balls for each wicket, the others 30.

In 27 first-class matches, only four batsmen (C. B. Fry, J. Hardstaff, snr, T. Hayward and L. C. Braund) scored centuries against the South Africans.

* In the 1909–10 South Africa–England series, which the home side won by three matches to two, Vogler took 36 wickets and Faulkner 29 – but in nine innings Hobbs averaged 67.

G. A. Faulkner

by Neville Cardus

On 10 September, 1930, Major Aubrey Faulkner, DSO, was found dead in his office at the Faulkner School of Cricket, Walham Green, Fulham. The room was full of gas, the doors and windows shut.

Only a week or two ago I lunched every day during the Manchester and Oval Test Matches with Aubrey Faulkner, and, as always, I enjoyed his splendid conversations on cricket, his personal charm, frankness, downrightness, his genius for the game, his own quick cricket sense, his readiness to listen to points of view other than his own, his simple humour, his boyish love of a joke at the expense of the solemnity of the professional attitude. The news of his death yesterday frankly knocked the present writer over. Cricketers have lost a rare friend, and the game has lost one of the greatest all-round players that ever lived.

In a certain respect he was the cleverest technician of them all, for not only was he a batsman who could be called a stylist and a master, but also he helped to develop, and in time became a commanding exponent of, the 'googly', the most difficult of all balls. To become a great 'googly' bowler a lifetime's study is required of most men; you don't expect a Freeman to go to the wicket and score a hundred with the art of an Aubrey Faulkner. In Test Matches for South Africa he scored over 1,700 runs at an average of 41·87, and he took 82 wickets at 25 runs each. During the first South African tour of Australia in 1910–11, Faulkner in Test Matches scored consecutively 62, 43, 204, 8, 56, 115, 20, 80, 52 and 92. He mingled, as a batsman, defence and offence in proportion. He could hit powerfully and beautifully all round the wicket; but never did he take his eye off the ball or let his body fall away from the ball's line.

During the season just over Faulkner frequently expressed his opinion that Bradman's success was the consequence of an ability to make late strokes with the body right over and on top of the ball. Faulkner made his great scores against some of the finest bowlers in the history of cricket. He exploited the 'googly' at medium pace, and, unlike other South African spin bowlers, he was not at a loss when he came from matting to the turf of this country. In 1912 he took 163 wickets on

English pitches at 15·42 runs each. At Leeds, in July, 1907, Faulkner in eleven overs accounted for Hayward, Tyldesley, Braund, Jessop, Arnold and Lilley – for 17 runs. He bowled the leg-break and the 'googly' so skilfully that there was little in the flight of each ball to disclose its essential problem. His pace off the pitch was killing, and his curve through the air was always thoughtfully directed. A more studious cricketer never played; he was constantly pondering principles and possibilities. When the time came for him to give up active service he could not leave the game alone; he established a school in London where he did invaluable work at a period when first-class cricket was badly in want of culture and experienced teaching. One or two Lancashire cricketers enjoyed instruction from Faulkner; I think Hopwood, Iddon and Booth will all agree that they learned points from Faulkner that will help them all their lives. It was Faulkner's insight that saw the promise in Peebles; he worked hard and patiently to hand on to the young bowler his own mysterious craft.

In 1921 Faulkner emerged from retirement and played for MacLaren's team at Eastbourne; he scored 153 in the second innings,* and in the match took six wickets for 63. At the crisis Australia were within 53 of victory and five wickets had to be taken. MacLaren then asked Faulkner to bowl. At the Oval the other week Faulkner laughed over this most trying moment of his career. 'I didn't want to go on,' he said. 'And I told Archie to try somebody else because I was out of practice, and a bad "googly" bowler can lose a match in a minute. But Archie was obstinate, and, with my heart in my mouth, I tossed up a leg-break to Andrews. He was clean bowled. Then Armstrong came in, and I remembered that he never liked the "googly". With my heart beating, I sent up the "wrong 'un". Armstrong, all at sea, got his legs there. Then I sent the straight top-spinner, and Armstrong again used his pads. He was out, didn't like it, but had to go.' MacLaren's team thus defeated the Australians for the first time in their wonderful summer of 1921, and Faulkner's genius can seldom, in all his magnificent career, have seemed so vital and resourceful as on that unforgettable mellowing August afternoon at the Saffrons.

He brought dignity to a game because he played it with his whole heart and mind – and they were big and manly, both of them. You could not conceive of a mean stroke by Faulkner, or a stupid, idealess ball. Cricket with Faulkner was his way of life. That his life is now ended, so soon after the Test Match at the Oval, where he seemed as

* 'I coached myself as I went along,' said Faulkner later, 'the Aussies must have thought I was mad.'

full of energetic love of the game as ever – this is hard to believe and cruel to believe.

*

G. A. Faulkner considered Trumper the greatest batsman he had ever seen or bowled against. However, asked the finest cricket he had witnessed – 'Taylor playing Barnes on matting'.

N.S.W. 2nd XI

How would this Trumper fare if he entered cricket today [1951], when a team plays to win only if there is time after making itself safe from defeat? He would be lectured on the need to respect the new ball and play himself in instead of adventurously challenging the bowlers from the start. He would find selectors attaching importance to something he never thought about – his average. This inconsistent spellbinder, who captivated the cricket world yet made blobs in three consecutive Test innings, would be moved down from opening batsman. He would be demoted to the second eleven and kept there until he learned restraint, learned not to advance so far along the pitch, not to steer fast yorkers to the leg boundary under his uplifted left foot – the stroke delicately described as the dog shot. He would be taught to forget the lofted drive (except as a liberty to be taken when the enemy bowlers were worn to a frazzle).

Ray Robinson

Tempi

ALLEGRO CON BRIO

In 1910–11 Australia and South Africa played five timeless Tests. At Adelaide the home bowlers, who included the very fast Cotter, achieved 20 overs to the hour but there was criticism of South Africa's dilatory progress – 482 at 60 runs an hour. Fortunately Trumper then restored tempers by making 214 not out in four hours. The average runs per match in this series was 1,210 in three and a half days.

MARCIA FUNÈBRE

In 1954–55 Pakistan and India played five four-day Tests, all drawn. Played to a finish, at the prevailing rate of scoring and fall of wickets, the runs per match would have been 951 scored in five and a half days.

On 16 January, 1977, at Madras, on what the England manager and captain called 'a perfect batting wicket', India and England passed a five and a half hour day by bowling 64 overs from which 152 runs were scored. In the not so distant past the Indian slow left-arm bowler, R. G. Nadkarni, controlled things far better. Between 1960 and 1965 in 19 home Tests against England, Australia, New Zealand and Pakistan, he took 44 wickets at 23·72 off 748·4 overs.

Had there been a Nadkarni bowling unchanged at both ends on 16 January, 1977, 64 overs would have realised 90 runs.

S. F. Barnes

by Bernard Hollowood

My father regarded Barnes as the greatest bowler of all time, though he invariably spoke disparagingly of him in other contexts than cricket. They had played together for Staffordshire during Syd's golden years and had battled against each other on numerous occasions in the League. Barnes, my father said, was as mean as they come, and 'difficult' – by which I understood him to mean that he didn't care very much for Barnes's brand of heavy sarcasm and bitter comment. But there was no doubt whatever about his genius. 'Oh, yes, he could bowl 'em all, but he got his wickets with fast leg-breaks. Marvellous, absolutely marvellous, he was. Fast leg-breaks and always on a length.' Others, Barnes included, have claimed that he bowled every known ball except the googly – swingers, off-breaks, top-spinners, the lot. But undoubtedly his *chef d'œuvre* was the leg-break. He took a long run, a bounding, springy run and as his arm came over in a perfect action, mid-on and mid-off could hear the snap of his long fingers as they rolled and squeezed the ball into its revolutionary parabola. There has been no one like him. O'Reilly could bend them from leg, but not with Barnes's consistency or devil; Douglas Wright could bowl fastish leg-breaks, but not on the length that destroys and goes on destroying.

He was a strange man, a social misfit in the cricket scene of Victorian, Edwardian and Georgian days. He might have been a Keir Hardie or a George Lansbury or a Frank Cousins if he had turned his mind to politics, for he was forever kicking against the pricks and quarrelling with the Establishment. He considered himself undervalued by his employers, insufficiently recognised, and overworked, and he would down tools as readily as an East End docker. Throughout his long playing career he carried outsize chips on his shoulder, and not one of the many clubs he played for could ever be certain of his unqualified loyalty and co-operation.

He resented discipline not because he wanted complete freedom but as a matter of principle. At all levels of the game he had to be handled with kid gloves – by captains, colleagues and committees. Outspoken himself, he resented outspokenness in others and displayed acute sensibility to any word or deed that slighted his personal Bill of Rights. Put on to bowl at the 'wrong' end, he would scowl and sulk and develop mysterious physical disorders, sprains and strains. Time and time again his career was broken by some real or imagined injustice. He would be on top of the world, the master bowler wanted by his country, a dozen counties, scores of League clubs: and then he would disappear from public view. At the height of his powers he dropped out of the England team for years at a stretch. He sampled county cricket, played a match or two and quit.

The most common reason for these surprising exits was finance. Cricketers are poorly paid today: in Barnes's time they scratched a living, and unless they found jobs during the winter – which wasn't easy – those with family responsibilities existed only marginally above the subsistence line. The old pro of the sentimental school of cricket writers is a dear fellow, nut-brown and salty-tongued, who reminisces cheerfully with pipe and pint at every opportunity. In reality, a majority of the county cricketers who ended their careers before the Hitler war found their middle- and old-age blighted by poverty. There were no pension funds for them, no large lump sums from benefit matches and only a handful, the spectacularly successful, picked up good money on the side from journalism, authorship, lecturing, advertising, coaching and sponsoring. There was no money in radio, and television was not yet in action.

The players had no union to protect them so that they were more or less compelled to accept whatever wage their counties thought reasonable, and the counties were governed by autocratic amateurs who treated the professionals with the kindly condescension that they reserved for their domestic servants, gardeners and local tradesmen. And it was this that made Barnes see red. His trouble, at root, was that he demanded equality of opportunity and the abolition of class distinctions fifty or sixty years before the rest of the country, and at a time when the lot of the vast majority was docile servitude.

His take-it-or-leave-it attitude of no compromise was a new phenomenon in industrial relations – on the employees' side – and obviously it produced deadlock when matched by similar obstinacy from the bosses. Barnes asked for travelling expenses on top of his wage: the county told him that the wage included the travelling expenses; Barnes said that if they didn't meet his modest request he would leave the club; the county said they couldn't be dictated to by players. End of contract. Barney retires fuming to his tent. He told the Lancashire secretary that he expected the county to find him a decent job during the winter and was rebuffed, the secretary saying that 'it couldn't be bothered'. Barnes was promised a benefit match if he served the club dutifully and successfully for eight years, and Syd asked for the Roses Match, Lancashire v Yorkshire, at Old Trafford on a bank holiday. The secretary explained that the club had never done as much for other players and couldn't make an exception for Barnes. So Barnes walked out.

On the field he was always a trier, always active mentally and physically. He wanted the game to be run his way and was openly critical of almost every captain he played under. If his advice was not heeded he grumbled and then retreated into cold fury. He set himself the highest standards of play and could not tolerate inefficiency in others. His masters paid by results and Barnes sweated and schemed to achieve rewarding figures, and anyone who reduced the effectiveness of his efforts through slackness, inability or misfortune had to suffer the consequences, scathing looks and words and a display of icy scorn.

His colleagues admired his skills, but were terrified of incurring his displeasure and found games with him a sore trial. So there was no great outcry when the selectors omitted the name Barnes, S. F. from their national elevens. I suspect that on these occasions – and they were numerous – all the more easy-going Players and most of the Gentlemen breathed a sigh of relief.

I was frankly afraid of Barnes, afraid of his scowling displeasure, his ferocious glare, his crippling silences and his humiliating verbal scorn, and I played with him and against him only when he was beginning to mellow! 'There's only one captain of a side,' he used to say, 'when I'm bowling – me!'

He could be an ogre on the field, but away from the business of the day he could relax with pipe and drink sufficiently to be vastly entertaining as he dealt in wry, economic humour, pontificated judgements and mechanical chuckles. At Colwyn Bay, Staffordshire against Denbighshire, a courting couple outside the ground on a rise above the sight-screen distracted a batsman and failed to understand the umpire's yells and gestures. Barnes got up from the grass, where he had been taking a breather, cupped his hands round his mouth and shouted 'Down 'er, man! Down 'er!' Then universal laughter, the magic twinkle in Barnes's eye and the 'funny haha' chuckle. Great.

But a few overs later his face was like a pea soup fog. I had just missed a sitter in the slips. Straight to me, knee-high, in and out. He found it hard to forgive, to utter the conventional comforts of 'Hard luck!' 'Never mind!' 'We all drop 'em sometimes' or friendly, assuaging banter.

Barnes's greatest admirer, I suppose, was A. C. MacLaren who picked him largely on the strength of his performances in the leagues. But even MacLaren was upset by Barnes's surly intractableness. When warned that the ship carrying the English team was in danger, the captain reacted philosophically: 'There's one comfort,' he said, 'if we go down that bugger Barnes will go down with us.'

Cricketers and cricket writers who did not know him in his playing days have the strange idea that Barnes was always the genial, cryptic conversationalist of his octogenarian years, the familiar memorable figure who sat with the blind Wilfred Rhodes at Test Matches, the dispenser of memorabilia and bonhomie. He wasn't. After a lifetime of groaning and bickering, Barnes began to enjoy the fame that had so long been denied him. His achievements were put into perspective and illuminated anew by the fantastic exploitation of cricket in the post-war years by radio, television, the press and book-publishing. He was fêted, honoured, befriended, wined and dined, and he thoroughly enjoyed his belated helping of jam on his bread. It surprised him, this adulation, for hitherto he had assumed that he alone was aware of his genius. And I suppose he must often have wondered as the plaudits rolled forth how different his life would have been had he been able to 'fit in' and accept discipline in his playing days. Nothing is more certain than that he would have broken every bowling record in the book.

On the field Barnes radiated belligerency. Like all the best bowling craftsmen he hated batsmen and believed that every ball delivered should be their last. Bradman triumphed mentally over the opposition because he really did regard his wicket as impregnable. Barnes scythed through batsmen because he believed in the divine right of Barnes.

[*1971*]

BARNES AT MELBOURNE, 30 DECEMBER, 1911

by Jack Fingleton

The band in Melbourne was playing comic-opera tunes as the Englishmen were led out by Johnny Douglas. The early morning was dull and close and around eleven o'clock there were a few drops of rain. The weather looked like developing into a thunderstorm. But Clem Hill, winning the toss, feared neither the light nor the moisture-laden atmosphere – lending swing to a new ball – nor even the pitch. 'Bad luck, Johnny,' he said to Douglas, 'we'll bat.'

There was a slight mist as the umpires walked out. Bardsley had been put through a pretty rigorous physical test and had been pronounced fit, although, after a battering from Foster in Sydney, he was well strapped up as he walked out with Kelleway to open the innings. Kelleway was very wary in playing the first over from Foster. Then Barnes prepared to bowl to Bardsley. Barnes, in collaboration with Douglas, took a long time to settle his field. He was most pernickety in this matter.

At last he was satisfied and over came the first ball. It was on a good length and Bardsley shaped at it very cautiously. He missed, and it hit him on the leg and went into his stumps – an in-swinger that would have had the Australian lbw had it not bowled him. Another left-hander, Hill, was next, and he took a single from the first ball, a fact to be noted because it was a long time before another run was scored from Barnes. Hill faced up to Barnes again for his next over, and a torrid one it was. There was an immediate and loud appeal for lbw but it was rejected, and Hill, defending desperately, saw the over through. Kelleway faced Barnes for his next over. He missed completely an in-swinger on his leg stump that straightened up and he was out lbw. Australia: two for 5.

In came Armstrong and he saw Hill in all manner of trouble. Barnes gave him one that was an off-break to him, and followed with an in-swinger. Then came one a little wider, going away, which Hill allowed to pass. The final ball of the over pitched on Hill's leg-stump and hit the top of the off-stump. Australia: three for 8.

As captain, Hill had put Trumper lower on the list so that he could bat with the sheen gone from the ball. But Trumper came now with the ball still almost new. Meanwhile, spectators were busy recalling an earlier tour by Warner's team when Australia batted in Sydney on a perfect pitch under a thundery sky, and Hill, Trumper and Duff were out for 12, leaving Noble and Armstrong to stop the collapse. This time, as Trumper walked out in the tense atmosphere, a great cheer went up. Trumper would succeed where the others had failed! Armstrong drove Foster for three and then faced Barnes. Immediate exit! He snicked his first ball and Smith caught him behind.

Four Australian wickets were gone for 11, and of that very modest figure only a single run had been scored from Barnes. He had taken four wickets for one run! Test cricket had not seen the like of this before. Ransford, on his home ground, now joined Trumper, and the latter brought a relieved cheer, like a clap of thunder, as he brilliantly back-cut Foster. The ball went like a streak, incidentally hitting Douglas on the shins, and the batsmen ran two. Rain began to fall now and the players came off after forty-five minutes of play.

They were back again fifteen minutes later. Barnes bowled a maiden to Ransford, feverishly defensive. Then in the next over, from Foster, Trumper made two delicious late-cuts to the rails. It looked like another maiden over from Barnes to Ransford, but the left-hander got Barnes away to leg for a single off the last ball. It had been an hour since the previous and only run had been taken from Barnes.

Barnes didn't seem himself in his next over. He bowled a full-toss that went high over Ransford's head for four byes. At the end of the over he spoke to Douglas. Barnes had been ill during the preceding week and there was a doubt whether he would play. He told Douglas that he couldn't see the other end. Everything seemed to be going round and round.

So, to the great relief of the Melbourne crowd – and also of the batsmen at the wickets – Barnes left the field. He didn't return until after lunch.

The Australian players, on their way from the dressing-room to lunch in another pavilion, had to run the gauntlet of many an anxious inquiry from the spectators. What was wrong? Was something amiss with the wicket? To all inquiries the humbled Australians gave the one reply, 'Barnes!'

Foster knocked Trumper's stumps back after lunch, and then Barnes took the ball again. Australia: five for 33. Minnett, a notable performer in the preceding Test at Sydney, came next and promptly snicked Barnes to third-slip. He was dropped. But after scoring two, he skied Barnes to cover, where Jack Hobbs was waiting. Six down for 38, and Barnes had the remarkable bowling figures – 11 overs, 7 maidens, 6 runs, 5 wickets. [*1958*]

*

England 265 (W. Rhodes 61, J. W. Hearne 114) and 219 for two (J. B. Hobbs 126 not out) beat Australia 184 (Barnes five for 44) and 299 (W. W. Armstrong 90; F. R. Foster six for 91) by eight wickets.

*

When Hampshire played Gloucestershire in 1911, Jessop scored a century in each innings, his 276 for once out coming at 79 runs an hour.

Inevitably after this, *Wisden* regarded C. B. Fry's 258 not out with misgivings, the great batsman playing with 'considerable caution'. Fry scored at 50 runs an hour.

H. W. Taylor

by Chris Greyvenstein

It is generally agreed that Taylor was the only batsman in the world ever to score consistently off S. F. Barnes during his heyday, yet their first encounters were certainly won by the Staffordshire bowler. Taylor told me: 'The first time I ever played against Sid Barnes was during the Triangular tournament in England in 1912. In those days the wickets were not covered and it was a horribly wet season. Dave Nourse, Aubrey Faulkner and I were technically the best equipped to deal with such conditions, but I'm afraid Barnes and F. R. Foster formed too good a combination. Barnes did not worry me as much as Foster. He was a fast left-hander and he was downright unpleasant to bat against. He employed a variation of the leg theory that caused so much trouble in later years and we just could not cope. I still rate Foster as one of the best quickies I ever batted against and it was a tragedy that his career was cut short by an accident which cost him a leg.

Barnes was a marvellous bowler. He bowled leg-breaks and off-spinners at about the same medium pace as Bill O'Reilly did for Australia years later. He could also roll one for a top-spinner that was very difficult to detect. In fact, in 1912 we just never saw it. In addition Sid often opened the bowling and he used to swing the new ball away from the right-handed batsmen at more or less the same speed as Eddie Barlow does these days.

On English wickets he was a real terror but I had a lot of experience batting against googly bowlers and I'd learnt to watch a bowler's finger movements as he delivered the ball. This made me quite confident that I would be able to handle Barnes under South African conditions. I made no secret of the fact that I was looking forward to batting against him on matting wickets, but I doubt very much if anybody took me seriously. In those days you only had to mention Barnes's name to have batsmen scurrying for cover. Overemphasis on forward play and poor footwork contributed to many a batsman's downfall against Barnes, but he was nevertheless the finest bowler I ever saw.'

In 1913–14 J. W. H. T. Douglas brought an MCC side to South Africa. Barnes had batsmen mesmerised from the start – except for small, slightly built, hawk-faced Herbie Taylor who was absolutely determined to show that Barnes was not unplayable after all, and this he proved in what must rate with the great innings of all time.

'I played Barnes the way I did those magnificent googly bowlers Vogler, Schwarz, Faulkner and White when I came into first-class cricket. I kept my eyes glued to the ball in his hand as he ran up to the wicket. And just before he delivered it I would switch my eyes to about a yard above his head to catch any finger movement as the ball left his hand. It was no use picking up the ball after it had left the hand of a bowler like Barnes because you would have no idea of what it would do off the pitch. Once I knew what sort of delivery it was going to be it was a case of forward to the ball you can meet and back to the ball you can't. Of course, you have to be quick with your footwork but what I have told you now is the really very simple secret of batting.'

South African wickets were tumbling with nerve-shattering regularity [in the Durban Test on 13 December, 1913], but Taylor never faltered. With machine-like precision, he reduced Barnes to the ranks of the mere mortals. Finally South Africa were all out for 182 of which 109 came from Taylor's bat. What is more, Barnes did not even have the satisfaction of taking his wicket. He was out caught Strudwick off Douglas.

An indication of how completely Taylor dominated the South African innings is the fact that Nourse, with 19, was second top scorer and Baumgartner, with 16, the only other batsman to get double figures.

In spite of Taylor's brilliance, it was still Barnes who wrecked the South African innings. He took five for 57 in 19.4 overs and when England went on to score 450 runs it was obvious that they would win. In the second innings, it was Barnes's turn to win the duel against Taylor and the Springboks folded for only 111 runs. Barnes again took five wickets, this time for 48 runs.

Taylor and Barnes continued to dominate events, with honours going ever so slightly to Taylor if you consider that he was a member of the weaker side and constantly under pressure.

At the end of the series, Barnes had the figures of 226 overs, 56 maidens, 49 wickets for 536 runs at an average of 10·93. Taylor topped the South African batting averages with 508 runs in 10 innings for an average of 50·80.

But the proof of Taylor's dominance over the greatest bowler of his day cannot really be found in the Test Matches. It was for Natal in the nineteenth match of the tour – and the only one lost by MCC – that Taylor once and for all tamed Barnes.

MCC had a poor first innings and could only reach 132, but Natal, with Barnes once again taking five wickets, would have been even worse off had it not been for Taylor at his incomparable best. He scored 91 out of a total of 153, giving his side a slender lead of 21. Taylor's must have been a remarkable knock because Chapman, with 11, was the only other Natal batsman to get double figures. The tourists did a little better in the second innings, totalling 235 and leaving Natal 215 runs to win. This is how Taylor remembers that golden day:

'Our first two wickets fell very quickly and then Dave Nourse joined me. From the start he was in the soup against Barnes but he somehow survived the few overs to lunch. He and I took a couple of sandwiches and went and sat apart from the others.

"Herby," he confided, "I can't play this blighter. That darn top-spinner of his is impossible to spot." So I told him to keep his head down and I would try to keep him away from Barnes as much as possible.

After lunch our plan worked like a charm. I was dropped with my score at 49 – off Barnes of all people. His wrath was something to behold. I decided then and there to try and hit him out of the attack and from his next three overs I took 32 runs. Johnny Douglas helped a little by keeping Barnes on too long. At the same time the tip and run tactics must have been very frustrating to a man of Barnes's explosive temperament.

Anyway, he was given the ball again to start another over. I was just about ready to take strike when he suddenly turned to the umpire, took his cap back, threw the ball to the ground and made a few rude remarks about me to Dave at his end. Then, without another word, he stalked off the field while Johnny Douglas pleaded with him to carry on. Douglas came over to me and apologised. I pointed out to him that I could not allow him a substitute fielder but I should have known better. This fine gentleman would never have dreamed of asking. So the game carried on without Barnes, certainly to old Dave's great relief. We were later told that Barnes had stormed into the dressing-room, whipped off his shirt and had a nice wash-up. Then he stretched himself out and drank several whiskies!

In the meantime we were going very well, safely and at a steady pace. Imagine my surprise when Dave, who had been stealing glances at the dressing-room between overs, suddenly and quite out of character tried to hit Rhodes out of the ground only to be caught on the boundary for 59.

"For heaven's sake, Dave! Why did you do that?" I asked him.

"That —— is coming back!" he hissed his answer as he walked past me to the pavilion. "I saw him getting ready on the verandah."

But by that time it was a little too late for even Barnes to stop us. I got my century and we won by four wickets.'

In later years, Barnes, who lived to the ripe old age of ninety-four, vehemently denied that he ever left the field because Taylor so persistently stole the strike. Taylor, on the other hand, insists that this was indeed the case, and Barnes's well-known temper and his frequent brushes with the cricket authorities during his career certainly loads the evidence in favour of Taylor's version. His performances against Barnes established Taylor as one of the best batsman in the world, but the Great War broke out shortly afterwards. Taylor joined the Royal Flying Corps and earned a Military Cross on the Western Front.

[*1971*]

*

For the information of Sir Donald Bradman, Mr Fingleton and others, an agency man asked Taylor (19 January, 1933) what he thought of England's 'bodyline' attack then rampant in Australia. The reply was succinct: 'There is no danger if the batsmen play forward.'

JUDGEMENT

Statistics didn't matter a tinker's cuss with me. I estimated capacity and individualism. I looked the subject in memory's eye.

Jack Fingleton, when selecting his master cricketers

Roll of Honour, 1914–18

The most melancholy of all reading is the casualty lists of the Great War. First, the names of regular army officers, whose best cricket years were far behind them, appeared; soon boys straight from school joined their seniors in the apparently endless sacrifice. Two mighty adversaries who had clashed in the Melbourne Test of January 1908 – K. L. Hutchings bowled Cotter 126 – died, the batsman in France, the bowler before Beersheba. Riley, who at Hove in 1911 had survived 19 deliveries while Alletson smashed his 142 in forty minutes at the other end, was killed; Lieutenant A. E. J. Collins, still remembered by *Wisden* for his 628 not out in a Clifton College house match, did not survive 1914. Sub-Lieutenant R. C. Brooke, the most successful Rugby School bowler of 1906, died after commending himself to anthologists of English poetry; Rear-Admiral the Honourable H. L. A. Hood, CB, DSO, who when in command of a battleship selected his officers for their cricketing prowess, went down with his ship at Jutland – doubtless remembering missed wardroom catches. Perhaps the game's greatest actual loss was Booth of Yorkshire; potentially, 2nd Lieutenant John Howell of Repton was regarded as a future England batsman. The brilliant young Worcestershire player, Frank Chester, lost a hand but at least survived to become the most famous of umpires.

The names below are limited to men who played in first-class cricket; university cricketers are included only if they were awarded Blues.

ENGLAND

Lieut.	C. H. ABERCROMBIE, RN	Hampshire
2nd Lieut.	C. BANES-WALKER	Somerset
Captain	P. D. BANKS	Somerset
Captain	G. BELCHER, MC	Hampshire
Captain	F. M. BINGHAM	Derbyshire
Lieut.	W. S. BIRD	Oxford University and Middlesex
Sergt-Major	H. G. BLACKLIDGE	Surrey
Sergt	C. BLYTHE	Kent and England

2nd Lieut.	M. W. BOOTH	Yorkshire and England
Colonel	Sir E. R. BRADFORD, Bt	Hampshire
Lieut.	D. R. BRANDT	Oxford University
Lieut.	W. M. BROWNLEE	Gloucestershire
2nd Lieut.	W. B. BURNS	Worcestershire
Captain	A. M. BYNG	Hampshire
2nd Lieut.	L. G. COLBECK	Cambridge University and Middlesex
Major	E. CRAWLEY	Cambridge University
Captain	W. J. H. CURWEN	Oxford University and Surrey
Captain	G. B. DAVIES	Cambridge University and Essex
Lieut.	C. G. DEANE	Somerset
Captain	G. C. W. DOWLING	Sussex
Lt-Colonel	H. A. DU BULAY, DSO	Kent
Captain	C. H. EYRE	Cambridge University
Corporal	T. H. FOWLER	Gloucestershire
Captain	H. G. GARNETT	Lancashire
Lieut.	H. F. GARRETT	Somerset
Rifleman	T. GREGORY	Hampshire
Lieut.	R. E. HANCOCK, DSO	Somerset
Lieut.	A. HARTLEY	Lancashire
Captain	C. E. HATFIELD	Oxford University and Kent
2nd Lieut.	R. E. HEMINGWAY	Nottinghamshire
Lieut.	H. E. HIPPERSLEY	Somerset
Lieut.	W. H. HOLBECH	Warwickshire
Captain	B. H. HOLLOWAY	Sussex
2nd Lieut.	G. W. V. HOPLEY	Cambridge University
2nd Lieut.	J. H. HUNT	Middlesex
Lieut.	K. L. HUTCHINGS	Kent and England

Captain	J. E. V. ISAAC	Worcestershire
2nd Lieut.	B. G. JAMES	Gloucestershire
Captain	A. JAQUES	Hampshire
	P. JEEVES	Warwickshire
Corporal	D. W. JENNINGS	Kent
Major	R. W. F. JESSON	Hampshire
Captain	R. O. LAGDEN	Oxford University
Lt-Colonel	L. J. LE FLEMING	Kent
Lt-Colonel	R. P. LEWIS	Oxford University, Surrey and Middlesex
2nd Lieut.	C. L. MACKAY	Gloucestershire
Captain	E. MARSDEN	Gloucestershire
Lieut.	G. C. NAPIER	Cambridge University and Middlesex
Captain	A. S. NESBITT	Worcestershire
2nd Lieut.	W. W. ODELL, MC	Leicestershire
Lt-Colonel	C. H. PALMER	Worcestershire
Lieut.	J. E. RAPHAEL	Oxford University and Surrey
Gunner	W. RILEY	Nottinghamshire
Captain	J. H. A. RYAN, MC	Northamptonshire
2nd Lieut.	T. A. TRUMAN	Gloucestershire
2nd Lieut.	F. N. TUFF	Oxford University
Lieut.	W. K. TYLDESLEY	Lancashire
Captain	G. L. WHATFORD	Sussex
Lt-Colonel	M. D. WOOD, DSO	Hampshire
2nd Lieut.	K. H. C. WOODROFFE	Cambridge University, Hampshire and Sussex
Captain	E. L. WRIGHT	Oxford University
Captain	H. WRIGHT	Leicestershire
Lieut.	W. E. YALLAND	Gloucestershire

SOUTH AFRICA

Captain	A. DIFFORD	Western Province and Transvaal
Captain	R. H. M. HANDS	Western Province
Lieut.	R. A. RAIL	Western Province
Major	R. O. SCHWARZ, MC	Middlesex and South Africa
Lieut.	G. C. WHITE	Natal, Transvaal and South Africa

AUSTRALIA

Trooper	A. COTTER, AIF	New South Wales and Australia
Private	A. MARSHAL, AIF	Queensland and Surrey
Gunner	E. F. PARKER, AIF	Western Australia

NEW ZEALAND

Lieut.	G. HOWE	Wellington

Wisden's Cricketers of the Year: Blythe 1904, Booth 1914, Hutchings 1907, Marshal 1909, Schwarz 1908.

*

Most Americans have heard of only one cricketer and, oddly, his name appears above. Indeed he is as well known in the United States as are the heroes of the Baseball Pantheon – DiMaggio, Gehrig, Gomez, Podres, Robinson, Ruth and Williams. This is due to the lifelong addiction to cricket of the former Dulwich College fast bowler, P. G. Wodehouse, who – a few years after the Great War – immortalised Jeeves of Warwickshire. Contemporary records all omit this player's army rank; in view of the Wodehouse transformation, this seems appropriate.

G. Gunn

by R. C. Robertson-Glasgow

Cricket is still scratching its head about George Gunn, Senior; and it will not readily recover from him. Technically, he was a genius. Aware and capable of orthodoxy, he mostly preferred to laugh at the book of words.

He mocked equally the rules of batting and the Rules of Cricket. He was silently and exquisitely amused at cricket's precise measurements and its neat pomps. Why twenty-two yards? Why not an acre or so? wherein a man might stroll about with bat and pads and play any ball jerked along by unseen agency, backhand or forehand, cutting half-volleys square to the boundary and driving long-hops for a single over mid-off's head. Why not? And, in these genial wanderings, he should have come upon Edward Lear, looking, as usual, perfectly spherical and wearing a runcible hat; and there should have been a single-wicket match of no time, no dimensions, no result; then an argument, over a glass of ale, on whether Aunt Jobiska was exactly right in her view that a Pobble is better without his toes, as everyone knows. Then they should have pledged a return match, to be played three weeks earlier, with Lewis Carroll as umpire.

As the great Frank Crumit might sing, 'He robbed the world of fancy.' In his late twenties, some six years before the last war, he found himself in Australia, trying to recover that health which so often, unhappily, eluded him. The England cricketers were also there, and their batting wasn't going right. Gunn was called from his restful meanderings to a violent struggle on the Sydney arena. He played an innings of 119; his first appearance for England against Australia. More recently, at the age of fifty, he and Andrew Sandham, touring with MCC, scored 322 for the first wicket against Jamaica, at Kingston.

There were some odd happenings on that trip. Gunn, at an age when it is often found convenient to prop the feet on the mantelpiece and discourse on cricket's decline, went out to open the innings in a Test Match against some very fast and very awkward bowling. In the intervals of taking the ball anywhere between the left armpit and the left thigh, he played beautiful strokes in an innings of just under 50. 'How did you like it?' a fellow-player asked him on his return. 'All right,' was the answer, with a wry smile, 'but I'd sooner play a hand of solo.'

On the same tour he was fielding in a solar topee near the leg-side crowd. A tremendous skier was hit, I think by Constantine. Gunn, after skirting around on his bearings, stood quite still under the ball. In his left hand he held his topee at full stretch, to suggest an infringement of Law 41; with his right he made the catch. It is said that this performance bewildered Wilfred Rhodes, who was riven between wonder and disapproval. 'Ay,' he said, in that confidential, husky, Yorkshire voice: 'Ay, a grand catch; but George shouldn't have done that.' Ah, Wilfred, you, if any, must know there were no shoulds and shouldn'ts with George Gunn.

I happened to be playing on the same side as Gunn in a match soon after the last war. It was a North-Western Festival. Experimental. They called it, I believe, North v South; though it might have been China v Japan, for all anyone seemed to know or care. There were queer occurrences both on and off the field. Gunn and another player opened our innings, and I noticed that the batsmen, before the start, were in earnest colloquy with the umpires. At the interval I asked Gunn what they'd been saying. 'Oh,' he replied, 'they were telling us there were to be no lbws in this match; and I was saying "Thanks very much; and if we have middle wicket knocked out, it's just a *nusty* incident, and we knock her in again and go on."'*

The faster bowlers will remember Gunn best. He loved to walk sideways towards them, like a grimly playful crab, till they seemed nearly to meet in mid-pitch. A flash of the bat, and the ball would be flicked away to third-man or glanced to long-leg. Of him alone I should say that words cannot describe his moods of batting. One hour you might find him plodding along like any old sedate number one; the next, he would be playing strokes for which the word 'brilliant' is just ridiculous. His view was that cricket is made for man. Perhaps it was a sunny morning, and he wanted to sit in a deck-chair by his family or friends. Very well. The pitch was true. Nottingham had plenty of batting. And, about noon there Gunn was, sitting in a deck-chair, watching the others at the wicket. He stood no nonsense from the game.

I see that, apart from his 62 centuries, an average of 26·71† stands against his name. 'How very funny,' I can hear him say. 'Why not 267·1, or 2·671 or 2671?' In genius, in pleasure given and enjoyed, the last figure is about the truth. [*1943*]

* This match at Blackpool found umpires A. E. Street and B. Tremlin unequal to their task, the first wicket to fall being A. C. Russell lbw, b Robertson-Glasgow.

† Lewis Carroll, a mathematician, would have corrected this figure; Gunn's career average was 35·95. However, as *Wisden* (1947) got it wrong, we may conclude that Gunn, even in retirement, bemused the statisticians.

F. E. Woolley

by Ian Peebles

Each innings was an event. There was always something almost dramatic about the appearance of this majestic figure. He walked unhurriedly but purposefully to the wicket amidst a buzz of anticipation on the part of the crowd and a well-founded apprehension on the part of most bowlers. On arrival at the crease there were no affectations or mannerisms, either of which would have been wholly alien to the scene. He would be given guard, glance down at the setting of the field and take stance. He stood upright, bending only so far as his height compelled him, feet slightly apart, hands high on the bat, the general effect being one of the ease and simplicity which characterised the whole performance.

There was about him an air of detachment, so that occasionally one got the impression that he was a casual, almost careless, starter. This was obviously not so, but I would say that, always eager to attack, it took him an over or two to get the feel of things and become warmed up. It might be added that this impression of indifference could be somewhat disconcerting to the opposition, acutely conscious that if they did not succeed immediately awful retribution was liable to befall them.

As the bowler reached the crease he would pick the bat up in a long, smooth circular sweep, parting his feet with a short, forward step of the right foot. The bat came down straight and firmly controlled close to the line of the off-stump. There was plenty of time to make the choice of stroke and whatever it might be it was never otherwise than a flowing, rounded gesture. Never did one see a hasty stab or unbalanced jerk. His defence, being based chiefly on attack, did not have the rock-like impregnability of his contemporary, Philip Mead, but it was enormously aided by the fact that he was a most difficult man to bowl at. Once he was going there was no area in which the bowler could seek shelter. He had all the strokes, and he lent to them an unequalled force and beauty. Thus, when one is asked what was his best shot, it is impossible to say, for whatever he did was enthralling. He was a beautiful off-side player off back and front foot, driving, cutting, slicing to all sectors. I have frequently quoted what I consider to be the prettiest compliment ever paid on the field of cricket. It was at Canterbury in 1930 that Frank took 60 undefeated off the Australians in double-quick time. The first burst came chiefly off Alan Fairfax, a very high-class quick-medium bowler, who was lathered against all sections of the off-side fence. Seeking reassurance, he asked that fine rumbustious character Vic Richardson if he thought it was 'all right bowling at his off-stump'. 'All right,' said Vic enthusiastically, 'it's bloody marvellous – we're all enjoying it.'

Frank was the most exhilarating straight hitter. The action seldom appeared to be more than a free-swinging forward stroke, but the ball would sail away to clear the longest boundary. He loved to treat fast bowlers so and when in frustration they dropped the ball short he would pull them square with the same unhurried venom. This was essentially a pull, made with the full long-armed swing of the bat as the striker lay back on his left leg. The hook was somehow too angular a movement ever to fit into this flowing repertoire.

It was a dominating as well as a graceful performance, the batsman sailing serenely on his chosen course in all circumstances, disrupting and ignoring opposing stratagems.

At Tonbridge, when Walter Robins and myself were young and cock-a-hoop at getting a couple of early wickets, Pat Hendren indicated Frank's dominating figure advancing on the scene. 'Here comes the lion-tamer,' said he. It proved an apt description and when we had been flogged out of sight Nigel Haig devised a somewhat desperate device. Harry Lee, at square-leg, was to keep dropping back until he was right on the boundary, and Nigel would then bowl the fifth ball of the over short. To a point the plan worked out. Nigel dropped the ball short and Frank slapped it away straight in the desired direction. However, it bisected the line of the fielder's upturned eyes about 8 feet above his head and went 'thwup' into a tent behind, so that the structure tugged at its moorings and shimmered like a belly-dancer. All, especially the fielder, were rather relieved that the plan had not worked out in the final detail.

He *hit* the ball beautifully on the leg side with the same full rhythmical swing of the bat. One stroke particularly pleases the memory and seems to be a penchant of left-handers, as Graeme Pollock also plays it to perfection. It is the pull-drive played off the front foot to the good-length or overpitched ball in the region of the leg-stump. Ideally, this is played to the faster bowling, when the rise of the ball aids the 'take-off' and it goes sweet and far between mid-wicket and long-on.

Like all true artists, he took a keen interest in the implements of his craft. He had very particular tastes in bats, and Gunn and Moore used to make him four bats each season which he calculated would cover his needs. These were produced exactly to his requirements. He liked a heavy bat, weighing about 2 lb 6 oz, but with the weight evenly distributed and not too low in the blade. Thus, although he had plenty of wood, the bat would come up easily and in good balance. Frank's bats were certain to come in for some hard treatment and when he had made an appreciable dent in the driving section he would rest the bat, for he thought at this stage it lost something of its resilience.

On his retirement in 1938 he had two of these specially made bats intact. He gave them to Charlie Barnett, who found them superb in every way and put them to very good use.

Frank never expressed any preference for, nor prejudice against, any particular type of bowling. One would surmise that he enjoyed himself to the utmost against the fast bowlers. It was against them that he produced his most startling effects, and it was inspiring and amusing to see him quell any ill-advised attempts at retaliation. He was not a man to be intimidated and, not unnaturally, he had a fine confidence in his own powers of counterattack. If he was hit he considered that he was the party to blame, and he was never heard to complain or speak a rancorous word against anyone who bowled aggressively. Indeed, he had little reason to do so, for the bouncer was ever grist to his mill.

He considered Macdonald and Larwood the fastest bowlers he had ever played, and thought the latter the fairest and best. To watch him opposed to either must have been to see the highest expression of the game of cricket. I never myself saw him tackle Macdonald, but I played in a North v South Trial match at Old Trafford where he opened the innings against Larwood and Voce at full blast. He got 50 out of 72 in less than an hour. Always having a slight flair for the anticlimax, he lathered this powerful combination into retirement with joy and ease, and was then caught at long-on off a full-toss from Tommy Mitchell.

At Folkestone in a Festival match where feeling ran rather high the West Indies fast bowlers let go such a burst of pace that certain of the home batsmen were visibly relieved when soon out. Frank and Bob Wyatt then made centuries. They provided an interesting contrast. Bob, rock-like and the more stubborn and immovable at the evidence of hostility about him, battled grimly. Frank, detached and apparently unaware that the bowling was intended for anything other than his enjoyment, serenely carved it to every point of the compass.

This scene rather underlined a very particular quality of Frank's play. He had at all times a quiet and unruffled dignity. This had no hint of pomposity, which is a highly assailable attitude, but sprang from a quietly determined personality allied to a natural physical grace. Amongst the innumerable charms of cricket is its power to inflict indignities and farcical situations on its lovers and practitioners. To these Frank seemed largely immune. Even when run out, an accident which befell him 44 times in his career, he seemed unruffled and unhurrying, in a situation where batsmen are inclined to look a trifle dishevelled.

The only instance I have heard of his being disturbed out of his Olympian calm was recalled by Leslie Ames. When he had thrashed the regular Glamorgan bowlers all over the field Emrys Davies appeared to bowl his seldom-practised left-handed 'chinamen'. These for some reason caused Frank great perturbation, which, in its turn, caused the purveyor and all else present great astonishment. There is something rather touching about this scene, which smacks of the elephant's unaccountable fear of the mouse. [*1969*]

*

When Woolley was in his fortieth year (1926), he stroked 114 against the Nottinghamshire of Larwood at a run a minute, and 137 against Macdonald's Lancashire. But these were trifling efforts compared with the masterpiece which adorned the Champion County (Lancashire) v The Rest match – 172 not out scored in 125 minutes: Macdonald 19–0–113–0. One extraordinary thing about this innings is that only 80 of the runs (2 sixes and 17 fours) came from boundary hits; Woolley progressed at a Jessopian pace merely by placing the ball.

In 1929–30 those present at an MCC v New South Wales game at Sydney witnessed centuries from Bradman, Kippax and Archie Jackson; among other stroke-makers taking part were Duleepsinhji and Woolley, the latter making 219 in four hours. In his forty-eighth year (1934) Woolley scored ten centuries for Kent, the average runs and time of these innings being 125 and two and a quarter hours; the following year his 229 off a Surrey attack which included A. R. Gover and F. R. Brown came at 72 runs an hour. In his fifty-second year he made a century before lunch against Worcestershire's three Test bowlers, R. J. Crisp, R. T. D. Perks and R. Howorth; this same summer, 1938, he played against the Australians for the last time.

*

by Oliver Warner

Woolley's last innings against the Australians, which was played for Kent at Canterbury on 13–16 August, 1938, was in a sense an epitome of his career. Bradman's very strong team batted first, and made 479. The Don himself contributed a skilful 67, S. G. Barnes being top scorer with 94.

Barnes would undoubtedly have made a century but for the fact that the young Kent captain, F. G. H. Chalk, at last bethought him of the most experienced bowler on the field, his regulars having been hammered. Experience paid. After a short spell, Woolley had Barnes caught by Todd off a thoroughly puzzling ball.

During the week-end there was rain, followed by bright sun. The wicket was at first difficult. Woolley went in first for Kent, as was usual in his last season. He pushed the opening ball defensively, and trotted down the pitch. In most county games it would have been a safe enough run, since fielders generally stood well back when he was batting, but the Australians knew all about such things, and Woolley, amid Kentish groans, was promptly run out. The team followed him in orderly procession. They were all out before lunch, and were forced to follow on.

Lunch itself had been, for the players, a ceremony of farewell to Woolley, and no doubt the visitors thought they had seen what was, but for courtesy, almost the last of him. Far from it! In the very first over of the second Kent innings he smote two fours clean over the bowler's head.

The Australians had had one experience that day of Woolley throwing his wicket away, and, if he was not even going to play himself in, his second life must also, surely, be short and sweet. At any rate, considering such disrespect mere bravado, they at first declined to place a deep field for him. Woolley was notoriously reckless, they understood. It must have seemed, to their serious and mathematical natures, almost like second cricket childhood. For once they were wrong in their judgement.

In half an hour, by means of correct strokes, but hit so hard that few were rash enough to try to stop them, Woolley had made 50. At that point his partner Fagg's score stood at 7; and the young man was as a rule no laggard. It was the 1930 Test Match batting over again. The spectators, amid the gracious tents with their fluttering flags, had had a taste of the champagne of cricket.

Tea was taken early, when Woolley had been batting well under an hour, and had made 67. Afterwards he treated himself to the one six of the innings, a huge, easy drive towards the pavilion. At 81, well within sight of his century, he played his first careless stroke, getting too much under the ball. He was well caught by Bradman, fielding at mid-on, and running in. It was a fitting end to an innings of which only one man was capable – and he about to retire! Although Kent batting is seldom dull, and although Ames afterwards scored a century, the light seemed to depart when Woolley had been cheered away.

Macartney, who saw the game, as did the present writer, called it the innings of a supreme artist. The assessment was accurate, and it should be added that Woolley's sense of audience was as acute as ever. He never showed off; it was an attitude of which he was incapable even as a youngster, but it pleased him always to give pleasure, and he left the game before that power in him had diminished. For that reason, he will always be remembered in Kent as a man who retained his youth until his fifties. [*1952*]

*

R. C. Robertson-Glasgow shall have the final word: 'There was all summer in a stroke by Woolley and he batted as it is sometimes shown in dreams.'

J. B. Hobbs

HAIL AND FAREWELL, 1934

by J. M. Kilburn

It is nearly thirty years since John Berry Hobbs, who has now announced his retirement from first-class cricket, played in his first championship match for Surrey; nearly thirty years since he made his first century in first-class cricket; nearly thirty years since he first trod that Oval turf which has known so many of his triumphs. From Hobbs (J. B.), a young man of great promise, he has travelled a long and glorious road to become Jack Hobbs, known the world over and accepted as 'The Master' of cricket. In his springtime cricket was a flourishing flower, full-blown and sweet-o'-scent, for with him on the fields were Trumper and Noble, MacLaren and Jackson, Hirst and Rhodes and a whole host of others whose names are immortal and memories green. Here Hobbs found fortune, for there was stimulating challenge to his genius and knights worthy of his jousting.

No batsman yet seen has evolved such mastery over all the vagaries of bowler and wicket. When the sun shone and runs came merely for the asking, he took them with a thankfulness beyond mere acceptance. He found no pleasure in painstaking effort, in watching the numbers go round; he made every innings a textbook of batting with illustrations entirely his own. A hard Oval wicket meant a good score for Hobbs – that was certain: but how the score would be made was beyond all hope of prophecy. Days were not always thus, for sometimes rain fell and spin bowlers snapped their fingers in glee. Into their hutches the rabbits went tumbling, but Hobbs, amazing the world, remained firm at his end. The pages of cricket reports echo again and again, 'Hobbs played a brilliant innings, where all others failed.' Nor was he a plant of one garden. In every cricketing county of England his magic was seen, and he charmed South Africa and Australia as he charmed the men of his own native land.

When Hobbs first carried his bat for Surrey and for England, bowling strategy was not as in these times. Fast bowlers were fast, scorning swing, and relying on speed, length and break-back. Hobbs mastered these. Medium-paced off-spinners, such as Trumble and Hearne, reaped their harvest of wickets. Hobbs mastered these. Then came the googly with all its attendant alarms. Where others were beaten or hesitant, Hobbs reigned supreme, scoring still with freedom and ease, sure of himself and his power.

The years passed and the fires of Hobbs's youth flared less brightly. A new theory of bowling brought a new batting technique, and nothing in post-war cricket has revealed more grandeur than the autumn of this man's career. From the brilliance of his classical foundation grew the safety and power of his on-side play. No longer was his bat a lance, pennant flying, eagerly routing the foe. The lance became a wand, charming the enemy to impotence and bringing success through calm and assurance. Nothing could have been more beautiful than this later quietening of Hobbs; there were no regrets for the passing of that amazing speed of eye and footwork that were essential to his earlier brilliance.

'Grow old along with me,
The best is yet to be.'

said Hobbs, and played as Victor Trumper would have played had ever the years grown over him.

Hobbs was never an inhuman, mechanical cricketer; he had a fine sense of duty to the game and its supporters. Runs as represented by marks in the score-book had for him only the value they had to his side. He has thrown away his wicket many times in an attempt to entertain the spectators; he has got himself out as though saying, 'You must be tired of me now.' His records, the bare framework to his picture, are in themselves a source of wonder. He has passed the century 197 times; over 61,000 runs has he made in the aggregate; 323 runs he shared with Wilfred Rhodes for a first-wicket partnership in Test cricket. On sixteen occasions in one season he made a score of more than 100. Is it credible that any one man will ever do more? Yet not for these things alone, or even mainly, will he be beloved in our memory. We shall think of him, trim and tidy, coming out to open the innings; we shall see the twirling of the bat before each ball, the easy, perfectly poised stance at the wicket, those dancing feet move swiftly back or forward, and we shall dream of him 'burning the grass with boundaries', his bat flashing forth every stroke known to cricket. With Grace and Trumper and Ranji he stands incomparable – our debt is beyond all hope of payment.

H. Sutcliffe

by Dudley Carew

There have always been those who affect to find him antipathetic because of his bland refusal to be rattled and confused like any normal man would be when the ball was beating him, he was giving chances, the wicketkeeper was wondering how it was the bails managed to stay on.

The manner in which he would hold up the proceedings to waft a refractory member in the pavilion back into his seat or cross his legs and lean on his bat at the end of an over which had given the bowler every right to blaspheme and claim that four balls out of six had undeniable moral claims to his wicket encouraged their distrust. 'Swank,' was what they were inelegantly wont to say, but swank was a quality in which Sutcliffe was entirely deficient. He had, however, what is the precise opposite of it, and that is a very exact idea of his own capacity, an abiding love for the tight corner and the hard battle, and a not unmischievous delight in staying at the wicket when by all the laws of cricketing decency he should have been back in the pavilion. 'Sutcliffe was repeatedly hit on the pads,' 'There was a confident appeal for lbw, against Sutcliffe,' 'Sutcliffe appeared to give a chance at the wicket when he had scored 4' – these phrases have constantly appeared in the newspapers, and they do give a fair enough impression of periods in some of the long innings he has played, and indicate one side of his cricket. He was fallible but, and this is the point, his poise, his manner of playing, his air of superintending the whole game as though it were an amusement expressly got up for his benefit, never betrayed the fact. A hair's breadth might divide the ball from the stump, but not one of his own glossy black hairs was ever out of its place for an instant of time. Just as this imperturbability has led to an overrating of Sutcliffe's own conceit of himself, so has it inclined people to underrate the essentially obstinate and combative side of his cricketing nature. Yorkshiremen are supposed to be hard and craggy with a bluntness of speech and behaviour which proclaims their own egotism and fighting courage to the world, and Sutcliffe, whose looks, behaviour and batting are gracious with a soft and southern charm, has often looked, from the superficial point of view, to be playing for the wrong side. Actually he is the dourest Yorkshireman of them all in his determination, his power of concentration and his relish for a struggle against odds. His style as a batsman has not the mastery of Hobbs, his partner in a series of first-wicket stands against Australia which would have inclined the balance of the inter-war Test Matches our way had they been at all adequately supported, and a curious turn of the wrists as he plays forward, while it is as unmistakable a signature to an innings as Whistler's butterfly was to a painting, is not attractive in itself. He had some lovely strokes, however, and a drive which sent the ball almost square was a joy, but his great value to a side lay in the cool, concentrated ability he brought to bear on any and every situation.

[*1946*]

Hobbs and Sutcliffe

When England and Australia began the Oval Test in 1926, the home side had won only a single match to the Australians' twelve since the Great War. A. P. F. Chapman replaced A. W. Carr as captain of England, and Wilfred Rhodes was included although nearing his forty-ninth birthday. The sides were:

England: J. B. Hobbs, H. Sutcliffe, F. E. Woolley, E. Hendren, A. P. F. Chapman, G. T. S. Stevens, W. Rhodes, G. Geary, M. W. Tate, H. Larwood, H. Strudwick.
Australia: W. M. Woodfull, W. Bardsley, C. G. Macartney, W. H. Ponsford, T. J. E. Andrews, H. L. Collins (captain), A. J. Richardson, J. M. Gregory, W. A. Oldfield, C. V. Grimmett, A. A. Mailey.

At the close on the first day, Australia had scored 60 for four in reply to England's 280 (Sutcliffe 76; Mailey six for 138); at the close on the second, Australia were all out for 302 (Collins 61, Gregory 73), with England 49 for none – Hobbs 28, Sutcliffe 20. That night a thunderstorm broke over south London.

*

by John Marchant

I am glad that storm came and that the rain fell as it did and that the wicket was turned into what Hobbs himself describes as one of the most difficult he has ever played on. For that storm with the consequent abominable wicket gave the opportunity for English cricket and two English cricketers in particular to rise so greatly to a great occasion that so long as the game is played the fame of what was done on that day will endure and be told among all generations, even as we are accustomed to tell with reverence of the deeds of the Hambledon men.

When the multitude of the utterly profane reached the Oval on that morning the sky was overcast, and remained so until noon. Then the sun came out, and for ninety minutes before lunch the drying wicket was one of those which all true bowlers feel sure they will find if they are good enough to go to heaven when they die.

Play began at eleven o'clock, Grimmett and Macartney bowling. From the latter Hobbs took two singles, from Grimmett, some singles, a two, and a couple of boundaries on the leg side, and for a matter of sixteen overs that was all. For the first forty minutes of play Sutcliffe's overnight score of 20 stood still below his number on the scoreboard. He was not idling or in any horrible difficulty. He was just watching everything very carefully, playing everything he had to play very skilfully, and biding his time. He knew, as we all knew – for the sky showed signs of clearing – that there was an uncommonly tough time coming, and it was his business to be there and ready for it when it came. When he decided that it was time to begin he hit Grimmett for a two and a three in one over, and brought the total score to 80. Richardson went on at the Vauxhall end.

At first he bowled over the wicket. Hobbs, who received the ball, hit it to the leg boundary over the heads of the assembled populace fielding just behind him, and brought his own score to 50, to the unqualified delight of the 28,000 or so of us who saw him do it. This time the members of the Australian team joined most heartily in the applause. Perhaps the warmth with which on the preceding day the English team had saluted the fifties of Gregory and Collins had something to do with it. The cheers died down, and Hobbs hit the third ball of that acceptable over for another four in the same direction, and the last for a single. From the second over, also bowled over the wicket, he obtained a two. Then Collins directed the keen-faced man in spectacles to bowl round the wicket and tucked his field a little closer round the batsman's legs.

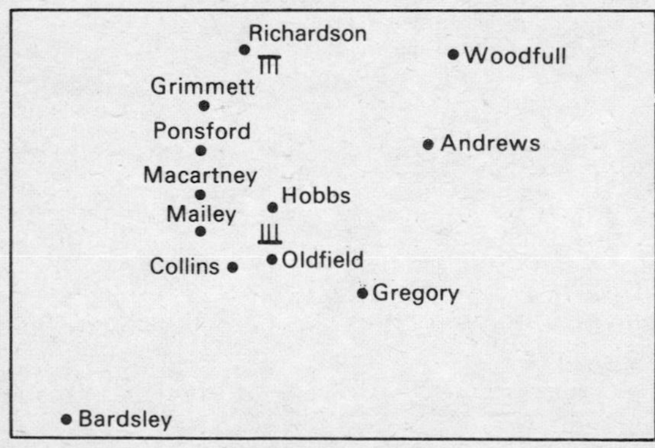

RICHARDSON'S FIELD

That arrangement, or something practically identical with it, persisted through ten overs from Richardson, in the course of which exactly one run was scored from him. Hobbs played eight of those ten overs.

Richardson was bowling the ball which pitches on the middle- or leg-stump, and breaks across the batsman's body. The sun grew hotter and hotter, and the wicket was doing the most incalculable things, and the ball was popping up at every angle. Just one false stroke, just one failure to kill the rising ball – and there were those five pairs of hands waiting with eager hope. The utmost that the batsman could hope to accomplish was so to play the ball that it should drop harmlessly at the fieldsmen's feet, but so far in front of them that there was never the semblance of a chance. And this Hobbs proceeded to do.

Over after over. Each spinning ball as it landed wrenched a tiny bit out of the turf, to be carefully picked up and thrown aside by Hobbs before the next ball came. Sometimes there was the ball he could safely leave alone; more often he was bound to play, knowing perfectly what the risks of playing it were. He watched each ball every inch of the way from the bowler's hand on to the blade of his bat, and not a semblance of a false stroke did he make in all that time.

The spell was broken at last. Richardson had tired, perhaps, with the continuous effort, mental and physical, of those ten overs. The eleventh contained two balls which Hobbs could hit, and hit them he did, for a two and a four, and it was as though St George had slain the dragon, or David had done all that was necessary to Goliath, or the siege of Verdun had been raised. It felt quite like that.

It is possible that people will never cease arguing about those ten overs. M. A. Noble started it by declaring that while they were being played Hobbs was carrying out a gigantic piece of bluff at the expense of Collins, a bluff that was so successful that it lost the match for Australia. His contention was that during that time when the wicket was so utterly unpleasant for the batsman, Collins himself and Macartney should have been bowling, and he holds that Hobbs was never in the least uncomfortable with Richardson, but simply pretended to be in order that Collins might be persuaded to keep him on instead of putting on somebody who would have been really dangerous at that time. Another view is that the person whom Hobbs really bluffed was Richardson, by standing, as he did, nearly a foot wide of his leg stump, and then moving into position to play the ball as soon as he had seen how fast and where it was coming.

But the end of the ten overs was very far from being the end of peril. Runs were coming from Richardson now in almost every over, but his bowling was still infinitely dangerous, and Macartney, bowling from the pavilion end, was as bad – or worse – with the still drying turf giving him full value for the spin that he put on the ball. But now that it was no longer a case of one end being closed against scoring, the figures began to creep up and up, slowly perhaps, but steadily on the whole.

In spite of the Ten Overs – really I think they deserve capital letters – Hobbs was scoring a shade more than twice as fast as Sutcliffe, though after that second four in Richardson's first over, he did not reach the boundary again till, by twos and singles, he had brought his total to 72. But always his figures mounted. At the luncheon interval he had made 97. Sutcliffe's score was 53, and England's total was 161 for no wicket. So teasing and incalculable had the bowling been that even Oldfield had not been able to prevent the addition of eleven extras to the batsmen's score of 150.

Those who were there will never forget; those who were not there can perhaps imagine the welcome the two of them received when they came back to the pavilion. We had come to the Oval that morning fearing, and with abundant reason, that there could now be only one end to the match. Since cricket no longer knows a Grace or a Lucas or a Shrewsbury or a Stoddart, it did not seem humanly possible that there could be for us any escape from the evil which that storm had wrought. It was no unreasonable terror, based on carefully nurtured fear of those terrible Australians; it was a belief, based on abundant experience, that the batsmen did not live who could withstand two and a half hours of absolutely first-class bowling, backed up by immaculate fielding on such a pitch as that was bound to become directly the sun shone.

The only answer is that at a time of greatest need they showed the greatest qualities, qualities not only of skill, but of temperament. Their valour found in their trained and disciplined bodies instruments proper to its service, but without that valour the instruments would have been worthless.

When play was resumed after the interval, Gregory was put on for the first time since he had bowled his three overs at the opening of the innings on Monday. In his first over Hobbs found his chance to score a two and bring his total to 99. He had to wait for the next over from Gregory to obtain the necessary single.

It was, when it came, the most audacious of short runs. He so put his bat on to the ball that, even though it came from Gregory, who was bowling fast just then, it had no more life in it, and trickled feebly in the general direction of point. Hobbs moved far more quickly than the ball, and so, too, did Sutcliffe, his ally in so many run-stealing expeditions. Even they have not often been so utterly audacious, but they succeeded in their adventure. Each was safe at his wicket, and a roar that would put any ordinary thunderstorm to shame was beginning to rise from that multitude of rejoicing people.

Honestly, we could not help it. All that morning we had been sitting tight, almost afraid to whisper for fear that the noise might put somebody off his game. We had lived through the long agony of the Ten Overs; we had watched all that a treacherous pitch and wily bowlers could conspire together to do to injure the honour of England, and except for those brief moments when two entirely deserving batsmen were hurrying in the direction of the luncheon table, we had had nothing that could be called a chance to say what we thought about it all. But this was an occasion when cheers were not only indicated but demanded, and we cheered. And we continued to cheer.

As for Hobbs, he was more outwardly and visibly joyful than I have ever known him to be. When he reached home safely at the end of that utterly impertinent run, he was waving his bat in the air. Then he waved his cap. Then, as the riot continued, he waved bat and cap at once. Our happiness was crowned, and we put a special violence into the next shout when Collins went across from his place to shake hands with him. And then, just when everybody was beginning to remember that after all there was some cricket to be attended to and that it might be as well to get on with it some crowd-compelling maniac in the seats more or less under the shadow of the biggest gasometer decided that it was our duty to give three formal cheers for Hobbs.

After that, cricket continued. It did not continue much longer for Hobbs. In the course of the next over, a single was run, and once more he had to face Gregory. The first ball was a beauty. It grazed the batsman's leg, and went on to remove the off bail. Hobbs's eleventh century in a Test Match against Australia was exactly 100.

*

England's first wicket had realised 172. Woolley stroked 27 elegant runs before falling lbw to Richardson, and was succeeded by Hendren.

*

It was while Hendren was with him that Sutcliffe made the stroke – and a boundary at that – which gave him his fifth hundred in a Test Match against Australia, and his first in such a match in England. Once again the game was held up while we congratulated and thanked him. It was our second real orgy of cheering within an hour and a half, but there was nothing of the anticlimax about it, and we dealt as faithfully by Sutcliffe as we had by Hobbs, and the Australian players helped us with hearty goodwill. And Sutcliffe showed that he was feeling very happy about it all by hitting another four directly we were willing for play to continue.

At that time he was hitting hard and often. Twenty-four out of the forty runs which led up to and came immediately after the century mark in his score came from boundaries. All the bowlers seemed alike to him. He was never rash, never hitting for the sheer love of hitting. But he was in that superb form when a man is able to detect the possibilities of a scoring hit latent in a ball which, in less happy mood, he would be content to play with a purely defensive stroke. He had been at work for more than four hours today already, but there was no sign of weariness, in spite of the scorching sun, and the terrible mental strain of the morning's play.

*

Hendren was dismissed for 15, and Chapman for 19. In the penultimate over of the day, Stevens fell for 22; Rhodes came in with the score 373 for five. By now Sutcliffe was 161.

*

Sutcliffe once again faced Mailey, bowling from the Vauxhall end. Two leg-byes were run, and Mailey sent down his fourth ball. It was a leg-break; Sutcliffe misjudged its pace off the pitch, and it bowled him. In utter amazement he looked at his wrecked wicket. Then he thumped the ground with his bat, and looked as though he would have liked to give himself a good, hard bang on the head with it. He looked also as if he would like to say Bother, and Blow, and possibly words more dreadful than these, and thumped the ground again. And then he woke up to the fact that if he did not make haste to the pavilion somebody would certainly catch him, seeing that vast numbers of people were trying to do even time from all parts of the ground.

So he ran, too, and won through to safety somehow. He had been batting, taking the two days together, for seven and a half hours. In all that time he had made no mistake. He had withstood all that the malice of the elements and the skill of man could do to make hard his way, and he had won for his country victory, and for himself fame which shall not pass while cricket is still played.

*

375 for six at the close, England were all out on the fourth day for 436, and then dismissed Australia for 125 – so winning by 289

runs and regaining the Ashes. The Australians found Rhodes's cunning too much for them, as sometimes their fathers' generation had. During the match his figures were 45–24–79–6, his victims Richardson (twice), Woodfull, Bardsley, Ponsford and Collins.

This was not Rhodes's last Test: at Kingston in April 1930, he found the young Headley on his way to a double century – Rhodes's match figures suggest containment: 44.5–25–39–2.

AN AWFUL SIGHT

He emerged from the pavilion with a strong, rolling gait; like a long shoreman with a purpose. He pervaded a cricket pitch. He occupied it and encamped on it. He erected a tent with a system of infallible pegging, then posted inexorable sentries. He took guard with the air of a guest who, having been offered a week-end by his host, obstinately decides to reside for six months. Having settled his whereabouts with the umpire, he wiggled the toe of his left boot for some fifteen seconds inside the crease, pulled the peak of a cap that seemed all peak, wiggled again, pulled again, then gave a comprehensive stare around him, as if to satisfy himself that no fielder, aware of the task ahead, had brought out a stick of dynamite. Then he leaned forward and looked at you down the pitch, quite still. His bat looked almost laughably broad.

R. C. Robertson-Glasgow remembering bowling at C. P. Mead of Hampshire and England

Armstrong's Circus

by Kenneth Gregory

The great Australian sides of 1902, 1921 and 1948 may be revered but not compared. The Tests of 1902 and 1921 were confined to three days while those of 1948 sprawled over five, 1902 was the wettest season on record and 1921 one of the driest, a ball lasted throughout an innings in 1902 but could be renewed after 200 runs in 1921 and 55 overs in 1948. However one common factor was the duration of matches against the counties – three days. If the primary concern of a touring side is to win the Test series, the great touring side should not experience any major problems when facing the counties, unless caught on a rain-affected pitch by, say, the Yorkshire of Rhodes or Verity. The county games should provide entertainment, this being related to the number of runs scored, and the rate at which they are scored, by the tourists, and to the speed and economy with which the opposition is dismissed.

Consider the great Australian sides of this century:

1902: V. Trumper, R. A. Duff, C. Hill, J. Darling (captain), S. E. Gregory, M. A. Noble, W. W. Armstrong, A. J. Hopkins, J. J. Kelly, H. Trumble, J. V. Saunders.

1921: W. Bardsley, H. L. Collins, C. G. Macartney, T. J. E. Andrews, J. M. Taylor, C. E. Pellew, W. W. Armstrong (captain), J. M. Gregory, H. Carter, E. A. Macdonald, A. A. Mailey.

1948: A. R. Morris, S. G. Barnes, D. G. Bradman (captain), A. L. Hassett, K. R. Miller, R. N. Harvey, S. J. E. Loxton, I. W. Johnson, D. Tallon, R. R. Lindwall, W. A. Johnston.

The following figures are based on runs per wicket, balls per wicket, and runs per 100 balls scored in the first innings of *all* matches between the Australians and the county sides in each of the three seasons. Because it was once normal for teams to average something like 20 overs to the hour, the scores are based on a six-hour day of 120 overs. For purposes of comparison, two other touring sides (both of which won their Test series) have been included – W. M. Woodfull's of 1934, with Bradman, Ponsford, McCabe, Grimmett, O'Reilly and Fleetwood-Smith at their peak, and R. B. Simpson's of 1964.

CLOSE OF PLAY ON FIRST DAY

	Australians batting first		County batting first	
1902	Australians	316	County	169
	County	70 for three	Australians	162 for three
1921	Australians	448	County	160
	County	28 for two	Australians	220 for three
1934	Australians	418	County	232
	County	to bat	Australians	90 for one
1948	Australians	436	County	146
	County	to bat	Australians	167 for two
1964	Australians	336	County	283
	County	30 for one	Australians	45 for one

The significance of the above becomes apparent when noting the size of the Australians' first innings lead, and the time on the second day when it was accomplished:

1902	147	by 2.20 pm
1921	288	by 2.45 pm
1934	186	by 5.00 pm
1948	290	by 3.40 pm
1964	53	by 5.25 pm

Why, then, did the 1921 Australians win only seven of their twenty-one county matches in two days? (They beat England at Trent Bridge in well under two days.) The answer was Armstrong. In amiable mood, he would agree to hours of 11.30 to 6.30, not so amiable perhaps noon till six. But if some misguided soul advertised the fact he had travelled far to watch the Australians (and the then Prince of Wales spent much of the summer doing this), or if Armstrong felt in a dark mood: 'Two till six!' Whereupon his batsmen would batter 400 runs or so for the loss of a few wickets before knocking off for the day.

Early in the season the cricket correspondent of *The Times* declared that the tourists' bowling was weaker than that of any other Australian side. As the attack consisted of Gregory, Macdonald, Mailey and Armstrong, this statement was inaccurate. Against the counties their figures bordered on the absurd:

Gregory	75 wickets at 13·[illegible], balls per wicket	[illegible]
Macdonald	78 wickets at 13·10, balls per wicket	30
Mailey	78 wickets at 16·51, balls per wicket	31
Armstrong	68 wickets at 12·48, balls per wicket	37

Armstrong, of course, was merely the 'end-stopper'.

True, English cricket was weak in 1921 after the disruption of war, yet there were many who, during their careers and after, were regarded as outstanding – some as great. Nine of the following totalled forty-two Test centuries for England – A. Ducat, George Gunn, J. W. Hearne,

E. Hendren, P. Holmes, V. W. C. Jupp, D. J. Knight, H. Makepeace, A. C. Russell, A. Sandham, H. Sutcliffe, E. Tyldesley, F. Watson and F. E. Woolley – but in thirty-two innings for their counties against the Australians they averaged 14·78. A similar fate befell some reputable bowlers: for their counties W. E. Astill, John Gunn, P. G. H. Fender, A. P. Freeman, J. W. Hitch, A. S. Kennedy, J. Newman, C. W. L. Parker, S. J. Staples and J. C. White combined to take 10 Australian wickets – average 113·00, balls per wicket 154.

Brilliant in the field (*The Times* conceded this), the Australians possessed two great batsmen, Bardsley and Macartney. Psychologically, the former had his problems, if he read the newspapers. Although 'as fine a left-hander as Hill' of the 1902 side, Bardsley was frequently reproached for slow scoring. On the first day of the tour at Leicester he crawled to 80 not out in a couple of hours; his 127 against Gloucestershire occupied two and a half hours, while Hampshire confined him unaccountably even if his second hundred did come in sixty minutes. Poor Bardsley! Time after time his partner was Macartney: 140 not out in two hours at Leicester, 105 in eighty-five minutes against Hampshire, 121 in two hours at Bristol, 193 in two and a half hours at Northampton. His adventures at Trent Bridge have never been equalled: a century in ninety-five minutes, a second in fifty (after which he sent for his heavy bat which drove better), a third in an hour – tiring, he was out for 345 made at 88 runs an hour.

Armstrong's circus provided rare entertainment, its ring master provoked much abuse. No cricket ball was ever the same again after Armstrong (best fighting weight twenty-two stone) had driven it. Which prompts the thought that had he played today, when balls lose their shape after being prodded for half an hour, there would have been a new ball every over.

C. G. Macartney

At Leeds, 10 July, 1926

AUSTRALIA
First innings

W. Bardsley (captain) c Sutcliffe b Tate	0
W. M. Woodfull not out	134
C. G. Macartney c Hendren b Macaulay	151
T. J. E. Andrews lbw, b Kilner	4
A. J. Richardson not out	70
B 2, lb 2, nb 3	7
Total (for three wickets)	366

To bat: J. M. Taylor, J. S. Ryder, J. M. Gregory, C. V. Grimmett, W. A. Oldfield and A. A. Mailey.

Fall of wickets: 1–0, 2–235, 3–249.

England: J. B. Hobbs, H. Sutcliffe, F. E. Woolley, E. Hendren, A. W. Carr (captain), A. P. F. Chapman, R. Kilner, M. W. Tate, G. Geary, G. G. Macaulay and H. Strudwick.

by Neville Cardus

Every cricketer in the land knows by now that on Saturday Leeds was a torment of argumentation. 'Why did Carr put Australia in?'

'If he thought the pitch was likely to get difficult, why did he leave out of his side Parker, the best slow left-hand spin bowler at his service?' These questions buzzed in the air of Headingley the afternoon long, but I can see now that they were only so many midges of controversy living their brief fretful moments in the glorious sunshine of Macartney's batsmanship.

This Test Match will be remembered for Macartney's innings long after we have ceased our multitudinous chatterings about the mistakes made by Carr and the Selection Committee. The very result of the game (whichever way the gods may turn round the adamantine spindle) will pass from memory sooner or later, but Macartney's cricket will leave its bright dye stamped there. The game, its chances and results, its ambitions and frustrations, with all our political talk 'about it and about' – all these things are by nature perishable, for they belong to the abstracts and brief chronicles of the time. Macartney's innings was a work of personal art and as much a revelation of man's power to create brave and lovely things as if it had been wrought substantially in poetry, prose, paint or stone. It was cricket that lifted the match, big as it was, far above the narrow pressure of partisan interests; the crowd at Leeds, though aware that every run made by Macartney was a heavy hindrance to England's chances and, moreover, a sting into the heart of England's captain – none the less, every man and woman, boy and girl, amongst us sat willingly under the spell of delight cast by this little wizard of cricketers. And when he broke his spell by getting himself caught, we came out of our enchantment with sorrow enough; we had been seeing visions, dreaming dreams of the great days of cricket – the days when batsmanship like Macartney's was not a miracle of refreshment in a stony desert. Macartney on Saturday let us see again the game as it was played by 'Ranji', J. T. Tyldesley, Spooner, MacLaren, Victor Trumper, R. A. Duff, F. S. Jackson, Kenneth Hutchings – to mention but a few of the artist-batsmen of a single period.

Young sceptics are nowadays constantly crying out, 'O you croaking greybeards; you sentimentalise the past and see old-time mediocrity with eyes that tell beautiful romantic lies'. Well, Macartney at Leeds provided the evidence the 'greybeards' would have chosen in support of their familiar claim that post-war cricket is compared with pre-war cricket, as sackcloth to silk, stale beer to new wine. If it is objected that Macartney, being a genius, must not be cited as a 'typical' batsman of a given epoch, the answer is that Macartney's school (and spirit) of cricket gave us its personal artists in the score, that even the average everyday batsman of that school (for example, Ernest Hayes) might well loom handsomely against the current background composed of dull standardised batsmen who hold to that negative 'safety-first' philosophy which belongs to the age we live in at the moment.

It was necessary to begin with this tribute, not only because the artist commanded our affection and gratitude, but because Macartney's innings came like the sign of a prophet showing cricket the way out of the wilderness. Let our batsmen throw away the common species of the moment – the 'two-eyed stance' quackery, and the rest; let them trust their love of cricket as a *game* to lead them to brave ways of their own of doing things with a bat delicious to the touch. Only a great passion for cricket could inspire Macartney to play as he does; the beauty he makes on a green field is his offering to the game which, because of its traditions of chivalry, has attracted and nurtured his own genius.

From the opening ball of the game Bardsley was out. Tate sent a quick-rising ball that swung away a little, yet kept dangerously close to the off-stump. Bardsley merely 'shaved' his stroke, and he fell to a splendid catch at first slip by Sutcliffe, who gripped the ball low to the earth with an action which was all curving young life and limb.

The crowd roared out its satisfaction at England's quick taste of blood; the English fieldsmen gathered round the wicket in a confident circle and Carr lived through his moment of vision. Then the iron was plunged into him – none of us watchers at Leeds will ever know the half of the bitterness that came into Carr's expectant heart after that moment of short-lived ecstasy. Two minutes following the game's outset Macartney came to the wicket. Against the second and third balls of the same over of Tate's in which Bardsley had fallen Macartney played defensive strokes, confidently but fruitlessly. The fourth ball Macartney cut for two, a stroke clean and aggressive. The fifth ball, which rose abruptly to the bat, Macartney flashed a swift catch to the left side of – Carr! England's captain flung all his being to the scudding hit – Lord!' he surely said, 'Macartney now is mine and for next to nothing.' Carr got the ball in his hands – got his net over the butterfly Macartney. And he let it go. Down to the ground fell the spinning ball, and with it fell England's hopes in this match. Macartney gave us no other opportunity; at the end of his innings his one mistake was no more than brief breath blown on the polished magnificence of his cricket.

Suppose Australia had put England in on a pitch of a sort England is not used to. And suppose, in these circumstances, England had lost Sutcliffe for nothing and then had nearly lost the wicket of Hobbs. Would not the common shout of 'Safety first' have gone through England's ranks with a vengeance? It was 'safety first' for England at Lord's the other week when our total read '150 for 0'. Macartney did not draw into his shell after his escape from a difficult chance. He is a great cricketer, and as such understands well that challenge and risk are body and soul of the game. From the next six balls he received after his 'escape' Macartney hit seven runs, including a superb off-drive. Macartney attacked the English bowling the moment he went 'to the middle'; in quick time he knocked it away from its length, reduced it to the dogged but unavailing work of schoolboys, played it here, there and everywhere to his heart's content – cut, drive, thrust and glance, each stroke a different facet on a diamond of an innings. Woodfull kept company with Macartney. Macartney's bat rippled its music, Woodfull's bat pat-patted all the time – sort of pom-pom-pom accompaniment in the bass to Macartney's sparkling valse caprice. As I looked on these two superb but wholly different batsmen, I thought of Dr Johnson's description of Pitt and Walpole – Macartney was the meteor and Woodfull the fixed star.

Macartney raced to his first 50 in 48 minutes, out of a total for Australia of 64; he reached his century in 100 minutes out of a total of 131. Victor Trumper once got a Test Match century before lunch –

at Manchester in 1902. It is only right and proper that Macartney should have been given the grace also to achieve this wonderful performance. For the same joyous yet dangerous spirit that moved the incomparable Victor also sets in motion the quicksilver cricket of Macartney, who indeed has inherited Trumper's own chivalrous blade – which he used in his own way.

From 11.32 on Saturday until 2.50, the English attack was a vain thing. Macartney never seemed likely to get out – this despite the prodigious risks he was always taking – while Woodfull's innings might have been growing before us like a tree with roots deep in the ground. If at long intervals we saw a ball beat the bat, we were astonished at the batsman's momentary negligence. After lunch Macartney was nearly bowled by Tate, and a run or two later he almost returned the ball to Geary. These slight mistakes only increased our admiration at the marvellous precision of Macartney's cricket on the whole; they were proof that, after all, it was mortal skill and not witchcraft that was doing it all. Macartney seemed to tire after he passed his 150; he suddenly sent a catch to mid-off, and the next minute he was walking back to the pavilion, and 35,000 people were standing on foot roaring him home. Macartney batted two hours and fifty minutes; in this time he and Woodfull made 235 for Australia's second wicket.

Macartney's innings seemed to contain every known stroke in batsmanship – and several of his very own. He gave us the wristwork of Spooner, the quick feet of Trumper, the fierce physical energy of J. T. Tyldesley. He proved once again that length bowling is relative, not absolute – that quick feet and versatile stroke play will turn the best-pitched ball into sorry enough stuff. Even so accurate a bowler as Kilner was unable to drop a length for long to Macartney; one quick jump to the ball made a half-volley; one quick backward motion of the right foot made a long-hop. In all his just less than three hours of brilliance, Macartney did not let us see a half-dozen 'ragged' strokes. His timing was amazing; every hit seemed born at his wrists' ends, and each went over the field with the speed of thought from the bat's middle. And often it was an audacious cross-bat – yet one moving according to the strict laws of Macartney's art, which, though apparently lawless to the common eye, has, like the art of every individual genius ever born, its own strict rationalism – right for Macartney, wrong for anybody else.

*

The match was drawn: Australia 494 (Woodfull 141, Macartney 151, Richardson 100); England 294 (Macaulay 76; Grimmett five for 88) and 254 for three (Hobbs 88, Sutcliffe 94).

M. W. Tate

by John Arlott

In the eleven months between the beginning of May 1924 and the end of March 1925, Maurice Tate, in his thirtieth year, placed himself among the really great bowlers of the modern, or overarm, age of bowling – F. R. Spofforth, Lohmann, C. T. B. Turner, S. F. Barnes, Maurice Tate and Bill O'Reilly. There have been other outstanding bowlers but, for attack, for ability to defeat the best batsmen on unhelpful wickets, for bowling the virtually unplayable ball, these men must stand alone. Even in such company, Tate has one unique quality, in that he lacked that support without which – it is an axiom of cricket – no bowler can achieve consistently great results. Each of the others had a partner little less mighty than himself – it was Spofforth and Boyle or Spofforth and Garrett, Turner and Ferris, Lohmann and Peel or Lohmann and Briggs, Barnes and Foster, O'Reilly and Grimmett – but Maurice Tate had no one of comparable stature to share with him the task of bowling out England's opponents. He achieved his great place in cricket history without real support, for the partnership of Tate and Gilligan which had promised to be so immense, was unhappily broken for ever as an effective weapon. Cecil Parkin, who had the gifts to be little lower than his Sussex contemporary, did not remain in the Test cricket world – for reasons not connected with his playing ability; what a great pair those two might have been. Thus, in two ways, Maurice Tate was unique among the great bowlers. When a master bowler lacks support, his opponents can regard him as a problem separate from the remainder of his team's outcricket. That is to say, a single defensive batsman can be deputed to 'farm' the outstanding bowler while his less safe fellows play themselves in and score runs against the lesser bowling: meanwhile the spearhead is slowly blunted by purely defensive batting directed to the end of tiring him out. Because escape from Spofforth meant facing Garrett, because at the opposite end to Sidney Barnes was Frank Foster, in each case a foil only a little less great than the principal, those great bowlers *had* to be played as an alternative to stalemate at both ends and a rate of scoring which could not hope to win a match. Tate, however, for many years, gave many wickets to his fellow-bowlers by driving the batsmen to them in a state of partly relaxed relief while, against him, resistance was the normal course of strategic batting.

Above all, Maurice Tate was unique in that he made the ball leave the ground faster, in relation to its speed through the air, than any other pace bowler in the history of the game. Great batsmen have said that he could be of medium pace through the air and positively fast off the pitch. Certainly, at the start of an innings, it was impossible to play back to him; the batsman who tried to do so would find his stumps leaping before his bat was fully down. Thus more than one young cricketer playing against Sussex has been sent out with strict instructions from his senior pro not to do anything but play forward to Maurice Tate until he has scored at least 20.

1923 had been a great season for Tate, but in 1924 he was the greatest problem batsmen had faced since Sidney Barnes. It was excitement to go to Brighton to watch him. At any moment he might whisk away the entire batting of a county in a burst of inspired bowling. For years, to win the toss at Brighton had been to take a day-long lease on the friendliest stretch of turf ever tamed by sun and groundsman for the delight and prosperity of batsmen. Now it was different; captains won the toss there and took first innings half-reluctantly.

When the sea-fret was on the wicket and Tate was playing, the Sussex team went out to field almost with joy. He would take the end which enabled him to bowl into the wind and measure out his run – seven full paces and a four-feet jump – and there he made his mark. 'Tich' Cornford – wicketkeeper of Sussex after the sad death of George Street – would crouch at the wicket, standing close, his head no higher than the bails, for Tate believed he could not bowl so well with the wicket-keeper standing back. Then you saw the most perfect bowling action that theory or practice can conceive. Two short walking steps, falling into six accelerating running strides and – midway between the fifth and sixth – the body rocked easily back. The left arm was thrown up, the ball held in the back-slung right hand so that, at one point of the swing, the left hand pointed high forward and there was a pure straight line from the fingers of the left hand diagonally across the body to the right hand. But this was momentary, and comes back only in the analysing memory, for the eye and mind at this time were consumed by the immense unchecking power of the bowler's movement. Then, with the final leap, came the full rhythmic swing of those heavy shoulders: he delivered at the highest point of his vertical swing and followed through with his hand seeming to press heavily into the air. The left foot, square, plunged into the ground just off the line of the stumps, so that, in any appreciable spell, he would dig a pit just where the batsman stood and which might have to be filled-in several times in the course of a single match. And, ask any man who ever fielded at cover-point for Sussex in Tate's day and he will tell you how, even there, he could feel the ground shake as that left foot pounded it in his follow-through. Tate's arm swept on after the delivery in a huge circle right round past his legs and, as he pulled away to the off-side of the wicket, he had completed the finest bowling action of our time. The approach, delivery and follow-through, fathered, concentrated and directed every fraction of their combined energy into the pace of the ball.

After he had bowled a few overs on a wet day, you would see his run clearly marked in sharp, complete footprints, showing black against the green, for he put his feet down in *exactly* the same place each time he ran up to bowl. And he always delivered from the same point of the crease – close against the stumps – he did not 'use the crease' – which telegraphs to the batsman the type of ball the pace bowler is about to bowl. There is no suggestion of strain or pressing in his action and, in his entire career, Maurice Tate never once bowled a no-ball! At Brighton, on one occasion, he threw up a slow 'floater' which a violent wind carried away – and that was his only wide. That delivery apart, every ball he ever bowled was finely controlled and, simultaneously, impelled with immense ferocity.

Bowling into the wind on a heavy seaside morning, he would make the ball dart and move in the air as if bewitched. The in-swing and the out-swing were there as a matter of course, but, as every man who batted against him at his best will testify, the ball would sometimes seem to begin to swerve and then straighten again before it struck the ground. Once it pitched, the bound was full of fire and, because Tate was a 'long-fingered' bowler, on a green-topped wicket the ball would sometimes strike back in the direction opposite to the swing. That is to say, an out-swinger would become, in effect, an off-break off the pitch, or an in-swinger a leg-break. Sometimes this happened to his 'cutter' because of the tendency of the cut break to swerve; but it could also happen to deliveries which were not 'cutters'. Tate, of course, like any other swing bowler, could only produce the swing *deliberately*, the subsequent tricks of the swung ball off the 'green 'un' happened, according, we may assume, to the angle of seam to ground on pitching, but not within the command of the bowler. When he bowled thus on a green wicket, no batsman in the world was too good to be his victim; the ball pitched and left an ominous black mark on the damp turf where it landed; that was the danger sign. Batsmen, when they saw Tate's mark on the pitch at Hove, resolved to play forward, hold their bats very straight and hope. The ball would whip into Tich Cornford's gloves with a villainous smack and the little man would hollow his belly and was lifted to, or off, his toes as the ball carried his heavy-gloved hands back into him.

There was no 'new' lbw rule in those days to prevent the batsman from covering up with his pads to the ball which nipped in late off the pitch. More than one batsman with a great record against the finest bowlers would shuffle across the wicket to Maurice Tate, keeping his bat away from the ball which, sinfully late, would swing away at fierce pace towards the slips – where Ted Bowley, Bert Wensley, Duleep, Tommy Cook, John Langridge, over the years, were great fieldsmen to the bowling of Maurice Tate. But when that out-swinging ball struck back off the pitch, the pads would be there, it would thunder against them in its denied course to the wicket and there could not even be an appeal. A fraction shorter and it would race across the face of the pad and rise high to hit the batsman's thigh and produce an excruciating agony so that even those batsmen who did not rub themselves because 'it encourages the bowler', broke their rule when this ball of Tate's crashed home on the unprotected muscle.

Because we have not his like among us today, it is difficult to convey the power of Maurice Tate's bowling for those nine years from 1923 to 1932. Certainly no batsmen in the world could expect with any real confidence to weather Tate's first hour of bowling in the morning. Of those who did survive, and their number is small, none ever 'middled' every ball at which he played. And, with it all, Tate, by the judgement not only of his team-mates but also of his opponents, was the unluckiest of all great bowlers. He was also bowling at the wicket or around the edge of the off-stump and he probably beat the bat more often than any other bowler of his time. Again and again the ball would miss the wicket when Cornford had turned his head away to avoid being struck by a flying bail: it would miss by the narrowest margin so that the bails seemed to shake in their grooves at its close passage. Then Maurice Tate would turn his follow-through into a gesture of suffering to the Gods at the narrowness of the batsman's escape. The next ball would be bowled to adjust the misfortune of the preceding ball and so, on and on through the hottest day, his ferocity burned beyond the power of sweat to quench it. His stamina was such that he bowled unwaveringly through the longest spells. Sometimes, coming back to the Sussex side after two days of bowling in a Test Match, he would, after ten or so overs, ask for one of the slips to be moved to short-leg – for the first sign of Tate tiring was the lapse of power of his out-swing. But, even when he was tired or the pitch denied him help, he still expected a wicket with every ball, still put the ferocity of five bowlers into stock-bowling, and again and again turned defence into attack.

Often he was bowling too well: batsmen just good enough to get an edge to his out-swinger were hit in the middle of the bat by the ball as it struck back: when he was bowling at his best with the new ball, only the greatest were good enough even to edge him in the early stages of their innings. Most dangerous of all was his out-swinger, which moved in at the line of the middle-and-off stumps and then, in the last yard, moved away towards the slips. No pitch was quite so dead but he could startle the batsman into the hasty stroke, no position so hopeless but he could muster enthusiasm and magnificent bowling to meet it. [*1953*]

APOCRYPHA

I caught and bowled Tate for 50, as I nearly stood on his huge feet. 'Why,' he said afterwards, 'you came down the pitch like Abraham.'

R. C. Robertson-Glasgow

A. A. Mailey and C. V. Grimmett

by Ray Robinson

Mailey and Grimmett were as different as it was possible for two short men to be whose bowling was founded on flight and turn and who both earned their living by deftness of the right hand – wisecracking Mailey as a cartoonist and journalist, and earnest Grimmett as a signwriter, whose favourite letter must surely have been the capital S. Caricaturist Mailey's brown eye took in more than the length of a nose or the set of a chin. A student of character, he sized up opponents off the field before he ever saw them bat in hand. If he judged them to be highly strung or easy-going, vain or modest, he adapted his bowling tactics accordingly.

Mailey began his run with a shuffle, then jogged up with five easy steps, weaving from side to side and carrying the ball in his left hand, as if to keep the batsmen guessing what he was up to. At the last moment he took the ball in his right hand and flung his right arm back until it was hidden behind him, while he peeped over his left shoulder at the batsman. His arm came directly over the top, in classic style, and as his fingers ripped across the ball it was difficult to tell from his hand and wrist action whether a leg-break or a wrong 'un was coming.

Grimmett stole up with a straight, quick, skippety run of half-a-dozen paces. Whereas Mailey was at full height in delivery, Grimmett bowled with his shoulders hunched. His arm whipped around like a boxer's right swing. He is the nearest to a round-arm bowler seen in big cricket since they ceased pressing trousers out sideways. Because his arm was one-third of the way down towards horizontal he had to drop his wrist to tilt his hand to the angle needed for his wrong 'un, which (like O'Reilly's) turned farther than his leg-break.

That tell-tale roll of the wrist warned observant batsmen which turn to expect. They were thankful for the small mercy. In a less-subtle bowler it would have been a great drawback, but Grimmett was too crafty to peg away with clear-cut leg-breaks and boseys. By varying the amount of wrist roll he sent along many in-between balls. Mostly they were overspinners which went straight on, but often there was a doubt in a batsman's mind because he could not be sure the ball would not turn a little one way or the other. In delivering his flipper, which darted from the pitch, he could not silence a snap of the fingers. So that batsmen could not play this one by ear he drilled the fingers of his left hand to snap out a similar sound as his right spun other kinds of balls.

Mailey bowled like a millionaire, Grimmett like a miser. Arthur went all out for curved trickery of flight and biting turn. To produce those effects in Australian conditions he had to put so much snap into his finger action that accuracy was left to take its chance. The legend grew that his full-tosses were intentional. Mailey alone knew and, rightly, he wouldn't tell. If practice makes perfect, they were the most finished full-floppers ever bowled.

Twice in Test Matches (at Melbourne, 1925, and the Oval, 1926) Mailey skittled the sagacious Hobbs with full-tosses. The fatal ball at Melbourne was the second consecutive full-pitch; Hobbs played hardly any kind of stroke at it, as if he were spellbound, and it landed between his feet and the stumps. The explanation of such staggering occurrences was that Mailey could bowl a ball which, when a few yards from the batsman, would dip in from the off as sharply as if it had glanced off some invisible object in the air.

Another time, his twirling fingers dragged the ball down so short that after three or four diminishing bounces it ran along the ground towards Leslie Keating (Victoria). Resorting to boyhood's method of dealing with a creeping grubber, Keating squatted on his haunches and swept his bat along the ground. At the last moment the ball fraudulently hopped over the horizontal bat and bowled him. As the out-generalled batsman departed, Mailey proudly demonstrated to nearby fieldsmen how he placed his fingers on the ball when he wished to deliver such a nonplusser.

Not one of the 73,000 balls bowled by Grimmett in first-class cricket was a double-hopper, or anything like it. He put the third dimension of length into googly bowling and never sacrificed control in attempts to get greater spin. He liked least bowling to nimble batsmen who advanced surely to drive the ball before it could turn. To them he pushed most of his deliveries along at a lower trajectory, but he ballooned them high and often enough to embarrass slow-footed players who weren't confident about venturing from the crease. When batsmen dealt it out to Mailey, he continued to float the ball well up, as if to encourage them to gorge themselves and burst. When Victoria made the world record score against New South Wales in 1926, Mailey paid out 362 runs for his four wickets, off 512 balls – heaviest outlay on record in one innings.

Grimmett simply couldn't afford to have such experiences. When quick-footed batsmen attacked him his first aim was to cramp their style, by pushing the ball through at accurate length, and await his chance for revenge. Sometimes he cunningly varied that method if he were hit for four. Pretending that he was losing control under punishment, he would waft the ball along at tempting height. But batsmen who leapt forward devouringly found that the ball would drop short enough and wide enough to be hard to reach; it put them in peril of being stumped or of lofting a catch. Apart from that, Grimmett's basic strategy when he was fighting rearguard actions on Australian pitches was to harp away on a restraining length, constantly varying his flight and pace until he snared the batsmen into playing back his favourite flipper, which skidded through to rap their padded shins in front of the stumps. One-fifth of Grimmett's victims in Tests against England were out leg-before-wicket, and on Australian turf the proportion rose to more than one-third.

Opinion is divided whether Grimmett, an unparalleled Test wicket-taker of his time, was a greater bowler than Mailey. This is like asking whether a mapping pen is better than a charcoal crayon. To decide, I believe you have first to define what you want in a googly bowler. Slower through the air, Mailey gave batsmen more time to move out to him but the risk of misjudging the ball was higher. In all Tests he got one-sixth of his victims stumped, Grimmett one in eight. On an average in first-class matches Mailey took a wicket for every 46 balls, compared with Grimmett's one in 52 balls.

In Australia I believe Mailey was more dangerous, because his flight was more deceptive in the light atmosphere and he screwed a snappier break from the granite-like turf. Grimmett got more turn on the Adelaide pitch than other Australian grounds. Too wise to wear his fingers to the bone for little gain, he often bowled more straight ones than anything else on the first two days, and relied on wily changes of pace and flight. Mailey's two Test records were put up in his own country – nine wickets in England's second innings at Melbourne, 1921, and 36 wickets in the rubber.

In England Grimmett was the better. In the denser atmosphere he could make the ball dip and duck, and he turned it enough on the less-laundered wickets to bowl some of the greatest batsmen behind their backs, by breaking the ball around their legs. On dead pitches which robbed the keenest breaks of sting and made other slow right-handers ineffective Grimmett's control enabled him to bowl away steadily and wheedle the batsmen out.

Summed up, if you wanted your googly bowler to be a shock-trooper, to be thrown in to capture wickets quickly without much heed to cost, you would vote for Mailey. He was more likely to come to light now and again with an unplayable ball (if there is such a thing) and leave a great and well-set batsman gaping. At 44, six years after he retired from Tests, the pranks he could make the ball perform astonished even such a deep student of bowling as Verity.

If you wanted your slow googly bowler to undertake a big share of the attack in all weathers and on all wickets your vote would go to Grimmett. Like the quicker O'Reilly he was a dual-purpose bowler: if conditions made the dismissal of the opposition a long task he could peg away with economical perseverance, keeping the batsmen playing hard in the protracted intervals between the fall of wickets. [*1945*]

GRAMMATICI CERTANT . . .

Mailey used to relate how Grimmett, a New Zealander, came to him soon after his, Grimmett's, entry into Australian cricket and asked questions about their gyratory art. Mailey told him all he knew. Years later, when Grimmett had won fame, there was some banquet or reunion at which both were present. Grimmett, probably elated by unaccustomed good cheer, for he was a man of abstinence, came up to Mailey and said in that voice like a ventriloquist speaking through a watering-can: 'Arthur, you told me wrong about the Bowzie.' Rather as if Virgil had been accused by Horace of giving misleading information on the number of feet in the hexameter! *R. C. Robertson-Glasgow, 1948*

Changing Fashions in Spin

by Kenneth Gregory

A. A. Mailey and J. C. Laker once took 30 wickets in three, and two, consecutive Tests respectively:

MAILEY	1920–21	Adelaide Melbourne Sydney	195.5 overs 21 maidens 746 runs 30 wickets
LAKER	1956	Leeds Old Trafford	138.3 overs 57 maidens 203 runs 30 wickets

All five matches were won by these bowlers' sides.

So that readers may acclaim or denounce certain decades, there follow the average match figures in Tests between England, Australia and South Africa of certain spin bowlers since 1920, also the runs their batsmen gave them to bowl against – these being based on two completed innings. Since it was formerly part of Australian mythology that Laker was a one-season bowler, his figures exclusive of 1956 are noted.

In all instances overs consist of six balls, Australia and South Africa having used both eight- and six-ball overs during the period.

CAREER AVERAGE MATCH FIGURES

		Own side's runs		Overs	Runs	Wickets (to the nearest)
Googly	1920–26	748	MAILEY	60	197	6
	1925–36	728	GRIMMETT	80	169	6
	1932–38	654	O'REILLY	72	136	6
	1952–64	616	BENAUD	55	112	4
Off-spin	1948–59	490	LAKER	48	90	5
			(less 1956)	43	92	4
	1949–60	452	TAYFIELD	77	158	5
	1932–36	714	GRIMMETT and O'REILLY in partnership	144	274	13
IN ENGLAND						
	1926–34	816	GRIMMETT*	91	175	6
	1934–38	712	O'REILLY	80	174	6
	1948–56	550	LAKER	48	100	6
			(less 1956)	43	108	4
	1955–60	444	TAYFIELD	72	146	5

* On his three tours of England, Grimmett was well supported by various batsmen who averaged thus: W. M. Woodfull 43, A. F. Kippax 45, S. J. McCabe 49, W. Bardsley 57, W. H. Ponsford 62, C. G. Macartney 75, D. G. Bradman 115.

IN AUSTRALIA AND SOUTH AFRICA

	Own side's runs		Overs	Runs	Wickets (to the nearest)
1920–25	778	MAILEY	68	224	7
1925–36	656	GRIMMETT	80	169	7
1932–37	588	O'REILLY	61	138	5
1952–64	680	BENAUD	57	118	4
1949–58	456	TAYFIELD	79	164	6
1956–58	416	LAKER	48	76	3
IN AUSTRALIA					
1920–25	780*	MAILEY	76	256	8

* Sometimes batting for Australia at nine were J. S. Ryder, C. E. Kelleway and J. M. Gregory whose combined 108 Test innings averaged 41.

Suppose the sides the above bowlers served were to win their matches by, say, 50 runs: throughout Grimmett's career, the other Australian bowlers had to take 13 wickets at 36 each, but Tayfield's South African colleagues 14 wickets at 18.

Similarly in England: Grimmett's partners required 14 wickets at 42, Tayfield's 14 at 18. In Australia Mailey's companions needed 12 wickets per match at 40.

The least awe-inspiring task faced the other Australian bowlers when Grimmett and O'Reilly were in partnership – 7 wickets at 56 runs each.

Long Odds at Edgbaston

by Kenneth Gregory

'He would win the toss, then retire to a hot bath, to perspire and exude last night's champagne.'

Neville Cardus on the Honourable Lionel (later Lord) Tennyson

Tennyson employed, as gentleman's personal gentleman, one W. H. Livsey who, besides preparing his lordship's champagne and drawing his bath, kept wicket for Hampshire. On 14 June, 1922, Tennyson won the toss at Edgbaston:

'A topping morning, Livsey, and a perfect wicket. I am putting Warwickshire in to bat.'

'Indeed, my lord?'

'We shall dismiss them right speedily, then run up a very big score.'

'I think your lordship would be well advised to...'

'Peace, Livsey! I have decided we shall bat all day tomorrow.'

'A most agreeable prospect, my lord. However, I would point out...'

'Inform the side of my plan, Livsey. By 5 o'clock it will be apparent how I have outwitted Warwickshire.'

At 5 o'clock on 14 June, 1922, the final editions of the evening papers included this intelligence:

WARWICKSHIRE

First Innings

L. A. Bates c Shirley b Newman	3
E. J. Smith c Mead b Newman	24
Mr F. R. Santall c McIntyre b Boyes	84
W. G. Quaife b Newman	1
Hon. F. S. G. Calthorpe c Boyes b Kennedy	70
Rev. E. F. Waddy c Mead b Boyes	0
Mr B. W. Quaife b Boyes	0
J. Fox b Kennedy	4
J. Smart b Newman	20
C. Smart c Mead b Boyes	14
H. Howell not out	1
Lb 2	2
Total	223

HAMPSHIRE BOWLING

First innings

	O	M	R	W
Kennedy	24	7	74	2
Newman	12.3	0	70	4
Boyes	16	5	56	4
Shirley	7	0	21	0

Fall of wickets: 1–3, 2–36, 3–44, 4–166, 5–177, 6–184, 7–184, 8–200, 9–219, 10 223

HAMPSHIRE

First innings

A Bowell b Howell	0
A. Kennedy c Smith b Calthorpe	0
Mr H. L. V. Day b Calthorpe	0
C. P. Mead not out	6
Hon. L. H. Tennyson c Calthorpe b Howell	4
G. Brown b Howell	0
J. Newman c C. Smart b Howell	0
Mr W. R. Shirley c J. Smart b Calthorpe	1
Mr A. S. McIntyre lbw, b Calthorpe	0
W. H. Livsey b Howell	0
G. S. Boyes lbw, b Howell	0
B 4	4
Total	15

WARWICKSHIRE BOWLING

First innings

	O	M	R	W
Howell	4·5	2	7	6
Calthorpe	4	3	4	4

Fall of wickets: 1–0, 2–0, 3–0, 4–5, 5–5, 6–9, 7–10, 8–10, 9–15, 10–15.

'I trust you saw my boundary stroke, Livsey?

'Yes, my lord, it appeared to bounce from the head of mid-off.'

'From the hands, Livsey, from the hands.'

'I stand corrected, my lord.'

'I congratulate you, Livsey, on the way you obstructed the wicket-keeper, thus acquiring four byes.'

'Your lordship's congratulations are scarcely merited, I was merely endeavouring to avoid the ball.'

'The fact remains, Livsey, that but for our combined efforts, Hampshire would have been dismissed for seven. I am now informed by Mr Calthorpe that he wishes us to bat again.'

'Again, my lord?'

'Again, Livsey. And do stop echoing me.'

'I am sorry, my lord, it was simply that being asked to bat again suggests we have already batted once.'

'Semantics, Livsey. By the way, divers Warwickshire members have laid long odds against Hampshire winning this match. I hope you have your salver ready to collect my winnings?'

'I will polish it at once, my lord.'

By close of play more wickets had fallen:

HAMPSHIRE	
Second innings	
A. Bowell c Howell b W. G. Quaife	45
A. Kennedy b Calthorpe	7
Mr H. L. V. Day c Bates b W. G. Quaife	15
C. P. Mead not out	12
Hon. L. H. Tennyson not out	14
B 1, lb 4	5
Total (three wickets)	98

Fall of wickets: 1–15, 2–63, 3–81.

Thursday, 15 June

'Livsey, what did I decide we should do today?'

'Bat until 6.30, my lord.'

Hampshire made a faltering start, Mead being dismissed at 127, Tennyson at 152, and Newman at 174. With only four wickets to fall, they still required 34 to avoid an innings defeat. Lunch was taken with Brown and Shirley at the crease.

'Livsey, I am not satisfied with Hampshire's progress. I expected a major contribution from Mead, and what happened? Gad, I shall send him a telegram. "Mead, c/o County Ground, Edgbaston. Why the devil did you get out? Tennyson." Send that off at once.

'Mead is sitting at the end of the table, my lord.'

'He is?'

'He has just asked for the pickles to be passed to him.'

'Pickles? At a time like this?'

'Mead is a left-hander, my lord.'

'I hope you don't partake of pickles, Livsey?'

'No, my lord.'

'Good! then you can make a century.'

'A century, my lord?'

'Think of Lord Curzon, Livsey. This afternoon he will play for Lords and Commons against Westminster School. Lord Curzon is a very superior person. I command you to make a supreme effort, Livsey.'

'I will do my best to be superior, my lord.'

At close of play Hampshire were still batting:

HAMPSHIRE

Second innings

A. Bowell c Howell b W. G. Quaife	45
A. Kennedy b Calthorpe	7
Mr H. L. V. Day c Bates b W. G. Quaife	15
C. P. Mead b Howell	24
Hon. L. H. Tennyson c C. Smart b Calthorpe	45
G. Brown b C. Smart	172
J. Newman c and b W. G. Quaife	12
Mr W. R. Shirley lbw, b Fox	30
Mr A. S. McIntyre lbw, b Howell	5
W. H. Livsey not out	81
G. S. Boyes not out	13
B 14, lb 10, w 1, nb 1	26
Total (nine wickets)	475

Fall of wickets: 1–15, 2–63, 3–81, 4–127, 5–152, 6–177, 7–262, 8–274, 9–451.

Friday, 16 June

'Is my bath drawn, Livsey?'

'Yes, my lord, and your stimulant is on the table.'

'By the way, Livsey, I read in *The Times* that yesterday you and Brown pottered about – 177 in 140 minutes, wasn't it?'

'Bearing in mind the example of Lord Curzon, my lord, and the difference in our social stations, I thought it best to be superior by stealth.'

'Quite so, Livsey. Oh, tell Boyes not to get out till I've had my bath.'

HAMPSHIRE

Second innings (concluded)

W. H. Livsey not out	110
G. S. Boyes b Howell	29
B 14, lb 11, w 1, nb 1	27
Total	521

WARWICKSHIRE BOWLING

Second innings

	O	M	R	W
Howell	63	10	150	3
Calthorpe	33	7	97	2
W. G. Quaife	49	8	154	3
Fox	7	0	30	1
J. Smart	13	2	37	0
Santall	5	0	15	0
C. Smart	1	0	5	1

WARWICKSHIRE

Second innings

L. A. Bates c Mead b Kennedy	1
E. J. Smith c Shirley b Kennedy	41
Mr F. R. Santall b Newman	0
W. G. Quaife not out	40
Hon. F. G. S. Calthorpe b Newman	30
Rev. E. F. Waddy b Newman	0
Mr B. W. Quaife c and b Kennedy	7
J. Fox b Kennedy	0
J. Smart b Newman	3
C. Smart c and b Boyes	15
H. Howell c Kennedy b Newman	11
B 6, lb 4	10
Total	158

HAMPSHIRE BOWLING

Second innings

	O	M	R	W
Kennedy	26	12	47	4
Newman	26.3	12	53	5
Boyes	11	4	34	1
Brown	5	0	14	0

Fall of wickets: 1–2, 2–77, 3–85, 4–85, 5–85, 6–89, 7–113, 8–143, 9–147, 10–158.

Hampshire won by 155 runs

Tennyson's winnings were said to be not inconsiderable. During the remainder of the season Livsey omitted to be superior with the bat, playing 23 innings average 6·73. Brown later evolved a way of countering Larwood's short-pitched deliveries: 'I shall let them hit my chest.' He did this – once. However when the Australians appeared at Southampton in 1930, Brown struck the first ball of the game out of the ground, a feat which Tennyson did not recognise with a telegram probably because he was in his bath.

W. A. Oldfield

by Ray Robinson

As the most courtly of all wicketkeepers, William Albert Oldfield, settled into his preparatory stance he seemed to greet the incoming batsman with a curtsy. He spoke a few words of welcome, as if he were receptionist for the fielding side.

He did not carry politeness to the point of graciously sparing a batsman – like a courtier in a duel allowing his disarmed adversary to regain his rapier. Oldfield darted in for the kill as eagerly as need be; but no matter how quickly he despatched his opponent he never forgot his manners. He did not cuff the stumps or grab rudely for catches. His appeals were not raucous – nor were they apologetic. His stoop to retrieve the bails was like a bow to a parting guest.

Oldfield's actions in pauses of play were similarly genteel. Between balls and at ends of overs he constantly patted his gloves together, almost daintily, first one on top, then the other. I asked the reason for this mannerism; he said he always liked to feel that his fingers were making a perfect fit in his gloves, so he patted the palms with a crosswise action like a slithering clap. A tidy soul, he would go pat-a-patting from end to end with precise stride, the knee-flaps of his pads giving rather a strutting effect which seemed to call for minuet music. The short, dapper man would have made a fine courtier in Louis XV's day. You could picture him in the ballroom at Versailles, with powdered wig, gleaming shoe-buckles and snowy lace at his wrists. On the field his flannels were as spotless as a cravat. Never a thing out of place – except a bail flicked from its groove as a dandy might whisk a speck of snuff from his jacket. As a courtier he would have fitted blandiloquently into the cultivated conversation between minuets and quadrilles.

When Bert Oldfield, as a fair-haired youth of seventeen, played his first match for Glebe against Waverley in Sydney in March 1915, the opposing keeper was Carter. The Test veteran's swift efficiency was an eye-opener to Oldfield, who assumed that his technique must be the best and ought to be taken as a pattern. Oldfield played only one more match before going to the war. Practising with the AIF team at the Oval in 1919, he saw Strudwick in action and perceived that the Surrey man's methods would repay study better than the brilliant unorthodoxy of Carter. Oldfield and Strudwick were the same height, 5 feet

$5\frac{1}{2}$ inches, but the Australian was heavier, 10 stone 7 lb. Looking back from the heights he attained, Oldfield told me he could not have done so well with Carter's method of starting farther back from the stumps. He was sure that Strudwick's policy of taking catches close to the bat was sounder, because the farther the deflected ball travelled the more the gloves had to be pushed sideways to cover it.

Oldfield differed from Carter in mental approach, too. When the pair shared Australia's keeping in 1920 and 1921 the older man occasionally borrowed Oldfield's fingerstalls, but he mostly preferred not to use them for fear of lessening the quickness of his hands. The punctilious Oldfield bound tape around the first joint of each finger and thumb, the most vulnerable spots. He wore two pairs of chamois inner gloves which he always wetted first. On each finger he placed a strong leather stall, like an outsize thimble about an inch wide and coming down almost to the second joint. Inside were rubber tips to absorb whatever shock penetrated from the outer world. By the time he drew on his brown leather gloves with reinforced palms his hands seemed to be as encumbered as a bankrupt's estate. He preferred to sacrifice brilliance, if necessary, to ensure safety and fitness. He never lost sight of the fact that a fielding side which lost its keeper was in a mess, that a substitute stump-jockey could lose the match, the bowlers lose heart and the fieldsmen lose aim.

As far as I could see, that sacrifice of brilliance was largely theoretical. Standing up to the fast-medium bowling of Ryder on the fast Melbourne wicket of 1925, Oldfield stumped Hobbs (66) on the leg side – the most brilliant stumping of his career. In the first over of England's next Test innings, at Sydney, Oldfield was standing back to the fast bowling of Gregory with a north-easter when Hobbs leg-glanced the sixth ball down-wind and started to run. Oldfield was already on the move to leg; yards across, he gathered in the catch at top speed, yet with the poise of a tennis champion taking a wide return on the backhand.

Oldfield's keeping began long before the ball passed the stumps or before he stepped on to the field. He was Bradman-like in his alertness to detect every factor that could contribute to success. He improved his fitness with deep-breathing exercises and early-morning walks. At the practice nets he studied the bowlers to familiarise himself with their deliveries and finger-spin, so that he could anticipate the ball's behaviour. His grey-blue eyes were ever watchful for clues to the nature of the pitch and the effect of the atmosphere on the ball's flight. As a result, he took up his stance full of unostentatious confidence in his ability to make the most of every opportunity. He was always wide-awake, never lulled by his own air of quiet certainty into mechanical routine. At Sydney, in the five balls which Gregory bowled before Hobbs's fatal leg-glance, Oldfield had noticed that a strong wind over mid-off was blowing the fast bowler's in-swinger farther to leg.

Oldfield was so correct in style that photographs of him in action could be used as models for young keepers. With feet slightly wider apart than his shoulders, he went down in two movements: as the bowler came to the crease he lowered himself from a stoop to a squat on his calves, heels down. His right toecap twisted out towards cover, and the left pointed past the leg stump. His arms lay along his thighs, his mouth was at bail level and his eyes just outside the off-stump. Usually he rose with the ball to whatever height was needed to take it comfortably. That rising with the ball helped keep the fingers down – No. 1 safety-first rule for keepers – but sometimes he had to move earlier, especially if he judged that the ball would come through on the leg side; then, he aimed to step across in time to see the ball pitch and to cover it without reaching to the left. In covering off balls he did not believe in transferring the body so far that he might unsight first-slip. He preferred to lunge smartly with the right leg to bring his hands to the line of the ball. That made it easier to avoid a ball kicking dangerously from a sticky wicket, he said.

His neat efficiency often made difficult chances look easy, as in stumpings after batsmen hit over yorkers. His methods were so quiet and undemonstrative that when he spilled chances on his unlucky days they went down so quietly that you were hardly aware of it and no angry buzz came from the crowd. His blackest days were in the 1928–29 Tests, when some gremlin caused him to miss half-a-dozen chances to stump or catch Hammond off Grimmett, and the times late in his career when Fleetwood-Smith's left-arm googly bowling turned everything topsy-turvy. It must save young keepers from disheartenment to know that even the greatest masters have sometimes been all fingers and thumbs. In such a difficult art the wonder is that misses do not exceed successes, even in Test ranks. [*1951*]

Perils of a Correspondent

by Dudley Carew

Every day for four and a half months in the years from 1926 to 1939, from the Seniors' match at Oxford to the end of the Scarborough Festival – I had telegraphed, on the special forms the Post Office thoughtfully provides for the purpose, an average of ten sheets a day; a sheet consists of eighty words. During that time never once had the copy, written in my own far from easy handwriting, failed to get to its destination in time. Misprints, of course, there were, but on the whole the entire process seemed a miracle of accuracy and despatch. A messenger would be ordered to be on the ground ten minutes before the drawing of stumps – and five minutes or so before his time he would appear. As the umpires took off the bails, the copy was handed to him and that, so far as the writer was concerned, was the end until the next morning when, there in its accustomed column, were the pencilled sheets metamorphosed into the neat severity of print with the full stops, to say nothing of the commas and semi-colons, in their (usually) right place. A daily miracle, indeed, and one on which the unscientific were apt occasionally to ponder. One day the unimagined, the impossible, happened and an agency report described the second day of the August Bank Holiday match between Notts and Surrey at Trent Bridge. It had been a busy and eventful day's cricket, the details of which are now vague, but busy and eventful it certainly had been. The Notts and Surrey Bank Holiday match had not, in the years before the war, the glamour and importance it possessed when Lockwood and Lohmann were on one side and William Gunn and Shrewsbury on the other, or even when Hobbs was No. 1 for Surrey and George Gunn for Notts, but still it was an occasion, and the Trent Bridge crowd, volatile and humorous, helped the illusion that great events were abroad. What is more, it had been an eventful day in the sense that much of the excitement and action had taken place in the last hour, and this lack of consideration on the part of the cricketers puts a severe strain on the nerves and intelligence of those whose duty it is to present a full portrait of the day's play. Let us suppose that in the morning A plays an innings of great worth and merit on a difficult wicket, or B does a bit of bowling which earns him an impressive analysis. These things live in their own right, and, like the figures on the Grecian urn, have an existence independent of time and circumstance. But suppose in the last hour of the day C comes along and knocks up a hundred in which there are 4 sixes and 15 fours, or six wickets fall unexpectedly – the balance of the picture which had tentatively set A or B in the foreground is upset and C, or the fall of wickets, has to be given a prominent place. And time and space in newspaper work are limited. A certain amount of jugglery with the copy is necessary. The practice stops short of 'cooking' the books, and the process, if applied to finance, would lead to a warning from the Bench rather than a severe sentence, but contrivance and alteration there have to be, and success depends upon the smoothness with which A, B, C and the collapse are fitted into the general design. On that day an unexpected turn in the game in the last hour or so had been duly wrestled with and, behold, all the labour had gone for nothing. 'What,' I demanded of the Post Office after breakfast, 'what had happened?' and the Post Office, sorrowful and apologetic, was ready with an explanation. 'You could not go through, sir,' it said, identifying copy and person in a confusing and indissoluble whole, 'you could not go through, for you were stuck in a pneumatic tube.'

[*1946*]

COMPROMISE

'Please God, let Victor Trumper score a century today for Australia against England, out of a total of 137 all out.'

Prayer of the thirteen-year-old Neville Cardus

1,107

On 24 December 1926, a Sheffield Shield match between New South Wales and Victoria began at Sydney.

by Jack Fingleton

After five hours of streaky endeavour, the New South Wales side was out for a rather colourless 221. The next day (Saturday) was Christmas Day so that the game was put aside for two days. It began again at 11.30 on a bright Monday morning.

As usual, the two Bills, Woodfull and Ponsford, opened for Victoria. A wicket should have fallen early. When Woodfull was 7, Ponsford mistimed a savage hit at a no-ball from McNamee, and the ball flew high to Kippax at mid-on. Woodfull, evidently, had not recovered fully from his Christmas dinner; anyway, his reflexes were muddled and he began charging towards Ponsford's end. As all schoolboys know, nothing is to be gained by running for a stroke off a no-ball unless the stroke is to the deep and there is more than a single in it – and, as all schoolboys further know, the only way in which a wicket can be lost off a no-ball (excluding the theoretical ways of interference, assault and so forth) is from a run-out. It follows that Woodfull – who, perhaps, was committing the only known indiscretion of his life – was badly at fault in going for the run. Moreover, it was Ponsford's call and he stood his ground, yelling at Woodfull, 'No, no: go back!'

Woodfull stopped and was stranded, half-way down the pitch, as Kippax caught the ball and sized up the situation. As so often happens on such occasions, time to think can lead to trouble. Quick, impulsive action is often best, ruling out errors of judgement.

McNamee crouched over his stumps, waiting for the return. Now, that same McNamee was a priceless wit but a hopeless fieldsman, one who was apt to grab at the ball. Bearing that fielding weakness in mind, and knowing there was plenty of time, Kippax sent in a perfect slow lob. It was destined to land plumb in McNamee's hands.

Alas, though, McNamee couldn't suffer the agony of waiting. The ball seemed to mesmerise him and it drew him forward. He grabbed at it – and at the same time – fell over the stumps, fumbled the ball, and then dropped it! In the midst of this horrible muddle, Woodfull raced safely back to his crease.

I have drawn the circumstances of this incident in some detail because, though the first wicket should have fallen for 17, it didn't fall until 375!

Woodfull made no other error until he snicked a catch to Ratcliffe off Andrews when 133. That was bad enough for New South Wales but at stumps the position was worse with Ponsford 334 not out; Hendry 86 not out. The one wicket had fallen for 573.

Mailey had bowled 28 overs that day, at a cost of 148. Only four maiden overs were bowled all day and Ponsford, who rarely scored behind the wicket, got many runs from a short-arm jab, a stroke he had learned at baseball, which carried the ball over mid-on's head. His on-side play was faultless, his feet getting his body into quick and perfect position. During the whole day he never gave anything that resembled a chance.

The spectators trooped to the ground next day in great numbers, wondering whether Ponsford would break Clem Hill's Sheffield Shield record of 365 not out, made for South Australia against New South Wales in season 1900–1.

But Ponsford didn't break the record. At 352 he snicked a ball on to his foot and it rebounded to the stumps. He turned, surveyed the fallen bail, and said with great feeling, 'By cripes, I *am* unlucky!' That remark staggered the New South Welshmen almost as much as did the score.

So, to the disappointment of the crowd and the relief of his opposition – who had come to perceive the genus of amaranth in his bat and his bulk – Bill Ponsford trudged reluctantly to the pavilion, not to sip nectar and tender thanksgiving to the gods but to meditate darkly on how Fate had cruelly crossed him at 352, only 14 short of the record he had set his heart on. Naughty Fate!

Hendry, a New South Wales player of other years, sacrificed his wicket at 100; Love, another former New South Wales player, was out for 6; King went for 7; but then came Jack Ryder, and he committed, first, assault and mild battery on the groggy attack and, finally, sheer murder.

Ryder made 295 – the first 100 in 115 minutes; the second in 74; his final 95 in 56 minutes.

His score in the book read thus: 1, 1, 1, 1, 1, 1, 1, 1, 1, 4, 4, 1, 1, 1, 4, 1, 2, 1, 4, 1, 1, 2, 1, 1, 1, 1, 1, 1, 1, 1, 4, 2, 1, 4, 1, 4, 2, 2, 1, 1, 1, 4, 1, 4, 4, 4, 1, 1, 2, 1, 1, 1, 2, 1, 2, 4, 4, 1, 3, 1, 1, 1, 1, 4, 1, 6, 1, 1, 4, 4, 2, 4, 4, 4, 1, 1, 2, 6, 2, 1, 2, 2, 4, 2, 2, 4, 2,

1, 1, 4, 4, 2, 1, 1, 1, 6, 1, 1, 3, 1, 4, 1, 2, 1, 1, 1, 2, 4, 2, 1, 1, 1, 2, 1, 2, 2, 1, 4, 4, 2, 4, 4, 4, 2, 1, 4, 1, 1, 6, 1, 1, 2, 4, 6, 4.*

Six times – a record for such games – Ryder hit the ball out of the ground. One hit, off a full-toss from Mailey, struck the verandah of the Smokers' Stand; another went into the reserve and narrowly missed smashing the clock. This caused a heartfelt sigh in the dressing-room, for the story was that six cases of champagne would be presented to any batsman smashing the clock on the Melbourne Cricket Ground – though a subsidiary item was that nobody, least of all Ryder, knew who had promised the champagne.

'Hard luck, Arthur,' somebody sympathised with Mailey in the dressing-room during an adjournment as the slow bowler was taking a much-needed rest.

'Well, you can't get wickets if the catches are not taken,' replied the whimsical Mailey.

'Catches?' asked the outsider, puzzled, 'I didn't see any catches.'

'There's a chap in the Outer dropped Ryder twice already off me,' said Mailey.

Off five overs from Mailey, Ryder hit 62. He was 275 when he faced up to Andrews, who also bowled slows. Ryder hit the first ball for four; the next for six; the next for four; the next for six, and, trying to reach his 300 in the grand manner, mis-hit the fifth and was caught by Kippax.

The carnage didn't finish with Ryder, Hartkopf, Liddicut and Ellis continued to push the New South Wales attack around and it fell to Ellis to hit the stroke that brought the 1,000 up. Jack Ellis was – he still is – a vital, cheerful fellow and as he made the eventful stroke to the outfield he whooped, 'Come on, there's three in it. Three in it and the thousand up! Long live Victoria!'

Fortunately for New South Wales, Ellis and Morton ran themselves out, but before the innings finished Victoria had tallied 1,107 – beating the 1,059 Victoria had made against Tasmania, which had been the world's record score in a first-class match.

The New South Wales players were leg-weary when they batted on the fourth day. They were all out for 230 and Victoria won by an innings and 656. Kippax was learning captaincy the hard way but he was a light-hearted chap who always saw the humour in things. One other point must be stressed. Despite the murderous onslaught, Kippax always had his bowlers aim at the stumps. There was no wide leg- or

* If you are academic enough to try and catch me out by adding up this glut of runs, I hope you go as cross-eyed over it as I did. Moreover, I intentionally left out Ryder's final scoring stroke, which was a six! J.F.

off-theory and this, undoubtedly, contributed greatly to the fact that Victoria's 1,107 was made in the incredible time of 574 minutes.

This was the Victorian scorecard:

W. M. Woodfull c Ratcliffe b Andrews	133
W. H. Ponsford b Morgan	352
H. L. Hendry c Morgan b Mailey	100
J. S. Ryder c Kippax b Andrews	295
H. S. B. Love st Ratcliffe b Mailey	6
S. King st Ratcliffe b Mailey	7
A. E. V. Hartkopf c McGuirk b Mailey	61
A. E. Liddicut b McGuirk	36
J. L. Ellis run out	63
F. L. Morton run out	0
D. J. Blackie not out	27
Sundries	27
Total	1,107

Fall of wickets: 1–375, 2–594, 3–614, 4–631, 5–657, 6–834, 7–915, 8–1,043, 9–1,046, 10–1,107.

BOWLING*

	O	M	R	W
R. McNamee	24	2	124	0
H. McGuirk	26	1	130	1
A. A. Mailey	64	0	362	4
N. Campbell	11	0	89	0
N. E. Phillips	11·7	0	64	0
G. Morgan	26	0	137	1
T. J. E. Andrews	21	2	148	2
A. F. Kippax	7	0	26	0

McNamee and Mailey each bowled a no-ball.

Just two weeks later, in Sydney, New South Wales made 469 in the return game against Victoria – and then toppled the champions out for 35! McNamee, who took 0–124 in Melbourne, this time took 7–21!

[*1958*]

*These eight-ball overs each averaged three minutes.

W. H. Ponsford

Who here receives the accolade of comparison with another

by Ray Robinson

Of all the batsmen I have seen, Ponsford's footwork was most like a boxer's. As the bowler's arm came over he began to shuffle in front of his stumps. When he saw the ball was coming well up, he extended the shuffle into a forward sidle until he had hunted it down with a crashing drive or a defensive smother. If it were short-pitched, he scuttled back into position to cut, glance or hook, all the while staring at the revolving ball as intently as if he were trying to decipher the maker's name. Bradman disliked playing forward in defence; usually he stood motionless as a statue until he learned the direction and length of the ball, then made all his movements in a flash. That is why, now and again, a flighted leg-break found Don with his mind not made up, and yielded a catch to slip or 'keeper.

Jardine once expressed the opinion that, curiously enough, Ponsford's wonderful sight did not produce quick footwork. Perhaps he was such a doctrinaire of formal foot placement (as if by numbers) that he could not class Ponsford's crab-like mobility in the category of proper footwork. I fancy that opinion would not be shared by any English spin bowler who tried to get Ponsford out – men like Peebles (who baffled Woodfull, Bradman and Kippax at Manchester in 1930 but was mastered by Ponsford), Freeman, Brown, Robins, Marriott and Tom Mitchell. I know it is not shared by Grimmett, a bowler to whom all batsmen deficient in footwork were pushovers, and against whom Ponsford made nine three-figure scores (ranging from 108 to 336) in the last fifteen matches in which they were opposed.

Ponsford himself ranked footwork as the first essential in batsmanship. He was so certain in his bent-kneed, short-paced advance to the pitched-up ball that he was never stumped in his thirty-five Test innings against England and only once (on the leg-side off Constantine, West Indies) in his fifty-one Test innings against all countries. If a bowler's hand action did not immediately reveal to him which way the ball was spun he did not worry; he was content to play each ball according to its length.

He concentrated so much on the ball, and on moving to deal with it, that I suspect he sometimes lost exact reckoning of where the stumps were behind him. This largely accounts for his having been bowled more often than other front-rank batsmen by balls that passed behind

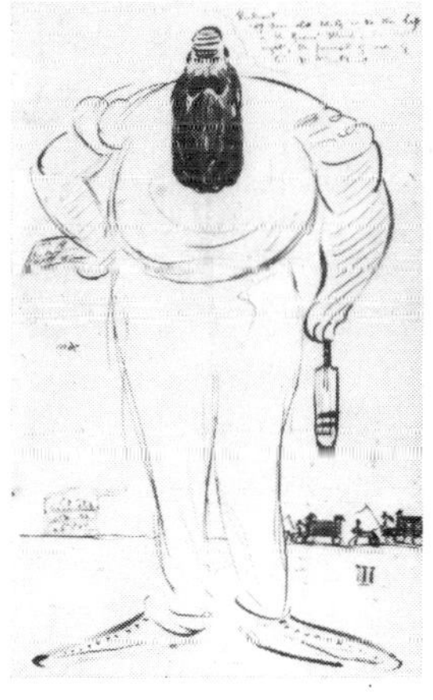

Top left: Martha Grace whose son 'turned the old one-stringed instrument into a many-chorded lyre' *Jubilee Book of Cricket*, 1897

Top right:
W. G. Grace

Bottom left:
W. G. Grace, Harry Furniss cartoon

Bottom right:
W. G. Grace, Max Beerbohm cartoon, 1895

A. Shrewsbury

G. A. Lohmann

The Australians in England, 1902
J. J. Kelly J. V. Saunders H. Trumble W. W. Armstrong M. A. Noble W. J. Howell
Major B. J. Wardill (manager)
C. Hill R. A. Duff J. Darling (captain) V. Trumper E. Jones
A. J. Hopkins H. Carter S. E. Gregory

RANSOMES' LAWN MOWERS.

THE BEST IN THE WORLD.

RANSOMES' 'HORSE-POWER' LAWN MOWERS FOR CRICKET GROUNDS

Are made from entirely new designs, embodying many improvements, and are believed to be the very best Horse-power Machines. They are especially suitable for large Lawns and Pleasure Grounds, Cricket Grounds, Lawn Tennis Grounds, Bowling Greens, &c. &c. The grass box is arranged for delivering the grass on either side at pleasure, without any complicated machinery. The frame is very strong, and the handles are adjustable. A new and simple adjustment is provided for setting the knives; the concave is also adjustable. There is a wind guard to prevent the grass blowing about; the gearing is automatic, working direct on the driving spindle; the box folds over the machine, which then can be stowed away in small compass.

PRICES:—26-in. (Pony), £14. 10s.; 30-in. (Pony), £18; 30-in. £20; 36-in. £24; 48-in. £32.

Boots for Pony, 25s.; Horse, 30s.

R., S., & H. also manufacture 'Automaton' Lawn Mowers for hand power; the best General Purpose Machines, sizes from 8 to 20 inches, prices from 55s. to £8, and 'Reversible' Lawn Mowers, the best Machine for Amateurs and for cutting borders, sizes 6 to 10 inches, prices 32s. to 52s.

All Lawn Mowers Carriage Paid to the principal Stations in England, also to Scotch and Irish Ports.

A month's free trial allowed, when, if not approved, the Machine may be returned without any charge, carriage paid.

RANSOMES, SIMS, & HEAD, ORWELL WORKS, IPSWICH.

Top: Engraving from Lillywhites Annual, 1879
Bottom left: The cricket bat maker, engraving, 1934
Bottom right: Inventive precautions against rain at Old Trafford

V. Trumper

G. L. Jessop

Top: The South Africans in England, 1907
A. D. Nourse H. Smith W. A. Shalders M. Hathorn G. A. Faulkner G. Allsop (manager)
J. H. Sinclair R. O. Schwarz Rev C. W. Robinson P. W. Sherwell L. J. Tancred A. E. Vogler
J. J. Kotze
S. J. Snooke G. C. White S. D. Snooke

Bottom: The West Indians in England, 1963
G. Duckworth (scorer) W. V. Rodriguez S. M. Nurse M. C. Carew
C. C. Griffith L. A. King, E. D. McMorris L. R. Gibbs B. F. Butcher W. Pye (physiotherapist)
B. Gaskin (manager) R. B. Kanhai C. C. Hunte F. M. Worrell (captain) W. W. Hall
G. S. Sobers A. L. Valentine H. Burnett (assistant manager)
D. L. Murray J. S. Solomon D. W. Allan

C. G. Macartney
G. A. Headley

K. S. Ranjitsinhji
S. J. McCabe

Top left: S. F. Barnes
Top right: M. W. Tate
Bottom: A. V. Bedser

J. B. Hobbs

Top: The Australians in England, 1921

W. Bardsley J. S. Ryder H. L. Hendry J. M. Gregory E. R. Mayne T. J. E. Andrews Sydney Smith (manager)

A. A. Mailey E. A. Macdonald H. L. Collins W. W. Armstrong (captain) C. G. Macartney H. Carter J. M. Taylor

C. E. Pellew W. A. Oldfield

Bottom: The Australians in England, 1948

R. N. Harvey S. G. Barnes R. R. Lindwall R. Saggers D. Ring W. A. Johnston E. R. H. Toshack K. R. Miller D. Tallon S. Loxton

K. O. E. Johnson (manager) R. Hamence I. W. Johnson A. L. Hassett (vice captain) D. G. Bradman (captain) W. A. Brown A. R. Morris C. L. McCool

W. Ferguson (scorer)

T. Richardson

H. Larwood

R. R. Lindwall

F. S. Trueman

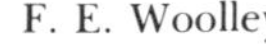

F. E. Woolley

W. R. Hammo

W. J. O'Reilly

D. G. Bradman

C. I. J. Smith: The Stroke

L. Hutton

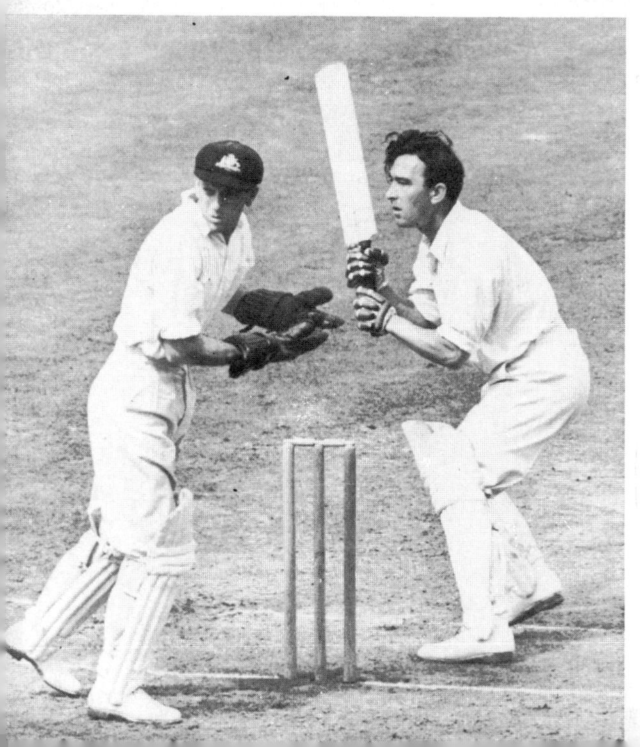

D. C. S. Compton

B. Sutcliffe

M. P. Donnelly

F. M. Worrell

J. C. Laker

G. S. Sobers

his legs. That happened six times in the fifteen innings in which English bowlers hit his wicket in Tests, and it occurred occasionally in inter-state matches in Australia. Either he did not connect with a leg-glance or (as happened twice in the bodyline Tests) he thought the ball would clear the leg-stump, and did not attempt a stroke for fear of giving a catch to the leg-trap fieldsman.

The tendency to shuffle too far across was acquired in correcting an earlier fault. When Ponsford entered international cricket he left too big a gap between bat and pads in forward strokes to balls near the off-stump, and drew away in playing balls on his leg-stump. That made him vulnerable to Tate's late and penetrating swing. In a year or so he had rebuilt that part of his play so thoroughly that no bowler could have got a marble, much less a ball, between his bat and his left leg. Except for one season (when bodyline introduced a new factor) Ponsford did not lose his leg-stump often enough to think of risking worse complications by meddling with the inward movement which gave him such advantages in getting properly over the great majority of balls bowled to him. And for every time his leg-stump was hit he made heaps of runs with glances and on-side placements.

He made a little more than half his scoring strokes with most of his weight on the front foot, whereas Bradman played three-fifths of his off the back foot and hit three-quarters of his fours with hooks, pulls and other forcing on-shots, cover-hits, cuts and glances. Though both batsmen hit three-fifths of their fours to the on-side, where the fielding population was smaller, for every four scoring strokes by Bradman to the off Ponsford played five.

This more even balance between forward and back play, and on and off strokes, explains why Ponsford sometimes scored as fast as Bradman. The Victorian was 11 when Don joined him for their Oval partnership and he was not overtaken by the harder-hitting player until he had passed 100. How many more strokes he played in that period is indicated by his having scored only 28 of his 100 in boundary hits, compared with Bradman's 60 in fours. At Leeds, where Ponsford had a 22 start, Don beat him to 100 by 20 minutes, yet Bill was first to 130. Bradman's greater severity in exacting maximum toll from every short-pitched ball made his score mount faster as the bowlers became wearier. He was about 40 ahead of Ponsford when each of the record partnerships ended.

Ponsford is the only batsman who has scored 300 in a day's play in Australia.* When he was 26, he hit up 334 in a day (5½ hours' play)

* The South African B. A. Richards has since scored 325 in a day–South Australia v Western Australia at Perth, 1970–71.

against NSW – an average speed of 60 an hour. Not that he ever gave much thought to his scoring rate. There was nothing of the showman in him, and his primary duty as an opening batsman was to overcome the bowling. If the bowlers deserved respect he gave them respect, playing each ball on its merits and patiently awaiting the opportunity to carve into the bowling and polish it off. Other times, he unashamedly used lesser matches for long batting practice for pending big games.

He is the only player who has scored 400 twice. He was the founder of total batting, the first to make a habit of regarding 100 as merely the opening battle in a campaign for a larger triumph. In his operations against bowlers he used everything that would serve his ends, from digging in for protracted trench warfare to launching summer offensives. In his defence-in-depth he backed up his bat with a set of bulky pads, strapped around a pair of the thickest calves ever owned by a man of 5 feet 9 inches. Yet not once in his fifty-one Test innings was he out leg-before-wicket.

O'Reilly said Ponsford was the greatest concentrator he bowled against. Constantine valued him 'worth two of any other batsman I have seen for a big game'.

Wisden (1935) records that the English bowlers thought him every bit as difficult to get rid of as Bradman. Ironmonger, last of the great Australian leg-spin left-handers, said Bradman did give a bowler a glimmer of hope, but Ponsford none. Ebeling,* fast-medium Test bowler of 1934, said he never tackled Bradman, for all his genius, with the same hopeless feeling as he did Ponsford, whose bat always looked too broad and whose impregnability smashed bowlers' morale (incidentally, neither this pair nor any other batsman even frayed the edges of Ebeling's morale).

Much the same with Verity. The Yorkshire left-hander dismissed Bradman eight times in Tests and a couple of times in other matches, but the only time Ponsford's wicket fell to him he did not know it had happened. The ball was well clear of the off-stump and Ponsford (181) stepped back and hooked it to the boundary wide of long-on. Verity was watching the ball being returned when he heard the Leeds crowd roar and was surprised to see Ponsford walking away. The batsman's left foot had swung back just after he hit the ball. It touched the leg-stump, dislodged one bail and he was given out, hit-wicket.

Part of a great batsman's stock-in-trade is ability to manipulate the strike by intentionally playing strokes for an odd or even number of runs. Bradman and Ponsford each developed the stratagem to a fine

* Who organised the England–Australia centenary Test at Melbourne, March 1977.

art. But, as both were right-handers and each was accustomed to running the show in partnerships with others, their manœuvring when they batted together caused knowing winks in the pavilion when both wanted to get to the one end – or to get away from it. Probably the greatest compliment Bradman ever paid Ponsford was an indirect one. On the night after their 451 partnership, Don mentioned that he thought Bill should have taken the greater part of the bowling with the new ball at 400! [*1945*]

*

The England bowlers at Leeds and the Oval in 1934 were W. E. Bowes, G. O. Allen, E. W. Clark, W. R. Hammond, H. Verity, T. B. Mitchell and J. L. Hopwood. They had a frustrating time.

The first day at Leeds England tottered to 200, play finishing with Australia 39 for three – Ponsford 22 not out. The next wicket fell at 5.51 pm the following day with the score 427. Rain saved England from certain defeat.

Batting first at the Oval, Australia lost W. A. Brown at 21 with the clocks showing noon. Then followed a repeat of what Cardus inevitably called 'the Leeds double concerto', the second wicket falling a few minutes before the close at 472. This time it did not rain.

In these successive Tests Ponsford and Bradman added 839 runs, progressing at 76 an hour. Ponsford's average for the series was 94·83, Bradman's 94·75.

L. N. Constantine

by R. C. Robertson-Glasgow

Learie Nicholas Constantine must rank as one of the best all-round cricketers within memory; though he would not be inclined to compare himself with this or that famous player, but rather with his own self-proposed standard, which is as high as the sky.

In recent times W. R. Hammond, Frank Woolley and Don Bradman have had the power, as batsmen, to take the whole crowd with them; among bowlers, Larwood, Grimmett, Freeman and, possibly, O'Reilly, have, when given the ball, been able to induce that tautness of expectation which can be felt rather than expressed. But, of them all, Constantine alone has been the one thing to watch, the magnet of the moment, whether batting, bowling or fielding. And what a wicket-keeper has been lost! Surely no man ever gave or received more joy by the mere playing of cricket.

Constantine has always come fresh to the cricket public, re-awakening them on each rare appearance not only by the violence of genius, but by some novelty of method, some different and startling arrangement of the eight balls in the over, some unsuspected place in the field, some unbelievable device for striking an off ball to the mid-wicket boundary. Sometimes the heat of the whole thing becomes too much. He boils over. Flames appear, and have to be extinguished by the blanket of orthodoxy.

He was born right into cricket. He has told us of the early family games, both sexes partaking, Uncle Pascall, that subtle left-hand bowler, joining in, and his father, L. S., who played cricket here in 1900 and 1906, admonishing in rapid tones, then hitting the young Learie every sort of catch till darkness drove all in to supper. When he was about nineteen he came over here with H. B. G. Austin's team. I remember his wonderful fielding at cover-point against us at Weston-super-Mare. He did not bowl, but watched Uncle Pascall. At Oxford he made 77.

In 1928 he reached full fame. The beautiful fielding remained; to that were added new and riper powers as a hitter; and he had become one of the few fast bowlers in the game who mattered. This was his only full season in English county cricket. He did the 'double'. Among many remarkable feats the chief was his defeat, almost single-handed, of Middlesex at Lord's. He scored 86 in the first innings; took seven for 57, five bowled, in a Middlesex innings of 136. West Indies were left 259 to win; they lost 5 for 121, then Constantine hit 103 in an hour, and they won by three wickets. That winter he passed into Lancashire League cricket and settled in England. This suited the Saturdays of Nelson and his own desire to study law. The rest of us suffered a loss.

That triumph and departure mark the beginning of what may be called his semi-mythical period. He continued to do wonderful things, but in cricket which, though fitted to his temperament, was seldom worthy of his genius. His art, now at its height, lacked the sharpest spur and provocation. So it was bound to rust somewhat, and, in his Test appearances of 1933, neither in batting nor bowling was he quite the early Constantine. For all that, his choice of life was right.

In 1939, once more joining in for the Tests, he came out as a medium-paced bowler with a faster ball and a variety of spin and flight most absorbing to watch. His five wickets for 75 against England on a perfect pitch in the first innings at the Oval, including those of Oldfield, Hammond and Hardstaff, were taken by a combination of high skill and intelligence, and his hitting in an innings of 79 was as fierce as ever.

I should not wonder if, among his preparations for peace, he has included a left-handed googly and a system for hitting sixes off shooters. [*1943*]

1928

The three cricketers of 1928 destined for the widest fame were the St Edward's School captain, century-maker and fast bowler, D. S. R. Bader, later to join the RAF; the Harrow opening batsman, T. M. Rattigan, already jotting down plays; and Lancing's fast-medium bowler, P. N. L. Pears, now associated with *Peter Grimes*, the *Serenade* and numerous other works by Benjamin Britten.

W. R. Hammond

by J. M. Kilburn

Hammond in his heyday offered all the glory and the colour of medieval chivalry. He graced a cricket field by stepping on it. He brought to combat the dignity, the skill, the authority of rightful rank. The trappings and the panoply surrounded him. He was never seen without being remembered. In his time a Test Match could not seem a Test Match in his absence.

Hammond's cricket reached the topmost peaks of the game. More than anyone else of his generation he reflected gleams of a golden age and carried us all beyond the care of local loyalties to an experience of the spirit. He thrilled us, held the imagination, raised us beyond ourselves in his presence and the darkening to his final curtain cannot obscure the unquestionable greatness of the whole play.

It was a satisfaction to watch Hammond do no more than walk from one position in the field to another, from first-slip to first-slip. His was the very poetry of motion, flowing, smooth and vital. Sometimes he made no runs and did not bowl, and still earned his keep by catches. Three times he held six catches in an innings and once he held ten in a match. He was everything the slip fieldsman is supposed to be in theory: he was balanced, he never 'grabbed' at the ball and though he used both hands whenever possible he had full confidence in either right or left alone. His timing often made his achievement incredible in retrospect, yet the most natural activity imaginable during the execution.

Hammond's bowling was as easeful as his fielding and his batting. There was a delicacy of touch and hidden vigour in it. An economical 'sideways' action gave him control and subtle variation of pace and helped him to swing the new ball. Had the gods denied him batting talent he could have found fame as a bowler.

There was no denial of batting talent; in technique, temperament, power and grace Hammond was superb. It was said that his on-side play had its limitations, that he possessed no hook shot; Macdonald at Old Trafford was not conscious of the deficiency one historic morning in May. When Hammond did not hook, it was because Hammond did not choose to hook. On the off-side, where Hammond mostly did choose to play, he was acknowledged as without peer. Fast bowlers of his time thought him the best player of slow bowling in the whole world; slow bowlers pointed out that fast bowlers also paid for his wicket. His magnificence was undeniable and his display of it was lavish.

He played incomparable innings for England over a period of nearly twenty years and the multitudes of Lord's and Sydney rose in homage to him, but it is not beyond argument that he gave the highest expression of himself at Bristol or Gloucester or, best of all, at Cheltenham. He could wear the robes of state with assurance and nobody ever saw him cheapen a cricketing occasion, but he was perhaps at his most comfortable and impressive when circumstances gave him a deck-chair to sit in until it was his turn to bat and he could stroll out to make a century for his own entertainment. In the end the game lost savour for him because he was too public a figure. His own genius and the responsibilities placed upon it spoiled his cricket—so he gave it up.

There is no need to make comparisons between Hammond and his contemporaries, or indeed between Hammond and any cricketers of any time. He stands among the few who can be excused the noun in apposition. It is sufficient to say W. R. Hammond, omitting as superfluous 'the Gloucestershire and England cricketer' [*1959*]

ET IN ARCADIA

There was some grand cricket played in the period between the wars, and if our children and grandchildren condole with us in having lived in those dreadful times, we can at least answer, 'Ah, but we saw Chapman field, Larwood bowl, Hammond bat, and we are not so much to be pitied as you think.' *Dudley Carew*

At Lord's, 24 June, 1938

ENGLAND

First innings

L. Hutton c Brown b McCormick	4
C. J. Barnett c Brown b McCormick	18
W. J. Edrich b McCormick	0
W. R. Hammond not out	210
E. Paynter lbw, b O'Reilly	99
D. C. S. Compton lbw, b O'Reilly	6
L. E. G. Ames not out	50
Lb 12, nb 9, w 1	22
Total (for five wickets)	409

To bat: H. Verity, A. W. Wellard, D. V. P. Wright and K. Farnes.

Fall of wickets: 1–12, 2–20, 3–31, 4–253, 5–271.

Australia: J. H. Fingleton, W. A. Brown, D. G. Bradman (captain), S. J. McCabe, A. L. Hassett, C. L. Badcock, B. A. Barnett, A. G. Chipperfield, W. J. O'Reilly, E. L. McCormick and L.O'B. Fleetwood-Smith.

Umpires: E. J. Smith and F. Walden

by Ronald Mason

At the outset McCormick found a little answering greenness in the wicket and made his slightly short-pitched deliveries whip and sing round the apprehensive ears of Barnett and Hutton. Barnett, a straightforward true batsman who liked straightforward true bowling, was prone to fence and swish at this kind of thing, while the Hutton of June 1938 on a sporty pitch was neither the Hutton of August 1938 on a shirt-front nor the Hutton of 1950 on anything that was offered. Accordingly there was a tentative air about the batting, and a dangerous tendency to prod; and the score was only 12 when Hutton prodded once too often and spooned a feeble dolly catch. Edrich, who followed, was defeated almost before he was in, missing a blind scared hook before being devastated trying a blind scared pull; and with the score at no more than 31 Barnett was bullied into giving just such another dolly catch as Hutton's. England 31 for three with the game barely forty minutes old and the shine still on the ball. The bottom fell out of all England spectators' hopes; or would have fallen out but for the emergence of the assured cocky figure of Eddie Paynter to assist the calm, detached authority of Hammond, playing the fiery imponderabilities of McCormick with apparently minutes to spare.

In these frightening straits Hammond proceeded to one of the greatest innings of his life: greatly set, greatly prepared for, greatly executed. Before he had been in twenty minutes it was clear, and to noboby was it clearer than to Bradman, who was master in this business. McCormick, in face of this impassive contempt, shrivelled into insignificance in a couple of overs. Fleetwood-Smith came on and was instantly thrashed twice for four in his first over, deadly murderous calculated blows off good-length balls, menacingly certain. The dangerous spinner wavered in his length, and Hammond drove another half-volley straight past his boots for four. Even the great O'Reilly, labouring up to the wicket in concentrated hate, found he could not spin the ball as he wished in face of such aggression. Paynter was every bit as calm, and once hit Fleetwood-Smith for six over fine-leg with engaging impudence. The initiative was taken right away from Australia. Against all probability and out of the unpromising depths of initial disaster, Hammond and Paynter took England's score to 134 for three before lunch. Hammond had made 70, beautifully in command, relaxed and serene, untroubled by the early disasters. In the interval he and the rest of the players were lined up and presented to King George VI, with Earl Baldwin in attendance; a gracious if distracting ceremony, but failing, one is happy to remember, to turn Hammond's concentration from the matter urgently in hand.

A man I know saw every ball of this day bowled, and for every ball he stood, packed in the overflowing crowd high at the back of the stands behind long-off as you face the pavilion; he was young then and he had an important examination pending, and he should have devoted his day to his books, but he left them on an impulse and came to Lord's. He stood there on his hot and aching feet all day and focused his gaze on the mastery unfolding before them; out of the fogs and frustrations of middle age he says he would gladly, ever so gladly, go through the whole of that day again, for he has remembered it in peace and war, in alien city and alien continent, through tension and tranquillity all his life. He remembers Hammond coming in with squared grim shoulders to the chaos and by the very force of skill and personality raising the England innings on those shoulders to honourable levels again; how after the first sighting minutes he settled compactly to the central task, how soon he flexed his shoulders in an experimental cover-drive, and how for several overs he would ever and again unship one of his great patent off-drives and tingle the palms of cover or extra-cover or mid-off; how Bradman dropped a man back on the crowd's toes at deep extra-cover and how Hammond off the back foot cracked good-length ball after good-length ball at this man in the deep, great reverberating drives that whistled and thrummed with the power of his wrists and shoulders, drives my friend remembers for their individual beauty and power after nearly a quarter of a century – then how as he came to certainty of timing and found at last his effective direction one drive at last cracked clean through the ringed field out of all possible reach and was followed at once by others like it, until the off-side seemed as full of holes as a colander and though the fielders never abated their energy and courage he seemed at the end able to place the ball, and place it at intimidating speed, precisely where he chose. 'It was a throne-room innings,' said Cardus, watching enraptured. 'He played greatly and deserved better bowling.'

McCormick on his return was as good as useless; Fleetwood-Smith and O'Reilly at least kept a length; but not a ball beat the bat for hours. Paynter's crusading lightfoot impudence well matched the crushing authority that Hammond had once and for all triumphantly assumed; he suddenly burst into brilliance, driving and late-cutting to charm the world. Hammond got to his hundred, one of the outstanding Test centuries of his own and his contemporaries' time, in just under two and a half hours; by this time he was playing at will from anywhere in his own half of the wicket, mobile and well balanced, on the easy hunt for runs. 'He only gave one chance,' says my friend reminiscently, 'and that broke Chipperfield's finger' – and he stifles a cheerful smile, for he is a kindly and humane man. Paynter was suddenly and unexpectedly lbw for 99, a sad oversight to end a glorious attacking innings and a record stand of 222. Denis Compton, chafing at the long wait, was fatally over-impetuous and underestimated the tiring O'Reilly; and at tea England had lost five wickets for 271 and Hammond, steady as Gibraltar, was 140 not out – 70 before lunch, 70 after, an excellent symmetry.

The last two hours were a duel between him and O'Reilly, bowling great-heartedly in the heat and intensifying his accuracy when he might have been expected to relax it. Never so O'Reilly; he plunged venomously to the crease with formidable aggressive energy never abating; he contained Hammond, though leg-stump tactics did not noticeably daunt him from on-drives and leg-hits. The cool reliability of the well-tried Ames supported him refreshingly for the whole of this session; no chance was given, no risk was taken, the day proceeded gravely to its appointed close. A symmetrical one, too; for in this last period he added precisely one more 70 to the other neat 70s of his day's compiling; it was as if he added to the artist's grace a mathematician's native precision. Hammond faced the last over of this racking day and played it coldly and forcefully as a maiden, laying the ball dead under his nose with uncompromising finality. 'All day he had carried a burden,' said Cardus, 'and with a calm which hid from us the weight and magnitude of it. He came to his 200 as easily and as majestically as a liner coming into port.' My friend on the terraces, resting his throbbing feet and stretching his paralysed muscles, took comfort in the reflection that Hammond was probably more weary than he and saluted him as he cheered him home with the rest of the packed crowd, for uplifting not only the corporate spirit of all England's supporters but a weary student's flagging morale, and for lightening not only his path to the examination room but his memory for the rest of his life. [*1962*]

*

The match ended in a draw: England 494 (Hammond 240, Ames 83) and 242 for eight, declared (Compton 76 not out); Australia 422 (Brown 206 not out, Hassett 56) and 204 for six (Bradman 102 not out).

W. J. O'Reilly

by Jack Fingleton

The first day O'Reilly appeared among the Mighty at the Sydney Cricket Ground nets Mailey came to him and suggested that he should change his grip of the ball.

Mailey was Mailey. His word would have been gospel to most up-and-coming young bowlers, who would have hastened to do his bidding. But not O'Reilly. If there was one thing he possessed it was a mind of his own. Politely he thanked Mailey for his interest, but he had always held the ball that way and, if Mr Mailey did not mind, he would continue to do so.

That was not cheek. If somebody years before had gone to Mailey and suggested he should have changed his grip, Mailey undoubtedly would have done as O'Reilly did. Individual art is created and little moulding is needed. The essence of the champion is either inherent in the individual or it isn't, and he prefers to work out a destiny along his own lines.

Mailey twined his fingers around the ball and cracked his fingers and wrist when delivering as a stockman would his whip. O'Reilly cupped his fingers around the ball and rolled it out. Mailey was not renowned for his length, O'Reilly was; Mailey was a slow bowler, O'Reilly medium pace, and between the two was a fundamental difference in all things, even to temperament.

I recall no bowler who resembled O'Reilly. At medium pace he bowled a leg-break, a bosie and a top-spinner. If the wicket took spin he could turn the ball the width of the stumps and more, as Jardine found to his amazement one Melbourne day in 1932; but generally his spin was modest and content to do all that was necessary – either miss the bat by a fraction or find its edge for catches.

He concealed his bosie as artfully as an expert cracksman would his fingerprints and therein was his great strength. There was some peculiar mixture of top-spin in his bosie that gave the ball a sharper rise from the pitch than his leg-break. This was the ball which brought many catches to his leg-trap. Unsuspecting batsmen played it with the bat the usual height from the ground. Bouncing higher, the ball kissed the bat higher up its face and, with the rising spin still operating, the ball flirted with the atmosphere long enough for the catch to be made.

But O'Reilly was not distinctive alone in the variety of balls he delivered. He had other rich gifts, none more tantalising to the batsman than his long, queer approach to the wickets. Edmund Blunden described it aptly when he wrote that O'Reilly's bowling began long before he got to the wickets. All batsmen like the bowler to come calmly and evenly in his run-up, but with O'Reilly a batsman's line of flight went up and down like a see-saw as O'Reilly came bobbing along like a kangaroo in the legs and a windmill in the arms. And then, finally, the ball hurtled at the batsman from a mass of erupting humanity.

All this was part of O'Reilly's technique and contributed to his greatness, but nothing in his make-up was of more importance than his temperament.

'I have never seen a bowler,' Constantine once told me, 'who seemed to suggest by his every action that he wished to goodness he was a fast bowler, a fast bowler who would carry every batting thing before him. That, all other things being equal, is the ideal bowling temperament to possess.'

Hot blood surged through O'Reilly's veins. It was quick to rise to the top, showing in veins that stood like whipcord over his temples if he thought he was being wronged by fate, umpires, conditions or cricket legislators – and I really think at no stage of his career did O'Reilly consider he and his bowling brothers were anything else but the victims of oppression. It might have been that the grudge he bore batsmen in the home paddock of his youth never really left him, but in his first-class career he always contended that bowlers were the playthings of the game, the legislators and the gates. The bowler was cricket's poor relation. He was a perpetual male Cinderella, always doing the interminable dirty work for his elder brothers, the batsmen and the legislators. [*1947*]

The Master Ball

It appeared that the Melbourne Test of 1932–33 would be won by England. At the close of the third day, with all ten wickets in hand, 208 were needed for victory:

Australia 228 (J. H. Fingleton 83) and 191 (D. G. Bradman 103 not out); England 169 (H. Sutcliffe 52; O'Reilly five for 63) and 43 for none.

by Denzil Batchelor

Who could doubt what the end must be?

And next day something happened which had been allowed for in nobody's calculations: the hearty, bonhomous wicket of the evening before instantaneously developed signs of something like senile decay. First-hand accounts of its condition vary with the part played by the cricketers involved. Bill O'Reilly has described it to me as the type of the wicket on which Australia hit up 404 on the last day at Leeds in '48: a wicket which made it possible for the ball to be spun. Douglas Jardine, in his fine account of the game, explains that his own innings on this pitch was limited to three balls, of which he smothered the first before it had turned more than 4 or 5 inches, while the second, left alone, broke a foot and a half, and the third turned 9 inches before he touched it into the slips.

It was clear that, after an apathetic youth and a hearty middle-age, the wicket was finishing its life in a mood of arthritic crotchetyness. This gave an opportunity which O'Reilly was quick to seize. Here at last was the chance – the lost game could be won. While Leyland was batting buoyantly enough, Sutcliffe was demurely exploring the possibilities of expansion and development. Yet it was Sutcliffe who stood between Australia and victory: get rid of Sutcliffe and you had rolled up the English flank.

And that is precisely what Bill O'Reilly did. The ball that turned the trick was of perfect length and pitched on the leg-stump, whipping across to hit the off-bail while the batsman groped down the line of the wicket. After all these years O'Reilly still remembers it as about the best ball he ever bowled in his life: and the point is, of course, that he bowled it at the exact moment when the best ball of a bowling genius (and nothing less) could set his side on the high road to victory.

After that, winning the match was a routine job. The only possible batsman who might alter the shape of the game was Hammond. In the face of much ill-informed criticism, he attempted to hit the bowlers off their length in a death-or-glory innings. For a while he prospered; and then his bat failed to get properly under a quickening leg-break as it left the pitch, and the majestic mashie shot ballooned into the deep, where O'Brien, with a quicksilver dart from the rim of the boundary, seized the shadowy chance.

Then, one by one, the hopes of the side came, half-saw and were conquered. Of them all, only Wyatt and Allen gripped the imagination as counterattackers with a mission. They went down making strokes to the end: and when, as in the first innings, O'Reilly claimed Wyatt as a leg-before victim, the game was virtually over. The last four wickets fell while 4 runs were added: Allen, being delectably stumped whilst prancing out to administer cavalier treatment to Ironmonger.

Australia have won a great Test; and all Melbourne has gone home happy. The players are happy, too; not least Don Bradman, for whom someone has taken up a collection of a hundred pounds in recognition of his contribution to victory. But if you are to reward people according to their deserts, I am not persuaded that the right man got the cherry on the cake on that particular occasion. Bradman was mighty; Bradman was invincible. In the second half of the game, when not another man of them all could scrape together 35, Bradman hit his superb century like a man from Mars toying with the playthings of a lesser star.

The game, however, was not won by Bradman, but by the bowler who took, in the match, ten wickets for 129 runs. That is, if such a game can be won by one man alone. If it can be won by one ball alone, it was won by the ball that kicked back from the on, to shave Herbert Sutcliffe's off-bail from his wicket. No one raised a collection of a hundred pounds for the man who bowled this ball. No one splashed his name in headlines in bolder type than you use for abdications or atom bombs.

After all, he was only a bowler. [*1950*]

. . . and Hammond

On the second day of the Leeds Test in 1938 Bradman had batted incredibly in appalling light; at the close C. J. Barnett and W. J. Edrich were in possession.

England 223 (W. R. Hammond 76; O'Reilly five for 66) and 49 for none; Australia 242 (D. G. Bradman 103, B. A. Barnett 57).

by Ralph Barker

All that Sunday the rain circled Leeds, falling in torrents a few miles away but shying away from Headingley. Like some hallowed museum piece the wicket was to be preserved in its exact state of Saturday. When play started on the Monday morning it looked dusty and worn. Estimates were that Australia might find a fourth innings target of 150 beyond them. That meant that England had to get another 120. They were expected to get considerably more than that.

Barnett and Edrich faced O'Reilly from the Kirkstall Lane end and McCormick from the pavilion end. It was a warm, sunny morning, but a hint of thunder was still in the air. O'Reilly at once made the ball turn sharply and quickly, and Bradman rearranged his field, bringing four men close in to the bat, two of them on the leg-side for the googly. The crowd gasped at the violence of O'Reilly's spin. His googly was bouncing like a tennis ball. One ball spun back from the bat and rested against the stumps, but the bails clung to their grooves.

Somehow Barnett and Edrich hung on. A no-ball from O'Reilly was despatched by Barnett for four. The England score crept to 60. Then McCormick bounced one at Barnett, and Barnett essayed a hook, only to sky the ball near the wicket, where it was easily caught. It was an inglorious end to an invaluable partnership.

McCormick was getting plenty of life out of the wicket and in his next over he rapped Edrich on the knuckles. It seemed to Bradman that the end opposite the pavilion was playing the less reliably, and he switched O'Reilly to the pavilion end and introduced Fleetwood-Smith at the other. McCormick had done his job in breaking the opening stand.

Hardstaff came in and promptly hooked O'Reilly down beyond the members' stand for four. O'Reilly, furious with himself, tried a faster ball but overstepped the line and winced as the umpire called no-ball. Hardstaff swept it contemptuously away for another boundary, the runs clicking up on the scoreboard with awful rapidity. O'Reilly's anger could not be contained. With dramatic emphasis he paced out his run again, gesticulated fiercely, as though the call of no-ball constituted a personal outrage, and thundered up to the wicket to bowl the next ball. Like the girl in the novelette, O'Reilly was never more thrilling to watch than when he was angry. This time he was livid with rage.

No one on the ground had ever seen a ball like it. It was the greatest ball O'Reilly ever bowled. It was not only fast, really fast, it was a vicious leg-break. Hardstaff sparred at it in bewildered fashion, and the ball just took the top of the off-bail. If O'Reilly was going to bowl like that, no batsman on earth could stop him, not even Hammond. And Hammond was next.

Just how far above their fellows Hammond and Bradman stood at this stage in their careers can be emphasised by quoting their figures so far that season. Hammond in 25 innings had averaged 86 and passed 2,000 runs. Bradman in 21 innings had averaged 126 and also passed 2,000 runs. They stood alone at the top of the English and Australian averages, separated from the next man by a distance. No England batsman was within 400 runs of Hammond's aggregate and no Australian within 600 of Bradman's.

With O'Reilly in this mood, Hammond was clearly England's first and last hope. As he made his way to the wicket, Hammond knew this well enough. Bradman knew it, too, and he motioned his two short-leg fieldsmen, Fingleton at silly mid-on and Brown just in front of square, to come in even closer. O'Reilly prepared to bowl.

Plunging and rolling like a ship in stormy seas, O'Reilly bucketed up to the wicket, wrist cocked, arms flailing, face contorted with pain and emotion. He gave Hammond the googly, pitching about middle-and-off so that Hammond would have to play at it, and he pushed it through at a full medium pace. Hammond went half forward, bat sloped back at an angle, stabbing the ball into the deck. But that tennis-ball bounce upset his calculations. The ball turned sharply, and Hammond could not quite keep it down. It darted away towards square-leg, a foot from the ground, just out of reach it seemed of Brown's outstretched hand. But Brown had seen the ball off the bat. Like some elongated mechanical grab his hand reached for it, perfectly cupped. The next moment the ball was in it, and Hammond was out. Out first ball.

A great sigh went up from the 36,000 spectators who were crammed into the ground, the biggest crowd ever for a Test Match at Leeds. Then there was a terrible silence at Hammond departed. In two balls O'Reilly had opened the way for an Australian victory, and the retention of the Ashes.

England were not entirely done with yet. Next man in was left-hander Eddie Paynter, and no man was a better fighter. As the diminutive Paynter took guard and prepared to stop the hat-trick he disappeared altogether behind the cluster of close fielders that Bradman had assembled for him. Somehow he scraped O'Reilly's next ball away, and the intolerable tension was lifted. But next over, without another run being scored, Edrich lost his balance playing forward to Fleetwood-Smith and was stumped. England were 73 for four.

Compton joined Paynter, and with their last two specialist batsmen together England were only 54 runs ahead. Another hundred runs were needed to give England an even chance. Both men decided to go for their shots, on the principle that O'Reilly on this wicket would certainly get them out in time so they must take what was offered while they were there. Paynter hit two successive balls from O'Reilly for four, a cut and an old-fashioned pull, and Compton sent another O'Reilly no-ball soaring into the deep and then cover-drove him for four, pushing the score into the nineties. Then Compton tried to sweep O'Reilly's googly. The high bounce deceived him, the ball brushed upwards off his glove and Barnett took the catch. 96 for five. England were only 77 in front, and the destruction of their batting was all but complete. The batsmen to come were Price, Verity, Wright, Farnes and Bowes.

Everything depended on whether Paynter could find someone to stay with him. Price did for a time, supporting Paynter and striking one or two lusty blows of his own, but when they had added 20 runs Fleetwood-Smith took three wickets in a row – Price, Verity and Wright. Farnes hit a four and a three, but Paynter could not get at the bowling again and O'Reilly finished off the innings by getting Farnes and Bowes. England were all out for 123, Paynter being left stranded with 21 not out. Australia needed only 105 to win. [*1967*]

*

Australia won by five wickets, O'Reilly's match analysis being 66–25–122–10.

C. I. J. Smith

And a last wicket stand

Christened Cedric Ivan James, Smith sounded like an amateur batsman of the 1890s. In fact he was a fast bowler good enough to be selected as one of the 1935 *Wisden*'s Five Cricketers of the Year, and known as Smith, J.

*

by Ian Peebles

When I first saw the St Lawrence Cricket Ground, Canterbury, in August 1939, my attention was distracted from its beauties by having to make a ticklish decision.

If Middlesex beat Kent, we still had a fair chance of winning the championship; so, as captain, I had to move with caution.

There had been a good deal of rain overnight, and the pitch lay lush and green under a strong but fitful morning sun. I had won the toss, and the question was – to bat or not to bat. Being no judge of turf, I found it a hard one to answer. Eventually, finding opinion amongst the bowlers divided and not having a weather prophet handy, I decided to play safe and take strike.

That great and unique pundit, Gerry Weigall, strongly disagreed with my decision. Never a man to underclub himself in the matter of words, he described it variously as 'criminal', 'lunatic' and 'pusillanimous'. This reminded me of one of Gerry's admirers, who, having listened to a similar denunciation, said he always regarded him as the most consistent authority he knew on cricket matters. The grateful light in Gerry's eye faded slightly when his friend added: 'I have only to reverse your opinion diametrically and I can't be very far wrong.'

Accordingly, I replied that whatever doubts I might have had were completely at rest now that I had heard his views. This sally he took, as ever, in good part, telling me to 'Wait and see, sir.'

As a matter of fact, I watched our progress with a good deal of anxiety. We had several awkward moments, but the first innings score had reached 200-odd when the ninth wicket fell. It was not brilliant, but a gamble might have proved disastrous, and I felt if we could scrape a few more runs my policy would be justified. This depended to some extent on myself, as it was now my turn to bat.

At the other end was Smith (J.), not out 4. He was not, at first sight, a much more likely batsman than I was, on a turning wicket with quite an array of spin bowling. The most entertaining batsman in the country, his technique was fundamentally confined to one stupendous stroke. The left leg was stretched massively in the direction of mid-on, and the bat (5 lb plus) whistled through the air with a powerful and remarkably supple swing.

The direction the ball took if struck, depended entirely on its length, width and any unforeseen variations in pace from the bowler. Thus the long-hop to the off might be struck, flat batted, over extra's head or, if laggardly from the pitch, come straight back like an anti-tank shell.

The good-length straight ball was Jim's favourite, as this could be driven off the rise far over long-on. But it was when he struck too soon at this type that the customer got the maximum value for his money. The ball would then hiss vertically into the stratosphere while an agitated gaggle of fielders would gather underneath to perform every manœuvre in drill book and ballet in their efforts to estimate its point of descent.

A frantic captain, if not actively engaged in the *mêlée*, would seek to gauge the likeliest catcher and make himself heard above the tumult of 'yours' and 'mines'. If he kept his head there was always ample time to summon up the wicketkeeper, but as often as not, the ball would descend with a thud in the middle of a circle dizzy from their exertions.

On this occasion Smith played his natural game, and it was soon apparent that it was his day. After several balls of a particularly good over from Watt had passed the stumps by a tiny margin, the last flew over the big tree at square-leg. This was largely the pattern of things to come, and soon the score was progressing by regular instalments of four or six a time.

At the other end I plied the 'dead bat', but was by no means idle. Backing up was not a matter of making a yard down the pitch but of gaining sufficient elbow room to take violent evasive action. To avoid loss of limb, or even life itself, one had to resort to the zooming vertical climb or the undignified crash dive, while averting collision with a bowler and umpire similarly employed.

Canterbury has seen bigger and altogether better stands, but surely never one so packed with improbable action. The ball whined and hummed to every point of the boundary, not excluding the screen directly behind the striker. Fielders, one moment breathing expectantly down the back of my neck, were next belting back to the very edge of the ground. If, at any time, the field bore a slightly orthodox pattern, it did so in deference to tradition, rather than to practical requirements. The captain must have sighed for the orderliness of Hammond or Bradman.

Watt bowled, Wright bowled, Davies bowled and periodically rain fell, possibly summoned by the ball's frequent excursions into the cloud belt. Eventually the momentous possibility dawned on all present – Smith was going to make a hundred. It was certain that this possibility would in no way affect his tactics, and there would be no question of 'nervous nineties'.

The climax was fittingly dramatic. At 96 Smith received a ball rather short and wide of the off-stump. He gathered his eighteen stone and let fly with that mighty bat, only to find the ball on him rather sooner than he had expected. The ball, meeting the flailing blade early in its arc, resulted in a square-cut as good as anything John Tyldesley could do. Third man had no time to move. Jim, grinning hugely, had the nerve to look as if he had meant it.

We had added 116, of which Jim had made 101. It was not the fastest hundred of the season, because of the rain, a highish percentage of complete misses, and the time it took to fetch the ball back or find another in similar condition. Still it won us the match, if not the championship.

The last word, however, lay with the delighted and unabashed Weigall. He dismissed our effort as a 'prostitution of the art of batting'.

[*1953*]

*

At Bristol, on 16 June, 1938, there were no interruptions. Smith made 66 in eighteen minutes after reaching fifty in eleven minutes. The STROKE was translated thus:

2, 4, 4, 6, 1, 6, 6, 6, 1, 6, 2, 6, 6, 2, 2, 6.

Legend has it that once, during his salad days with Wiltshire, Smith was sent in at 6.10 pm as nightwatchman. Twenty minutes later he returned to the pavilion, 80 not out. The spectators of Corsham were delirious; the cows, several fields distant, indignant.

Decline of the West

by C. L. R. James

Bodyline was not an incident, it was not an accident, it was not a temporary aberration. It was the violence and ferocity of our age expressing itself in cricket. The time was the early 1930s, the period in which the contemporary rejection of tradition, the contemporary disregard of means, the contemporary callousness, were taking shape. The totalitarian dictators cultivated brutality of set purpose. By now all of us have supped full with horrors. Today cruelties and abominations which would have immeasurably shocked and permanently distressed earlier ages are a commonplace. We must toughen our hides to live at all. We are now like Macbeth in his last stage:

> 'The time has been my senses would have cool'd
> To hear a night-shriek, and my fell of hair
> Would at a dismal treatise rouse and stir
> As life were in't. I have supped full with horrors;
> Direness, familiar to my slaughterous thoughts,
> Cannot once start me.'

It began in World War I. Exhaustion and a fictitious prosperity in the late 1920s delayed its maturity. It came into its own in 1929. Cricket could no more resist than the other organisations and values of the nineteenth century were able to resist. That big cricket survived the initial shock at all is a testimony to its inherent decency and the deep roots it had sunk.

The violence of the cricket passions unloosed in the thirties is what strikes the observer today. There was no absolute necessity for Voce and Larwood to take the actions that they did on their return from Australia. Rather than submit to the opinions of a large majority, A. W. Carr preferred to go out of the game altogether. Jardine seemed to be at war not with the Australian eleven but all Australia. The history books tell us that he carried his relentlessness to India: there were no Bradmans in India. What objective necessity was there to introduce bodyline into England after the Australian tour? Yet the attempt was made. Jardine soon went, never to return. Ponsford abandoned the game when he was only thirty-four. Sir Donald Bradman assures us that but for the intervention of the war, 1938 would have been his last visit to England, and he contemplated only one more season in Australia. He was younger than Ponsford. No balls had whizzed past his head for years. Yet he had had enough.

It is in Bradman's autobiography that we can today see conveniently the mentality of the time. The most remarkable page in that remarkable book is his account of his feelings after he had completed his hundredth century. He had played big cricket for nearly twenty years. In that time he had scored as no one had ever scored before. He had made his runs at the rate of fifty an hour. He had scored centuries and double centuries and treble centuries in cricket of the most demanding type. He had conquered bowlers and decided series. Yet what are his sentiments after he had made the hundredth run of the hundredth century? He felt it incumbent upon him, he says, to give the crowd which had so cheered his achievement some reward for its wonderful feelings towards him. He therefore proceeded to hit 71 runs in 45 minutes. This, he adds, is the way he would always wish to have batted if circumstances had permitted him. However, as circumstances did at last permit him the luxury, he classed 'that particular section of my innings as the most satisfying of my career'. In all the years that I have been reading books on cricket this remains the strangest statement that I have ever read, and one to which I frequently return; to it, and to the writer. If Sir Donald Bradman was able to play 'in the way I would always have loved to do had circumstances permitted' only after he had made one hundred centuries, we have to ask ourselves: What were these inhibiting circumstances?

This much at least is obvious. The game he had played between 1928 and 1947 was a game quite different from the one that had been played by Grace and Shrewsbury, Trumper and Ranjitsinhji, Hobbs and Rhodes, the game we had played in the West Indies. Grace, Ranjitsinhji, Trumper and their fellows who had played with them lost infinitely more matches and series than Sir Donald Bradman ever lost. They were painstaking men who gave all they had to cricket. Yet I cannot conceive of any of them thinking of batting in the way Sir Donald thought of it. He has been blamed for machine-like play. He has been blamed for the ruthlessness with which he piled up big scores. This is absurd. I have seen some of his greatest innings and I do not wish to see anything finer. George Headley has explained to me that people speak of Sir Donald's heavy scoring as if each and every great batsman was able to do the same, but refrained for aesthetic or chivalrous reasons which Sir Donald ignored. Speaking with authority, Headley is lost in admiration and even in wonder at the nervous stamina and concentration which Sir Donald displayed in making these mammoth scores so consistently over so long a period. In the autobiography Sir Donald maintains that he played cricket according to the rules as he saw them. There is no need to question this. Every page of his book shows that he has been deeply hurt by what he considers unfair criticism. Every accusation that I have ever heard made against him he has taken care to answer. The slightest wound still gives pain to this tough, relentless opponent. He is conscious of righteousness. His sincerity is patent. He feels himself a victim, and a victim he is, but not of petty jealousies of individual men. The chronicles of the time (far more then than now), when re-read today in the light of after events, tell the story clearly enough. The 1930 Australian team which broke all previous records took a little time to get going and was left in no doubt as to what spectators and pressmen thought.

By 1928, when he began, big cricket was already being played everywhere with the ruthlessness that Bradman is saddled with. He never knew any other kind of cricket. Ponsford and his triple and quadruple centuries had set the tone for Bradman. If Bradman made 974 runs in Tests in 1930 he had experienced when a boy of eighteen a far more merciless 905 from Hammond in the season of 1928–29. His gifts and his cricket personality matured at a time when the ethics, the morals, the personal impulses and desires of cricketers were quite different from those who had played the game in the decades that had preceded. Cricketers already mature when Bradman appeared might want to play like Bradman. They couldn't. They hadn't the outlook. They hadn't the temper. They had inhibitions Bradman never knew.

The new ones could learn. Hutton at the Oval in 1938 showed that he had learnt well. I have never had so painful an experience at any cricket match as when watching Hutton and Hardstaff together during the England innings of 903 for eight declared. Bodyline may have vanished. Its temper remained. Other men had stood out above their fellows. W. G. had. But 1865 was not 1930. The spirit which Sir Donald Bradman could release only after a hundred centuries was present, I am sure, in every single one of the hundred centuries that W. G. Grace made, was always present in Trumper and Ranjitsinhji, Fry and Hobbs. That spirit was dead. If Hobbs had been born in 1910, or later, England would have bred another Bradman. Sir Donald first ran the cricket mile in under four minutes and unloosed the floodgates. Circumstances conspired to place the blame on him. I have gathered that even in Australia the attitude to him is ambivalent. They admire him, they are grateful to him, they love him, but they know that the disregard of the compulsions of everyday life, the chivalry that was always a part of the game, began to fade at the time he came into it. Sir Donald is not to blame. He was unfortunate in his place and time. The fact remains that he was in his own way as tough as Jardine.

This was the situation faced by 'It isn't cricket' in 1930. It was not only a Test series at stake. Everything that the temple stood for seemed threatened within and without. If Bradman continued his portentous career a way of life, a system of morals, faced the possibility of disgrace and defeat just at the particular time when more than ever it needed the stimulus of victory and prestige. The men who had made it their special preserve were threatened not only in cricket. They were threatened everywhere. As is usual in such cases, they fought back blindly and were driven into extravagance and immorality. The bodyline upheaval shocked everyone and made the cricket world pull itself up and tread carefully. The spirit was not exorcised. The Oval match of 1938 was followed by the long-drawn-out siege in Durban. Luckily the war put an abrupt end to cricket as it was being played in the thirties. The relief was only temporary. Today the same relentlessness is abroad. Cricketers try to preserve the external decencies. The tradition is still strong. But instead of 'It isn't cricket', now one hears more frequently the cynical 'Why isn't it cricket?' Scarcely a tour but hits the headlines for some grave breach of propriety on and off the cricket field. The strategy of Test Matches is the strategy of stalking the prey: you come out in the open to attack only when the victim is wounded. No holds are barred. Captains encourage their bowlers to waste time. Bowlers throw and drag. Wickets are shamelessly doctored. Series are lost or believed to be lost by doubtful decisions and immoral practices, and the victims nurse their wrath and return in kind. Writing in the *Cricketer* in the early 1920s MacLaren said that in all his career he had known batsmen duck short balls only on two or three occasions. In the West Indies up to when I left in 1932 you took the short ball round to the leg-boundary (or you underwent repairs). Today statisticians and metaphysicians seek to impose a categorical imperative on the number of bumpers the fast bowler may bowl per over. To legislators for relief batsmen of all nations, like Cherubim and Seraphim, continually do cry.

A corps of cricket correspondents functions as an auxiliary arm of their side, but is ready to turn and rend it at the slightest opportunity. What little remains of 'It isn't cricket' is being finally stifled by the envy, the hatred, the malice and the uncharitableness, the shamelessness of the memoirs written by some of the cricketers themselves. Compared with these books, Sir Donald's ruthless autobiography of a dozen years ago now reads like a Victorian novel. How to blind one's eye to all this? Bodyline was only a link in a chain. Modern society took a turn downwards in 1929 and 'It isn't cricket' is one of the casualties. There is no need to despair of cricket. Much, much more than cricket is at stake, in fact everything is at stake. If and when society regenerates itself, cricket will do the same. The Hambledon men built soundly. What Arnold, Hughes and W. G. brought is now indelibly a part of the national life and character, and plays its role, the farther it is away from the pressure of publicity. There it is safe. The values of cricket, like much that is now in eclipse, will go into the foundations of new moral and educational structures. But that they can be legislated to what they used to be is a vain hope which can only sour on the tongue and blear the eye. The owl of Minerva flies only at dusk. And it cannot get much darker without becoming night impenetrable. [*1963*]

PERSPECTIVE

There is a man who during the summer months can keep a mental diary of his private life by reference to cricket events. He can say, in effect, 'it was on the day that Leyland made 165 against Glamorgan that my wife left me'; or, 'Yes, it must have been on a Wednesday that I was made bankrupt, for that was the first day of the Surrey and Lancashire match at the Oval.' *Dudley Carew, 1946*

D. G. Bradman

Figures reveal nothing of a batsman's style but, in the case of Bradman, they state with precision the essence of his genius. His 338 innings and 117 centuries in first-class cricket may be analysed thus:

TEST MATCHES

80 innings { 51 innings of less than 100: average 34*
29 innings of more than 100: average 234

Once he had passed 200, as he did on twelve occasions, he averaged 275.

OTHER FIRST-CLASS MATCHES v Australian states, English counties, etc.

258 innings { 170 innings of less than 100: average 40
88 innings of more than 100: average 204

Once he had passed 200 in these matches, as he did on twenty-five occasions, he averaged 337.

It has been argued that some of the bowling he faced in Australian state cricket was below par; however his thirty century innings in England, against bowling continually faced by his contemporary, Hammond, averaged 203.

RATE OF SCORING – Test Matches

Bradman naturally adapted himself to the state of the game, his time to reach 100 varying from one hour 38 minutes to four hours 13 minutes.

Sometimes after reaching his century he would accelerate madly (a further 144 in 146 minutes at the Oval, 1934), sometimes he would slow down as fields became more defensive.

Average time to make 100: two hours 46 minutes

Average time to move from 100 to 200: two hours 18 minutes

* Sobers's 134 Test innings of less than 100 averaged 32.

RATE OF SCORING – other matches

In making the first 100 runs of these 88 centuries, Bradman averaged two hours 17 minutes; thereafter he advanced to 200 in a further one hour 36 minutes. In the four non-Test innings in which he made over 300, he proceeded from the 200 mark at 80 runs an hour. His average for these four innings, twice not out, was 759.

*

Between 16 December 1927 and 5 March 1949, Bradman played in 62 Sheffield Shield matches, 31 apiece for New South Wales and South Australia. In 52 innings for New South Wales he averaged 107·74, in 44 for South Australia 112·97.

In eight seasons he averaged over 100 runs an innings.

On tour in England, Bradman batted six times at Leeds and averaged 192·60, twelve times at the Oval averaging 139·20. He scored centuries on each of eighteen English grounds.

Throughout his career he scored 25·47 per cent of his side's runs, in Test matches 26·03 per cent. Against South Africa in 1931–32, he was responsible for 38·25 per cent of Australia's runs – the other batsmen including Woodfull, Ponsford, Kippax and McCabe.

He shared in 41 partnerships of 200 and more runs, 164 partnerships of 100 and more.

The average runs added while Bradman was at the crease was 143, his share 57 per cent.

The average runs added in Tests while Bradman was at the crease was 154, his share 56 per cent.

Throughout his career Bradman scored at 42 runs an hour. His brightest spell occurred over the Australian seasons 1933–34 and 1935–36 and the English tour of 1934 (he played no cricket in 1934–35) when he played 47 innings with an average of 104·40, his scoring rate 52 runs an hour.

Bradman did not believe in hitting sixes, preferring to keep the ball on the ground. During his career he hit only 46 sixes – generally late in his innings.

D. G. Bradman

by H. S. Altham

What then, is the secret of this astonishing phenomenon? Let us consider first the physical equipment. Bradman is a small man and were a stranger to meet him standing still in ordinary clothes he would notice nothing remarkable about him except a pair of exceptionally high shoulders, an unusually resolute jaw and a keen pair of eyes. But see the same figure in flannels and in action and the first secret is not far to seek. For here is obviously a perfectly co-ordinated body, balanced on feet as neat, and at the same time as strong, as any professional dancer's, which ensure maximum speed and accuracy of movement: add to this that flexibility of hip which is a hall-mark of nearly all great games-players, great power of forearm, wrist and (often forgotten) hand, and you have some idea of the machine that turns out the runs. Machines need looking after and Bradman has always known how to keep his not merely, it would seem, in good running, but in racing trim. But greatest of all his natural assets is a speed of reaction which, I believe, scientific tests have proved to be quite abnormal; perhaps only with Ranji was there so small a time-lag between conception and execution, and this is the secret of his stroke play whether in defence or attack. He sees the ball sooner, watches it longer and can play the stroke later than anyone else. Remember, too, that in his case each stroke decision is regulated by a singularly acute cricket brain and a, by now, immense batting experience.

It would be illogical to expect in a man of his build the effortless ease of stroke play which one associated with Frank Woolley or the power of Walter Hammond's driving, though in all conscience there is power enough; nor can he rival one of the greatest of English batsmen – George Gunn – in giving the impression that he has 'all day to play his shot in': the tempo of his batting is staccato. But the power and versatility of his stroke play are astonishing; unlike the vast majority of his contemporaries he can fight a war on two fronts, for he seems equally at home with an off-side or leg-side attack: he can hit the ball through the covers with equal facility off the front or back leg, and he is a brilliant cutter, both square and late; but it is on the other side of the wicket that his mastery is most impressive. He is the finest hooker in the world and can direct this stroke at will anywhere from wide mid-on to fine-leg with the vital, and very rare, security of hardly ever lifting the ball, whilst to bowl even a fairly accurate length on the line of his leg-stump or legs is to ask for punishment; here, perhaps, his peculiar genius is most pronounced, in his ability to force the ball through any inviting gap, generally off the back foot, meeting it very near his body, and with a combined thrust of the forearms and flick of the wrists played with a perfection of timing that makes a utilitarian stroke into a work of art. Allied with this great variety of stroke play there goes an extraordinary facility for placing the ball, and only very accurate bowling and the most skilfully adjusted placing of the field has any chance of keeping him even moderately quiet on a good wicket. In his earlier years, and even now when the whim takes him, he could and can go the pace of a pure hitter, and for a time in the early part of the 1934 tour he seemed practically to have selected that role for himself: then I believe an almost stern remonstrance from Woodfull sobered him, with the monumental result that we all remember, and since then, though his stroke play could never be anything but remarkable, runs rather than strokes appear to have become his main objective.

For the extraordinary consistency with which he pursues that aim we must look beyond the mere technique of a superlative defence coupled with outstanding physical fitness and a stamina that sustains him through the longest day. If I may borrow terms from another sphere, Bradman is not a romantic but a realist: he finds his satisfaction in achievement rather than in method; he is not tempted, as Jack Hobbs often was, to try dangerous strokes simply because the mere making of runs by ordinarily secure means had begun to pall, or to regard a mere century as the signal for 'chancing his arm', either as a concession to his physical nature or from the feeling that made Michelangelo want to give up painting in favour of sculpture, 'because it was too easy'. He will always play to the clock and the state of the game and very rarely fails to take drastic toll of a tiring attack during the last ninety minutes of a day's play; but, other things being equal, he is content to go on his way from his first century to his second and from his second to his third with the same deliberate speed, unwearied, unexcited and, above all, undiverted.

It is sometimes said that 'Bradman cannot play on a sticky wicket': that is nonsense. With his natural gifts he could not help being good under those conditions, when the ability to move the feet quickly and play a delayed stroke accurately mean so much: in the Leeds Test Match of 1938 the ball was consistently on top of the bat, but he made his century as usual and that century settled the match, whilst in that absorbing game, in which all Yorkshire to this day believes they were robbed of victory by rain,* he played Verity, on his own admission, as well as he ever remembers being played.

Another statement that I have sometimes heard made, in a sort of vague disparagement, against Bradman is that he is 'inhuman'. If this means that he is uniquely immune from the ordinary frailties of the cricketing flesh, he certainly stands condemned, for he does not tire, he does not relax, and even on the days when he is, for him, palpably out of form, a long score remains more probable than a short one. But if it implies that he lacks personality or the capacity to enjoy the game himself and make others enjoy it, it is ludicrously false. His immense vitality, for one thing, gives it the lie: one cannot be bored with a man who is so tremendously alive every moment he is on the field. But it was finally and utterly disproved by his captaincy of the Australians in 1938. No one can have been surprised at his tactical shrewdness on that tour, but I doubt whether anyone was quite prepared for the personal ascendancy which he established over his team. I do not think I have ever admired anything on the cricket field so much as his leadership through those heartbreaking days at the Oval in August: his own fielding was an inspiration in itself, and as hour succeeded hour with nothing going right and the prospect of the rubber receding over a hopeless horizon, it was, one felt, his courage and gaiety that alone sustained his side. And when the tragic accident† came, the game was over, the balloon was pricked and his team was a team no more.

If Falstaff in a tavern in Eastcheap 'babbled o' green fields', may we not find comfort in remembering our own Arcadies? I am the happier now for having seen 'W. G.' bat and Kortright bowl, for having fielded to 'Ranji' and Archie MacLaren, and for having been comprehensively bowled by Colin Blythe. But, as I have written in another place, 'In the many pictures that I have stored in my mind from the "burnt-out Junes" of forty years, there is none more dramatic or compelling than that of Bradman's small, serenely-moving figure in its big-peaked green cap coming out of the pavilion shadows into the sunshine, with the concentration, ardour and apprehension of surrounding thousands centred upon him, and the destiny of a Test Match in his hands.'

[*1941*]

* Yorkshire needed 67 to win with seven wickets to fall; Hutton, Wood and Verity were out, Sutcliffe was not out – hence the county's belief in ultimate victory.

† With England's score approaching 900 for seven, Bradman injured an ankle so badly, when bowling, that he played no more during the tour. As *Wisden* put it, 'Hammond probably would not have closed the innings during the tea interval on the third day but for the mishap to the opposing captain.' Fingleton had also retired, with a strained muscle.

H. Larwood

FROM THE PRESS-BOX

by Dudley Carew

For sheer perfection, for an instrument precisely adjusted to the work it had to do, Larwood's action seems to me incomparable. Macdonald's held dark hints of power and savagery; Larwood's threat was as open and unequivocal as an ultimatum. There were no subtleties in it, no tricks of run-up or delivery. It was a long run and Larwood would consistently gain pace in the course of it. There was no jerk or check, and then at the end the arm would go over, the body swing beautifully through and the left leg would take a considerable strain – there always seemed the chance that it would get jarred on hard grounds as the years went on. It was thrilling, in the true sense of the word, and the memory of it comes back as sweetly as the memory of the May flowers did to Nyren. It was a great experience to sit on the pavilion roof or in the press-box, which is opposite it, and watch Larwood in action during the brief seasons of his real greatness before controversy and publicity dulled the flame and dammed the inspiration. The Trent Bridge crowd, a keen and knowledgeable one – too partisan, the purist might object, and prone during the afternoon in two or three of its units to indulge in not always coherent or logical comment on the proceedings – would stir when the ball was thrown to him, and the ground would hum with expectation as the Coliseum in Rome must have done when the number promising some particularly blood-thirsty business went up on the board. For there was no doubt at all that when Larwood bowled there would be action and more than an even chance of wickets tumbling and a general slaughter of batsmen. It all too often happens that people are mesmerised into an appreciation of batting at the expense of the other departments of the game. Sixes, fours and hundreds, averages up to rival the sun temperature in the tropics – these enchant the senses of the indiscriminating, and a maiden over bowled on a perfect pitch by an artist goes for all too little, and a piece of unobtrusively good fielding often for nothing at all. The fast bowler, however, compels attention and does something to restore an unfair balance, and Larwood, although he had no spectacular tricks, was perhaps the most spectacular of them all. It has never been my ill-fortune to witness what has been described as 'bodyline' attack by Larwood – his attack as I saw it for the full space of his years in county cricket was founded on the classic principles, and the field he used would not have caused a 1900 eyebrow to raise itself in surprise. I have never seen him 'bumping' the ball while a gaggle of short-legs hung round the back of the batsman's pads, but I have seen the perfect length ball pitched outside the off-stump whip back to hit the top of the middle and off, and I have seen the ball swinging late away towards the slips with first-class batsmen making tentative, involuntary, reflex stabs of the bat at it in an attitude reminiscent of the little figure in the automatic machine on the pier. Larwood could make all but the greatest look second-rate, and the greatest had to be at their best against him. [*1946*]

1932–33

FROM MID-ON

by Bill Bowes

The big scoring by the Australian batsmen, and in particular Don Bradman, during the 1930 tour of England was something that Jardine intended to counter if it was at all possible. He was certain the Australians had such an all-round ability to make strokes that it was impossible to bowl to them using a standardised 4/5 field placing. That is, five men on the off, four on the leg or vice versa. He wanted a 7/2 field placing if possible and nothing more than a 6/3. You must attack off-stump and just outside, or you must attack leg-stump and just outside,' he said. 'By confining stroke play to one half of the field we can contain the batsmen. My chief concern is whether you bowlers can produce the control needed,' he added.

Jardine, a man who planned his every move like a chess player, had no intention of revealing his tactics too early. In the opening match of the tour against Western Australia he only gave Larwood six overs of off-theory and in the second game of the tour against a Combined XI when four of Australia's batting stars (including Bradman) were in the opposition he faced them with all the slow bowlers and G. O. Allen. But he gave Allen only four overs in the first innings and seven in the second.

In the third game of the tour, against South Australia, he gave Larwood only five overs and did not play him against Victoria; but then brought him in for the fifth game, against a Combined XI in which both Woodfull and Bradman figured for the opposition. Jardine had Larwood start with off-theory and against Bradman he switched to leg-theory. He had Voce and myself try both theories, too, but it was Larwood who took the eye. I say this purely and simply as a bowler judging another – Larwood was magnificent. He had a spot-on accuracy in direction. He could switch easily from off-stump to leg-stump attack ... and at what a terrific pace!

Larwood seemed to skim off the hard Bulli soil surfaces of Australia like a pebble skimming off water and with a bounce equally unpredictable. He had such pace that any delivery pitching more than halfway down the pitch was good length. He had the additional great asset (which he said he noticed on his first trip to Australia) that whereas most deliveries would go flashing through at less than stump height, one out of every three or four deliveries would skim off the surface to be chest height at the batsman. He did not have to dig the ball in deliberately. It happened naturally. If Voce, Allen or myself wanted to make the ball get chest height at the batsmen we had to dig it in, and it bounced like a tennis ball and with all the speed taken out of it.

Lol skimmed 'em, and to such purpose he claimed four wickets for 54 runs in the first innings and two wickets for 5 runs in four overs in the second. He got Bradman out in both innings and the Don confessed later he disliked the method of Larwood's attack so much he immediately complained to the Australian selectors present at the match.

Jardine, and the England players, were delighted. The skipper had really hit upon something good and the first Test Match, even though Stan McCabe hit leg-theory all over the Sydney Oval for a not out score of 187, did nothing to quell that delight. All the other batsmen failed. England went to a ten-wicket win and Larwood in the two innings had 5 for 96 and 5 for 28... wonderful bowling.

Flushed with success, Jardine decided to play all of his four fast bowlers in the second Test, but the Melbourne groundsman proved too wily. On a pitch that crumbled badly, a century by Bradman and some fine slow bowling by Bill O'Reilly saw Australia through to a win by 111 runs. Yet, England's bowling on this unsuitable pitch had seen Australia out for 228 and 191. There was still a lot to be said for the theory of attack.

A lot to be said! A hard pitch at Adelaide for the third Test, with Larwood again finding that disconcerting 'skim', saw the start of a controversy which split cricketers and administrators the world over. One delivery from Larwood pinged Woodfull over the heart and sent the Australian skipper reeling. Bertie Oldfield, going for a pull stroke at Larwood, deflected the ball to his right temple and it felled him like an ox. Prior to this Fingleton and Ponsford had taken knock after knock high on the thighs – and in the middle of the back, too, as they had tried to get away from the 'skimmers'. The crowd went mad. They hooted and booed. An Australian journalist coined the word 'bodyline'. Amid scenes never before seen on a cricket ground England won by 338 runs (Larwood seven wickets in the match) and cables between the Australian Board of Control and MCC brought an offer from MCC to cancel the tour immediately.

Jardine called a meeting of his players and asked if they wanted him to abandon his ideas of off-theory and leg-theory bowling. They voted overwhelmingly to have it continued. With Larwood as the spearhead of the attack, claiming 33 wickets at 19·5 each on the tour, England took the series by four–one. Wherever Larwood played there were packed grounds. Larwood's 'skim' was unpleasant for batsmen but my word it was thrilling to watch.

On the tour Larwood got Bradman out six times in ten meetings. The Don's average, from 139 an innings during the tour of England, was reduced to 56·5 an innings on this tour by England. Of course, other batsmen and bowlers, especially Allen, had moments of glory. Jardine, for his unswerving approach to the job of beating Australia, deserved special praise. But the real hero of the piece was Larwood. He rounded off the series by scoring 98 in the first innings of the Fifth Test and how those Australian barrackers 'rose' to him. Although they booed and jeered and shouted, they knew his worth. They loved him. He had great entertainment value. [*1968*]

FROM TWENTY YARDS

by Jack Fingleton

I will never see a greater fast bowler than Larwood. I am sure of that, and at this moment pay a tribute to him as a truly magnificent bowler. His genius in 1932–33 with the ball was of the same mould as Bradman's with the bat in 1930. He had the advantage of a canny, astute captain in Jardine, who carefully nurtured him in quick, small bursts of bowling and who, moreover (apart from the bodyline placing), was as artful a skipper as you would meet in a day's walk in smelling out the weaknesses of batsmen.

I, for one, will never cease to sing Larwood's praises as a bowler. I saw so much of other fast bowlers from all other lands that I do not hesitate in placing him on the highest pinnacle by himself (I never saw E. A. Macdonald). One could tell his art by his run to the wickets. It was a poem of athletic grace, as each muscle gave over to the other with perfect balance and the utmost power. He began his long run slowly, this splendidly proportioned athlete, like a sprinter unleashed for a hundred yards dash. His legs and arms pistoned up his speed, and as he neared the wickets he was in very truth like the Flying Scotsman thundering through an east coast station. He was full of fire, power and fury – or so he looked at the batting end just before he delivered the ball at you at an estimated speed of 90 miles an hour.

The first time I was in runs with Larwood bowling I was watching, naturally, the batsman at the other end as Larwood ran up. Just as Larwood approached the crease I heard a loud scraping sound and the thought flashed across my mind that Larwood had fallen. He had not. A few yards from the crease he gathered himself up and hurled all his force down on to a stiff right leg which skidded along the ground for some feet. How his muscles and bones stood this terrific test over the years is a mystery to me. Curiously enough, this leg gave out on him in the final Test of the bodyline series.

I had this interesting experience from batting against Larwood. The first dorsal interosseous muscle, between the thumb and the index finger, ached for a week after batting against Larwood, so severe was the concussion of the ball hitting the bat. I experienced this against no other fast bowler.

I still retain my mental picture of Larwood and I remember that he could move the ball in the air when it was new. A ball that came to me one day in Adelaide on my leg-stump in the air knocked my off-stump flying. He could move the old ball in from the wicket with what is known as a body-break, and the pity of it all was that a bowler with such rare gifts of art and nature should, whether at his own or another's desires, have prostituted his genius when it was at its full lustre.

[*1947*]

CAUSE AND EFFECT

In retrospect it is not difficult to appreciate at least one reason for 'bodyline'. Whereas prior to 1932–33 the Test averages of certain Australian batsmen were, so to say, decent – Woodfull 53, Ponsford 42, Kippax 39, McCabe 33, that of Bradman was not. In his 26 innings he averaged 112.

That a batsman should have reached 100 twelve times in twenty-six innings was bad enough, but Bradman was not satisfied with mere centuries. To illustrate his significance, let us imagine that certain leading batsmen had, throughout their Test careers, been compulsorily 'retired' at 100:

Retired at 100 average		Career average
41	R. N. Harvey	48
44	W. R. Hammond	56
44	G. A. Headley	60
45	G. S. Sobers	57
46	L. Hutton	56
48	C. L. Walcott	56
48	E. D. Weekes	58
48	R. G. Pollock	60
49	J. B. Hobbs	56
50	K. F. Barrington	58
52	H. Sutcliffe	60
59	D. G. Bradman	99

S. J. McCabe

A cricketer sometimes plays an innings which entitles him to be regarded as a supreme master. McCabe played three such innings – at Sydney in 1932–33, at Johannesburg in 1935–36 and at Trent Bridge in 1938.

by Jack Fingleton

At Sydney four wickets had fallen for 87 with Bradman out of the game when McCabe came to the wicket. The prospects were poor. As if to show her capriciousness and how surely she held destiny in her hands, Fate permitted McCabe when 5 to play a ball from devastator Larwood towards Voce in the gully. The ball flew high off the bat and came to earth a few inches short of Voce's clutching fingers. In such manner does Fate toy with history, granting or denying favours by the flimsiest of margins. Did not A. W. Carr write the first page of an immortal chapter when he dropped His Excellency, Charles Macartney (known far and wide as the Governor-General because of the way in which he lorded things at the wicket), when he was 2 at Leeds in 1926? Had Carr taken that chance cricket would have been infinitely poorer by the loss of an innings which yielded a century before lunch, a century out of the team's total of 131 in eighty minutes, and an innings everywhere acknowledged as unexcelled in the history of the game for sheer artistry and brilliance.

So, too, had Voce got his fingers to the McCabe shot in Sydney the game would have lost one of its gems. McCabe first had to master an English attack which included Larwood at the very apogee of his greatness. After the attack had been mastered, McCabe switched to defiance, taking the crowd of fifty thousand enthusiastic Australians from the depths of despair to the heights of happiness.

How the crowd surged into ecstasies that day at the temporary slaying of the giant Larwood! To that time Larwood's deeds had been a challenge not only to Australian cricket, but to Australian manhood. He flowed in an unforgettable current of rhythm to the creases like a wave gathering itself smoothly up before crashing down on the beach. Larwood's speed, his physical danger to the batsmen were such as to strike awe into the hearts of those watching from over the fence, but

McCabe first checked him, then cheeked him, and finally laughed at this English colossus – though be it noted that the Englishman had most of the other laughs with McCabe in that 1932–33 season.

With Richardson, whose share was 49, McCabe put on 129 for the fifth wicket, the most able and impressive of all Australian partnerships of that series. With Grimmett, who made 19, McCabe added 68, and with Wall whose contribution was four, McCabe added 55 for the last wicket. This amazing last-wicket partnership, in which McCabe guided Wall away from the strike and himself hit boundary after boundary, was the one which caused the record crowd of that Sydney Saturday morning to burst itself and the picket fence (though some said the hundreds of pickets were pulled off the fence to give the crowded spectators a better view) in uncontrollable frenzies of acclamation.

When stumps were drawn at the end of the first day's play Australia was six for 290; when the innings finished before lunch of the next day the total was 360, of which McCabe was 187 not out.

Considering the terrific odds he had to face, I am inclined to the opinion that this Sydney innings was McCabe's greatest, but as soon as one tries to become dogmatic on this subject there floats before the vision the epics of Johannesburg and Trent Bridge. I saw all three innings, batting for a long period with him at Johannesburg, and it was here he had to face disabilities unknown to him at Sydney and Trent Bridge. At each of the latter places he batted on a glorious wicket, the type of wicket a batsman dreams about. At Johannesburg, on the contrary, he did duty on a dusty wicket, a pitch worn cranky and irritable by 898 runs, and of all wickets, even a wet and sticky one, none is more difficult than that off which the ball shoots and bites.

*

Australia required 399 to win at about a run a minute. McCabe joined Fingleton at 17 for one on the third day; forty minutes later bad light stopped play with Australia 85 for one, McCabe not out 50.

*

McCabe ran to a flowing century before lunch, joining Macartney and Bradman in the feat, but in the afternoon, if it were possible, he pulverised the South African attack even more into dust.

McCabe never put a foot or his bat in a false position. To me, at the other end and fully aware of the difficulties of maintaining even a defence on such a wicket, McCabe's batting bordered on the miraculous. He made 100 in 91 minutes, 150 in 145 and in that total was the amazing tally of 24 boundaries.

In the middle afternoon lightning flashed with startling vividness in the mineral-laden Johannesburg air. Peals of thunder rolled over the Wanderers, but not even the wretched light of the impending storm could dim the Australian's brilliance.

No better compliment could have been paid McCabe than this. With Australia still 125 runs behind and three hours to play, Wade, the South African skipper, did the most extraordinary thing of appealing against the light from the field. It was quite apparent that the pending heavy rain would stop the match at any moment. There was thus no fear that South Africa could be beaten, but Wade was nonplussed, mesmerised and indeed stampeded by the profuse profligacy of McCabe's boundaries. Some said that there was the flavour of unsportsmanship in Wade's appeal, but Wade was one of cricket's gentlemen. I knew from close quarters that McCabe had woven a spell over him.

Trent Bridge differed somewhat from the others, because here McCabe had to contend with strictly orthodox tactics on a perfect wicket.

[*1947*]

*

At Trent Bridge in 1938 England declared at 658 for eight (L. Hutton 100, C. J. Barnett 126, E. Paynter 216 not out, D. C. S. Compton 102), Australia losing Fingleton, W. A. Brown and Bradman for 134 on the second day, whose close saw McCabe 19 not out with F. A. Ward as 'nightwatchman'.

*

by Denzil Batchelor

Monday's play began according to pattern. Farnes, no mild-eyed deer now but a snorting war horse again, overthrew Frank Ward immediately, and both the remaining new batsmen with pretensions to class promptly fell to Douglas Wright. Hassett and Babcock revealed themselves as complete tyros against our spin bowlers on a grass wicket. Little Hassett, dapper and elegant, black-browed Badcock, a sawn-off shotgun of a fellow, with a forearm like a Wiltshire ham: between them they had not a stroke fit to be aimed at a googly. The prodigious off-break that spurned in to wreck Badcock's wicket was the best ball of Wright's first Test Match; and for long he bowled like a master of his craft. His pace was above medium, and his length nothing like so colourless as to be branded as impeccable. He followed his short bouncer, which lured high-spirited Australians into the hook, with a length ball which seduced Hassett into raising a modest catch within range of the infallible Hammond at first-slip.

The fieldsmen, grouped conventionally and effectively, were playing their part, with Hammond conspicuous with magnetic fingertips for every ball that came from the bat's edge off the in-swinger. Recalling this fielding, years later, I once at Lord's persuaded Hendren and Sandham to assess Hammond's worth as a slip field. Their judgement was instant and unanimous. 'Wally!' apostrophised Patsy Hendren, 'he picked 'em out of thin air as if with a humming's bird's tongue.' They agreed that he was unquestionably the finest slip field either of them had ever seen in action. But what about Constantine? 'Ah!' said Hendren, 'Learie is the best field I have ever seen in my life in *any* position.'

Well, with the grand and hostile fielding, the steady, less than benevolent bowling, with the enemy's willingness to fall back into a state of defence, all seemed set for justice to be done, and the Australian at the bar taken out and punctually executed.

But before the condemned man's last lunch something went wrong. At one wicket, flesh withered like grass: at the other, McCabe stood defying the lightning. This batsman bore a home-made nickname by which he was never known in this country. It was Napper. He had earned it in an earlier tour when with the rest of the Australian team he had suffered himself to be shown around Versailles. When the guide reached the Emperor's personal apartment he drew a haunting word picture of the final conflict between the man of destiny and the onrush of history. The stodgiest materialist from the bush could almost feel the palpable presence, and there was a sudden freezing of blood when McCabe (who had lost himself in Josephine's boudoir) suddenly reappeared through a door facing the party. The reincarnation of Napoleon stood forth in a lounge suit from Pitt Street, Sydney. Napper he became from that moment. But never till this June afternoon, when England were perfectly poised to complete the rout of Waterloo, did he prove himself spiritually entitled to the nickname.

He challenged the bowling as if defeat were inconceivable; as if he only had to race the clock to a huge score to cut down victory in full flight. It was no rearguard action in the last ditch, but a counterattack of the phantom battalions of the Grande Armée against all the King's horses and all the King's men. Not for nothing had his prototype declared that in a war there are two forces, the spiritual and the material – the spiritual being to the material as ten is to one.

By lunch-time McCabe's forays and sorties had brought him 88 trophies: mere runs on the scoreboard, but splendid as the captured banners of an army. He had hooked Farnes furiously. He had left his ground to savage Wright's double-edged attack. Already the initiative had dropped from the nerveless hands.

But it was after lunch that McCabe swelled to his full grandeur. When Hammond came on to bowl with classic nip from flawless pitch, McCabe whipped him off his toes for two boundaries, whistling south of square-leg off successive balls. When Farnes, now merely pegging away, dropped a bouncer outside the target area, which must have hissed like a hornet towards the little man's ear, his huge hooked shot rattled high among the seats in the eastern stand. As the afternoon wore on it became clear that by one man's gallantry the tide of battle had been swung.

In one over the position was deteriorating. Before the next it was out of control. The fieldsmen, glued to their routine positions, had become so many laughing-stocks – McCabe never wasted a hard hit where one stood on rigid sentry duty to cut off the boundary.

Once again, Hammond's captaincy failed when confronted with the crisis of the unexpected. He delayed the new ball. He bowled Verity much too late in the day, and quite vainly. He persisted with the humbled Wright, who twice running saw balls of ragged length cracked with a trip-hammer to the sight screen behind the bowler. Then, to prove that there were moments when McCabe thought the slaughtering drive and the majestic pull a vulgar type of technique, he fell back on the refinements of the cut. Thrice in an over he conjured pace out of his own well-sprung wrists to augment the flagging speed of Farnes's out-swinger on its way to the boundary behind third-man.

He reached his own second century in a tremendous over which must have chilled the cockles of Wright's heart. Off one ball he smote his emperor's drive at which mid-on had not time to blink before the thing was a memory. A presage of the V2, that on-drive. Next a lumbering donkey drop was served up, and contemptuously heaved first bounce over the square-leg boundary. Then the perfect length ball on the off-stump was met by dropping back to the wicket and, with a flash of disciplined wrists, steered off the right foot in a great arc of speed to outflank extra-cover. Finally, to the last ball, a knock-kneed long-hop, was assigned the grandee's hook that carried mid-wicket. Sixteen runs off four balls, and each stroke eclipsing the loftiest textbook standards. It came to an end at last, that noble innings, like every famous reign or time of ecstasy. It came to an end with a steepling mis-hit off Verity that Compton engulfed at extra-cover.

With the assistance of three left-handers, none of whom had any pretensions to batting virtuosity, McCabe had done a unique thing. Many men have won matches off their own bat. On this wicket and with England's sky-scraping score, such a feat was not possible – so McCabe had done more. He had come in at a moment in history when it seemed certain that the sun was about to set on a long period of Australian ascendancy. McCabe, by his own efforts, had stopped the sun, and saved the Australian empire. [*1949*]

*

The scores in this drawn match were: England 658 for eight, declared; Australia 411 (McCabe 232) and 427 for six (W. A. Brown 133, Bradman 144 not out).

*

As McCabe was working his miracle, Bradman called to the Australian team from the pavilion balcony: 'Come and see this. Do not miss a moment of it. You will never see the like of it again.' What the eight miscreants were doing is not clear.

NON-SPONSORED

'For a cricketer thoroughly out of condition I should prescribe a preliminary course of walking exercise extending over three weeks or a month – say, three 5-mile walks at a pace of four miles an hour, and one 10-mile walk at a slower pace each week.' *C. B. Fry, 1903*

G. A. Headley

by C. L. R. James

George Headley would be my candidate for a clinical study of a great batsman as a unique type of human being, mentally and physically. So far as I know no one has probed into this before.

Mentally. George is batting against an Australian slow bowler, probably Grimmett. To the length ball he gets back and forces Grimmett away between mid-wicket and mid-on or between mid-wicket and square-leg. He is so quick on his feet and so quick with his bat that Grimmett simply cannot stop ones and twos in between the fieldsmen. Every time Grimmett flights the ball, out of the crease and the full drive. Grimmett, that great master of length, can't even keep George quiet. He has a man at fine-leg. He shifts him round to square and moves square to block up the hole. Next ball is just outside the leg-stump. George, gleeful at the thought that fine-leg is no longer there, dances in front of the wicket 'to pick up a cheap four'. He glances neatly, only to see Oldfield, the wicketkeeper, way over on the leg-side taking the catch. The two seasoned Australians have trapped him. That sort of thing has happened often enough. Now note George's reaction.

'I cut that out.'

'What do you mean, you cut it out?'

'I just made up my mind never to be caught that way again.'

'So you do not glance?'

'Sure I glance, but I take care to find out first if any of these traps are being laid.'

'Always?'

'Always.'

And I can see that he means it.

Similarly with placing. For George, to make a stroke was to hit the ball (he had a loud scorn for 'the pushers') and to hit it precisely in a certain place. He couldn't think of a stroke without thinking of exactly where it was going. Whenever he had scored a century and runs were not urgent, he practised different strokes at the same ball, so as to be sure to command the placing of the ball where there was no fieldsman. Those who know George only after the war don't really know him. In 1939 he was, in addition to on-side play, a master of the cut, both square and late, and though he was, like Bradman, mainly a back-foot player, half-volleys did not escape him. This placing to a shifting field must also be to a substantial degree automatic. Having taken a glance round, *and sized up what the bowler is trying to do*, the great batsman puts the ball away more by reflex than conscious action.

Now physically. Headley has told me that the night before a Test he rarely slept more than an hour or two. (The night before the second century in the Test at Lord's he never slept at all.) But he isn't suffering from insomnia, not in the least. This fantastic man is busy playing his innings the next day. The fast bowler will swing from leg. He plays a stroke. Then the bowler will come in from the off. He plays the stroke to correspond. The bowler will shorten. George hooks or cuts. Verity will keep a length on or just outside the off-stump. George will force him away by getting back to cut and must be on guard not to go too greedily at a loose ball – that is how in Tests he most fears he will lose his innings (a revealing commentary on his attitude to bowlers). Langridge will flight the ball. Down the pitch to drive. So he goes through every conceivable ball and makes a stroke to correspond. This cricket strategist obviously works on Napoleon's maxim that if a general is taken by surprise at anything that occurs on a battlefield then he is a bad general.

Morning sees him in the grip of processes he does not control. He rises early and immediately has a bowel motion. At ten o'clock he has another. And then he is ready. He is very specific that these automatic physiological releases take place only on big-match days. He is chain-smoking in the dressing-room. But once he starts to walk down the pavilion steps he would not be able to recognise his father if he met him halfway. Everything is out of his mind except batting. Bumpers? Bodyline? He is not concerned. He gets out to good balls (or bad), but such is his nervous control that no bowler as such has ever bothered him. Near the end of an English tour he is physically drained except for batting. He has a few days' leave, he sits and smokes. His companions plan expeditions, make dates to go out with girls. George sits and smokes. From where he sits he doesn't want to budge an inch. But when they return to the tour, as soon as he has a bat in his hands, he is as fit as ever; fit, however, for nothing else except batting. When the season is over the fatigue remains and it takes him weeks to recover his habitual self. I watched the West Indians in the nets at Lord's in 1933 before the tour began. George never to my knowledge practised seriously. He fooled around playing the ball here and there. It was his first visit to England, but he was as sure of himself as if he were in Jamaica. In 1933 he ended the season with scores of 79, 31 (run out), 167, 95, 14 and 35. He was third in the averages for the season, Hammond and

Mead averaging 67 to his 66. If he had thought about it in 1933 he would have made the runs needed. With him batting was first, not second, nature. In 1939 he was 72 with Hammond next at 63. He was a fine fieldsman and of the great batsmen of his day only Bradman was faster between the wickets.

He once gave me a vivid account of what constituted fine batting and I have never known him to be so consistently passionate as he was on this occasion. To explain himself he walked about the room using a flat bamboo ruler one foot long to illustrate the motions of the bat. It seems that two famous players had come to Jamaica in 1963 and paid him a visit. George switched the conversation to modern defensive batting.

'I told them: what is this business of opening batsmen batting for two hours and making 40 or 60 runs? I told them that to do that was to play in the hands of the bowlers and captain of the fielding side. When an opening batsman behaved in that way and got out he left the bowlers and fielding side in full command of the situation. The business of opening batsmen is to break up the bowling and make it easy for the batsmen who follow. They gave me some explanation which I could not accept.'

'What do you think is wrong, George?' I asked him, because this has now been a point of heated discussion in England for a number of years.

George began to swing the ruler in his left hand up and down.

'The point,' he said, 'is in the left hand. Too many of these modern batsmen are playing the ball in front of the wicket off their right hand. That is quite wrong.'

Over the years I had never seen him so emphatic.

'Every stroke in front of the wicket has to be guided, controlled and given its force by the left hand and the left wrist'; the bamboo ruler swung up and down.

'All you have to do is to get there in time and then whatever the pace of the bowling you use the left wrist and left hand and you can put the ball wherever you please.

For strokes behind the wicket you use the right hand and the right wrist. But as long as these batsmen are playing the ball in front of the wicket off the right hand and the right wrist, they will never be able to make runs off the fast bowling, it will always pin them down.'

What does he remember most? Or rather what do I remember most about his talk on cricket? George rarely raises his voice. He never raised it louder than when he spoke of the West Indian failure in Australia to deal with the bumpers of Lindwall and Miller. 'West Indians couldn't hook,' he says, his eyes blazing. '*West Indians!*' To this day he remains adamant in his view that as far as he is concerned bowlers can drop the ball where they like and put fieldsmen where they like. 'If they catch it when I hit it they are welcome.' There is not the slightest trace of braggadocio; I have not known a more genuinely modest cricketer. For all I know, George may be quite wrong in his views of short fast balls though he had plenty of them in his time and dealt faithfully by them. He speaks as he does because it is part of his outlook: never to have his equanimity disturbed by anything that a bowler may do.

[*1963, 1967*]

10 for 10

On the morning of 12 July, 1932 – the third day of the match between Yorkshire and Nottinghamshire at Leeds, the pitch was still saturated after a thunderstorm. At lunch the visitors were 38 without loss in their second innings, the Yorkshire left-hander, Hedley Verity, having the figures: 9–9–0–0.

During lunch the sun appeared, and Nottinghamshire soon slumped to 67 all out. Verity not only performed the hat-trick in dismissing W. Walker, C. B. Harris and G. V. Gunn, but also accounted for A. Staples and H. Larwood, W. Voce and S. J. Staples in another twelve deliveries. His post-luncheon analysis appears thus in the scorebook:

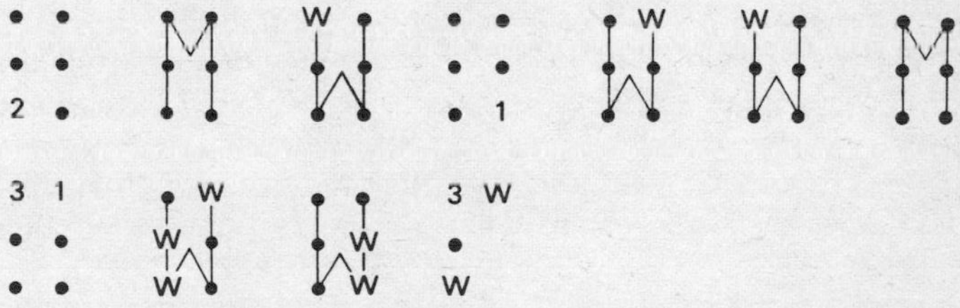

19.4–16–10–10

Captain Verity died on 31 July, 1943, of wounds received in battle. His grave at Caserta is adorned with white roses.

Lord's

by Jack Fingleton

A touring cricketer should jot down the impressions which crowd in on him when first he sees famous cricketing grounds. For years they have been delectable names to him, and as he reads about them, feeling intimate with their every characteristic, his mind boggles at the thought that some day he, too, will tread their sacrosanct turf. I grew up within five miles of the Sydney ground, and knew it well from the Hill as a youngster in the pristine days of Collins, Bardsley, Hobbs, Gilligan and other heroes. We used to gaze in enthralment through the palings at the top of the Paddington mound as the players went to the nets on the Number Two ground and then, later, watched with an almost overpowering awe the umpires and players as they emerged for play from the mysterious and hallowed depths of the Members' Stand. Melbourne and Adelaide, which I knew first as a player, have each their own individual atmosphere, Adelaide, with its hills in the distance and immediate parklands and cathedral spires, possessing a beauty all its own among famous grounds. Brisbane is the sad sack of all Test grounds, lacking in everything but a paradise of a wicket. Johannesburg, Durban and Capetown sparkle with distinctiveness – the latter surrounded by the incredible beauty of trees and Table Top, with a brewery peeping into the ground for good measure – but it is Lord's, of all grounds, that holds most interest for the touring cricketer. I could not imagine cricket without Lord's; it is truly, as has been so often acclaimed, the mecca of the game, and one is filled with reverence and tradition as he enters the ground itself. Some have told me that they have been disappointed on first seeing Lord's. I cannot imagine why. To be true, it lacks the huge concrete stands of the Melbourne amphitheatre, and the Australian is at first struck by the absence of the towering scoring boards so common to all first-class Australian grounds. Everything that goes before in the trip through London – from Tralfagar Square, through Admiralty Arch, past Buckingham Palace with its Royal Standard and red-black attired sentries spanking it along the side railings, through Hyde Park – all this prepares one for the majestic grandeur and old-world charm of Lord's, dozing in the watery sunlight of a late April afternoon. Its Mound Stand is immaculately white; from the nursery nets in the distance comes the soft music of ball on willow to play around the aged face of the Long Pavilion, pleading with it to rouse from its winter hibernation and gives its hoary benediction and indulgence to yet another cricket season. It must be grand to play in Lord's first game of the year. At this time the tourist is down in Worcester, listening to the peals from the adjacent cathedral. Lord's is all I ever expected it to be, brimful of years, tradition and ghosts. I hope it never changes, not even to taking unto itself a modern scoring board. I could not imagine, for instance, the huge Adelaide scoring board towering over Lord's. It would make the ground out of proportion. I listened to a very brilliant speech one evening at Lord's by our Right Hon. R. G. Menzies,* in which at a dinner, presided over by Lord Baldwin, he cleverly twitted the MCC for its unmodern conveniences. Most English grounds stand in need of useful scoring boards, but, please, not at Lord's! The clank-clank of the printing machine as it slowly turns out its scoring card, identifying batsmen and bowlers with their numerals on the meagre board, is part of the general Lord's set-up. I walked slowly around Lord's, looking into every nook and cranny, feeling even a familiarity with The Great One, Grace, as I peered down into the depths of the aged baths. With what vigour must he have splashed away here at the end of a long sunny day at the creases, a hundred or two behind his name – sorry, his number – and plenty of bathing room to take his bulk. I walked the Lord's outfield and saw not a soul in sight. I put a foot on the unprepared square of wicket and immediately groundsmen, messengers, net bowlers, printers and gentlemen in the dress of the city appeared gesticulating from all quarters of the ground. I saw no harm in what I did, testing the spring of the turf as a captain does when he pokes a forefinger into the wicket, but Lord's is Lord's and the wicket is holy, untouchable ground. I explained to an impressive-looking gentleman that in Australia the wickets are torn to shreds in the off-season by football boots. He was not impressed. I left Lord's – very impressed. Nothing is more English than the manner in which the spectators parade the ground during the luncheon interval, gazing long and intently at the wicket, which is guarded off by ropes. A bell rings, everybody goes back to his seat (which is never molested, as far as I could see), and not a scrap of paper is left on the ground as the umpires and fieldsmen walk out. I am rather afraid this would not be practicable in Australia. Some spirit would be bound to attempt taking a piece of the wicket as a souvenir. [*1947*]

*Knight of the Thistle, 1963.

by Dudley Carew

Mr Edmund Blunden has written of the feeling of ghostliness, of unreality, which attacks those who watch cricket in war-time, and nowhere has it been more pervasive and insistent than at Lord's. In 1940 it was possible to watch the flow of white down the pavilion steps, not indeed with that tranquillity which is one of the essences of the game, but with a vivid concentration, at once joy and anguish. 'Look thy last on all things lovely every hour,' wrote Walter de la Mare, and the line ran like a refrain through that summer of glorious weather and tragic history, but when the unthinkable and the imminent did not happen and the long slog up to the summit of victory began, cricket receded in the mind, and, even when it was watched and played, it was as though some intangible substance had found its way between act and appreciation. It is best, then, to remember Lord's as it was in that fabulous last season before the war, or even to put the clock further back and imagine it as it must have been when hansoms went jingling up the St John's Wood Road and a huge man with a flaming cap and a black beard led his team on to the field. Urbanity is surely the keynote of Lord's, urbanity added to a proper sense of its importance in the cricket world and as a national possession. There is still a hint of a cross between eighteenth century and Victorian manners to be found in the Long Room, and not only in the Eton and Harrow and the University matches are civilised elegance and ease to be found there.

... and a connoisseur

In 1941 Kenneth Farnes* paid a team of schoolboys at Lord's the compliment of bowling seriously at them, and, while they lost the match, they must have gained a valuable insight into what first-class fast bowling really meant ... we were standing talking at the back of the pavilion when there came along an extremely small boy with an autograph book in one hand and a cigarette card, which obviously had Farnes's picture on it, in the other. Stolidly, and without a word, his eyes travelled up the six foot two of Farnes and rested on his face. He was a cautious infant who had evidently heard of forgery and impersonation. Methodically he compared the features on the card with those above him. Finally, he was satisfied, and still without a word, held out his book. In equal silence and gravity Farnes signed and, still silent, the phenomenon walked slowly away. The whole solemn transaction was infinitely absurd, and it appealed greatly to Farnes's own grave sense of humour. [*1946*]

*Pilot Officer Farnes was killed on 20 October, 1941.

Roll of Honour, 1939–45

Many of the following had, like Farnes, played with distinction at Lord's; more than one of the Australians were lost on operations over Europe a few days after playing at headquarters for the RAAF.

ENGLAND

Lt-Colonel	F. G. B. ARKWRIGHT, MC	Hampshire
S/Leader	C. T. ASHTON	Cambridge University and Essex
Major	T. G. L. BALLANCE, MC	Oxford University
Lieut.	P. H. BLAGG	Oxford University
Captain	J. P. BLAKE, RM	Cambridge University and Hampshire
P/Officer	R. E. C. BUTTERWORTH	Oxford University and Middlesex
F/Lieut.	F. G. H. CHALK, DFC	Oxford University and Kent
Sub-Lieut.	E. J. H. DIXON, RNVR	Oxford University and Northamptonshire
Lieut. (A)	P. T. ECKERSLEY, RNVR, MP	Lancashire
P/Officer	K. FARNES	Cambridge University, Essex and England

Major	R. A. GERRARD, DSO	Somerset
B/S/M	J. W. T. GRIMSHAW	Cambridge University and Kent
W/Commander	J. G. HALLIDAY	Oxford University
Major	C. P. HAMILTON	Kent
Captain	G. F. HODGKINSON	Derbyshire
Brigadier	B. HOWLETT, DSO and Bar	Kent
Captain	R. H. C. HUMAN	Cambridge University and Worcester-shire
Captain	G. D. KEMP-WELCH	Cambridge University and Warwickshire
Private	J. W. LEE	Somerset
Lieut.	G. B. LEGGE, RNVR	Oxford University, Kent and England
P/Officer	G. G. MACAULAY	Yorkshire and England
Surg.-Lieut.	F. M. McRAE, RNVR	Somerset
Sub-Lieut.	M. H. MATTHEWS, RNVR	Oxford University
Lieut.	R. P. NELSON, RM	Cambridge University and Northamp-tonshire
Major	C. W. C. PACKE	Leicestershire
F/Lieut.	W. J. PERSHKE	Oxford University
Captain	P. W. RUCKER	Oxford University
Major	K. B. SCOTT, MC	Oxford University and Sussex
Captain	R. G. TINDALL	Oxford University

Major	M. J. TURNBULL	Cambridge University, Glamorgan and England
Captain	H. VERITY	Yorkshire and England
F/Lieut.	D. F. WALKER	Oxford University and Hampshire
Lieut.	P. M. W. WHITEHOUSE	Oxford University and Kent
S/Leader	R. de W. K. WINLAW	Cambridge University and Surrey

Chalk, Dixon, Legge and Walker were captains of Oxford, respectively, in 1934, 1939, 1926 and 1935, Ashton, Kemp-Welch and Turnbull of Cambridge in 1923, 1931 and 1929.

The death occurred in 1944, of typhoid contracted while on active service in Italy, of one who never played first-class cricket – Captain E. M. GRACE, RAMC, grandson of E. M. ('the Coroner') and great-nephew of W. G.

SOUTH AFRICA

Lieut.	C. M. BARKER	Transvaal
Major	A. W. BRISCOE, MC	Transvaal and South Africa
Captain	P. H. B. CLOETE	Western Province
W/Commander	G. L. CRUICKSHANKS, DFC	Eastern Province
Private	C. DOYLE	Orange Free State
Lieut.	R. J. EVANS	Border
Air/Sergt	C. M. FRANCOIS	Griqualand West and South Africa
F/Officer	H. D. FREAKES	Transvaal
Major	J. D. E. GARTLEY	Transvaal
Lieut.	E. P. HAMILTON	Transvaal

Private	C. HART-DAVIS	Natal
F/Lieut.	A. B. C. LANGTON	Transvaal and South Africa
Air/Sergt	C. F. B. PAPENFUS	Orange Free State
A/B	D. PRICE	Western Province
AUSTRALIA		
F/Sergt	C. P. CALVERT	New South Wales
Sergt/Obs.	R. G. GREGORY	Victoria and Australia
Sergt	K. L. RIDINGS	South Australia
F/Sergt	W. A. ROACH	Western Australia
Sergt	F. W. SIDES	Queensland and Victoria
P/Officer	F. THORN	Victoria
F/Officer	C. W. WALKER	South Australia
NEW ZEALAND		
Major	W. N. CARSON, MC	Auckland
Private	R. CROOK	Wellington
F/Officer	F. S. HADEN	Auckland
2nd Lieut.	N. W. McMILLAN	Auckland
Lieut.	D. A. R. MOLONEY	Wellington and New Zealand
2nd Lieut.	A. P. MONTEATH	Otago
Private	C. WAREHAM	Wellington
WEST INDIES		
Deputy Flight Cdr	D. MERRY	Trinidad

Wisden's Cricketers of the Year: Farnes 1939, Macaulay 1924, Turnbull 1931, Verity 1932.

Cricket under the Japs

*by E. W. Swanton**

It is strange, perhaps, but true, how many of us agreed on this: That we were never so thankful for having been cricketers as we were when we were guests of the Japanese. There were periods when we could play 'cricket' if our antics do not desecrate the word. There were occasions when we could lecture, and be lectured to, about it. It was a subject that filled countless hours in pitch-dark huts between sundown and the moment that continued to be euphemistically known as lights-out. And it inspired many a daydream, contrived often in the most gruesome setting, whereby one combated the present by living either in the future or the past.

In the days that followed shortly on the fall of Singapore, before work for prisoners had become widely organised, there was a certain amount of play on the padangs of Changi camp that really deserved the name of cricket. It is true that one never seemed able to hit the ball very far, a fact probably attributable about equally to the sudden change to a particularly sparse diet of rice, and the conscientious labours of generations of corporals in charge of sports gear, for whom a daily oiling of the bats had clearly been a solemn, unvarying rite. These Changi bats must have reached saturation point in the early 1930s, and I never found one that came up lighter than W. H. Ponsford's three pounder. However, the pitches were true – matting over concrete – and there were even such refinements as pads and gloves. After most of us had been moved to Singapore City on the first stage of the journey up to Thailand, Lt-Colonel A. A. Johnson, of the Suffolk Regiment, promoted some excellent matches with the Australians, whose captain was none other than B. A. Barnett; I cannot write of these from first-hand knowledge, but this was, so to speak, Cricket de Luxe, and our jungle cricket bore little outward relation to it.

This first of the camps on the Thai–Burma railway in which we played cricket was Wampo. Christmas Day, 1942, was our first holiday, I think, since our arrival in October, and it was perhaps the fact of our so occupying the afternoon that caused our guards to receive subsequent requests to play cricket with suspicion, as having some religious significance and being therefore good for morale. (It was always the

* Major E. W. Swanton, RA.

policy to keep prisoners' morale at the lowest level compatible with their being considered able to undertake whatever work was on hand. It was no doubt on this principle that, later on, the Allied chaplains were solemnly and sternly forbidden to pray for victory!)

This particular game was notable, I remember, for what is probably the fastest hundred of all time. It was scored in about five overs by a very promising young Eurasian cricketer called Thoy, who, with graceful ease, kept hitting the tennis ball clear over the huts! Nothing, of course, could have been more popular than the victory of the Other Ranks over the Officers, but the broad lesson of the match was that the merit of any contest depends on the preservation of the balance between attack and defence. (One could not help wondering, earlier in the war, when bombs were raining down on the Oval, whether the Surrey Committee were taking the hint.) For jungle cricket our bat, surreptitiously made by the carpenter, was obviously too big.

Our cricket for the next twelve months was confined to theory and reminiscence, but lower down the line, at the base camps of Tarsao and Chungkai, various forms of play were improvised, while still later, at Nakom Patom, the hospital camp, the technique was exploited in front of large and happy crowds of men anxious to forget the tiresomeness of dysentery, beri-beri and malaria.

Cricket at Nakom Patom reached its climax on New Year's Day, 1945, when a fresh, and certainly hitherto unrecorded, page was written in the saga of England v Australia. The scene is not easy to put before you, but I must try. The playing area is small, perhaps 60 yards by 30, and the batsman's crease is right up against the spectators, with the pitch longways on. There are no runs behind the wicket, where many men squat in the shade of tall trees. The sides are flanked by long huts, with parallel ditches – one into the ditch, two over the hut. In fact all runs by boundaries, 1, 2, 4 or 6. An additional hazard is washing hung on bamboo 'lines'. Over the bowler's head are more trees, squaring the thing off, and in the distance a thick, high, mud wall – the camp bund – on which stands a bored and sulky Korean sentry. (Over the bund no runs and out, for balls are precious.) In effect, the spectators are the boundaries, many hundreds of them taking every inch of room. The dress is fairly uniform, wooden clogs, and a scanty triangular piece of loin-cloth known (why?) as a 'Jap-Happy'. Only the swells wear patched and tattered shorts. The mound at long-on is an Australian preserve, their 'Hill'. The sun beats down, as tropical suns do, on the flat beaten earth which is the wicket. At the bowler's end is a single bamboo stump, at the other five – yes, five – high ones. There is the hum of anticipation that you get on the first morning at

Old Trafford or Trent Bridge, though there are no score cards, and no 'Three penn'orth of comfort' to be bought from our old friend 'Cushions'.

The story of the match is very much the story of that fantastic occasion at the Oval in August 1938. Flt-Lieut. John Cocks, well known to the cricketers of Ashtead, is our Hutton; Lieut. Norman Smith, from Halifax, an even squarer, even squatter Leyland. With the regulation bat – it is two and a half inches wide and a foot shorter than normal – they play beautifully down the line of the ball, forcing the length ball past cover, squeezing the leg one square off their toes. There seems little room on the field with the eight Australian fielders poised there, but a tennis ball goes quickly off wood, the gaps are found, and there are delays while it is rescued from the swill basket or fished out from under the hut. As the runs mount up the barracking gains in volume, and in wit at the expense of the fielders. When at last the English captain declares, the score is acknowledged to be a Thailand record.

With the Australian innings comes sensation. Captain 'Fizzer' Pearson, of Sedbergh and Lincolnshire, the English fast bowler, is wearing *Boots*! No other cricketer has anything on his feet at all, the hot earth, the occasional flint being accepted as part of the game. The moral effect of these boots is tremendous. Captain Pearson bowls with shattering speed and ferocity, and as each fresh lamb arrives for the slaughter the stumps seem more vast, the bat even punier. One last defiant cheer from 'the Hill' when their captain, Lt-Colonel E. E. Dunlop, comes in, another and bigger one from the English when his stumps go flying.

While these exciting things proceed one of the fielders anxiously asks himself whether they will brew trouble. 'Should fast bowlers wear boots? Pearson's ruse condemned – where did he get those boots? ... boots bought from camp funds: Official denial ... Board of Control's strong note ...' headlines seem to grow in size. Then he remembers gratefully that here is no Press box full of slick columnists and Test captains, no microphones for the players to run to – in fact, no papers and no broadcasting. The field clears at last. As he hurries off to roll-call he thinks of a New Year's Day six years before when the bund was Table Mountain, the field was the green of Newlands, and he decides that even the South Africans who jostled their way cheerfully back into Cape Town that evening had not enjoyed their outing more than the spectators of this grotesque 'Cricket Match'.

There was much more 'cricket' at Nakom Patom of similar sort, and not a few who came to jeer stayed on to cheer. One was reminded how hitting a moving ball demands the observance of certain principles, whatever the circumstances, while, as for bowling, I defy anyone who does not obey the cardinal rules to pitch six running to a length with a tennis ball.

Talks on cricket were given at many camps, and there were cricket quizzes too, wherein a few so-called experts were showered with questions from all sides. These occasions were never lacking in humour, and there were generally enough Australians among the audience to give, as one might say, a bite to the thing. Sometimes the game was presented from a particular angle. Thus Len Muncer, of Middlesex, a sergeant in the Sherwood Foresters, described the life of a cricket professional, while Lt-Colonel D. V. Hill, of Worcestershire, showed the game from the point of view of a county captain. Admittedly in a prison camp there was not much in the way of alternative diversion. None the less the interest was wide enough and genuine enough to emphasise what a tremendously strong hold cricket has in England; a hold that among Australians is even stronger.

A few days after the Japanese surrender our camp at Kanburi began to assemble frequently for news bulletins. Emissaries, we heard, were flying hither and thither, instructions and encouragement were being relayed from Governments to POWs; the air was heavy with the most momentous happenings. Moreover, many of those present had had no news of the outside world for months, or longer; yet, no item commanded so much attention as the Test Match at Manchester.

I had, by then, already taken my first walk for three and a half years as a free man. We found ourselves in a Thai village on the edge of the jungle. In the little café our hosts politely turned on the English programme. Yes, we were at Old Trafford, and a gentleman called Cristofani was getting a hundred ... [*1946*]

*

After Victory in Europe, England and Australia played five unofficial Tests – two wins to each side, and one drawn. During the fourth match at Lord's, a former captain of cricket at St Paul's School, B. L. Montgomery, arrived – the pavilion standing to welcome him.

At the end of August, England played the Dominions, the latter winning an heroic encounter by 45 runs with eight minutes to go. Lt-Colonel S. C. Griffith, DFC, who less than a year previously had been busy at Arnhem, kept wicket for England, S/Leader W. J. Edrich, DFC, made 78 and S/Leader W. R. Hammond a century in both innings; Major M. P. Donnelly of the New Zealand Division enchanted with 133, F/Officer K. R. Miller, RAAF, progressed on the third day from an overnight 61 to 185 in ninety minutes, Sergt D. V. P. Wright took ten wickets.

W/Officer A. L. Hassett was prevented by illness from leading the Dominions who thereupon showed their sense of occasion by unanimously choosing a civilian Welfare Officer as captain, a gesture which greatly moved L. N. Constantine.

INITIALS

'Of course any self-respecting boy revels in his heroes' initials and a good many of the amateurs had three apiece.' *Bernard Darwin*

Darwin, golf's incomparable stylist, wrote a book on W.G., so must be honoured here.

Do boys, self-respecting or otherwise, still revel in the initials of their heroes, or do they think of the Titans as Chris, Mike, Tony and Ted?

Middle-aged and elderly boys are here invited to fit initials to names, the owners having appeared for the Gentlemen between the wars and, with one exception, played in Test cricket. Time allowed: one minute.

H. G. O.	Stephenson
G. E. C.	Yardley
M. J. C.	Stevens
W. H. V.	Jupp
E. R. T.	Owen-Smith
V. W. C.	Allom
J. W. A.	Wood
N. W. D.	Holmes
G. T. S.	Levett

And which Australian Test cricketer was A. E. V.?

L. Hutton

Sir Leonard Hutton announced his retirement from cricket during the winter of 1955–56.

by Alan Ross

Self-sufficiency, I suppose, is one of the true marks of the artist, and Hutton has been self-sufficient as a cricketer to the point of often seeming disinterested.

Like probably all men who can do one thing better than anyone else in the world, he seemed at moments unutterably wearied by it. The context of Hutton's cricket, the bleak decade when he almost alone in England – Compton and Bedser were allies – preserved its dignity, has been such that grace and levity seemed almost excluded as indecencies.

Compton, born under a warmer star, has combined all these attributes, as it were in defiance. His genius is romantic and individual. Hutton has never made such an appeal; his art has existed within precise technical limits. It would have been as unthinkable for Hutton the man to step outside the figure of Hutton the batsman as it would have been for Nijinsky suddenly to assert his own personality while dancing the Faun.

It is in precisely this subservience of the personal to the impersonal, this sacrificing of the imp of human impulse to the demands of situation, that classicism consists. Hutton has been the embodiment of so many classical ideals – discipline, restraint, concentration, correctness and elegance of execution – that he came to be thought of as an abstraction, infallible and incapable of improvisation. But he was neither of these things. In 1948 he conquered majestically a fallibility against fast, hostile bowling; in 1946–47 in Australia he showed, when forced to it, powers of improvisation never hitherto suspected, of an order of which only the greatest are capable.

It was known, of course, that he could play every stroke – except perhaps the hook, but then the hook is a luxury and Hutton's technical vocabulary, though complete, was spare in character – but he showed flashes during his great post-war seasons, flashes as rewarding as his own smile, the lightening of his eyes, that he took pleasure in playing the rarer, more dangerous ones. Only, however, when necessary; it remained an axiom of Hutton's batting that economy was all, that flourishes were an indulgence and no part of perfection, no matter how esoteric and complex perfection may be adjudged to be. 'I refrain from saying too much,' he wrote to me not long ago, 'I am Yorkshire bred and born you know, I have bought a drink but not too often.'

In his youth, he was, in fact, as near infallible as a great player can be: he was so, by cutting down on, by almost completely eliminating, risks. Cardus, in one of his most memorable essays, 'Hutton and Hobbs and the Classical Style', has written:

'He is perfect at using the dead bat – rendering it passive, a blanket of a buffer, against which spin or sudden rise from the pitch come into contact as though with an anaesthetic.' This defensive resourcefulness, based on a perfect and calculated technique, was certainly part of his genius: he made no moves that were not absolutely certain of success. His strength and superiority were likewise in his preparations, in his asceticism, his conservations of energy, his power of withdrawal till the right moment. He had the single-mindedness which Bradman also possessed, which enabled him to be solitary and to convey through the rigours of his own self-communings an air of nobility. He inspired admiration, rather than love, but that was his birthright, rather than, I suspect, his wish. The age and the situation created his character, and he respected them as forces to which the wise man bows assent.

Unexpectedly, but logically, he came to captain England: and to new problems he brought the same professional skill, the same monastic care as he had previously devoted to the problems of batting. Batting now became the lesser thing, indulged in with no less responsibility, but with greater abstractedness, as if his mind was on deeper strategies. His captaincy on the field was as evidently controlled and rehearsed as used to be his every innings, though it had limitations and obscurities. Nevertheless, he was a successful, as well as a lucky, captain, and his record against Australia will remain for everyone to see.

Whatever criticisms can ever be laid against him, he never spared himself; he seemed often on the point of exhaustion. I remember saying to him at Sydney that I should like to see him play a handful of innings in which, free of worry, he could bat 'just for fun'. He nodded thoughtfully. At Leeds last summer, when he was already out of Test cricket, he turned to me and said: 'A hundred or two will put me right, a few runs,' and he looked up quizzically, as if he found them strange words to say, 'made just for fun'.

It seems we shall have to do without the fun. We shall not again in serious play watch the beautiful ease of his stance at the wicket, the tugging of the shorter left arm at the cap peak, the thoughtful walk, toes slightly turned out, between the overs, the barometric sounding of the pitch. His mannerisms are part of contemporary cricket. A writer, a painter, however, live on through their work: a cricketer leaves only statistics and memories. Hutton's statistics require no repetition. But I shall remember, among many things about him, the unique drama of his last great Test innings at Lord's against Australia. He had, not long before he went in to bat, put down three catches, none easy nor greatly difficult either, and some unkind mockery had greeted him each time he subsequently stopped the ball.

When he went out to open the England innings with Kenyon, he looked even paler than usual, a frail, feverish magnetic figure, with an audience more critical than fond watching him walk to where Lindwall performed his tigerish preliminary antics and Miller lazily fondled the shining red ball. I felt then he would make nought – or a hundred. He made 145, a flawless innings. He cut exquisitely, drove gorgeously square, flicked the ball off his legs as it swung late into him. Next day the Members rose to him, and so they should have done. It was a peculiarly Huttonish triumph. [*1957*]

*

On 20, 22 and 23 August, 1938, at the Oval, Hutton played an innings of 364 against Australia.

*

by Edmund Blunden

As I read it, the debate lay essentially between him and W. J. O'Reilly, whose bowling begins so long before the ball leaves his hand. Australia breeds 'demon bowlers', and he is of that lineage. Australia once produced poets who were English poets a little out of touch; now she has her own; and O'Reilly with ball in hand is quite the parallel of an Australian poet, territorially distinct in rhythm, passion, scheme and transition. Within him, an experience decidedly different from even the dales or the hills of Yorkshire is for ever prompting and proposing. On this day (the second of the match) he was not less formidable than usual, though in recognition of the difficulties of his task he looked (like the lovers in Thomson's *Seasons*, which probably he has taught his school classes) 'unutterable things'. The wicket was officially easy, over-prepared – yet we saw the ball bounce enough to escape the wicketkeeper's jump. All day O'Reilly was a menace, and all day Hutton played him as a perfect pupil, sedulous in his use of instructions – he has since had barely time, yet time enough, to advance beyond that stage. Report had it that in this Test Match he was directed all along by older cricketers, instructed in every point of subjection to his high calling, even to the devouring of a banana for his lunch, and it looked so; the fact diminishes his glory not a shade, indeed it makes it greater. Hardstaff and Leyland, as it appeared to me, met the occasion in a more majestic style as seasoned troops, but the English cause rested upon Hutton's immensely virtuous studentship.

The second day was one of clouds and darkness, and had the rains descended it would have surprised few. Play was delayed in the morning and cut short in the evening. Hutton walked into the pitch with a score of 160 and when he had increased it to 300 (a fantastic figure) the umpires accepted the conclusion, darkness, without a second's deliberation. The Australian plan appeared mainly to be packing the field on the off-side in the hope that a spinner would some time lift up from Hutton's outstretched bat – caught. He parried that challenge, and he did not allow O'Reilly to bowl at him until the ball was actually in the air – all that hobgoblin work in the run-up discounted. The young batsman might have been writing a book on the art which he had acquired. All was performed so that C. B. Fry might have analysed all and gone home with classical satisfaction – *Omne tulit punctum.* The batsman's body and his bat were as truly one as love itself. 'Constancy to an ideal object' inspired the boy, and no doubt many young temptations to chance this or that piece of pyrotechnics were rejected with speed like light. 'That would be just what I was told not to try.'

Approaching the 300th run of his own innings, Hutton gave the impression of being accustomed to such a situation, and, as the London sky grew really sinister, he collected his runs without passion but thriftily, one here, one there; on his taking the 300th with a suitable little push (to say in such a prominent place just as in any old game that a run is a run whether first or 300th) the umpires instantly allowed an appeal against bad light and the day's play ceased. But not the innings. 'Hutton – Continued', said the posters next day, and on the train to town I saw the engine driver escape from his post at one of the stops in order to snatch a glance at the latest news. It was just as he and the passengers wished – Hutton had set up a record in Test Match scoring; and in consequence of this immensely patient and serious yet charming innings – thirteen hours of temptation repelled – the match became an overwhelming victory for England. [*1943*]

*

At Brisbane in 1950–51, a storm decided the game. England began the final day – having been set 193 for victory – at 30 for six, which soon became 46 for eight. Hutton, who had been held back, made 62 not out, only one other batsman (F. R. Brown 17) making double figures. The bowling consisted of Lindwall, Miller, W. A. Johnston and J. Iverson.

*

by Denys Rowbotham

Hutton not only shot the match through with greatness for the first time in three days: he made the efforts of all the rest look like those of pottering journeymen. He commanded the day with a majesty that has rarely been seen since Hammond and he was undefeated at its early close.

He did so on a wicket which though now generally true in its pace and responsiveness to bounce still allowed Johnston and Iverson to spin the ball much and sharply. He did so for the most part with only Brown and Wright as his frail, fallible partners. He proved to the large Australian crowd that he is still the world's greatest batsman in technical resource and the mastery of measured risk on a difficult wicket, and the crowd were not slow in letting him know that they knew it . . .

The rest was all Hutton. Before even Evans was out he had shown that Iverson's cleverly concealed spin was never likely to deceive him, and throughout his innings he was never once drawn forward either by Iverson's slower-flighted ball or his faster dipping one. He cut his top-spinner at once the moment it was dropped short and he turned or glanced his sharp off-spin with a leisured grace which disguised its pace off the wicket.

When Brown joined him he began to jump out and drive Iverson high to the sight screen, and when Iverson then only slightly shortened his length he was pulled with defiant pugnaciousness to mid-wicket. Within half an hour Iverson was bowling to a deep defensive field on both sides of the wicket. It was a hurting pointer to what might have been.

Only when Brown at last was drawn forward fatally by Iverson's flight and gave a simple catch to short mid-on did Hutton unleash his most terrible thunder. Then no bowler could restrain him. Hassett had replaced Johnston by Miller, who today bowled fast over the wicket. Hutton drove him past mid-off for four with the imperiousness of a MacLaren. He straight drove him for a four that was nearly six, and pulled every bumping short ball to the long-on boundary or to mid-wicket for two.

He lay back and cut Iverson high down the empty gully, daringly and dazzlingly as Washbrook, then straight drove him again to the sight-screen for the four that brought his fifty out of 76 in seventy minutes. The crowd cheered him as if Australia had won, not as if he were doing his utmost to hammer her to defeat. And when Hassett at last was compelled to call on Lindwall, hammer indeed Hutton did. He drove more of Lindwall's balls than he pushed forward. He drove him high over extra-cover, steeple high over mid-on and straight to the deep field in front of the sight-screen.

He did not score boundaries repeatedly only because Lindwall had deep and three-quarter deep fielders everywhere – a mockery of a fast bowler's field. Much more, Hutton's driving was so cool, so neat, and so compact, so powerfully wristed and poised on footwork so swift that one felt that each shot was the one which his impulse would have had him play, not his last desperate effort to bring England victory.

That he could not do so was because at the last Wright attempted a shot. For forty minutes Wright had abjured such a liberty. He had watched Hutton's drives flashing everywhere. The temptation of one long hop he resisted. A second proved too much for him. That was that, and Hutton's great fight was over.

*

Australia 228 (R. N. Harvey 74) and 32 for seven, declared, beat England 68 for seven, declared (W. A. Johnston five for 35) and 122 (Hutton 62 not out) by 70 runs.

BELT OF HIGH PRESSURE

I remember at Worthing one morning the Sussex dressing-room in an uproar of mirth over a copy of the *Morning Post*. Robertson-Glasgow, in writing of the weather the day before, had described it as 'windy and warm like bottled lemonade', and the surprise in the last two words had sent them into hysterics. *Dudley Carew*

R. R. Lindwall

by Denys Rowbotham

Lindwall was one of the greatest fast bowlers of all times and at the height of his power – with his partner in arms, Miller – dominated Test Match cricket as all the runs of Bradman, Barnes, Morris, Hassett and Harvey hardly did comparably.

Even at its most formidable the Australian run-making machine could sometimes be contained. The two firebrands who could not be were Lindwall and Miller. And what a contrast the two made: Miller unpredictable, tempestuous, a creature of mood and moments, a player great by nature rather than by disciplined art and artifice; Lindwall perhaps the most athletically trained, technically ordered and tactically organised fast bowler there has been. When Miller struck there was something of elemental, unpremeditated cataclysm about the abrupt happening. It is doubtful whether Lindwall bowled an unpremeditated ball in his life. He bowled batsmen out. He had them caught and leg before wicket. But, above everything else, he first thought them out.

Lindwall's thinking began with his action. It was organised from first step to last. His first loping strides were so relaxed, his acceleration thereafter so imperceptibly cumulative, that only just before he flung himself into his long delivery stride did one realise he was travelling at top speed. His action was not high for the purists, but the right arm was extended in its cycle and with the left made the classical opposing spokes of the cartwheel. There was no open-chestedness either. The left shoulder pointed ominously to the batsman. The back was arched. Every ounce of body action was added to maximum impetus and not a particle of energy was wasted.

Ordered action bred such strict control that it is doubtful if there has been a more accurate fast bowler. Lindwall bowled straight and to a length always. He could bowl a yorker almost at will. When in frustration he unleashed a bumper it may not have risen so alarmingly as did Miller's but rarely was it pitched wide or too short. It threatened chest, bone or throat, and was difficult to avoid. These qualities, allied to a control of late swing either way, would have made Lindwall menacing had they been the sum of his possessions. They were not. In Australia seam and shine generally are only transitory allies. So Lindwall, like all his great predecessors, cultivated that other and most subtle classical deception – variation of pace.

It was his mastery of pace variation, along with his ability to read quickly the technical strength and weakness of incoming batsmen and his cunning in playing on them, which made Lindwall distinctive even among the greatest fast bowlers. These are the qualities hardest to detect from the ringside, and most unpleasant in their swift, rueful appreciation by the batsman at the wicket. There were times over a long stint when Lindwall's pace looked fast-medium. Then only the departing batsman knew how an unchanged action had disguised a ball of exceptional pace or held another back just too disarmingly. Within this context batsmen of generous backlift or with a tendency to become grooved under persistent uniformity were meat and drink to Lindwall.

Lindwall also made another simple discovery early on. It was that the transition from back-footed to firm-footed forward technique had made English batsmen particularly vulnerable to a ball pitched on or near the length of a half-volley. Such a ball compelled a positive shot. Late swing, pace, unerring control of direction and Australia's swooping close fieldsmen did the rest. No fast bowler has plagued a batsman with a greater variety of stratagems nor, sustained by a trained, toughened fitness which as easily could have made him a distinguished full-back at Rugby League, maintained his challenge over longer hours and years.

Yet had Lindwall not been a great bowler he would still have been a notable cricketer. For at his best he was a considerable batsman, sound in defence and comprehensive of shot with a superb drive past mid-off or through the covers. He transformed the third Test in 1946–47 by scoring a century in 115 minutes and with Tallon adding 154 in only 87 minutes. And at Lords in 1953 his hitting was memorable in a match of fine batting. His fielding was safe and when the chances came not less consuming than that of his brilliant colleagues. That he could so nurse a harassed mother's air-sick small boy on a plane flight that the mother slept and the boy so enjoyed himself as to forget to be sick was only the other side of a man soft and lovable as in combat he could be austere and formidable. *[1960]*

AT THE OVAL, 14 AUGUST, 1948

ENGLAND

First innings

L. Hutton c Tallon b Lindwall	30
J. G. Dewes b Miller	1
W. J. Edrich c Hassett b Johnston	3
D. C. S. Compton c Morris b Lindwall	4
J. F. Crapp c Tallon b Miller	0
N. W. D. Yardley b Lindwall	7
A. J. Watkins lbw, b Johnston	0
T. G. Evans b Lindwall	1
A. V. Bedser b Lindwall	0
J. A. Young b Lindwall	0
W. E. Hollies not out	0
B 6	6
Total	52

AUSTRALIA BOWLING

	O	M	R	W
Lindwall	16.1	5	20	6
Miller	8	5	5	2
Johnston	16	4	20	2
Loxton	2	1	1	0

Fall of wickets: 1–2, 2–10, 3–17, 4–23, 5–35, 6–42, 7–45, 8–45, 9–47, 10–52.

AUSTRALIA

First innings

S. G. Barnes c Evans b Hollies	61
A. R. Morris not out	77
D. G. Bradman b Hollies	0
A. L. Hassett not out	10
B 3, nb 2	5
Total (two wickets)	153

To bat: K. R. Miller, R. N. Harvey, S. J. E. Loxton, R. R. Lindwall, D. Tallon, D. T. Ring, W. A. Johnston.

ENGLAND BOWLING (to date)

	O	M	R	W
Bedser	15	4	35	0
Watkins	4	1	19	0
Young	19	6	38	0
Hollies	32	7	50	2
Compton	2	0	6	0

Fall of wickets: 1–117, 2–117.

by Denys Rowbotham

It has been a disastrous day for England in the Fifth Test Match here today. Yardley won the toss and at twelve o'clock England went in to bat on what before lunch was the slowest and most lifeless wicket we have had in the series, but at a quarter past three England had been dismissed for 52 – her lowest total in a Test Match against Australia in England and nearly her lowest total ever. Then, as if to prove beyond doubt that the wicket held no hidden venom – though it was visibly more difficult in the late afternoon – Barnes and Morris put on over a hundred for Australia's first wicket, and at the close Australia's score was 153 for two. England's only consolation was the bowling of Bradman second ball before he had scored.

Perhaps never has England known disillusionment so swift or unequivocal as this. In 1888 when England was dismissed at Lord's for 53 the match was a low-scoring one. Australia made only 116 in her first innings, and 60 to England's 62 in her second. In Australia two years before England scored only 45, but she won a low-scoring match by 13 runs. Today's cricket was not of this sort. Only once before lunch did a ball lift unexpectedly and nastily. That was at one o'clock, and it was bowled not by Miller or Lindwall, but by Johnston to Crapp. Yet at lunch England had lost Dewes, Edrich, Compton and Crapp for 29 runs, and only Hutton had shown normal watchfulness and a first-class player's competence.

England's last six wickets fell to the greatest hour of fast bowling that has been seen in this country since Larwood. It was pure straight fast bowling on a wicket which, for all its dead heaviness, was helpless to retard it, and with a ball that had long since lost its shine. But its energy and its accuracy were beautiful. This was sustained hostility at which hitherto Lindwall had only hinted. It was terrible bowling, yet the lovely lithe rhythm of it, the gathering of its impetus, the knitting of its energies in the last vicious leap of its delivery was as much a delight to the senses as any leisured leaning shot by Compton. It left England's last six batsmen as helpless as puppets. They had neither the quickness of eye nor the technique to deal with it. Yardley was bowled before he had half completed his shot. Evans played on as he tried vainly to drive a good length, and Bedser and Young merely held out helpless bats. Only Hutton played this bowling with the coolness of an everyday occurrence.

The attack would have tested to the limit the resources of England's other first four batsmen, but they did not give themselves a chance to receive it. In the morning, when one was remarking with what fortitude and keen hopefulness the Australians attacked on a pitch which offered no encouragement, they were out to shots of bad judgement and poor execution. Edrich and Compton were caught at close square-leg from crude hook shots to rising balls of a length nearly that of a long-hop. Crapp pushed out his bat vaguely to an out-swinger, and only Dewes was beaten by a ball which might properly have deserved a wicket.

Hutton's batting by contrast seemed cooler, more compact and more impersonal than ever. It was as immune to mortal temptation as it seemed beyond reach of error. He alone was sound in the basic technique of his craft, and he was never anxious or hurried. He scored slowly, but he made many wristy, attacking shots which on a drier ground would have brought fours; for Hutton is a crisp hitter, not a hard one. He was caught at the last by Tallon, who dived yards to his left and held at full stretch a fine-leg glance which might well have reached the boundary. It was the most brilliant of three brilliant Australian catches.

In the game's last two hours and three-quarters the Australians batted as soundly as England had batted inaccurately. Though Barnes and Morris were most watchful they were clearly looking for runs on a wicket which they must have deduced would only get worse as the sun shone on it. All that they could have asked was that someone should bowl them long-hops before Hollies could threaten disaster. Watkins obligingly did so, with a forthrightness which would have shocked a school captain, and Barnes cut and hooked them with a schoolboy's wicked glee. It remained only for Bedser to mix some generous half-volleys and full-tosses with his good length so that Morris could drive them through the covers, and in spite of Young's steadying influence England's total would be passed before tea. So, in fact, did it happen.

Afterwards Hollies flighted and spun the ball more enticingly than has any other English bowler in a Test this season, and he received the rewards of his courage. He drew Barnes forward with his leg-break and had him beautifully caught at the wicket, and drew Bradman even farther forward and bowled him with his googly. Even these encouragements, however, could not prevent his bowling far too many long-hops to Morris, whose broad stylish bat swept them gratefully, if sometimes, it seemed, almost sorrowfully, to the boundary. Hollies, at least, provided the long-needed virtue of mixed flight and spin. But unless both he and Young find greater accuracy on Monday England will field a long time against batsmen much more exact in defence than her own and much quicker to see and more pitiless to punish each loose ball that is bowled to them. [*1948*]

*

Australia 389 (Morris 196, Hollies five for 131), beat England 52 and 188 (Hutton 64) by an innings and 149 runs.

*

According to the BBC commentator Rex Alston (27 July 1948) – or so memory insists – Bradman declined to win the preceding Leeds Test with a boundary in that game's penultimate over so that R. N. Harvey might have the honour. Had Bradman hit this boundary, his Test aggregate – regardless of his Oval failure – would have been 7,000, average 100.

The 1948 Australians were undefeated, winning 23 of 31 matches, including 4 Tests. Seven batsmen averaged over 50 (Bradman, A. L. Hassett, A. R. Morris, W. A. Brown, S. J. E. Loxton, S. G. Barnes and Harvey), Miller a mere 47·30.

The least successful bowler was the leg-spinner D. Ring with 60 wickets at 21·81. Above him, in ascending order, were Loxton, E. R. H. Toshack, I. W. Johnson, C. L. McCool, Miller, W. A. Johnston and Lindwall.

Essex was the only county to dismiss the Australians in a day, the tourists being put out by 6.20 p.m. at Southend for 721.

Bradman celebrated his 40th birthday at the end of the season, his figures for four tours:

Inns. 120 TNO 18 Runs 9,837 Average 96·44

He hit 41 centuries. On 1 January 1949 he became Sir Donald Bradman.

On Making '0'

by R. C. Robertson-Glasgow

It has fallen to my lot to see, make and inflict 0 in many places. But the largest and most illustrious 0 that I remember was made by Miles Howell, the distinguished Oxford and Surrey batsman.

He was playing for Surrey against Yorkshire at the Oval, and the artful left-hander, Rhodes, was bowling at his deadliest. Howell was just then at the top of his form, and he played the Yorkshire bowlers, mostly Rhodes, during forty-three mortal minutes, firmly and in the middle of the bat – for 0.

Any spectator who entered the ground at any point in that innings and failed to observe the score board might reasonably have thought that Howell was in the comfortable thirties or forties. But that ball would not pierce those fielders. And then he was run out, bravely answering a call from his rash partner. Run out 0; with the sweat of battle pouring from his forehead. As he remarked in the pavilion: 'Not a run; not even a little one, dammit; and I feel as if I'd sprinted to the House of Commons and back!'

There are those who fancy that it is something to have scored 1 or 2 or some other disreputable and insignificant digit. They are wrong; it is nothing, or, rather, worse than 0. They have but enjoyed a span too short to show a profit, long enough to show their ineptitude. They have but puttered and poked and snicked in wretched incompleteness.

No; give me the man who makes 0 and doesn't care. As numbers go, he has achieved nothing; but equally, because he has never started, he has left 0 unfinished.

Instead of the fly-blown phrases that we read and, alas! too often write, on a century made at cricket, how relieving, if unlikely, it would be some summer morning to knock back a mid-Victorian breakfast while reading something like this:

> At Tootling yesterday Mr O. E. Jugg, batting at number ten, a singular promotion, made yet another of those noughts with which the cricketing public is rapidly becoming familiar.
>
> Mr Jugg, who, as usual, wore his own patent deer-stalker cricket cap, done in the club colours, a white

background picked out with maroon rabbits, and a snake-belt ditto, appears to have brought the technique of failure to an unprecedented pitch of excellence; further, he seems actually to enjoy it.

His appearance on the field of play, slightly delayed by an argument with an intoxicated member, followed by another with the last step down but one, was greeted with that burst of applause, perhaps not unmingled with affection and hilarity, which the cricket public, bless their hearts, reserve only for the heroes of the game.

And that there exists in Mr Jugg, not to mention those who ask him to play, something of the heroic, who can deny? His last six innings before this one have been as follows:

v Gas, Light and Coke (Home) – o (3rd ball; snooted by a double bouncer).

v St Luke's Choir (Away) – o (without receiving a ball; fast asleep, and run out by an old tenor).

v Tootling GPO – o (c and b by the head sorter).

v The Pirates – o (1st ball; shattered by a long-hop).

v St Luke's Choir (Home) – o (2nd ball; lbw from behind).

v Gas, Light and Coke (Away) – (1st ball; run out, after a quarrel).

Yesterday, against the Wessex Electric and General, Mr Jugg once more walked to the wicket with the air of a man who has left a lighted cigarette in the dressing-room. He had difficulty in obtaining the right guard, and seemed to be at variance with the bowler's umpire who, I am able exclusively to reveal, told him he had better drive a nail into the end of his bat, prop it in front of the wicket and go home to sleep it off.

This sally evidently so incensed Mr Jugg that he took guard on the wrong stump, and was caught off the back of his bat at third-man when trying to glide to long-leg his first ball, which chanced to be a full-pitcher. At this humorous feat spectators and players alike applauded, and the ovation followed him till he disappeared into the pavilion. This is the seventh consecutive o compiled by this now celebrated batsman. As his brother, Mr Lance Jugg, the eccentric wicketkeeper,

> so deftly puts it: 'O.E., with two matches to go, needs only one more o to string 4 pairs of cuff-links.'

In general, the research in o is difficult. Practitioners and annals of o are shy and obscure. Men of o are found to be talkative about everything else. And if, in one of those mental flights which are said to inspire the grasshopper, you chance to say to an acquaintance, 'Ah, Prendergast, my dear fellow, how did you enjoy your o at Lord's yesterday? I arrived just in time to see you in and out,' a brittle silence falls, as if a bottle of the old and nutty had exploded in your pocket at a temperance talk.

Even *Wisden*, so rich in the scattered cipher, *Wisden*, which has garnered cricket's yearly harvest, has left us to glean the os as best we may. They have to be picked out, like a few pearls from legions of oysters. True, we may read at rare intervals of whole teams shot out for o, not even a bye flicked off the stomach past the stumper; and that is admittedly remarkable, even though, as we are apt to suspect, the outgoing side consisted of subnormal batsmen assailed by a crazy sergeant major who was bowling on a pitch of broken glass. Remarkable, yes; but not exclusive; for eleven os, even if one of them be perforce o not out, are ten too many; like eleven pies thrown by eleven comedians in one act.

The essence, the aristocracy of o is that it should be surrounded by large scores, that it should resemble the little silent bread-winner in a 'bus full of fat and noisy women. Indeed, when the years have fixed it in its place, so far from being merely the foil of jewels, it should itself grow, in the fond eye of memory, to the shape and stature of a gem.

That is the true philosophy of o. [*1943*]

D. C. S. Compton

by E. W. Swanton

It is a dangerous thing when the crowd sets up an idol who tends to be of more moment than the game itself, as the great career of Sir Donald Bradman illustrates. To any who think on these lines I would say that the only thing that might ever spoil Compton as a cricketer is the effort of trying to live up to the dizzy standards his admirers have set for him; and that perhaps the best safeguard I can offer against this is an attempt to give an impression of the man himself, as he is on the cricket field.

When Compton first came into the Middlesex eleven at the age of eighteen he was quickly appreciated in his true colours by all who see a little more in cricket than the players taking exercise in the sunshine, and a series of numbers flicking round on the scoreboard.

Here, it was plain to observe, was a natural player of games, who combined the eye of a hawk with an instinctive gift of balance. To be analytical for a moment, it is an unusual measure of harmony between the eye and the brain controlling the movement of the body that produces the perfection of timing which differentiates the masters from other very excellent players. This formula applies equally to the exponents of all games played with a moving ball. In cricket one has seen it exemplified by such artists with the bat as Hobbs and Woolley and K. S. Duleepsinhji. To put the thing slightly differently, the secret of the skill of the Hobbs and the Comptons is surely the exceptionally swift and sure transference in their brain of the knowledge of what to do with the ball, that they see so quickly, to the limbs which are brought into the making of the stroke. There is no conscious process but an instinctive reflex action. Similarly instinctive is the acknowledgement of this virtue by the spectator. You might say that balance and timing add up to rhythm, and that it is rhythm which the unsophisticated spectator is appreciating when an especially delicious stroke evokes murmurs of 'Lovely, sir, lovely!'

There are many cries of 'Lovely!' when Compton is at the wicket, and there are plenty of those amiably sadistic chuckles which acknowledge the outwitting of the poor, honest bowlers and fielders. He is one of those lucky people whose genius the crowd is always quick to recognise. He can hardly help entertaining them. Batsmanship comes as naturally to him as golf came to Bobby Jones and to Miss Joyce Wethered, as she was; or football to Stanley Matthews and to Cliff Jones.

Let us take a look at Compton as he begins an innings. You will notice the breadth of shoulder which, with all else in proportion, suggests the strength of his frame. There have been great batsmen who were anything but powerful, and brute force must be subservient to the more delicate items of machinery. But there is no denying that good muscles are a great help, as the famous golfer somewhat brutally reminded his anaemic pupil who asked him what he should do to increase his length. 'What should you do?' barked the old warrior, 'I'll tell you what you should do. Hit it a damn sight harder!'

Compton then, without being unduly tall, is well made and powerful and I would say that the particular characteristic that has most strongly affected his style of batting is his remarkable strength of forearm. People seeing him for the first time sometimes find him a little ungainly. That is a thing one tends not to notice when one has spent many hours watching him play. But it is not hard to see what is meant. It is as though when the construction of this creditable machine was completed no one thought to go round and give the nuts and bolts a final turn. Some of the joints are a shade on the loose side.

Having noticed this peculiarity or not on his way to the wicket, and remarked the serene, confident smile which he usually wears as he walks down the pavilion steps, we can settle down to watch his method. What is the first thing the expert would observe? I think it is probably the fact that from the moment the bowler reaches the stumps until the stroke is completed Compton's movements are deliberate, almost leisurely. That is an unfailing sign of quality, meaning that the batsman has both focused the ball very early in its flight and followed it until it has come almost on to the bat. Thus he has been able to give himself ample time to decide on the stroke and also to execute it. Lesser mortals, who achieve only a briefer focus of the ball, often in their haste choose the wrong stroke, and when they choose the right one dangerous faults are apt to interfere with their hurried making of it.

It will be unusual if we have to wait long before he begins tuning up his strokes. Going clockwise round the field, there is first the leg-glance in all its varieties, and so keen is the eye that he rarely fails to make contact with even the finest flick he attempts. Then comes the leg-sweep that he is so fond of, made with right knee bent, an almost horizontal bat and a quick turn of the wrists. If, by the way, this is not a situation of any particular moment or gravity Compton might choose the wrong ball for this stroke and pay the penalty. It is one that allows a very small margin of error, and it is not to be recommended strongly to ordinary mortals. It would be a very expensive bait for a bowler to go on pitching a fraction wide of the leg-stump hoping for a mistake, for on a true pitch Compton generally times and controls his sweep to perfection; but it represents one of the very few possible chinks in his armour. Personally I never like to see him playing the stroke if the ball is coming slowly off the turf, or if the bowlers have cut up the pitch with their follow-through.

The hook (that is the leg-side hit off the back foot) is another and more orthodox favourite, and woe betide the bowler, fast or slow, who drops them short! The on-drive he plays too, and plays well, with a characteristic touch of wrist in the finish of the stroke, though the pet sweep absorbs some balls that the average batsman would hit wide of mid-on. Next comes a narrow segment of territory that Compton chooses rather to neglect. Perhaps because he is so very strong from elbow to wrist he rarely swings straight-armed from the shoulders, and thus, in contrast to Edrich, for instance, he uses the drive between mid-on and mid-off much less frequently than the other strokes in the book. The captain who allows the same field-setting to serve for these two betrays weak powers of observation.

Anyone who has discovered to his cost on the golf course what impressive distances Compton cracks a golf ball with a short sharp forearm punch probably comprehends why he normally prefers to hit a cricket ball in the same way rather than through a wide arc from the shoulders. I am reminded, however, of a diverting moment at Lord's which indicates his ability to drive if he wishes, and also perhaps sheds a light on his attitude towards the game.

One afternoon Compton came in from batting at the tea interval, and was enduring with his usual indulgence the shafts of genially abusive humour which are a long tradition of the Middlesex dressing-room. Someone, probably Walter Robins, said: 'It's a funny thing a strong chap like you can't drive the ball straight. We never see you hit it over the bowler's head.' Compton said: 'Yes, it is funny; look out for the third ball after tea.' A few minutes afterwards the third ball bowled came whistling straight and true into the Members' seats in front of the pavilion, and, as the umpire was signalling 'six' Compton waved his bat cheerfully to his companions. A slight incident perhaps, but significant of his outlook: least of anyone is he in danger of forgetting that cricket is a game to be enjoyed.

Proceeding still clockwise round the field we come next to the favourite Compton country. It ranges really from mid-off right round to second-slip, but the angles in most frequent use are those to either side of cover-point. And I write advisedly 'to either side' because of Compton's remarkable knack of beating the fielder there by disguising the direction of the stroke. One of his captains describes him as the best teaser of cover-point he has ever seen. His off-side strokes off the forward foot are not orthodox because normally he does not bring that foot right across on to the line of flight. He prefers to give himself more room, to bring his wrists into the stroke and, in consequence, to aim the bat squarer than he strictly should. In theory this is a dangerous departure from the textbook, and it is a sure indication of Compton's unusual gifts of eye and timing that he makes the stroke look safe – almost obvious.

The ball is hit off the back foot as severely as might be expected from his physique, all the way round the off-side, except that when it comes to the square-cut he still is apt to prefer to use the wrist and play forward. The later cuts, including the one very late and therefore very fine, complete an armoury which is more varied than that of anyone playing today. [*1948*]

PRECEDENCE IN TRINIDAD 1953–54

Denis Compton had a specially warm memory of an aged coloured gentleman of the old school, who having enjoyed the three 'Ws' to the full, plucked slyly at his elbow as he stood in the deep.

'Mistah Compton,' said this ancient, 'Mistah Worrell, Mistah Weekes and Mistah Walcott comes first, den comes de Lawd above.' *Ian Peebles*

K. R. Miller

by Ray Robinson

To young eyes, quickest to perceive the things that make cricket, Keith Miller is as an Olympian god among mortals. He brings boys' dreams to life. He is the cricketer they would all like to be, the one who can hit more gloriously and bowl faster than anybody on earth. When Neville Cardus called him a young eagle among crows and daws Miller was not a champion playing out of his class; sharing the field with him were the elect of the world's two greatest cricketing countries, Bradman, Hammond and bearers of other famous names, Compton and other men of personality.

Since World War II Miller has made his mark on pavilion roofs across half the earth. He was not clear of his teens when the war began; before long it hid from view a youth from Melbourne High School who at 17 had scored 181 against Tasmania in his first innings in first-class cricket and, just twenty, overcame the difficulties of Grimmett's bowling in making 108 against South Australia in his fourth match in the Sheffield Shield competition. As a Flying-Officer of twenty-five he gave up piloting Mosquitoes in 1945 to become the mainstay of the Australian Services' batting. As such, he seldom lifted the ball in the Victory Tests, but towards the end of the season he began coping with coping-stones and other upstair targets around English cricket fields. In his 185 for the Dominions he drove England's bowlers to seven spots among the buildings enclosing Lord's ground. *The Times*' own R. B. Vincent, discriminating and droll, began to wonder whether Lord's was a big enough ground for such terrific hitting. The first and farthest six crashed into the top-tier seats between the towers of the pavilion. Next morning one with less carry struck the southern tower, above the broadcasters' eyrie. They were among the highest blows Lord's pavilion had felt this century though they left intact the all-time record by an earlier exile from Victoria, Albert Trott, who in 1899 drove a ball over the hallowed edifice. Miller lifted his overnight total by 124 before lunch on the last day of the match. Only such an innings as his 185 could have won the game.

Even at tense moments in Test Matches he is as ready for a bit of fun as for a good ball or a sharp catch. When a bowler goes through an experimental run-up and delivery without the ball he promptly hooks an imaginary long-hop to the fence. The crowds share his enjoyment of cricket and he enjoys their presence. In a Test at Lord's he was in line to be third victim of a hat-trick; as the next ball struck his leg the crowd excitedly shouted: 'How's that?' Miller shook his head sorrowfully to the mass appealers, as if it grieved him to disappoint them. Onlookers are amused by his mimicry of the umpire signalling a wide against him, his drop-kicking the ball to the wicketkeeper after a running catch, his boyish exuberance in the scrambling horseplay for souvenir stumps at the end. No stage villain looks more melodramatic than Miller the bowler, staring at an umpire who refuses one of his whirling appeals. Once he toppled over backwards and appealed sitting on the pitch. When a bowler stops Miller's hard drive and menaces to throw him out, the tall batsman does not scamper back to the crease but holds up a stern hand, forbidding all tomfoolery.

Superb technique has enabled Miller to look for runs where others look for trouble. He blends with Melbourne forthrightness the allurements of style typical of Sydney, with a dash of Kent and Gloucestershire to bring out the full flavour. Watch him stride into the field, toes straight ahead but eyes looking about, following the fieldsmen's throwing to become accustomed to quick focusing in the outdoor light. At the wicket he takes in the positions of the backing-away fielders as he spins his bat upright with his left hand and stops it revolving with his right. Taking 'two legs' block, he marks the spot between middle and leg stumps by drawing a V back from the crease with two geometric strokes of his right toe. He adjusts his shirt-neck and smooths his long brown hair back with his left hand as he settles in his stance, the most easy and natural stance of all. In this he combines everything to produce dominating reach. His legs are straight but not taut, his body leans just enough for him to hold the bat comfortably. Comfortably and commandingly, because Miller's hands clasp the handle high – as unwelcome a sight as bowlers and fieldsmen can see.

Miller's forward play is unrivalled in splendour. He is the grandest player of cricket's grandest stroke, the drive. Left shoulder and elbow lead his body in unison with the thrust of his left foot towards the ball. As a thermometer responds to the sun's warmth, the height of his backswing varies in accordance with his estimate of the ball's quality. If he judges it to be coming within range of his matchless drive his swing is as full as a six-footer can keep in control throughout its menacing arc; his hands extend back to neck-height and cocked wrists point the bat skyward. At the moment of impact straight arms transmit the energy of true-lined shoulders to whipping wrists. Usually the ball is close to his front pad before the bat smashes through and onwards in

the direction the shot has taken. To put the kernel of his style in one sentence he wields the straightest bat with the greatest power. When Miller springs a stride or two forward both feet grip the pitch for the drive as firmly as when he advances only the front leg, and the purchase they obtain forces his knees inward.

His bowling has been chock-full of life and personality, and full of shocks for batsmen – some of them nasty shocks. He gathers momentum in a much shorter run than other fast bowlers, shorter than Wright takes for a slow-medium googly. Nine loose-jointed strides are usually enough, sometimes fewer. He is the only Test-class bowler with such a flexible approach, and the only one I have seen drop the ball as he ran, scoop it up and deliver it without a trace of the interruption. Once he bowled in odd boots, one size nine and a borrowed ten, because the stress of fast bowling had broken his own. After his short run Miller generates pace with such a convulsive body effort that it is a wonder his back and sides have not troubled him more often. His delivery is high-handed (in more senses than one), especially for his in-dipper. Not satisfied with late swerve either way, break-backs and a wide range of pace-changes, he rings in a leg-break or a round-armer now and again. Batsmen find it hard to understand Miller's bowling. Some of it is well over their heads.

We came to expect one like that whenever he was hit for four. That indignity stung the same combative streak in him as a bowler that a crisis did as a batsman (I preferred to see him hit the roof when he was batting). Tossing back his mane like a mettlesome colt with dilated nostrils, he would stride back, giving a hurrying clap to the fieldsman and thrusting out his hand to command a quick return, in eagerness to get at the batsman again. Rushing up, he would fling down a bumper that made the batsman duck penitently; or occasionally it would be an exaggerated full-toss instead. For the most frequent bouncer in post-war cricket he seldom hit a batsman – the ball usually bounced too high – but such moments transformed him from hero to villain, and he has been hooted at Nottingham, Madras, Perth, Adelaide, Brisbane and other points east and west. How much of his apparent anger was simulated only those close at hand could tell. As he ran up Miller did not always look at the batsman, and once started to bowl without noticing that the umpire's arm barred his path because the striker was not ready. When he almost collided with it he changed in a flash from his bowling action to shake the umpire's outstretched hand. His personality abolishes the boundary and brings the crowd into the game with him.

[1951]

*

The Scoop

by R. C. Robertson-Glasgow

Years ago, before Science got us down, the Scoop must have been quite a jolly affair. The King Stanislas of Ruritania dies, after a fifty-year reign devoid of excitement except an occasional change of mistress or variation in the design of military helmets. Resident in the Royal capital are Colonel Jenkins, a correspondent of *The Times*, and Commander Funnel, ditto for the *Morning Post*. There are no telegrams or telephone. Railways are unknown, steam-ships still in a laughable infancy. Letters to England, when collected, take two years. So the Colonel and the Commander get together over a few bottles of the best Hockburgheimer. The Colonel, dismissing the wine-drops from his moustache with an old-fashioned sweep of the hand, says: 'Funnel, I suppose you have heard that His Majesty King Stanislas died the day before yesterday while reviewing his cavalry in the Palace Yard?' The Commander, breaking a silence of forty-eight hours, replies: 'Jenkins, I have. Silly fool would review in the afternoon heat without his hat on.' The Colonel, disregarding the backhander at the Army, pours out a half-pint, then passes the bottle.

After a short interval of swallowing, the Colonel says: 'I shall take the news by land; horse-back, diligence, and so on.' 'And I,' says the Commander, 'shall take it by river and sea; Danube, Black Sea, Bosphorus, Aegean, Straits of Messina, Gibraltar. And I bet I get there first.' 'How much?' says the Colonel. 'A champagne dinner at Brookes,' says the Commander; and off they go. The Colonel is mistakenly arrested in Budapest on a charge of fraudulent impersonation and incitement to rebellion, and, when he comes out, finds he has missed the last drosky for six months. The Commander, meeting contrary winds off Cape Spartivento and losing his compass and half a spinnaker, is driven steadily backwards to Sevastopol. Disgusted, he returns to Ruritania via Odessa and the Carpathians. Both are recalled to London, which they reach in time to read of King Stanislas's life, reign, and death, in *Chambers' Encyclopaedia*.

A. V. Bedser

by John Woodcock

Alec Victor Bedser was more than a great bowler. He was, and is, a very dear man, abounding in integrity, softened by a gentle nature, and inspired by an unshakeable desire to give of his best. It is always a pleasure therefore, to meet him, and a privilege to write about him.

If, in this one paragraph, I have made him sound a paragon, he will be embarrassed. He has no time for flattery, or for things fanciful, or for praise that might sound too fulsome. His success, both on the cricket field and now in business, has been based, he will say, on those simple virtues which the young of today tend to look upon as being 'square' or old-fashioned.

On the most recent of his many visits to Australia, in 1962–63, this difference in outlook between Alec and the modern generation was there for all to see. He travelled as assistant to the Manager, the Duke of Norfolk. Besides being in charge of the net profits of the tour as well as the net practices, he liked to bowl at Ted Dexter's team whenever he could, and he had, to some extent, to familiarise the Earl Marshal with managerial routine. It was a full-time job. Yet at Adelaide, on successive mornings, Alex was up by six o'clock searching his accounts for a few shillings that had gone astray. To him, the players tended to take their responsibilities too lightly. To them, Alec was seeking perfection in an imperfect world. The two, while being incompatible, were the best of friends.

This then is the man who, with his great strength and wonderful natural rhythm, carried England's hopes of bowling Australia out in the years after World War II. He and his twin brother, Eric, joined the Surrey staff in 1938. When the time came to enlist with the Royal Air Force in 1939 they had each played twice for Surrey. Within a few weeks of their coming back from the war, in 1946, Alec was being compared with Maurice Tate. By 1948 he was a household name, and the comparison with Tate still stands, these two and Sidney Barnes being the greatest of all medium-paced bowlers.

Between 1912 and 1937 Tate took 2,783 first-class wickets, 155 of them for England. Between 1939 and 1960 Bedser took 1,924 wickets, of which 236 were for England. For the best part of fifty years one or

the other was pounding in to bowl in his outsize boots, the ball sounding like the crack of a whip as it hit the wicketkeeper's gloves. If the work of these two in their cricketing years could be collected and piled up around them in visible shape, what a vast mound there would be! And each carried unrepining the heavy harness of labour – in all weathers, winter and summer. They were idols in their own country and immensely popular abroad. There was something about them (though I can speak only of Bedser at first hand) which told you that if victory was possible no effort would be spared to achieve it.

You always knew when Alec was in the mood. His head would start to bob about as he came in from his mark. Sometimes the earth would seem to shake. No one was safe on such days as these. Bradman described the ball from Bedser that bowled him at Adelaide in the Fourth Test Match in 1946–47 as the best ever to take his wicket. 'It was delivered', wrote the Don, 'on the off-stump, swung very late to hit the pitch on the leg-stump, and then came back to hit the middle-and-off . . . There is no doubt in my mind that I found Bedser harder to play than Tate, especially in England in 1948.' After qualifying this assessment by saying how his own advancing years had caused his reactions to slow down by the time he met Bedser, Bradman paid both men the same tribute. 'They were magnificent bowlers, delightful personalities and ornaments to the game.'

Arthur Morris, one of the finest of all left-handers and a prolific scorer for Australia after the war, was so harassed by Bedser, particularly on the leg-stump, that in the end he conceded him a telling psychological advantage. In the 21 Test Matches in which they were opposed to one another, Morris lost his wicket 18 times to Bedser. Against Australia alone, Bedser took 104 wickets, a number surpassed only by Barnes with 106 and Wilfred Rhodes with 109. Barnes's wickets came in 20 Tests, Rhodes's in 41, Bedser's in 21; and the majority of Bedser's were taken at a time when only Doug Wright, the most mercurial of bowlers, could offer him any high-class support. Between 1946 and 1953, whenever England came near to beating Australia Bedser played the leading part.

Happily, before his powers began to wane he saw to it that England regained the Ashes for the first time after the war. Not all the methods employed by England to overcome Australia in 1953 were entirely creditable. Had they bowled at Leeds as they would have thought the Australians, in similar circumstances, should have bowled at them, they would have lost the Fourth Test. Instead they bowled altogether too wide. But when, after England's victory at the Oval, the final count

was taken, it was Bedser's bowling that had won the series. His 39 wickets in the five Tests was the highpoint of his career.

*

The Trent Bridge Test of 1953 began with Australia scoring 249 (A. R. Morris 67, A. L. Hassett 115 and K. R. Miller 55. The other eight batsmen totalled 7 and Bedser took seven for 44). England replied with 144 (L. Hutton 43, Lindwall five for 57).

*

by Jack Fingleton

Morris and Hole walked in slowly, making sure of only one over before lunch, and Hole escaped his 'pair' by glancing Bedser's first ball for four.

Something must have given Morris inspiration at lunch. It might have been something he ate; it might have been the flaring colours of the I Zingari tie our Prime Minister was wearing when he met both teams on the field (Dr Evatt, Australian Opposition Leader, was also present this day) but, whatever it was, Morris sailed into the English attack. He twice hooked Bailey for four and back-cut him for another four and beautifully forced Bedser for two. He ran to 20 out of 27.

Then the inevitable happened as Bedser again clean-bowled Hole. Bedser gave Hassett a nightmare of an over. One popped off a good length and hit Hassett in the chest, the Australian doing well to get his bat out of the way. It was like an inquest as Hassett patted the spot and Hutton and Compton looked over his shoulder. They all had similar thoughts – a 'spot' developing on the pitch.

That ball upset Hassett. He luckily edged Bedser through the slips and next over might have been stumped by Evans off Bailey on the leg-side – a difficult but definite chance. Morris continued to attack and had 32 out of 44, 25 of them off Bailey.

Now Hassett fell to Bedser. Bedser caused another one to bite but this time Hassett played it and it slowly rose to Hutton, a 'sitter' catch, at short-leg. Hassett was never comfortable and Harvey showed his concern for the 'spot' by patting it before he took guard. I could imagine some agitation in the Australian dressing-room regarding Bedser and the behaviour of the pitch. The pitch began looking dry and short of grass. Here was evidence that it was beginning to lift its face. And suddenly Harvey was hit on the neck by another flier.

Morris's tactics to get quick runs off Bailey were therefore excellent. The fight was now intense and the crowd were in great spirits, cheering Bedser tremendously. It took Harvey ten struggling minutes to get off

his 'pair' and it was amusing how the crowd roared with the players whenever an appeal was made.

Bedser hit Harvey on the fingers and Hutton looked just as concerned about the pitch as Harvey. The way it was going England would be finding things difficult in the fourth innings. Then Harvey went. He swung hard at a short one from Bedser and Graveney, ten yards behind square-leg, held the quick-moving catch. This led to tumultuous crowd scenes. The Australians were three down for 50, two of their best out in Hassett and Harvey. Bedser now had ten wickets for the match.

There were signs of panic in the Australian batting to Bedser but this was nothing as compared to what was soon to follow. Morris hung tenaciously to the other end but he was doing something about it. He twice smote Wardle for four but had a life at 15 when Evans missed stumping him off Wardle.

Much depended upon this Miller–Morris partnership but now Bedser got Miller out with a rank bad ball, that is, if a ball that gets a wicket can be called a bad ball. He bowled the only full-toss I have seen him bowl. Miller opened his shoulders at this 'gift' – and hit it straight to Kenyon at wide mid-on. Miller looked as if he could have kicked himself, falling to such a ball, but he and Bedser seemed to enjoy some wry joke as Miller passed him on the way out.*

Benaud came and was turned completely inside out by Bedser. He moved across the pitch, the ball went behind his legs and his three stumps went whirling. Benaud stood there, dumbfounded, and the umpire raised the finger of doom to him – very seldom is it that an umpire has to give a batsman out for being bowled. Bedser had taken five for 22 in 11 overs. He had sent this Notts crowd completely delirious. A passing engine-driver joined in the chorus for Bedser by giving a vigorous recital on his whistle.

Bedser had the Australians demoralised. He is a grand bowler but though the pitch had now given reason for suspicion there also had been some very bad batting by the Australians.

Morris moved to a grand fifty in 78 minutes and continued to keep the other end with profitable results but now Tattersall surprised him with a big leg-break, hitting his stumps. Morris had hit 60 out of 81, with 7 fours.

Davidson tried his luck with a haymaker off Tattersall and

*Bedser was in the Australian dressing-room at Lord's when Miller got two MCC batsmen with odd balls – one a full-toss and another a round-armer. When Bedser teased Miller about getting wickets with such balls, Miller replied, 'Oh, Alec, you want to try slinging up some muck now and then. It comes off sometimes.' As Miller passed Bedser on the way out, Bedser said to him, 'Thanks very much for that tip at Lord's.' Hence the big laughs (J. F.).

Graveney, running hard along the boundary, took a splendid catch. Tallon and Lindwall played Bedser better than anybody who had been before. Lindwall believes the way to play Bedser is forward and he was certainly proving the success of this theory. Lindwall, too, showed great interest in the 'spot', an interest surpassed, however, by Hutton who gave it a glance every time he passed it.

A delightful story came out about Tallon's innings. For some minutes before Tallon left the dressing-room, Hassett was discussing with his fellows whether an appeal shouldn't be made against the light. When Davidson's wicket fell and Tallon was leaving the room, Hassett said to him, 'All right, then, Don, give it a "go".' In cricket language, Hassett meant to appeal against the light. Tallon completely misinterpreted the word 'go'. He thought Hassett meant to go after the runs and there were gasping Australians in the dressing-room when Tallon didn't appeal against the light but began, instead, a blaze against the attack – a hit or miss effort.

Tallon now chanced his eye and arm against Tattersall and Simpson plucked out of the air an incredible one-handed catch as he was running back. This catch would have even brought down the house at a baseball game in America. Coming from Simpson in front of his own people at Nottingham it led to minutes of unrestrained cheering and clapping.

It was Tattersall who finished off the Australian innings but this time with catches off Bedser. Lindwall and Hill had terrific hits that were mistimed and the ball soared straight up into the murkiness. These are extremely hard catches to take, with the eyes of thousands upon the fieldsman, but Tattersall positioned himself and made no mistake with either.

So the Australians' innings finished for a meagre 123, of which Morris had hit 60. Tallon was next with 15; Lindwall had 12; the rest practically nil.

Bedser was cheered from the middle of the ground to inside the pavilion. He had taken seven for 44 in 17 overs. His bag for the match was fourteen wickets for 99 runs.

The ball that turned the Australian innings inside out on this unforgettable day of dramatic cricket was a ball that didn't get a wicket. The ball of consequence was the one that popped and hit Hassett on the chest. This paved the way for the catch that later followed – and, being watched closely from the pavilion, it paved the way for a lot of indiscretions that followed. The plain truth, however, was that Bedser was just too good. He had done it once again for England and, in doing so, joined our own Spofforth, Verity and Rhodes – who was at this game – as one of the immortals who have taken fourteen wickets

or more in a Test between England and Australia. No wonder Trent Bridge rose to Alec Bedser on this dull afternoon of 13 June, 1953.

[*1952*]

*

Rain prevented a result in this match. Requiring 229 for victory, England scored 120 for one (Hutton 60 not out).

SPIRIT OF BLANDINGS

Cover-point is a vain fellow who loves applause and the spotlight; wicket-keeper is tough and speaks to convince, not to amuse. Short-leg is an acrobat and pantaloon. Slip is a man of the world, glib and sharp, long-stop is an occasional waiter, once a young and ambrosial butler. Third-man is a hermit. But mid-on is best. He is a genial club gentleman, seasoned with the right stuff; and he knows that the ball the hand misses will yet bounce off the boots. *R. C. Robertson-Glasgow*

M. P. Donnelly and B. Sutcliffe

The four-match series between England and New Zealand in 1949 marked the end of three-day Tests, in this instance all drawn. Both sides averaged 120 overs a day, both scored at a run a minute or, in England's case, faster; at the Oval England included three spinners – Wright, Hollies and Laker, at Lord's Bailey (not yet called upon to frustrate Lindwall and Miller) rivalled Compton in brilliance of stroke-making. Superb in the field, New Zealand relied much on their slow left-hander T. B. Burtt who bowled to a packed off-side; V. J. Scott was obdurate as Woodfull, and the very young J. R. Reid gave more than a hint of rare days to come. But the chief glory of W. A. Hadlee's team lay in the batting of Sutcliffe and Donnelly, the former one who might have opened with Trumper without looking lost. His career 2,727 runs for New Zealand, average 40, was a remarkable achievement considering he never appeared on the winning side in more than forty Tests. Donnelly, of course, had excited greater enthusiasm in 1946–47 at Oxford than any undergraduate batsman since the turn of the century.

But to appreciate the spirit of 1949, we should note that in the New Zealanders' second innings described below, Lancashire bowled 25.5 overs in 68 minutes. Just as remarkable was the finish at Southampton when the tourists were set 109 to win in 35 minutes. That Sutcliffe and Donnelly raced to 50 in ten minutes, and that the runs were knocked off with five minutes to spare may seem odd, that D. Shackleton's 5.5 overs cost 56 runs even odder. In the context of the 1970s, it was all the fault of Hampshire's captain, E. D. R. Eagar, who – perhaps bemused after making 82 – forgot to order his bowlers to take their time. In the event they achieved 11.5 overs in half an hour.

Great Batting at Aigburth, 23 August, 1949

Lancashire 318 (C. Washbrook 125, P. Greenwood 50) and 224 for five, declared (C. Washbrook 68, J. T. Ikin 57, G. A. Edrich 53); New Zealanders 390 (V. J. Scott 87, M. P. Donnelly 80, B. Sutcliffe 61).

NEW ZEALANDERS

Second innings

B. Sutcliffe not out	79
M. P. Donnelly st Barlow b Tattersall	56
J. R. Reid not out	7
B 4, lb 7	11
Total (one wicket)	153

LANCASHIRE BOWLING

Second innings

	O	M	R	W
D. Stone	2	0	14	0
P. Greenwood	4	0	18	0
M. Hilton	11	0	60	0
R. Tattersall	8.5	0	50	1

by Denys Rowbotham

Those who stayed away from Lancashire's cricket match with the New Zealanders here today may well not forgive themselves for the rest of their lives. They missed not only a great victory for the New Zealanders but some of the greatest batsmanship that is likely to be seen in a generation.

Few of the spectators today could have anticipated after lunch the magnificence that was still in store for them. At a quarter to three Lancashire were 193 for three wickets, at five past three 218 for four, and all that seemed left for the crowd to do was to watch some cheerful hitting by Lancashire of not always accurate bowling and to drowse on this lovely ground in the falling afternoon sunshine. Then unexpectedly at twenty past three Howard declared at 224 for five wickets. It was a fine gesture but would have seemed against most counties a reasonably safe one. It left the New Zealanders an hour and a quarter in which to score 153 runs on a dusty wicket on which neither side had scored at a much faster rate than one run a minute.

In the matter of scoring runs quickly, however, the New Zealanders

are not a normal side, and when Wallace sent in Donnelly and Sutcliffe it was certain that they would not be so today, unless one or both of them was dismissed quickly. Neither batsman comitted an error for over fifty minutes. Then Donnelly jumped to drive a fast good-length ball from Tattersall, missed and was stumped easily. But the New Zealanders were 120 for one wicket, and when Reid dispelled any suspicion that he might fall into rashness through over-eagerness victory for the New Zealanders was assured. It came with a furious high on-drive by Sutcliffe. There were still seven minutes to spare.

It had been wonderful batting indeed that had attacked from the first ball it received. Both Sutcliffe and Donnelly drove, hooked, pulled and placed pushed shots for singles it seemed just how, when and where they might choose. Much more they did so without a hint of risk and without the giving of a chance. Only Stone at the start bowled erratically, and Greenwood, Tattersall and Hilton were about as accurate in length as they were yesterday. That the runs came as freely as they did was because wherever a ball was bowled within a length not short enough to be hooked or pulled Sutcliffe and Donnelly found its pitch. They did so by the quickest footwork that most of today's crowd will have seen. At one moment they skipped down the wicket like dancers, at another like sprinters from their starting-blocks. Sometimes a short leap would seem to propel them with the sudden fury of a missile from a catapult. But though the speed of their footwork was remarkable, the judgement which made it possible was more so. Scarcely once did either batsman miscalculate a ball's length or pace. If they did so, the withdrawal of a foot or a step backwards made like lightning would transform a drive into a brilliant hook or cut.

How confident was their judgement was seen best when Hilton was bowling. Almost at once Howard was compelled to set two long-ons and a deep mid-wicket for both of them. It reduced their drives to singles or twos immediately. Yet for nearly an hour even this could not worry them. It merely meant that if Hilton pitched outside the off-stump he was driven on the instant through the covers or past mid-off to the boundary. Hilton, indeed, was the most ruthlessly treated of all. Except when he was hooked it seemed that almost three-quarters of his balls were driven. Both batsmen jumped 5 yards, sometimes 6, to meet him and each shot, except for the high straight drive, was made along the ground and from the middle of bats which by some miracle seemed to have been deprived of edges. So sure did they seem that after the score had reached 80 all sense of a race against time vanished. Before this and after it their batting was so finely controlled that their purely defensive shots or pushes for singles did not seem outnumbered by their

hits. How master they were of their task is revealed by the steadiness of their scoring. Including 11 extras the runs that came from each over were as follows: 9, 8, 5, 4, 4, 5, 6, 5, 5, 3, 2, 5, 4, 1, 14, 10, 7, 16, 4, 3, 4, 11, 2, 1, 7, 8.

Stone bowled two overs and Greenwood three. The rest were bowled by Tattersall and Hilton. Stone was as erratic as he was yesterday, and in his first over Sutcliffe and Donnelly each hooked him for singles to long-leg and Sutcliffe drove him past point for two and turned him off his toes to square-leg for four. Although Greenwood's length was much steadier he was driven more remorselessly. If he bowled on the leg-stump he was glanced and when he shortened his length he was pulled. The first fifty came in less than 25 minutes, and though Tattersall steadied the scoring appreciably and once reduced it to a single from one over it made matters only worse for Hilton. Sutcliffe twice drove the latter in his next over for fours with such casual ease that Hilton, perhaps in despair, dropped the last ball nearly at his toes. Sutcliffe hit that for four too off its second bounce and grinned as impishly as the schoolboys who were watching him. The score was now 80 after only another 15 minutes' batting. It was now Donnelly's turn and Tattersall's. Donnelly celebrated Sutcliffe's fifty out of 97 by twice driving Tattersall off his toes to mid-wicket and then with wicked venom to long-on. He and Sutcliffe next glanced him for singles with such delicacy that one felt that one's eyes had deceived one and that two balls earlier such naked violence had not been. Ten minutes later the score was 120. Donnelly at last was out, and in a quarter of an hour the game was over.

The contrast in manner of the two batsmen was as fascinating as a student of style could have asked. Sutcliffe was all easeful flow no matter how far he jumped to drive. His body leaned into and over his shots still, and he was all grace and leisure however vigorously he sometimes hit. His footwork was as light as it was rapid and made his body seem without weight, and his bat weaved this way and that more like a wand when it did not flash brilliance like a sword. Always he was smiling, elegant and unruffled, eager but not grasping, attacking but not laying waste. Even though his purpose was clear-cut and his resolution as determined as his partner's, he was always a self-conscious stylist, and he seemed to cherish each shot he made.

By contrast, Donnelly was a compact mass of savage violence. Each crack of his bat was like a hammer blow. Where Sutcliffe's shots ran into smooth lines and curves, his were close-knit, short-armed and made, it seemed, with wrists of steel. Much more than Sutcliffe he made the bowler's length what he wished it to be. He took more risks, made

more creative strokes, but never did he smile. His mastery was austere and unrelenting, his mood tempered to hostility, and even his defensive shots were pouncing and dynamic. He was more calculating, too. He never wasted energy. His bat was a cudgel to be used only where and when it could do most batter. Sutcliffe would have scored consistently and charmingly off Tattersall. Only Donnelly could have shattered his length in one terrible over. So different were these two batsmen in temper, yet so alike in technical mastery, that it was impossible to subdue either of them so long as both were together. Donnelly beat the bowlers into subjection after Sutcliffe had persuaded them to error. Then Sutcliffe reaped the harvest of his partner's devastation. The like of both of them on this day may not be seen for years again.

T. G. Evans

by John Arlott

He is the most unquenchable man in all cricket. He will greet the batsman at the crease with a wink, pull his leg, stump him with an appeal paralysing in its speed and sharpness, commiserate with him, replace the bails and be waiting impatiently for the next man in – all within bare seconds. Never, surely, was a cricketer so boiling over with vitality or so prodigal of energy. Compact of muscle – not muscle for muscle's sake, but the muscle of purposeful activity – he seems almost to bounce as he moves. If he throws himself ten yards to take a catch, you may be sure he will be on his feet, throwing up the ball before the echoes of his appeal have died in the pavilion rafters. If he whips off the bails in an attempted stumping which finds the batsman's foot still grounded, then the bails will be back in position before the umpire can shake his head.

Until the Kent cricket committee, anxious for the safety of his eyes, demanded that he choose between cricket and boxing, Godfrey Evans had an unbeaten record as a professional boxer. I suspect he chose cricket because it promised longer and more frequent periods of activity and, as a cricketer, took to wicketkeeping because the wicketkeeper never gets any rest.

No one has ever seen him tired. Sometimes on the South African tour of 1948–49, the English team came off the field virtually sun-stunned after an entire day battling for a win on an iron-hard pitch in the pitiless glare of the Rand or the steam-heat of Durban. Very humanly, they wanted a cool bath and an ocean of rest – except Godfrey Evans, to whom a day keeping wicket was no more than a prelude to a swim, a party, a drive, a walk on his hands, a few cartwheels and, to crown the evening, his own rendering of 'The German Band' – with actions – the most physically exhausting song in the world.

He has the fastest and cleanest hands for the ball that the mind of a cricketer can imagine, and he tries for everything. He takes his innings as if he were certain of hitting any bowling out of sight: he does not always succeed, but when he does, the spectator sees the champagne of batting. Yet, when the game demands it, he can bat the other way. England had almost lost the Adelaide Test of 1947 when Denis Compton was joined by the No. 10 batsman – Evans – who batted for an hour

and a half before he scored. That innings was historic: it saved England – and it is almost the only time Godfrey Evans has admitted, even tacitly, that a bowler *might* be worthy of respectful batting.

... Godfrey Evans would bowl, simultaneously if he could, *and* field in the deep. For this very reason wicketkeeping alone can seem to him – as we may fancy – almost an unsatisfying day's work. He makes chances and he misses them, but, faults included, he is the finest wicketkeeper in the world by a clear margin. [*1952*]

TARGET

On 17 December, 1977, the Test and County Cricket Board said they would expect England, New Zealand and Pakistan to achieve a rate of 17 overs an hour (about 3½ minutes an over) during the Tests of 1978.

At Leeds in 1930, an occasion already referred to in the Introduction, Australia made 566 in 7 hours 40 minutes. As each incoming batsman took 2 minutes to reach the middle, the effective time was 7 hours 22 minutes, i.e. 442 minutes.

The bowlers concerned, and their overs, were: Larwood 33, Tate 39, Geary 35, Hammond 17, Tyldesley 33 and Leyland 11.

So in 442 minutes, while Australia scored at 74 runs an hour, England bowled 168 overs – that is 22·3 overs an hour.

If Larwood, Tate, Geary and Hammond had achieved the target of 17 overs an hour urged by the TCCB, then the spinners Tyldesley and Leyland must have bowled each of their 44 overs in *10 seconds*.

Character of a Decade

by J. M. Kilburn

As long as cricket continues to be a living game it must experience the cycles of change that mark decay and renaissance, rejection and development of ideas and consequent techniques. Until all resources of play and players have been exhausted the balance of bat against ball will waver to and fro, initiative and dominance rising and falling.

There have been one or two periods of violent revolution in cricket history, all brought about by bowling experiments, but in the main the changes in the game have been based on the peaceful acceptance of logical trends and the determination, conscious or unrealised, to find the maximum satisfaction from the given circumstances.

The decade following World War II was essentially a period of bowling pressure. The well-behaved pitches of the 1930s and the hasty dispersal of 'bodyline' bowling by legislation brought batting to one of its peaks, and when first-class cricket had to be put aside in 1939 bowling had not yet exploited the full scope of the concession in the altered lbw rule. From 1946 onwards bowlers, in keeping with the character of their times, began to concentrate on the easier way of earning their money. The age of the in-swinger followed. Batting was cribbed, cabined and confined by the so-called negative attack of bowling, at all paces, directed towards the leg-side and supported by constraining field-settings. Batsmen had no option but to limit themselves. The bravest of spirits cannot contrive a flowing cover-drive from the ball pitched outside the leg-stump. The test of temperament became patience, the touchstone of success became endurance. The brilliance of cricket lay in fielding of notable courage and skill in the leg-trap positions and, incidentally, in unimagined capacity of wicketkeepers in taking the ball on the leg-side. Evans and Tallon and a dozen others of lesser sparkle were not accidents of time and space.

With the redeployment of resource the foundations of judgement and appreciation required revision. Older standards ceased to be applicable. Economy as an ideal involves the encouragement of inactivity. An intention to restrict progress by bowling where the batsman cannot easily score is logically supported by making the overs last as long as possible. An intention not to be dismissed in creative enterprise finds virtue in not playing a stroke at all. Cricket becomes the concern of

the head much more than of the heart. It is to be reviewed as a balance sheet, as distinct from a spiritual experience. It is prose before poetry. It is, in the immortal summary of one distinguished exponent, 'not played for fun'.

The first-class cricket of the period was essentially mundane in outlook. Its aim was to take the cash and let the credit go. Professional concerns – in the conception of the times – became paramount and, as in every other game or business where professional and amateur live together, the professional drives out the amateur in an adaptation of Gresham's Law. There has been scarcely a sign of the traditional amateur approach to cricket since 1945, not even in the universities. Several successful players, more or less unpaid by direct financial reward, have, of course, appeared, but they have accepted the business-like approach to the business of batting and bowling and general cricket strategy. They have had no option. They conformed or they were unsuccessful and therefore unrequired.

Never in the whole of cricket history has the game been undertaken more grimly. Never have so many cricketers, cricket followers, cricket administrators and cricket writers been under such a strain of nerves. Light-heartedness became a condemnation, the occasional cap-over-the windmill a crime. Commercialisation represented the keyword of the decade.

An inevitable development has been the elevation of the major occasion to the neglect of the minor. Where the product of a performance takes precedence over its intrinsic value, only the Test Match or some comparable undertaking is regarded as significant. Players come to view their day-by-day, bread-and-butter cricket with an eye on its relation to international renown and the attendant perquisites. Cricketing success has tended to grow into a means far separated from its ends. The character of the age has permeated the game, and the character of the age is an egotistical cynicism. 'I'm all right, Jack...' extends from the juvenile market-value of autographs to the literary burgeonings of sporting personalities in authorship once- or twice-removed. A century at the wicket contained a cash-value (tax-free if possible) and offered such range of exploitation that there was scope for a business manager and profit in becoming a limited company.

In such an atmosphere it would have been difficult for cricket to avoid dullness. The game was played for profit and the profit was not to be measured in pride of performance or contentment in a way of life. There can be no disputing the fall in attractiveness of first-class cricket during the period. It served as an endurance test round the boundary edge as well as in the middle. It became necessary to revise recognised rates of progress in relation to the clock. Sixty runs an hour was to be regarded as an exception approaching the fanciful instead of as an average. Even 300 runs in a full day's play became worthy of remark.

The general fall in scoring rate was a characteristic feature of the period and the responsibility for it could not be laid entirely upon the batsmen. The batsmen were products of their time and it was not, on the whole, a time of distinguished batsmanship; but attractive batting, in the sense of rapid scoring and enterprising stroke-play, was severely discouraged. It was discouraged by the type of bowling – the concentration on the in-swinger; it was discouraged by the manner of bowling – the leisurely walk-back and the time-wasting between overs; it was discouraged by the development of tactical field-placing; it was discouraged by the change in pitch-preparation. The fast, true pitch virtually disappeared from the county fields and from many Test Match grounds. The most certain way to score runs was to wait for their accumulation.

A feature of the county cricket, a feature condemned but persistent, was war of attrition for two days followed by a flourish of artificiality on the third with complete misrepresentation of the 'sporting declaration'. Match after match proceeded to a sedate first-innings decision and ended in offers of complete cricketing illogicality in which teams without any hope of winning by their show of all-round strength were invited to hit or miss for an hour or two in denigration of the whole art of the game.

To the older mind there is no sense in a declaration that gives opponents the greater or an equal chance of victory. The primary purpose in a competitive game is to establish, maintain and conclude the advantage. The purpose of declaration is to drive home an advantage already gained, declaration being necessary because of circumstances involving time or playing-conditions such as a change in the pitch or the weather. The true 'sporting declaration' merely involves acceptance of a risk in the search for a further gain from an advantage already held. There is nothing 'sporting' in asking opponents who have been steadily outplayed for two-and-a-half-days to attempt, say, 150 runs in 75 minutes for the sake of creating a hectic and totally uncharacteristic finish to a match. 'Sporting' behaviour involves generosity of outlook on a basis of self-respect and equally high respect for the others.

Some cricket writing and much cricket broadcasting have extolled the meretricious and falsified standards of judgement. All cricket and all cricketers cannot be of the heroic mould, but editorial demand is inclined to insist that they be so regarded at all times. The sickening sycophancy of uninformed journalism and dramatised broadcasting sows the seed of its own eventual destruction, but in the meantime over-praised cricketers fail to develop and over-stimulated play turns to anti-climax. The skilful salesman can sell anything once or even twice, but there is no substitute for quality in the product over a long period.

Cricket never was and never can be a game of continuous excitement or of great achievements every day. The quiet hours, the simple strivings, are as much a part of the attraction as the unforgettable moments of high drama. Cricket is a composite joy, a blending of the modest and the magical. The cricket-lover cannot sup for ever on superlatives without a diminution of appetite and a jading of palate. Cricket cannot be made first-class merely by calling it so and assuming a virtue that is absent.

True greatness in play or player is inescapable. False presentation and standards obscure the issue but cannot change it. For the greatness in the cricket of the decade following World War II there should be gratitude. For the shortcomings and pretentiousness there need be no undue sympathy or apology – only understanding. [*1959*]

EGO (ii)

County cricketers will not be wearing advertising motifs on their clothing in the coming season, but 173 members of the Cricketers' Association agreed, at their annual meeting in Birmingham, that talks should take place for a national agreement in 1978. *News item, April 1977*

J. C. Laker

Ten minutes after lunch on 27 July, 1956, the second day of the Old Trafford Test, England were out for 459.

by Alan Ross

The Australian innings, an account of which gives one the feeling of telling an absurdly tall story, began respectably enough. The light roller had been on – Johnson having learnt his lesson at Headingley – and it was an hour and a quarter before the pitch changed from waltz time to rock 'n roll. During this period McDonald and Burke, without strain, scored 43 runs. McDonald, guiding Statham's second ball into the vacant covers for four, was generally the livelier, though Statham early on all but yorked him. Statham bowled six overs, Bailey three: at nine Laker came on from the railway end, and together he and Lock bowled seventeen overs without causing a flutter. At five to four May switched them round: the effect was as the sudden access of power after the repair of a faulty connection. McDonald, pushing forward, steered Laker heedlessly to Lock at leg-slip: to his third ball, also from Laker, Harvey played back, and inside, and was bowled. Craig came in for the first time in a Test Match in England, but though Lock now made the ball fizz up off the length, he stayed with Burke until tea: the score 62 for two.

Lock's first ball of the evening spun sharply away, hit Burke on the glove and Cowdrey at slip dived on it. Laker's first ball had Craig playing back, and, beaten by both break and pace off the pitch, lbw. Mackay, as ill at ease as one playing Blind Man's Buff in a roomful of strangers, jabbed nervously at his second ball and was caught by Oakman at second slip. Miller drove Lock for a straight six: then, aiming to drive Laker, was held very close in by Oakman at short-leg, the ball skidding off the inside edge. Two good catches these, at a shortness of range that makes any catching instinctive. Benaud, with unerring accuracy, delivered his second ball from Laker to Statham back by the fence at long-on: and Statham is as safe a catch as he is deadly a throw.

Archer, making a demented, tube-station rush, was stumped by feet: Maddocks and Johnson, both playing back to off-breaks pitched well up, were convincingly bowled. In 3.4 overs since tea Laker had taken seven wickets for 8: struggling to disguise the disbelief and pleasure that chased each other across his features he led England off the field for a rest and gossip.

At twenty past five they returned. Once more Statham and Bailey did the formalities: once more McDonald cut and Burke defended, for all the world as if it were the first innings. Twenty equable runs were scored, and then at a quarter to six, Laker, soon joined by Lock, resumed the exercise of his proprietary rights. McDonald, playing handsomely, now limped off for treatment to a knee.

Harvey, as if intent on instant reparation, made rapid ground to Laker's first ball; he hit it hard and low on the volley but, alas, straight to Cowdrey who, squatting like a Buddha in an odd position at shortish wide mid-on, threw the ball delightedly up. Harvey, in a rare moment of self-expression, tossed his bat in the air like a pipe-major, acknowledging with dismay one of the quickest 'pairs' in test history.

Burke, with Craig as partner, played Lock and Laker in a manner to suggest that, if his example were followed, all was not yet lost. Of Australia's closing score of 53 for one he had made 33.

THIRD DAY

After rain, play began at ten past two and Statham, in his opening over of the afternoon, bowled from the Stretford end under recognisable sun, hit Burke twice on the legs, the first time painfully striking the instep with a full-pitch.

Lock, from the railway, began with two maidens to Craig and was then replaced by Bailey, off whom, after twenty minutes, Craig scored the first run. At twenty to three Laker took over from Statham, using three short-legs, no slip and the rest of the field fairly deep. Burke immediately made an optimistic appeal against the light, which was rejected, and in the same over played an off-break stiffly and gently into Lock's hands at leg-slip. McDonald, continuing his overnight innings, lay back and cut Laker to the cover boundary, a stroke better than almost any played by an Australian on Friday.

Rain now came bustling up very fast out of a deluding sky, and, in no time at all, the water on the wicket was as clearly defined as on the Manchester Canal and about as muddy. The ground flooded, and a sizeable crowd returned to Old Trafford railway station as quickly as it had hurried in after lunch.

FOURTH DAY

For the second day in succession there was no play worth discussing: as a result the Australian reprieve verged on full pardon.

Lock bowled two maidens, Laker one: the drenched pitch was too dispirited to offer signs of life. Craig looked correct and poised, with a cap sitting baggily over a slim frame. Twice he played Lock splendidly off his legs for four: once he snicked a quicker ball fine of slip to the sight-screen. McDonald's bat and body were not always as close together as they might have been, but he looked rather safer than houses in this howling wind. A sudden squall after forty minutes sent everyone in for an early tea: but Bailey and Statham had not long been showing that the pitch still held nothing for them when a second, heavier shower finished it. Australia were 82 for two.

FIFTH DAY

At lunch Leonard Hutton, not a foolhardy gambler, bet five shillings the match would be over by five o'clock: he lost his bet, but the premises on which he made it held good. At Old Trafford, once the drying process is properly under way, the sun takes instantaneous effect: it came out soon after one o'clock, and blazed with flapping wind from a clearing sky. An island or two of obscuring cloud, and the pitch becomes as devoid of life as a Victorian miss with the vapours. From a quarter past three until tea the sun withdrew, and again the bowlers were rendered helpless. But vital damage had been done. Finally the clouds sailed out of sight, and it was on a golden evening, with the wicket taking notice, if not exactly lively, that Laker bowled England to victory and his own way into the legends of the game. In 51 overs he took all ten wickets for 53; making nineteen wickets for 90 in the match, a feat unlikely ever to be equalled or surpassed. S. F. Barnes, on Johannesburg matting, took seventeen wickets in 1913, the record hitherto.

The previous best in Tests between England and Australia were Verity's fifteen at Lord's in 1934, and Rhodes's fifteen at Melbourne in 1903.

The measure of Laker's achievement are the figures of Lock, who bowled three more overs in the match and took one for 106. At no time was the wicket truly a sticky; from time to time it quickened up and took varying amounts of spin, but Laker rarely, more rarely even than Lock, got the ball to pop. He took his wickets by unrelenting accuracy, by varying flight, length and intention with such imaginative skill that the batsmen were first hemmed in, then driven to surrender.

After the usual tactical disagreement about the fitness of the wicket for play, Bailey began the bowling only ten minutes late. He immediately found the edge of Craig's bat, but the ball just failed to carry to Cowdrey at first-slip. It was the nearest to a chance all morning. Neither batsman had either excuse for, or interest in, runs and they were content to push the ball gently down, with time and elbow room to do so. Bailey and Laker having made no impression, Oakman and Lock bowled until twenty past twelve, when May gave Statham the new ball. Statham made only one lift uncomfortably, and it was not long before Lock and Laker were renewing their blandishments with such violent flicking of the fingers that one felt only the most drink-sodden of pitches could resist them. Lock, trying perhaps for too much, began to pitch short and McDonald cut and pulled him. The last few balls of the morning from Lock showed a rising perkiness, but it was with 28 runs added, and no wickets lost, that Australia went in to lunch.

Craig, already over four hours at the crease, scored only two more: he went back to Laker, was beaten by the turn and plainly lbw. Lock's next over to McDonald cost ten runs, including further cuts and a pull. Mackay had followed Craig, and, with seven men breathing down his neck, he stabbed a good-length ball into Oakman's stomach. Miller, having made up his mind to play every conceivable ball with his pads, floundered inelegantly, until, scooping belatedly at a yorker, he was bowled. Archer groped at his second ball, it spun off his bat, and Oakman snapped him up at short-leg, low and a bare 3 yards square of the bat. Four wickets had fallen since lunch for 18 runs: Laker, who had reverted to the Stretford end, had taken four for 3 in 9 overs. Lock, still hopelessly short, was repeatedly pulled by McDonald, so May tried Oakman from the railway, rested Laker and switched Lock to Laker's end in an effort to improve his morale. The sun being temporarily hidden, the pitch was again devitalised, and Benaud, taking guard twice an over, flattening divots with the slow ponderousness of a Shakespearian grave-digger, found as little to trouble him in the bowling as McDonald. Together, with Australia 181 for six, they made their way in to tea, having been in composed partnership for eighty long minutes.

The sun, and the interval, unsettling for them and refreshing for Laker, brushed them quickly from the scene. Laker's second ball turned very sharply, McDonald was hurried in his stroke and Oakman took the crucial catch, his fifth of the match, at short-leg. McDonald, out only eleven short of a hundred, had shown wariness and resource for five and a half hours: his feet were not always in the right place, but, unlike several more illustrious colleagues, his heart was. It was a warm persistent innings, one which, considering its context, had surprisingly few dull passages.

Laker's first two balls to Lindwall, turning enough to surprise both batsman and wicketkeeper, went for four byes each: but Lindwall stuck, growing more adhesive every over, and by five o'clock he and Benaud were once more causing apprehensive glances at wrist-watches and furtive scurryings to the bar. Benaud's was the essential wicket and it came unexpectedly: having played consistently at the pitch of the ball, he suddenly misjudged the flight, went back to almost a half-volley and was bowled.

Lindwall and Johnson offered token resistance for twenty minutes, then Lindwall edged an off-break to Lock at leg-slip. Maddocks, shuffling back as in his first innings, was at once lbw; it had by now become almost as important to the crowd that he be out to Laker, as be dismissed at all. Lock had sensibly not slackened effort at the other end.

Laker, in response to a chanting crowd, appeared on the balcony, pink and pleased, a glass of beer in his hand: so modest a drink can rarely have been as richly deserved. [*1957*]

ENGLAND 459 (P. E. Richardson 104, M. C. Cowdrey 80, Rev. D. S. Sheppard 113).

AUSTRALIA

First innings		*Second innings*	
C. C. McDonald c Lock b Laker	32	c Oakman b Laker	89
J. W. Burke c Cowdrey b Lock	22	c Lock b Laker	33
R. N. Harvey b Laker	0	c Cowdrey b Laker	0
I. D. Craig lbw, b Laker	8	lbw, b Laker	38
K. R. Miller c Oakman b Laker	6	b Laker	0
K. Mackay c Oakman b Laker	0	c Oakman b Laker	0
R. G. Archer st Evans b Laker	6	c Oakman b Laker	0
R. Benaud c Statham b Laker	0	b Laker	18
R. R. Lindwall not out	6	c Lock b Laker	8
L. Maddocks b Laker	4	lbw, b Laker	2
I. W. Johnson b Laker	0	not out	1
Extras	0	Extras B 12, lb 4	16
Total	84	Total	205

ENGLAND BOWLING

First innings	O	M	R	W	*Second innings*	O	M	R	W
Statham	6	3	6	0	Statham	16	10	15	0
Bailey	4	3	4	0	Bailey	20	8	31	0
Laker	16.4	4	37	9	Laker	51.2	23	53	10
Lock	14	3	37	1	Lock	55	30	69	0
					Oakman	8	3	21	0

Fall of wickets: *First innings* – 1–48, 2–48, 3–62, 4–62, 5–62, 6–73, 7–73, 8–78, 9–84, 10–84.

Second innings – 1–28, 2–55, 3–114, 4–124, 5–130, 6–130, 7–181, 8–198, 9–203, 10–205.

Guide to Cricket for Visiting Americans

OR
A NATIVE RETURNS TO OLD TRAFFORD

by Alistair Cooke

Yesterday (24 July, 1954) so far as I could gather, England was beating Pakistan in a game whose swift conclusion is so foregone that Monday's crowd will have to be shanghaied or coaxed in with free beer. The connoisseurs at my elbow also instructed me that Bedser beat a Test record, that Wardle hit three home runs, that the Old Trafford pitch has astonishing powers of recovery, that the Pakistanis are not so bad as they look and that the English fielding was as snappy as it ought to be for a team that is going to Australia.

I dutifully quote the experts on these obvious conclusions because none of them was obvious at all to a renegade separated by time, and the corruption of baseball, from the gentle pleasures of cricket. My own impression was one of marvelling admiration for the endurance and gallantry of English crowds, who sit for hours in a dank wind and watch thirteen anonymous men in white, and two barbers with hats on, move in stealthy slow-motion on a public lawn; who ask so little here below that when the pitcher bowls six balls, and nothing at all happens, they rise in grateful applause with all the delirium of a Liberal fête saluting the prize dahlia at a flower show. Walking behind the stands on a circular tour of the field, I would hear these little rounds of clapping, disturbing the general hush at four-minute intervals. I inquired for the cause of them. They were always for maiden overs.

There must be some irresistible property in the drug of cricket, for this ceremonial coma and the grateful murmur that occasionally breaks it is practised all around the world, in the fetid winds of Pakistan, under the Renaissance skies of Jamaica, alongside the sheep-hills of New Zealand. Anyone inclined to make fun of cricket should consider that, though Mr Eden may be having a little trouble persuading the Egyptians, the koala bear is entirely familiar with the sound of a leather ball 'climbing the air from the thick of the bat'. It all goes to support the American conviction that although an Englishman on a trade-mission may be easy to handle, the secret agent to watch out for is the cricketer who settles modestly in your own neighbourhood and stays for twenty years because, he says, he 'just happens to like it'. It reminds me of an aged Texas lady asked to recall the types who settled West Texas. 'Mostly,' she replied, 'they were men who had shot their uncle in Tennessee or jumped a mortgage in Maryland. Nice, straightforward people mostly.' Then she elbowed herself up on her death-bed. 'Course,' she said, 'there were black sheep. Ah remember a man came here, said it looked like mighty handsome country, good for cattle. Just thought it was a likely place to settle. He was a suspicious character from then on.'

The United States immigration authorities should be alerted to any incoming Englishman carrying a cricket bat. At first glance, he may seem as inoffensive as Robert Benchley's typical Englishman, whose charm 'is not that he takes his pleasures sadly but that he takes pleasure in such tiny, tiny things'. But give him ten years and a heavy roller and the natives will be drinking tea, voting for a Governor-General and applying for secession.

Thirty years and three thousand miles away from Old Trafford is long enough, and far enough, to qualify any returning native as a man from Mars. And the following account, though strictly accurate in all matters of fact, may possibly strike the cricket fan as naïve or insensitive to the finer shades. I am simply trying to help any visiting American to a deeper appreciation of the game. And then, a man whose eyeballs are burnt by the summer sun – striking him every hour on the hour from May to November at the latitude of Corfu – is not likely to figure out very expertly what is going on in the encircling gloom. Cricket has to have 'fine shades' since it is played so often in the dark.

We got to the ground just after noon and there was a long, silent queue. But the cops, and the gatemen, the committee members and the programme sellers were in a dither, arching their eyebrows and hissing some gorgeous secret behind the back of their hands. I assumed that Marilyn Monroe had arrived, suffocating in a Bikini. But what they were saying was, 'Twelve thirty!' This miracle was made possible by Harry Williams, the groundsman, who had been up all night sucking away on some new sort of pipette and transforming the wicket from a flood into a treadable bog. And sure enough as the half-hour struck a file of little men in sweaters (and red flannel underwear, I'll bet) trotted on to the field, and were followed by two men carrying long slim spades. One was a Mr Evans, a vigorous hitter, I was told. But he was walking back before I learned to distinguish him from the fielders and the barbers (they turned out to be umpires). A great peace descended for a half-hour or so, irritated only by the alarming shout of 'Shot!' from the men in the pavilion. It was a false alarm. There wasn't a gunman in sight. It is simply what you say when a man makes a line-drive. Ho-hum.

Suddenly, the ball was dropped and they all came striding back to the pavilion again. England, I was told, had 'declared'. They stayed in the pavilion long enough to eat lunch, without a ripple of protest from the spectators. Eating lunch, it seems, is part of the game's strategy. At $2.16\frac{1}{4}$ (it is essential – in American newspapers it is compulsory – to get these incidents properly timed) they all came out again. But for some unexplained reason, having to do with that 'declaration' of war, it was the English team that came out. Now the Pakistanis were at bat. There are evidently different rules for visiting teams, or maybe there is a limit to the freedom you can grant newly freed Colonials, but anyway they weren't allowed to stay half as long as the English team. They played with great correctness, trapping straight balls with the left toe perfectly pointed, swinging back to the short-pitched ones, doing everything that would guarantee a couple of comfortable centuries on the hard ground, under the hot sky, of Pakistan. But they were playing on a lake against men bred to seafaring. And the Pakistanis' obedient textbook demonstrations of how they had learned to play cricket were pathetic in view of the obvious fact that Bedser and Wardle were cradled in mud. It is no accident that the television stand is built at the top of two nautical ladders and is a sort of mizzen-mast. It was the best place (and on a wet day perhaps the only place) to watch the Pakistanis all at sea. I went up there once in the hope of sighting a submarine, but achieved no greater distinction than that of stopping the game. The television crow's nest is spotted just above the bowling screens and if you wave an arm there it distracts the batsman as a fly might perched on his eyebrow. So Mr Hanif Mohammad waved at the umpire and the umpire turned and waved at your correspondent, who hastily beat it back to the main deck.

There were only three other events that disturbed the day-long hush of the crowd. After lunch Waqar Hassan, fortified by English carbohydrates, jumped into a fine drive and while the crowd was springing awake to applaud him McConnon had clapped the ball in his hand. McConnon was on his toes again when Wazir cracked at a half-volley. Apart from these two fine catches, and a couple of routine ones also from McConnon, the fielding looked to a baseball fan as if the English team had been up all night helping Mr Williams to drain the turf.

With wickets dropping like the drizzle from Heaven, the game began to take on the appearance of a competition, but just when it was warming into life they all walked to the pavilion again. This time it was tea, even cricketers apparently feeling that if you go much longer than two hours without a meal you will just dissolve into the rain and good brown soil from which this happy breed sprang. At 2.34 a strange light broke over the field. And again at 5.26. It was reliably reported to be the sun. At 6.30, when the Pakistanis were going in and out again in an embarrassing procession, they all decided to go back – for tomato-juice cocktails, I assumed. But it was the end of play, and now they are allowed one whole day, or six meals, to recover from this exhausting minuet. Will Rogers, I am afraid, had the answer when, on his only visit to a cricket match, he was asked by the then Prince of Wales for any suggested improvements in the game. He pulled at his forelock and said: 'Well, your Highness, if I was in charge I'd line up all the players before the game began and say. "Now listen, fellers, no food till you're through."' [*1954*]

F. S. Trueman

by Frank Tyson

Physically he hardly seemed destined for athletic greatness. Indeed his sporting prowess was limited to the soccer and cricket fields and an amazing adeptness on the more restrictive, yet nonetheless demanding billiard table. He was no Greek statue, but the truncated breadth of his characteristically square fast-bowler's frame was lined with an even strength from shoulder to hip. His feet, those ploughmen of many a batsman's wicket, like those of most great athletes, turned in and imparted their bent to his pillared legs. Even the square lines of his jaw – always prematurely dark-bearded around five o'clock – bespoke a certain pugnacity and power. He was puissant in back and long in arm, just like all of the mining fast bowlers who, over the years, Yorkshire, Derbyshire and Nottinghamshire have all whistled up to the surface. His upbringing never deserted him and even in the torrid sun and climate of Australia and the West Indies he retained his inborn underground fear of sunburn. On Bondi Beach, amongst so much bronzed flesh, his pallor made me realise why Australians call Englishmen 'Pommies'.

But there was nothing incongruous about Trueman's bowling. His parabolic approach from the regions of a straightish mid-off was rhythmically smooth, and stridingly long. Only the portly advance of years curtailed the long circular swing of his classically erect left guiding arm. At the bowling wicket his action was faultless in its body-swing, his bared, sparsely-haired chest affronting the sensibilities of mid-on and his metalled right toe braking the pent-up power of his troublesome final seven-league stride until the last volcanic moment. His follow-through was the batsman's nightmare and the umpire's bane, churning up large arable areas outside the suffering left-hander's off-stump. But such was Trueman's control of the mere mechanics of bowling that he seldom permitted such trivialities as a no-ball or a request to run off the pitch to disturb his confidence. He merely adjusted his drag or ran wider on the crease. His delivery, like that of his hearty fellow-tradesman Lindwall, was perfectly suited to out-swing, a ball on which most of his effectiveness was based. By comparison to his boomeranging out-curve, his in-swinger was a puny thing – at least to everyone except Fred. Even the Australian wickets, enervating on man and ball alike, could not curb his movement to the slips.

His very first ball in Australia, in 1958, resulted in West Australian batsman Jack Rutherford being caught in the slips: a moving performance which had the succeeding batsmen probing for another five overs. In 1963, his magnificent use of the second new ball in the second innings of the Melbourne Test and his subsequent five wickets tipped the balance in England's favour; I can still remember his dismissals of Benaud and O'Neill – the flashing bat, the edge and the surprising agility of Cowdrey at first-slip. There was an amazing resilience in his bouncer – enough to send it steepling over the head of many batsmen. To the ambitious hooker it always presented a challenge – sometimes successfully met, at others, painfully suffered. Even when he bowled a standard length, Trueman elicited disproportionate bounce from the pitch; it was just as if he hit the wicket as hard as he would have liked to strike the batsman.

Outwardly at least, he assumed the mantle of greatness with complete self-assurance. He was the Cassius Clay of fast bowling and whilst he did not always state that he was the greatest, one always felt that his mastery was founded on this confidence. Other bowlers toiled when the air was swingless, the ball without shine and the wicket barren of response. But Fred knew, as if with the certainty of faith, that he was still moving, cutting off the pitch, deviating off the seam – even if the wicketkeeper himself was not aware of it. It was a graphic experience, to listen to his description of a straight ball, missed by some wretched batsman – how it swung late to the slips and came back off the wicket. It was a brand of confidence based on the knowledge that in fact he could perform these feats when conditions suited him. Allied to it was a fierce pugnacity towards all batsmen, but more particularly towards those who were unwise enough to bat in that harlequinade headgear which Fred loathingly termed a 'jazz-hat'. Cambridge and Oxford batsmen have been known to lose all heart for the game after having met Fred on these colourful terms. Only rarely did his mask of confidence and hate slip – when as at Sydney in 1958 the wicket was hopeless in pace. But even then it was but a momentary lapse. It only needed the encouragement of a wicket to bring him roaring back.

I suppose that deep down Trueman was motivated by that unreasoning, mad-cap, fast-bowling force – the earnest desire to bowl really quick. In his declining years he still considered himself just as fast as on the day in Hull in 1949 when I saw him for the first time. Then he was a raw eighteen; at the moment of delivery his head was flung back and his gaze intent upon loftier things than the stumps. Nonetheless the Army batsmen, Geoffrey Keighley, the Yorkshire captain, and his fellow-fieldsmen will tell you that he was, even at that early stage, very fast. This was a painful testimony which was to be vouchsafed by the unfortunate Indian batsmen when they met him for the first time in Tests some three short years later. In that particular rubber he collected no fewer than twenty-nine wickets.

I often wonder whether that first Test of Trueman's in 1952 was all the more important because he was representing his country or because he was performing before his very own Headingley crowd. Certainly there stood behind his whole cricketing career the ultimate pride in his status as an international player; but the very prop of his cricketing existence was his unswerving allegiance to Yorkshire and his joy in all things emanating from the County of the Broad Acres. [*1968*]

*

At Edgbaston on 9 July, 1963, England declared their second innings, setting West Indies 309 to win in 280 minutes.

*

by Denys Rowbotham

The West Indians' second innings lasted little more than two hours. They lost their last seven wickets in 55 minutes for 36 runs, Trueman taking six of them in 24 deliveries which conceded only four runs.

That was the measure of a consuming skill and fury which brought Trueman seven for 44 in the innings and match figures of twelve for 119, which statistically he has never bettered in Tests. Rarely at this level and in English conditions moreover can he have bowled better. He attacked the off-stump aggressively. He found at once and maintained a length that imperilled forward play as much as it did back. He moved the ball in the air and off the pitch. He found a lift from barely short that had eluded Hall and Griffith with old ball or new. Yet with such shrewd economy and insight did he use this lift from still shorter that from a mere handful of bumpers or near-bumpers two brought him wickets.

Trueman sounded a note of challenge with his first ball, which reared over Hunte's ducking head. Another, which jumped from barely short to the batsman's right hand, hinted more sinisterly the technical method. Shackleton could not match Trueman's pace, but he could his taxing length and power to move the ball. In one over Trueman had pointed the hazards of forward play. As if sensing Carew would play back, Shackleton pitched an in-swinger fully and had him leg before wicket. In Trueman's second over, Hunte tried to drive an outswinger and edged it; again length anticipated a back shot and Hunte was caught off the edge at second-slip. Two for 1 had become a worse ten for 2.

Thereafter that was the way of it. Butcher and Kanhai would play forward and cleave the air. They would play back as often with the same bleak result. Trueman's out-swingers played round their bat's edge like lightning. In-swing rapped their pads or moved them to last-minute stunned shots and involuntary deflections. Their judgements were bemused so repeatedly that within minutes desperation ran them headlong into foolhardiness. Butcher hooked, steered and cut, and Kanhai drove on razor edges of danger. Yet somehow both survived for half an hour and in putting on 28 not all their shots courted suicide. Then Dexter took a hand by himself resting Trueman. His second ball bowled Butcher, who played back quite horribly across his line, and even now beyond prophecy the rout had begun.

Kanhai and Sobers survived until lunch, Kanhai punishing each delivery falling from strict length as he had from the start, but that was the end of all ordered resistance. The combination of Trueman's snaking out-swing, whipping in-swing and unpredictable lift, and Shackleton's subtly varied but always nagging restrictiveness set problems, it seemed, beyond the West Indians' ebullient temperaments and judgements to master. In his first over after lunch, Shackleton dropped only just short, yet Sobers must needs slash and edge a fierce catch to first-slip, which Sharpe took brilliantly head high. Did Solomon and Kanhai threaten momentary sanity in spite of their confusion? Trueman hurled down two bumpers in succession and Kanhai mishooked the second to backward short-leg. Without need, if not provoked unease, the West Indians were 78 for five.

It required only one of Trueman's barely short out-swingers to rise so abruptly that Worrell could not get his back shot away from it and at 80 for six the West Indians were finished. Even then the speed of Trueman's destructiveness strained belief: Murray offered a feeling back shot to an out-swinger in his next over; Hall's forward and Griffith's back shot confounded to the point of caricature in the following over; and Solomon caught from an edged hook to another bumper before the end of his next. Trueman had swept the West Indians from his presence with swashbuckling contempt. Yet he had done so in conditions which he relishes by indulging the classical canons of length and direction of an academic's fanatical precision.

*

England 216 (D. B. Close 55; G. S. Sobers five for 60) and 278 for nine, declared (E. R. Dexter 57, P. J. Sharpe 85 not out, G. A. R. Lock 56) beat West Indies 186 (Trueman five for 75) and 91 (Trueman seven for 44) by 217 runs.

Watching Benaud Bowl

Leg-spinners pose problems much like love,
Requiring commitment, the taking of a chance.
Half-way deludes; the bold advance.

Right back, there's time to watch
Developments, though maybe too late.
It's not spectacular, but can conciliate.

Instinctively romantics move towards,
Preventing complexities by their embrace,
Batsman and lover embarked as overlords.

Alan Ross

Tovarich at the Test

by Kenneth Gregory

As the 1961 May Day Parade in Moscow was covered by the BBC, reciprocal arrangements might have been made for the Lord's Test.

The time is three in the afternoon, Mackay has yet to add to his one o'clock score and the England captain signals for drinks. E. W. Swanton, J. H. Fingleton, B. Johnston and P. West are interpreting the excitement to television viewers at home while the Russian commentator Y. K. Slobin initiates his countrymen into the mysteries of the game.

FINGLETON: I liked the way Mackay let that long-hop pass safely outside his off-stump. Wouldn't you agree, Brian, that Australia are definitely getting on top?

JOHNSTON: Well, it's a bit early to say. Anything can happen in cricket as you well know.

FINGLETON: True. I remember in 'thirty-eight ...

SLOBIN: English viewers are at present hearing the views of the Australian Fingleton. He is a member of his country's ruling class, his last book was introduced by Prime Minister R. Menzies, the reactionary oppressor of the Canberra Communist Party.

JOHNSTON: By Jove! that was a near thing. Mackay nearly hit that one. Let's ask Jim Swanton what he thought about it.

SWANTON: Pretty good ball. Moved a bit off the seam.

JOHNSTON: I should have thought more than a bit.

SWANTON: A good 'un. Incidentally I must tell Jack Fingleton that I've just seen in the pavilion an old friend of his, Sir Holtby Humby. Looks very fit.

FINGLETON: All Australians will be pleased to hear that. We remember Sir Holtby when he was Governor of Northern Territory.

SWANTON: Played for Harrow in 'ninety-eight.

SLOBIN: At one end of the ground there is a fortress called the pavilion. Only aristocrats are permitted to sit in it. The names of all English babies of the ruling class are written down as they are born in the pavilion book. Many of the people who sit there are princes; their leader is the Grand Duke Altham.

JOHNSTON: And Mackay has taken a quick single. Risky in the circumstances. Still, four and a half days left.

WEST: My word! Indeed! Yes!

FINGLETON: I think I can see a beard growing out of the press-box. It must be.

SLOBIN: No member of the English Communist Party is allowed in the pavilion.

SWANTON: It's Alan Ross of the *Observer.*

FINGLETON: If Mackay doesn't soon get out we shan't be able to distinguish Alan from Father Time.

SLOBIN: Nowhere in England is the mastery of the English aristocracy so perpetuated as here at Lord's field. On top of a stadium there is the figure symbolic of the depressed classes. The Lords who owned this field once seized a serf called F. Time and compelled him to cut the grass with a scythe.

JOHNSTON: The Tavern seems to be doing a good trade.

FINGLETON: Probably the press-box emptying.

SLOBIN: In England the majority press is in favour of the cult of personality. Only this morning the *Express* openly encouraged cricket player Trueman with the words 'Freddie! Slam! Wham! Whoosh!' The newspapers like *The Times, Guardian, Observer* and *Sunday Times* which are the organs of the ruling class all employ journalists carefully conditioned by the university at Oxford.

SWANTON: Our spinners are not flighting the ball as Laker did five years ago. I think Jack Fingleton would agree?

FINGLETON: Well, Jim, as one who was not unacquainted with the prewar generation of England spinners ...

SLOBIN: To enter this field one has to pass through the Grace Gates. It is noteworthy that when tribute had to be paid to the medical profession the English chose a man who did not work under their National Health Service. For daring to criticise this and other decisions of the ruling class cricket player J. Laker was recently purged.

SWANTON: Looking through my glasses I can see some very comely young ladies at the top of the open stands. We'll ask Peter West what he thinks. Peter?

WEST: My word! Indeed! Yes!

SLOBIN: The English bourgeoisie are not allowed to sit in the pavilion but use a covered stand. Their spokesmen, the plutocrats Clore and Cotton, slobber as they think of taking-over the pavilion but the Whites will defend their privileges by calling in the Brigade of Guards.

FINGLETON: I prefer the ladies' stand at Sydney.

SLOBIN: Pictured now is the English proletariat herded together in a stand where there is no protection from the snow. They are dressed much as their forefathers were when the novelist C. Dickens visited Muggleton.

FINGLETON: There's one question I should like to ask Jim Swanton – has he ever seen Colin Cowdrey wearing a Harlequin cap?

SLOBIN: Patrolling the nursery and preventing the proletariat from realising their political aspirations are members of the Secret Police. Their uniform explains why they are called White Shirts. They are Fascist beasts, the dreaded Lord's PROs.

SWANTON: I've never seen Cowdrey wearing a Harlequin cap.

SLOBIN: English cricket players are either aristocrats or members of the proletariat. The aristocrats used to wear the so-called Harlequin caps but these enraged the masses and the aristocrats now wear them only in the House of Lords.

JOHNSTON: Trueman is taking the new ball. I'll ask Jack ...

SLOBIN: The expression on the face of English bowler Trueman contrasts strongly with the happiness displayed by our glorious Soviet athletes. Trueman is a member of the proletariat, he is clearly outraged that he should be compelled to carry the cricketing bags of E. Dexter to and from Dexter's hotel. Dexter is a member of the ruling royal family.

FINGLETON: Interesting to see two short-legs. Let's ask Jim ...

SLOBIN: To play cricket at Lord's field a country must be a member of the Imperialistic Cricket Conference.

SWANTON: We haven't seen two short-legs since half-past twelve.

SLOBIN: The men and women now debauching themselves is a sure indication that capitalism is working itself out in the Tavern.

JOHNSTON: Well, look who's here! John Arlott having a rest from the old steam radio. Enjoying Mackay, John?

ARLOTT: An amiable man, Mackay, square-shouldered ...

SLOBIN: English viewers are now hearing the voice of J. Arlott who speaks to those Wessex serfs too poor and exploited to own a television. Arlott was once a member of the State Police until he started writing bourgeois poetry.

SWANTON: That was mighty close to a catch at the wicket.

WEST: My word! Indeed! Yes!

SLOBIN: The first full description of a cricket match was written in 1706. That was exactly five years after Peter the Great introduced the game to England ... [*1961*]

Captaincy and F. M. Worrell

by C. L. R. James

A Test cricketer, above all a captain, is not an automaton, not an abstraction, not a kind of computer who responds to happenings with instruction. He is a man of like passions like ourselves. And Worrell, captain of the West Indies, had one passion – not to lift Test cricket to what it was. That was an effect, not a cause. Worrell's passion was to prove that West Indian Test cricketers could be as good as other Test players. To put it negatively, nothing was inherently wrong with us. When he was appointed captain of the team to Australia in 1960–61, he knew what he had to do and he knew how it had to be done. Those of us who fought the campaign to make him captain had a feeling that he *ought* to be the captain. In addition we felt that with him the team would do better, and *in time* find itself. More than that we did not expect. Strictly speaking, that campaign for Worrell as captain was a moral issue. But beside Worrell himself there was one notable exception.

For the West Indies cricketers, as cricketers, at least one man had complete belief in them, technically and spiritually. That was Learie Constantine. For nearly forty years Constantine had bombarded my scepticism with his conviction. After 1923 and particularly after the West Indian trip to Australia 1931–32, Constantine insisted to me, like a fanatic, that the West Indies team was as good as any other team, could play with any other team and win. 'They are no better than we,' was his belligerent statement, belligerent I believe because I could not be convinced and he respected my judgement and my opinions.

They are no better than we, he used to say: we can bat and bowl and field as well as any of them. To my – as I thought – devastating query, 'Why do we always lose and make such a poor show?' he would reply: 'We need a black man as captain.' I was stupid enough to believe that he was dealing with the question of race. I should have known that it was not so, because he used to speak with the utmost respect and admiration of H. B. G. Austin as a captain. He also had an immense respect and admiration for C. G. Macartney. What he used to tell me was that the West Indian players were not a team and to become a team they needed a captain who had the respect of the players and was able to get the best out of the team. Not too far from his argument was the sentiment that a good captain would respect all the men.

The captain does not only depend on fine players. He makes the best of them and he makes players who are high class players into men who play above themselves.

That explains Worrell's captaincy on the field. It wasn't merely knowledge; it was a conviction that guided everything that he did. At Leeds in 1957 he bowled fast-medium for many hours, taking seven wickets in 38.2 overs. It was suggested to him that someone else should open the batting. He refused; the duty of an opener was to open. He obviously was not himself and was soon out. It is quite probable his judgement was wrong.

The fact remains that that was the kind of thing for which he was known among the members of his side. He had been invited to go to India as captain after the 1957 tour. He was studying at Manchester University and could not go. When the MCC visited the West Indies in 1959–60, Worrell had been away from the first-class game for two years. However, he felt it his duty to go to the West Indies and play and found himself in the First Test at Barbados, short of any kind of first-class practice. However, he played himself into some sort of form in the Test, making 197 not out and helping the West Indies to reply to England's 482 with 563 for eight.

These qualities were a solid foundation to any captaincy, strategic insight into the capabilities of individual men and the capacity to get the best out of them, not only in general but for a particular situation. Added to this was the sentiment that Frank not only was prepared to do everything. He knew everything, at least everything that could be known. He had been a slow bowler and he had made himself into a fast-medium bowler. He had been a tremendous stroke player and now during the MCC tour had shown himself able to defend for hours. As a captain he was already legendary. On a Commonwealth tour to India the captain had fallen ill, Frank had taken over and had convinced everyone that here was a born captain. Furthermore, it was not merely the judgements of people in authority that had made him captain. He had been appointed captain of the team to Australia by what could be called a popular campaign and a popular vote.

As a result of his previous training (as a member of the black West Indian middle class of Barbados) Frank had certain other qualities which expressed themselves in his captaincy. For one thing he was always calm and unruffled even in times of crisis. I am told that that is very obvious in the photograph of the last run-out in the famous tied Test in Australia. His team remember also at a very critical moment at the Lord's Test in 1963, that when Hall began his last over eight runs were needed by England to win the match. Off the second ball, and the third, came sharp singles but the batsmen attempted another run when the ball was played to Frank at short-leg. First-class players are of the opinion that it was an open question whether a fieldsman under those circumstances would throw at the wicket or not. Frank did not throw. He ran to the wicket with the ball, determined to beat the batsman to the bowler's end and not to risk missing the wicket by a throw. Others might have thrown. His fellow-players thought it natural of their captain not to take the chance.

He was noted for the care that he always paid to apparently small, but in essence highly significant, events or episodes. Take the situation at Brisbane when the scores were tied and the last Australian batsmen were at the wicket. Hall had two more balls to finish the over, and Frank from mid-on walked over to him. What he said is worth noting as being symbolical of his methods as captain: 'Remember, Wes, if you bowl a no-ball, you'll never be able to go back to Barbados.' Hall reports that this so terrified him that he made sure to put his foot a good yard behind the crease. Kline, the batsman, turned the ball to square-leg and Solomon made his throw which tied the match. The team as a whole laughed at the particular kind of warning which Hall had been given by his captain – only to discover afterwards that Frank had calculated carefully what he should say. If he had told Hall seriously to be careful not to bowl a no-ball, Hall might have bowled one. But he put it with humour as a passing but necessary consideration and it had the effect required.

When Frank was appointed captain of the team to Australia he knew what Constantine always used to insist upon, that technically they were a body of fine individual players. What he had to do was to build a team. In discussing the tour in Australia, which I did very often with him, I was amazed to find that his main judgement of an individual player was whether he was a good team-man or not. It seemed that he worked on the principle that if a man was a good team-man it brought the best out of him as an individual player.

Frank led the West Indians in a type of cricket which he knew they could play, which was the only game they could effectively play. This approach to Test cricket, dead for a generation, was met halfway by Benaud and the result was the finest series of Tests that had been known during the century.

*

After the final Test of the 1960–61 series there was speech-making.

*

Sir Donald Bradman was remarkably reminiscent of a chairman at a party celebration meeting. Only in the intervals of the return to habitual self while he was being applauded did you catch a glimpse of the relentless scorer of centuries and the watchful, tireless captain. Benaud was fluent, with carefully chosen phrases, full of affection and respect for Frank Worrell and the West Indians (and not forgetting his own team); definitely a man of feeling, not ashamed or wary of it, but a man seeing the whole of his world and steadily. But Frank Worrell, speaking last, was crowned with the olive. Beauty is indeed in the eye of the beholder. I saw all the West Indian ease, humour and easy adaptation to environment. It was after our conversations and I could see his precise and uncompromising evaluations, those it seems are now second nature. But they were draped with that diplomatic graciousness which has apparently so impressed the Australian Prime Minister. If I say he won the prize it is because the crowd gave it to him. They laughed and cheered him continuously. He expanded my conception of West Indian personality. Nor was I alone. I caught a glimpse of what brought a quarter of a million inhabitants of Melbourne into the streets to tell the West Indian cricketers good-bye, a gesture spontaneous and in cricket without precedent, one people speaking to another. Clearing their way with bat and ball, West Indians at that moment had made a public entry into the comity of nations. Thomas Arnold, Thomas Hughes and the Old Master himself would have recognised Frank Worrell as their boy. [*1963*]

PHILOSOPHER

I had always laughed when playing cricket, except when slip fielders showed signs of lumbago, and I saw no reason to stop laughing when I wrote about it. *R. C. Robertson-Glasgow*

Final Overs at Brisbane

With half an hour left for play on 14 December, 1960, Australia – at 206 for six – needed 27 runs to beat West Indies in the First Test. The two batsmen at the crease, A. K. Davidson with 73 and R. Benaud with 42, had come together at 92 after the dismissal of C. C. McDonald, R. B. Simpson, R. N. Harvey, N. C. O'Neill, L. Favell and K. D. Mackay.

*

by Jack Fingleton

Divine Providence, with Doctor Grace the chairman of the advisory committee, must have ordained and controlled the tumultuous final minutes of this Test. No earthly mind could have conceived such a finish. Had it been presented in fiction publishers would have told the author to take it away; it was beyond the bounds of human credibility.

Everybody now knew that Hall alone could win this match for the West Indies but it was a desperate chance. Benaud viciously cut his first ball for a single. Davidson flashed at the next and missed and one wondered what were the thoughts in the dressing-room of Grout, next man in. Or, for that matter, the thoughts of the remaining Australian batsmen. Then came a no-ball from which the Australians took a single. Then Benaud skied one to the leg-side that fell only inches away from the grabbing hands of Hunte. That yielded another run so that 24 were wanted in twenty-five minutes.

Hall's long, slow trudge back to his mark, thirty-four paces away, gave everybody a chance to gain their breath. It intensified, too, the drama on this sunny, Brisbane late afternoon. Hall came down with a bouncer and Davidson, in peerless fashion and without a thought of physical hurt, moved inside it and hooked it thrillingly high to leg for four. Twenty runs to go. Next ball Davidson pushed, and off the Australians scampered for a ridiculously short run. Hall charged in but couldn't pick the ball up for the run-out. He stood there, arms on hips, despondent. Worrell patted him comfortingly on the stomach and, as I learnt afterwards, said to him, 'No more bouncers, Wes, no more bouncers.'

There was a frightful mix-up in that same over. Benaud pushed one to point and started for a run. Davidson shouted 'No' and then, strangely, began to run to Benaud's other end. Valentine, in the muddle, sent the ball to Benaud's end with Davidson almost there, too. Davidson began his long, hopeless run back but Alexander, taking Valentine's return, sprawled and for the life of him couldn't get the ball back to Hall in time. Davidson scrambled home, a fortunate escape. The West Indians looked most depressed. The ground rocked with excitement.

Hall takes a very long time to bowl an over. There were loud shouts from the outer of 'Get a move on – get a move on.' The umpires removed small boys from the top of the pickets and Sobers took the new ball at the other end at twenty-one minutes to six, Australia needing 19 to win.

A leg-bye came from Sobers's first ball. Benaud got a single next ball. Davidson played a drive that finished a cut, got a single, and 16 were needed in nineteen minutes. It was as good as over, surely, and particularly when Benaud played a scorching on-drive off Sobers that left Ramadhin bereft at deepish mid-on. A no-ball and now 11 were needed to win. Benaud took a sharp single that gave him his fifty in 124 minutes, with 6 fours, and at a quarter to six Australia needed 10, only 10, in fifteen minutes.

Hall came again. Benaud pushed at one, dangerously, and missed. A rearing bouncer (Hall ignoring Worrell's instructions!) nearly took Benaud's nose with it. Then Benaud just managed to keep out a lovely, swinging yorker, and they ran a quick single to Worrell, mid-wicket. Hall was making a last-ditch fight but it seemed hopeless. That over ended, at ten to six Australia needed 9 runs.

Davidson had come to bat at 2.19 pm; Benaud at 3.21 pm. Every single minute for them both had been heavy with responsibility and endeavour.

Two quick singles were taken from Sobers but then came disaster for the Australians. Benaud pushed one wide of square-leg, a very short run. Davidson came on but the little Solomon, picking up and throwing with the one action, hit the stumps over from the acute angle and Davidson was out. His innings was a masterpiece in temperament and skill, rigidly defensive for a long time and then inordinately brilliant. He had batted 194 minutes for his highest score in Test cricket, 80, and he had hit 8 fours.

The West Indies chivalrously clapped the gallant Australian all the way to the pavilion. Few greater Test innings, considering the mounting tension, have been played in Australia, and all this came upon

Davidson's tremendous success with the ball and his distinguished first innings. Eleven wickets and 126 runs!

Now, as if we had not had sufficient in this day to make it already memorable, purple drama mounted upon purple drama. Grout met Davidson halfway in. No minutes would be lost so far as Grout was concerned. Australia needed 7 runs to win in six minutes. There would be one more over, if necessary, after this one by Sobers, which had four balls to go.

Grout had the strike and scurried for a quick single from the seventh ball. This surely, was an error as it left Grout at the other end to face Hall's last over. That was if Benaud did not get a single from the last ball of Sobers's over. Six to win, nine balls to go. Sobers one ball left.

This ball was in itself to provide a supreme battle of wits. Quite obviously, Benaud meant to get a single and get down to the other end to face Hall. Quite obviously, the West Indians intended that he would remain where he was and Grout would be the sacrificial victim for Hall. Sobers put the last ball down on a perfect length with every tissue of strength he had in his left arm. Benaud tried desperately but he couldn't get it away. I counted some six converging West Indians who were almost in Benaud's pocket before he had finished his stroke. No stolen single from this important ball! Grout must face Hall at all costs.

And so Hall came to bowl the last over of the day to Grout at four minutes to six, Australia needing six to win, three wickets in hand.

I will never forget the sight of Hall, a magnificent specimen of a man, as he came back slowly to his mark to begin this last death-or-glory over. He wears a cross on a chain around his neck and I could see him fingering the cross as he walked. I could imagine him saying a prayer: 'Please, Lord, I'll do my best – you know I always do – but what I want is a miracle. And yet not one miracle but two or three. Please, Lord!'

The shadows were lengthening quickly across the ground. Hall poised on his mark, taking huge gulps of air into his lungs for the final fling. He got his balance and then he was away, legs and arms flaying, surely a terrifying sight to Grout at the other end. It was a ball of length and pace and it got up to hit Grout in the groin. Under ordinary circumstances, Grout would have fallen prone but as he was in the process of doubling-up he saw Benaud charging down at him. Benaud didn't call. To do so would have alerted the West Indians – and so, with the ball in the very block-hole and under the noses of some three fieldsmen, Benaud stole what should have been not half a run.

Five runs to win, seven balls to go!

Slowly, back trudged Hall, bitter, no doubt, that Grout had been spirited away from him – but now came a miracle. Contrary to Worrell's orders, Hall bowled another bouncer. It tempted Benaud's bat up with it as it rose high, there was a touch of bat or glove, Alexander had the ball in both hands, screaming his appeal in concert with his fellows, and Benaud was out. Hall had given that ball everything he had. Benaud played an unforgettable innings for 136 minutes, 6 fours.

Five runs now to win, six balls to go, two minutes to six but the clock now of no account because an over started must be finished.

Meckiff, walking in slowly as if to make sure his arms and legs all stayed with him, got the first ball in the middle of the bat. No run. Now came a flash of genius on Grout's part. Hall's next ball went wide down the leg-side to wicketkeeper Alexander and Grout began to run and call as he saw the ball going through to Alexander.

Like a startled hare, Meckiff took off, helter-skelter, for the other end. Hall had followed down the pitch in his run and Alexander threw to him. Hall gathered, wheeled, threw at his own end, missed (Meckiff would have been out otherwise), some West Indian hurled himself at the ball to save overthrows and Australia had gained another golden run in perhaps the strangest manner seen on a Test field. A run to the wicketkeeper! The inspired Grout had comfortably made good his ground.

Four runs now needed to win, four balls to go.

The whole ground, already delirious, went completely crazy over the next ball. Grout went for a big hit to win the match, but mistimed his stroke and the ball spooned up high to the leg-side, about midwicket. At least four West Indians could have taken the catch. Kanhai – one could imagine his teeth clenching in concentration – positioned himself perfectly right underneath the ball. This, one could almost hear him saying, was one catch he would never miss. But, alas, as Kanhai waited, the frenzied Hall charged in, jumped over Kanhai's head, and muffed the catch!

Horror of horrors! The crowd just simply roared. The West Indians stood around, stunned and dumbfounded.

One run came to Australia from the tragedy and so Australia needed now three runs to win with three balls to go.

Hall trudged back in despair and disgrace. In the tense and anguished hush I could hear the evening Angelus tolling from the nearby hill. I could imagine Hall hearing a chiding voice in his ear, much as Don Camillo did: 'You asked for ordinary miracles, you know. Not stupid ones.'

Again Hall got back to his mark and took in big gulps of air. Meckiff was now at the receiving end. Hall glared at him and the message obviously got through to Meckiff – 'Look out for this one. It will have everything I can give it.'

Down came Hall. Meckiff stood impassive and then he swung – trusting his all to good fortune – and he connected. The ball flew high, wide and handsome to the square-leg outfield where no man stood. A four, of a certainty! A win to Australia! So shouted the crowd; so said the announcer over the radio to hundreds of thousands of listeners; so screamed all the Press in the maddest scene ever seen in a Press-box.

But the little things are sometimes the important ones. Because of some oversight, the grass in the outfield had not been cut and a ball that looked all-over a boundary lost pace and was picked up on the verge of the boundary by Hunte, who had chased it as if in the Olympic 100 metres.

So, too, had the Australians sprinted furiously between the wickets. Up for one, down for two, a turn for three and the winning run as Hunte turned and threw.

Never, in all cricketing time, was there a better throw from the boundary. From some 90 yards away, the ball flew low and unerringly straight to Alexander. A fraction either side of the wicketkeeper and he could have done nothing about his objective. But it came to his hands and he took it perfectly and he threw himself at the stumps as Grout dived at the line like a winger in an international rugby match at Twickenham. A roar of appeal and Grout was out. The umpire's finger was up.

Grout rose from the ground, dishevelled, covered in dust, and slowly walked away.

Had the third run succeeded, Australia would have won. The two from the stroke made the scores level – 737 runs all.

And now two balls to go and one run to win.

As all felt who were watching, I had the strange feeling that what had taken place wasn't real. I couldn't believe my eyes. It was, I told myself, an incredible dream that would suddenly end with me crashing on the floor.

But now came the perfect climax to this mad, surging day. Kline got Hall's first ball to him away to leg and both batsmen charged off. From 12 yards away, completely side-on so that only one stump showed to him, Joe Solomon swooped one-handed and threw as he picked up – and the one stump visible to him went over! Up went the umpire's finger.

This was the miracle superb. Solomon couldn't pause to take aim. Had he taken his eye off the ball coming to him, he would have misfielded – and, fielding, he had to throw at the stump by instinct. Haste was the essence of his movement. Nobody was quite there to take the throw. Had somebody been there, the delay in taking it and putting it on the stumps might have enabled Meckiff to get home. The throw had to hit the stump. Had it missed, Australia had got the winning run.

And so it ended – a tie, one ball left to bowl after 3,142 balls had been bowled and 1,474 runs scored. A tie had never happened before in the whole history of Test Matches.

Everybody in the Press-box stood and roared and clapped at once. Worrell, shoulders drooped in near-exhaustion, was smacked on the back by his fellows and, very quickly, by the invading, cheering and acclaiming crowd. Benaud, with his flair for the proper gesture, walked on to the field, draped an arm around Worrell's shoulder and escorted him off. The crowd stood in front of the dressing-room, cheering and calling for the players to show themselves. They waited there until the ground was closed. Ninety minutes later, Hall was still singing calypsos in the dressing-room.

WEST INDIES *First innings* 453 (G. S. Sobers 132, F. M. Worrell 65, J. S. Solomon 65, F. C. M. Alexander 60, W. W. Hall 50; A. K. Davidson five for 135)
AUSTRALIA *First innings* 505 (C. C. McDonald 57, R. B. Simpson 92, N. C. O'Neill 181; Hall four for 140)
WEST INDIES *Second innings* 284 (R. B. Kanhai, 54, Worrell 65; Davidson six for 87)
AUSTRALIA *Second innings* 232 (Davidson 80, R. Benaud 52; Hall five for 63)

MATCH TIED

G. S. Sobers

THE BATSMAN

by Sir Donald Bradman

With his long grip of the bat, his high back-lift and free swing, I think, by and large, Gary Sobers consistently hits the ball harder than anyone I can remember. This helps to make him such an exciting player to watch because the emphasis is on power and aggression rather than technique – the latter being the servant, not the master. The uncoiling of those strong, steely wrists, as he flicks the ball wide of mid-on, is a real joy to watch because it is unique and superbly controlled, whilst the full-blooded square-cut is tremendous.

by Trevor Bailey

How did Gary strike a cricket ball so hard? What was his secret? First, he is tall and well built, with strong wrists, arms and shoulders. Second, his back-lift is both high and straight with a full follow-through. Although one can hit a ball very hard with a short back-lift the higher it is the greater the momentum of the bat at moment of impact. Finally, and most important, is Gary's timing: combined with his lovely full swing, build and natural strength, this enabled him to hit out with a destructive force very few have been able to equal. Incidentally, his carry at golf – over 300 yards – is longer than that of many professionals.

Gary's batting philosophy is refreshingly straightforward. He considers himself, with every justification, an entertainer, and says quite simply: 'We have got to give the spectator entertainment when we are batting.' This does not mean he despises defence. He knows he has to keep out the good balls, or he cannot score with the consistency required. Therefore his defensive technique is excellent. From his long stay in England Gary has learned to adapt to all types of conditions. However, he has always been an attacking player by nature, seeking to wrest the initiative from the bowler, and is convinced the bat is primarily an offensive rather than a defensive weapon.

At a very early age he realised that bowlers tend to be less effective and menacing if runs are being taken off them and they are seldom beating the bat. What I always found frustrating was when my good ball was despatched to the boundary by means of a true stroke. I considered the four that resulted from a long-hop or half-volley was my fault and was never worried if a perfect delivery was 'hoicked' for four, hoping the batsman would try to take another chance and thus increase the odds of my obtaining his wicket.

The man to fear was the one who scored off a ball of immaculate length without chancing his arm. This was downright disheartening, and was something Gary was able to do more frequently than most. I asked him if he preferred any particular style of bowling; whether he was happier against pace than spin – because most batsmen, even the greatest, are more suspect against one type than another. For instance, Sir Len Hutton was more likely to lose his wicket to an in-swinger or an off-break than to a ball leaving the bat; while the reverse applied to Denis Compton. Arthur Morris was wont to have some problems against Alec Bedser's late away swing, and most of the present England side have looked distinctly uncomfortable against real pace.

However, as far as Gary was concerned, once he had established himself at the crease for about twenty minutes he did not mind what was bowled at him – pace, swing, seam, spin. He felt capable of dominating them all, and did. He had no physical fear of fast bowling, being so sure of himself that, like Compton before him, he never bothered with a thigh-pad, even against bowlers of the speed of Wes Hall and Dennis Lillee. He argued that he had a bat and that was more than enough protection. Throughout his long first-class career he was hit badly only once, by an unexceptional English fast-medium bowler, when a ball lifted sharply off a length.

Like most West Indian cricketers, Gary was very strong off his legs. He is frankly perplexed when English players deliberately take a ball on their thigh-pad rather than using their bat. This may have stemmed from his early days when a hard ball was used and there were no pads.

Gary tended to relish the bouncer, aiming to hit it flat and down just behind square if it was travelling through at the right height. He occasionally lost his wicket by mis-hooking, but over the years it brought him a great many runs. The speed merchants soon became aware that he was not frightened by short fast-pitched deliveries, and that he was inclined to regard them as a welcome invitation to easy runs. Fred Trueman found that bumpers against Gary on a good wicket were an expensive luxury, and seldom bowled them at him, much to Gary's regret.

His method of negotiating the bouncer was simple. If hookable, he used the hook off the back foot; if they were too high he watched them sail by; if they had not risen sufficiently he fended them down off his body with his bat. He always had sufficient time and his footwork was invariably quick and correct. He never ducked, first because it meant taking his eyes off the ball, second because it was never necessary. Wes Hall claims triumphantly that he once forced Gary to duck in Australia – both were representing State teams. Gary says this was an act of courtesy to a great fast bowler, rather than a necessity. I am not going to argue with either version.

Spinners, like all bowlers, usually found bowling against Gary a testing and unrewarding task. Once settled, he refused to let them pin him down and was ever eager and willing to use his feet against them. The wrist spinner probably had more chance than the finger spinner because Gary sometimes failed to pick the googly early on. He recalls that Subhash Gupte troubled him in this way in the West Indies and rates the little Indian leg-spinner as the best he encountered, with Australia's Richie Benaud the most accurate. He also experienced difficulty in reading George Tribe. Like myself, he found picking the googly of the left-hander usually harder than that of the right-hander. Neither of us can understand why. It could be that they are an even rarer breed, but this solution does not really answer the problem.

There was no real flaw in Gary's batting or technique. He was equally at home against all kinds of bowling and was equally happy playing both his attacking and defensive shots off either the front or the back foot. The ideal strategy against him before he was set was to pitch a ball of full length on his off-stump and make it hold its own. This should be immediately followed by one of exactly the same line and length, but which then left him fractionally in the air, or, better still, off the wicket. The outcome might well be either a catch behind, or in the slips. If the chance was unaccepted, however, the bowler was liable to regret the lost opportunity for a very long time, as Gary is not the type of batsman who makes many errors.

Although in general it pays to move into line, Gary believes that there are many occasions when it is better to give oneself room to play attacking strokes. This is especially true against quick bowling, when there is little time. As a result he would often force quick bowling without his left foot being in a textbook position. Although the bat might be some way from his body, he could still play through the line with a full, straight swing. This meant there was a risk of his being snapped up behind, if the ball happened to move away, but it also provided him with many spectacular boundaries which delighted spectators and worried the unfortunate bowler.

Gary, when driving off his front foot, would also on occasion deliberately give himself a little extra room by keeping his right leg outside the line, especially when aiming to send the ball square.

I remember bowling to him in a Test during the West Indies tour of England in 1957. He was still in the apprentice stage, and I was certain I had found the 'gate' with a delivery pitching off-stump and coming back really sharply. Just when it seemed the ball was through Gary adjusted so that he not only kept it out of his stumps, but did it with the middle of his bat. [*1976*]

Batting at Bath in 1963 for the West Indies against Somerset, Sobers scored 112 in two hours. One delivery from the fast-medium K. E. Palmer pitched on his middle-and-leg stumps before moving sharply outside his legs; Sobers swung round and drove the ball with a straight bat to fine long-leg. The late W. T. Greswell, then Somerset President, blinked: 'I bowled at Trumper and Woolley, but I've never seen anything like that.'

THE BOWLER

by C. L. R. James

It is the business of a fast bowler opening the innings, to dismiss for small scores two or three of the first-line batsmen on the opposing side. If he does this and does it dramatically, then good captaincy will keep him in trim to make short work of the last two or three on the side, so ending with five or six wickets.

In 1964, his last session for South Australia, Sobers, against Western Australia, bowled batsman No. 1 for 12, and had batsman No. 2 caught by wicketkeeper Jarman for 2. Against Queensland Jarman caught No. 2 off Sobers for 5, and Sobers bowled No. 3 for 1. Against the history-making New South Wales side, Sobers had Thomas, No. 1, caught by Lill for 0. He had No. 2, Simpson, caught by Jarman for 0. He then had Booth, No. 4, caught by Jarman for 0. He thus had the first three Australian Test players for 0 each. In the second innings he bowled Thomas for 3.

South Australia's last match was against the strong Victoria side. Sobers had Lawry, No. 1, caught by Jarman for 4; Potter, No. 3, caught by Lill for 0; Stackpole, No. 5, caught by Lill for 5. In the second innings Redpath, No. 2, was caught by Jarman for 0; Cowper, No. 4, was caught by Hearne for 0; Lawry, No. 1, was caught by Jarman off Sobers for 22. (Let us note in passing that in this match against Victoria, Sobers scored 124 and had also scored 124 in the game against New South Wales, the same in which he dismissed the three Test batsmen each for 0.)

It is impossible to find within recent years another fast bowler who in big cricket so regularly dismissed for little or 0 the opening batsmen on the other side.

His action as a pace bowler is the most orthodox that I know. It is not the classical perfection, above all the ease, of E. A. Macdonald. Sobers gathers himself together and is obviously sparing no effort (a rare thing with his cricket) to put his whole body into the delivery. The result is that the ball leaves the ground at a pace quite inconsistent with what is a fast-medium run-up and delivery. It would be worthwhile to get the pace of his delivery mechanically timed at different stages, as well as the testimony of observant batsmen and observant wicketkeepers.

THE CAPTAIN

We had talked about the future captaincy of the West Indies. Worrell was as usual cautious and non-committal: yes, so-and-so was a good man and capable; and so on. Then when that stage of the conversation was practically at an end, he suddenly threw in:

'I know that in Australia whenever I had to leave the field, I was glad when I was able to leave Sobers in charge.' The timing, the style of the remark was so pointed that I felt I could push the unlocked door right open.

'He knows *everything*?' I asked.

'Everything,' Worrell replied. For me that settled one aspect of the question. The other I would be able to see only on the field. I saw it at Sabina Park at the first Test against Australia in 1965. Sobers was completely master of the situation from the moment he stepped on to the field, most probably before. He was aware of everything and at no time aware of himself. He was more in command of his situation than the far more experienced Simpson, though he did not have to face the onslaught that Simpson had to face, a problem not only collective but personal. Hall at one end and Griffith on the other. To see in the course of one day Sobers despatch the ball to all parts of the field with his bat, then open the bowling, fielding at slip to Hall or Griffith, change to Gibbs and place himself at short-leg, then go on to bowl slows, meanwhile placing his men and changing them with certainty and ease, this is one of the sights of the modern cricket field. I cannot visualise anything in the past that corresponds to it...

I believe Garfield Sobers has it in him, has already done enough to become the most famous, the most widely known cricketer of the century and of any century barring of course the Telstar of all cricket, W. G. This is not so much a quality of Sobers himself, though without his special qualities he could not fill the position. It is rather the age we live in, its material characteristics and its social temper. [*1969*]

R. G. Pollock

TRENT BRIDGE, 5 AUGUST, 1965

by E. W. Swanton

An innings was played here today by Graeme Pollock which in point of style and power, of ease and beauty of execution, is fit to rank with anything in the annals of the game.

Pollock came in when after fifty anxious minutes South Africa's score stood at 16 for two. Between this point and lunch he batted easily and without inhibition or restraint while two more wickets fell, and his companions struggled in every sort of difficulty against some very good swing bowling by Cartwright.

When the afternoon began the scoreboard showed 76 for four, Pollock 34. An hour and 10 minutes later it said 178 for six, and Pollock was walking back with 125 to his name, and the crowd standing in salute to a glorious piece of batting which must have carried the minds of the older ones among them to Stan McCabe's great innings here against England in 1938.

In cold fact this young man of 21 had made the 125 out of 162 in two hours and 20 minutes, and in the 70 minutes since lunch 91 out of 102. In his whole innings were 21 fours, and the two of these that came off the edge from Cartwright's bowling were the only false strokes of any kind that I saw.

The other 19 were either hit with a full, easy swing of the bat, or glanced or cut to every point of the compass. No one could find any way of containing him because (like E. R. Dexter, G. Sobers and R. Kanhai, perhaps alone among modern players) he uses every stroke.

He saw the ball so early that if it were of good length or more he met it with an almost leisurely movement, and drove off the front foot with a freedom and certainty that left the field standing.

When the length faltered, as it did of course under such assault, he lay back and clipped the short stuff with a crack that must almost have echoed the other side of the river.

It may perhaps be said by anyone trying to evaluate this innings that to have deserved the label of greatness it would have needed to be confronted by bowling of a higher quality than much that was seen. Well, when South Africa were at their worst pass, at 43 for four, with Bland just gone, he made three strokes to the cover boundary inside a few minutes, two off Cartwright and one off Titmus, and all three from balls that would have looked a good length to anyone else, with a precision of timing and consequent speed over the field that had everyone gasping.

With these strokes the moral balance shifted dramatically and South Africa must have begun to see the vision of recovery so long as their young hero could stay. It may be that after lunch as his assault reached its climax the bowling began to look somewhat ragged. The fact is, though, that until Pollock got into his stride almost anyone on the ground would have estimated South Africa's probable total at around 120, and there would have been a great many words spilt about the difficulty of getting modern bowling away, the impossibility, indeed, in conditions which allowed the ball to move as much as it did today.

Pollock has been spoken of in the same breath as Frank Woolley, and so far as the multitude of admirers of that great man are concerned such words are close to blasphemy.

There is no one who holds Woolley in greater esteem than myself, and I believe that he would have been proud, at his best, to have played as well as Pollock did this afternoon. Indeed, in the left-handedness, in the height and reach, and in the clean-cut simplicity of his striking of the ball, the comparison with Woolley is the obvious one that applies. And if any young cricketer asks how the very best of the pre-war players batted he could be safely told: 'Just like Graeme Pollock did against England at Trent Bridge.'

*

South Africa won this match by 94 runs.

South Africa 269 (R. G. Pollock 125; T. W. Cartwright six for 94) and 289 (E. J. Barlow 76, R. G. Pollock 59, A. Bacher 67; J. D. F. Larter five for 68); England 240 (M. C. Cowdrey 105; P. M. Pollock five for 53) and 224 (P. H. Parfitt 86; P. M. Pollock five for 34).

B. A. Richards

by Henry Blofeld

Barry Richards is undoubtedly the supreme batsman of his generation and arguably he is the best the game of cricket has ever known. It is inconceivable that any other batsman of any period could have reduced the art of batting to such absurdly simple dimensions. He has played countless strokes which have left bowlers and spectators alike gasping with astonishment at their beauty, their authority and their elegance of style and yet while these are all characteristics of genius in batsmanship the great impression, for me at any rate, is of an overwhelming sense of simplicity.

I wonder if any batsman has given bowlers an inferiority complex quicker than Richards. He bats through the opening few overs of a match as though he has been at the crease for two hours and then when he has scored twenty or thirty he gives the impression that he is already finding the game too easy. He begins to amuse himself by attempting the most outrageously improper strokes as if to relieve the monotony of batting. An off-break is cut delicately away from in line with the leg-stump, a half-volley on the leg-stump is somehow driven beautifully past cover and then a good-length ball which seems destined for a defensive stroke to extra-cover is despatched with an unhurried twirl of the wrists preceded by precise, unfussy footwork, into the gap between mid-wicket and square-leg.

There is never an ungainly movement or an appearance of anything but complete and absolute control. There can surely be no more fortunate people in the cricket world than the members and spectators of Hampshire for they know each April that during the summer months they are going to have the chance of seeing Richards play, say, thirty innings a year. Even when he is out to the first ball of the match it is a memorable experience for then it leaves an emptiness and a sadness which I am sure no other player is capable of producing.

There can be no doubt whatever about Barry Richards the batsman and yet Barry Richards the man is an enigmatic figure. He plays cricket as he talks about it, with a rather puzzled detachment, almost with the appearance of boredom. For a man who is capable of batting so beautifully and arousing such strong emotions in those watching him, he seems himself to be devoid of all emotion. However brilliant the stroke he just played, his face never flickers. When he acknowledges the applause for a hundred, he is doing it because it is the accepted thing to do in the circumstances and not because there is any sense of communication between the spectators and himself. When he is out he walks back to the pavilion in identical fashion whether he has scored a hundred or nought. Head down, the strolling walk, chewing rhythmically almost absent-mindedly, bat and glove in one hand and not even a faintly irritated tap of the bat on the ground at the time of dismissal, he climbs the pavilion steps maybe doffing his cap and retires from view leaving behind him an unreal sense of inconsequentiality.

How can a man who is so good at what he does, remove himself so completely and clinically from the means of doing? He is a fascinating character who, the more one gets to know him, becomes even less easy to understand, although he is able to rationalise and to explain his outward attitude with comfortable logic. There is an innate and dignified arrogance of manner in Richards, but not a semblance of conceit. When he says 'You see, with due modesty, I've done it all apart from Test cricket which I can't play now. It doesn't mean that much to me any more. Playing every day is not really my scene for I find I can't motivate myself too well for county cricket,' it is nothing more than the truth.

It is almost as if he is puzzled by his own approach to the game. It slightly irritates him to be called the best batsman in the world. It is a title which gives him no great pleasure and, as it surely would with another person, it does not give him the stimulus each time he goes to the crease to make sure that it stays with him. He does not like to talk about individual innings and indeed doesn't really remember them for long. He will occasionally and rather grudgingly admit that an innings was 'quite a good knock'. He once said to me, 'Some days you know it basically won't work from the moment you wake up. I suppose it's all to do with temperament. It's like waking up with a negative attitude. I haven't got the dedication. I accept this one hundred per cent. The times I've thrown it away are unbelievable. Yes, I feel guilty at times. On an easy wicket I get to fifty and then start playing a few shots and get out. Why do I do a silly thing like that as I know there are bad wickets about where I'll never get fifty? I should cash in.'

I am sure some people will feel upset that a batsman who has been given such remarkable natural talents as Barry Richards should react to these gifts in such an impersonal matter-of-fact way, as if being born with such gifts automatically brings with it the responsibility of nurturing and looking after them. If he was a dedicated student of the game in the way that many lesser players are, I have no doubt that he would still be a wonderful player, that his batting average each year would be higher still. But that is not Barry's character and I think each man bats according to his character and that if Barry was not the man he is he would not be capable of providing thousands and thousands of people with such marvellous entertainment year after year. If he was for ever in the nets or dissecting some aspect of the game, he might not late-cut off his leg-stump any more and although his off-drive would still go for four, it would not give the watcher the same feeling of exuberance, it would not force him instinctively to turn speechless to his neighbour as if to say, 'Did you see that?'

All of this may point to Barry Richards being distant, maybe even a rather cold personality. This could hardly be less true. He is a man who walks alone more than some and he cannot be blamed for that. He has one of the friendliest smiles in cricket and I personally enjoy his company as much as anyone I know. He is an individualist both on and off the field and in an age of grey conformity one should be grateful for that. [*1977*]

*

Although English and Australian crowds have never seen Richards play Test cricket, the innings described by Henry Blofeld below was doubtless watched by more people than saw Trumper during the whole of his career.

*

Southampton, 18 July, 1976

For seventy-one minutes yesterday evening Barry Richards did exactly as he pleased with the Essex bowlers and, for what it is worth, Essex had begun the afternoon as leaders of both the Championship and the John Player League. He scored 101 off 24 overs and gave the impression that if he had been bothered he could have gone on for as long as he liked.

In the circumstances it seemed almost incidental that Hampshire went on to score 169 for three. This enabled them to beat Essex, who largely as a result of a good innings by Gooch had reached 168, by seven wickets, with five overs to spare.

Everyone has his own favourite innings to remember from Barry Richards. For me, the hundred scored against Leicestershire at Bournemouth in this competition at the end of last August, when he made no less a bowler than Ray Illingworth look stupid, was supreme – that is, until yesterday when this latest innings joined it in the same bracket.

Bradman once saw Richards score 300 in Australia and had no doubt that he himself had never played a finer innings. There can be no higher praise than that.

Going faithfully through his innings would be to catalogue an unending stream of wonderful strokes almost certainly without being able to give them that extra dimension which Richards bestowed upon each of them. One over of description should be enough.

East bowled the fifteenth over and Richards played his first ball to mid-wicket for two. He then pranced down the pitch and drove him through cover for four. He played the next ball off his toes to mid-wicket for four as if doing no more than shrugging his shoulders and then East bowled a half-volley wide of the off-stump which he late-cut very fine for four more. Never can a more daring or cheeky stroke have been played with such total certainty. While everyone was recovering from this he again sauntered down the pitch and drove past cover for four. They were moments of pure gold.

Later on he stepped away and late-cut Acfield from well wide of the leg-stump past slip for two, he lay back and drove Lever over deep square-cover for four, he drove Acfield over extra for six and pull-drove the next ball high into the stand in order to reach his hundred. The second fifty had come off 21 balls. He skied a catch to cover next ball leaving a fine crowd and a television audience limp with excitement, and with something to talk about for years to come.

Cricket's Last Romantic

A BROADCAST TRIBUTE TO NEVILLE CARDUS ON HIS 75TH BIRTHDAY, 2 APRIL, 1964

by Kenneth Gregory

In the whole of recent English literature there was nothing more remarkable than the cult which grew up during the inter-war years, the cult of Cardus. Parsons wondered whether they should take a text from Cardus, the pianist Schnabel enjoyed one of the early books without having the faintest understanding of cricket. Birkenhead saw Cardus as 'an enchanter', Barrie sought him out in front of the Tavern at Lord's. If to many professional cricketers Cardus was a suspect character who insisted on divining the spirit within their solid flesh, he was to himself the most fortunate of men – 'I have met Richard Strauss and Bradman,' as it were the two master scorers of the century. Today the essays of Neville Cardus are studied by teenagers for their GCE.

Perhaps before long he will be chosen by some graduate in search of a PhD thesis – say, 'The Relationship between the Chord of C major and Hammond's cover-drive in 1938.' So let us for a moment ponder on the Cardus background and sources of inspiration. He was educated not at a university but in the Manchester public library where he immersed himself in the novels of Dickens. He did not qualify for the Press-box by compiling a tedious innings for Oxbridge at Lord's, but after serving as assistant professional at Shrewsbury and occasional drama critic-cum-leader writer on the *Manchester Guardian* of C. P. Scott. Indeed, had it not been for illness, he would not have been sent to recuperate at Old Trafford. Cardus might never have written about cricket. When he did, he was as much at home in the world of the novelists, poets and philosophers as he was in his northern streets. Small wonder he saw cricket not only as a game but as an integral part of the English scene; the English scene, past and present, became irrevocably interwoven with the game's seasonal comedy. In short, Cardus dedicated himself to 'the entrancing art of changing raw experience into the connoisseur's enjoyment of life'. He determined to make his readers see life whole – cricket in terms of music, economics, H. M. Bateman, the Theory of Relativity and much else. That he succeeded was due in part to the passion and persuasiveness of his pen, but also to the nature of his fellow-countrymen. Distrusting the arts, the English found a substitute in cricket – a timeless blend of formal dancing, rhetoric and comic opera. If we allow, as Cardus contended, that cricket is an art form, then it must be permitted its high priest, one who will truly comprehend its mysteries, regard it with an indulgent affection and seek to perpetuate its golden hours. So Cardus was able to do for Spooner and Woolley what Lamb had done for Munden and Agate for the Millamant of the young Edith Evans; he arrested the transitoriness of their medium, fastened upon their manners and movements, and gave them to posterity. In case posterity should require that PhD thesis, I myself have started researching. After all, we should hate misconceptions to undermine the reputation of our author. Posterity might come across a reference to Fabian tactics, find the essay on Sidney Webb and look forward to a critical analysis of the leg-spin bowling of Bernard Shaw. To be honest, the leg-spin potential of Shaw was touched on by Cardus, but the Sidney Webb in question was a Lancastrian who skittled Surrey on 15 June, 1900, the Fabian tactics those of the Roman general who foiled Hannibal. Still, I trust I have shown the need for research, at least where the earlier books are concerned. The one with which Cardus voluntarily declared his innings eight years ago, *Close of Play*, I shall ignore, as its only non-cricketing allusion is to Australian girls who – while pretty – 'are lacking in charm'. This, I hasten to add, is another way of saying that Australian girls do not sound like Elisabeth Schumann, a lady Cardus revered as he did Mrs Wilkins Micawber. The Micawbers bring me to vintage Cardus – *Days in the Sun*, *The Summer Game*, *Good Days* and *Australian Summer* – to the books which, with the classic *Autobiography*, are his abiding legacy. Now, although there are in the Cardus canon only three references apiece to Sterne and Meredith and two to Hardy, the creations of Dickens are mentioned no fewer than eighteen times. The Micawbers, Mr Mantalini, Mr Pecksniff, Mr Chadband and Mrs Gamp were all brought in to emphasise the decline in the art of late-cutting, or whatever. Yet it is strange that although Bach and Edward German, Handel and Mozart, Rossini and Wagner – Strauss's *Til Eulenspiegel* when Bradman was batting – all entered the Press-box with Cardus, there was never a mention of Tchaikovsky. Still, the mind of cricket was adequately propped by Aristotle, Hobbes, Hume, Herbert Spencer and Dan Leno, also a philosopher of sorts. Dr Johnson and Mark Twain came and went, Max Beerbohm was proved never to have entered Lord's, Oscar Wilde was called upon to explain the bowling of Fleetwood-Smith in Adelaide, Lewis Carroll and Albert Einstein . . . But let me end this inventory on a sombre note. At forty-five Cardus introduced Karl Marx on the subject of congealed labour, at sixty he succumbed to Gertrude Stein. Perhaps he had not heard Miss Stein sing.

Probably not, for Cardus believed we must turn to old-fashioned music for mellowness and simple song, as to old-fashioned batsmanship for simple beauty. He was, to adapt Yeats, the last romantic who chose as theme traditional sanctity and loveliness. Looking back to the cricket that bewitched him in his boyhood – the cricket of MacLaren and Trumper, of Ranji, Fry and J. T. Tyldesley – he could readily fathom its secret: 'the age was simple, which was the beauty of it'. He could go further. 'There was an enjoyment of ordinary everyday activities and vistas not known now.' Such a judgement was not, of course, a moral one but a statement of fact. There are technological advances in cricket as in everything else, but they do not necessarily lead to a deeper aesthetic appreciation of the game. The cricket whose heyday caught the young Cardus at his most impressionable had arrived at a state of grace, it had yet to become bogged down in sophisticated detail. He summed up the essence of cricket, the satisfaction it affords to both the rudest and most tutored of onlookers thus: 'When all is said and done, our heroes of cricket are the creation of the faith which all happy boys live and die in.' But if, like many other great essayists, Cardus was at heart a romantic, he was also a journalist and therefore a realist. His realism was, however, less attuned to the spirit of his age than to his own discerning vision. Some time after World War II he could write of 'the amateur influence and the patronage of wealthy families, now impoverished, [which] enabled cricket to develop not only as a game but also as an art'. Compare that dispassionate statement with a recent comment by Mr Alan Ross: 'Cricket, like the upper classes and standards in general, is in permanent decline. No one would have it otherwise.' Do we detect whimsical resignation or defiance in that 'no one would have it otherwise'? Cardus, I fancy, would have responded differently; we know that we cannot have it otherwise, but we certainly would if we could. That was the realism of Cardus – northern, hard-headed, devoted to cobbled streets yet able to cherish aristocracy in all its forms. He could dote on the past, but moved with the times without relinquishing ideals. Yes, Cardus moved with the times. Consider perhaps the most famous of all his phrases – it dates from the mid-1920s – concerning the Trent Bridge wicket: 'a Lotos-land for batsmen, a place where it was always afternoon and 360 for two wickets'. Such a felicitous phrase that Cardus used it again a quarter of a century later. The Lotos-land, always afternoon, but now cricket reflected the Welfare State, so Cardus changed the score from 360 to 304 for two wickets. A great realist, say I, even in his subconscious.

And because he was a realist, he was a master of the relevant simile or metaphor. I emphasise this because it used to be argued by those who had not fallen beneath his spell that he over-wrote and dragged in erudite comparisons for the sake of sight or sound. Nothing was further from the truth. The apparent embroideries of the Cardus style were as essential as the figures on a scorecard. Listen to his tribute to a cavalier Australian batsman: 'Mitchell provided opportunities for hard hitting to McCabe whose tempo suddenly ran away with him as Sir Thomas Beecham's does in the last movement of the Jupiter symphony.' I have an old Beecham recording of this work, and can point out the precise moment Cardus had in mind when he wrote of McCabe's abandonment of strict Test Match counterpoint. If you complain of such writing, you are really in rebellion against C. P. Scott, who once said, 'Our readers must educate themselves up to us.'

Whether or not we educated ourselves up to Cardus, we most certainly agreed with J. L. Garvin that he was 'first in his subject'. But was his subject worth it? That depends on our acceptance of any essayist's subject. We accepted the Cardus vision without question, we had no alternative. In retrospect we may smile at some of his dicta which have become as archaic in their application as Hazlitt's description of Neate's guard in 'The Fight'. How quaint to read that 'the ball which breaks away is more difficult to play than the off-break, no matter how well the latter be bowled'. Yet the truth behind this has not been affected by Laker's skill but by the attitude and skill of the batsmen facing him. We recall what Macartney once did to Macaulay in a Test Match, we know what he would have tried to do to Laker; instinctively we agree with the Cardus dictum, for it has within it the seeds of poetic truth.

It was for his mastery of poetic truth that we reverenced Cardus. For us, he told tales of gods and heroes, of supermen like Tom Richardson who bowled 110 overs in the Manchester Test of 1896 and took thirteen Australian wickets. Richardson was the most Herculean of all fast bowlers, on this famous occasion he attacked for three hours, but to no avail.

> 'Australia won by three wickets, and the players ran from the field – all of them save Richardson. He stood at the bowling crease, dazed. Could the match have been lost? His spirit protested. Could it be that the gods had looked on and permitted so much painful striving to go by unrewarded? His body still shook from the violent motion. He stood there like some fine animal baffled at the uselessness of great strength and effort in this world . . . A companion led him to the pavilion, and there he fell wearily to a seat.'

How, you may ask, could a companion lead him from the field if Richardson was the only man left there? James Agate professed to know the answer. 'Cardus was seven at the time, but I was there. I recall that Richardson legged it from the field and downed three pints before anyone else could reach the pavilion.' No matter, we still insist that Cardus is a master of poetic truth, which is one reason why he is a classic author. He always wrote humanely, and never far from tears. He could be witty when he chose, but at the expense of his readers, not of the cricketers he loved so well.

At his best he was a supreme lover, for ever fastening his eyes on the beloved, re-acting and analysing, digesting, until for example he had fathomed the secret of Rhodes.

> 'Flight – the curving line, now higher, now lower, tempting, inimical; every ball like every other ball, yet somehow unlike; each over in collusion with the rest, part of a plot; every ball a decoy, a spy sent out to get the lie of the land; some balls simple, some complex, some easy, some difficult; and one of them – ah, which ? – the master ball.'

His green and salad days? Would they might have lasted while cricket continues to be played! Other writers may delight us, yet there is always the suspicion that one has outshone them all.

In paying this tribute, I appreciate I have caused some offence to Cardus. 'I remain to this day subject to occurrent fits of irritation,' he once wrote, 'whenever someone praises my writings on cricket, and then adds as though by an afterthought, a word of recognition of my music criticism.' Ah, the perverseness of the man! Of course he has opened our ears to Mahler's ninth symphony, to Bruckner and the songs of Hugo Wolf. But if he hadn't, we might have discovered their genius for ourselves. A single performance of Mahler by a Walter or Klemperer tells us more than all the books in the world. But without Cardus, the fleeting brilliance – fleeting, because impromptu – of a Trumper or MacLaren would be lost and beyond recall. As it is, I sometimes wonder if Cardus did not create Trumper as some ageless symbol of chivalry. *Wisden* proves, I suppose, that Trumper did exist; Cardus tells us how he existed. Only when writing of Trumper did Cardus fuse the romantic and the realist in his make-up. Trumper, he agreed, is not a name likely to guide anybody towards sweetness and light. But 'Trumper's Christian name was Victor; the poetry in "Victor" neutralised the (let us say) prose in "Trumper"; had Trumper been named Obadiah . . .' Most wondrous fusion of romantic and realist!

It is not fanciful to suggest that writing gloriously about cricket is as worthwhile as playing the game gloriously. What better conclusion to a birthday tribute can I think of than to quote Cardus himself. Substitute the appropriate geographical changes, believe that playing and writing can be synonymous, and here you have Cardus on 'Cricketer' of the *Manchester Guardian*.

> 'I see his long, happy life always with the West Country for a background, a far-off England now, peaceful and simple of heart. Morning after morning the summer's sun rose for him, and he went forth and trod fresh grass. Every springtime came and found him ready for cricket; when he was a boy he learned the game in a Gloucestershire orchard white with bloom. He grew in the sunshine and wind and rain; the elements became flesh within him.'

That was Cardus on Grace. And who is Cardus save the Grace of cricket writers?

*

Knighted in 1967 for services to music and cricket, Sir Neville Cardus died on 28 February, 1975, aged 85.

Cardus on Bradman

Leeds, 11 July, 1930

AUSTRALIA

First innings	
W. M. Woodfull (captain) b Hammond	50
A. A. Jackson c Larwood b Tate	1
D. G. Bradman not out	309
A. F. Kippax c Chapman b Tate	77
S. J. McCabe not out	12
B 1, lb 8	9
Total (three wickets)	458

To bat: V. Y. Richardson, E. L. a'Beckett, C. V. Grimmett, W. A. Oldfield, T. W. Wall, P. M. Hornibrook. Fall of wickets: 1–2, 2–194, 3–423.

England: J. B. Hobbs, H. Sutcliffe, W. R. Hammond, K. S. Duleepsinhji, M. Leyland, A. P. F. Chapman (captain), M. W. Tate, G. Geary, H. Larwood, G. Duckworth, R. Tyldesley.

Nature, they say, breaks the mould when she has made a masterpiece. It is not true: nor is it true that history repeats only her humdrum pages. Beauty changes her modes and aspects, but the substance, the ultimate vision, is the same. Nature is never tired of her good things: every year she repeats the miracle of the spring-time's rapture and the summer's fulfilment. Today in a game of cricket Nature has lived again in a bygone experience, lived it as though with greater intensity because the genius of it all had once before thrilled her sensibilities.

Four years ago on this very same field of Headingley the Australians began an innings disastrously: they lost the wicket of Bardsley for none, then Macartney came forth and scored a hundred before lunch. Today Australia lost Jackson with only two runs made: then Bradman before lunch made a hundred also. Woodfull, who was Macartney's good companion and audience, was Bradman's. But whereas Macartney gave a chance when he was only 2, Bradman sent no catch at all before lunch and was guilty of but a solitary mis-hit, when he was 35 and a high cut flashed yards wide of Chapman at backward point. But this great innings will best be appreciated if I let an account of it emerge from a plain narrative of the match and thus gain the significance of dramatic context.

The wicket was dead easy: at the outset it contained enough moisture to prevent Larwood from getting the ball to rise higher than half of the stumps. His first few balls satisfied me that with reasonable luck Australia would bat all day. But Jackson was out in Tate's first over: he played too soon at an in-swinger, the stroke of a cricketer who is out of form and terribly anxious to get going again. The ball was played straight into Larwood's hands at forward square-leg.

Woodfull soon drove Larwood straight for two – and whenever a fast bowler allows himself to be forced in front of the wicket during his first overs, and by a scrupulous batsman, then can we conclude as a matter of logic pure and simple that a cricketer so pugnacious as Bradman will most certainly take the hint and jump at the opportunity of scoring quick runs on a perfectly tame stretch of turf. Bradman immediately hit Tate hard and forward for four – an aggressive back shot. He knocked Larwood out of action almost contemptuously by plundering eleven runs in one over – an off-drive, a square hit in front of the umpire, a leg hit and a single. Bradman seemed a disappointed man when he scored only singles: it was as though he was saying to himself, 'Only a one – that means I've lost the bowling for a while, and I do so like it.' Geary as soon as he came on saw Bradman achieve a violent on-drive of that very same length which in county cricket is always most tenderly and solicitously caressed and regarded.

In three-quarters of an hour Bradman reached 51 of 62: he hit fours nearly every over and let us enjoy every stroke of the game save the leg glance. He cut Tate dazzlingly for four: as soon as Tyldesley went on Bradman jumped out of his ground and crashed two straight drives. Yet despite the rare pace of Bradman's batting it was eminently secure and sound. He has a marvellously quick eye for the ball that is at all short or overpitched: but, better still, he is as wonderfully quick to see a good ball. I have never before seen a batsman play at Bradman's pace and take so few risks. Shall I describe him as a forcing defensive batsman? The paradox is more apparent than real. Bradman treated all the bowlers alike – as grist to his busy mill. The speed of his strokes rendered even the outfields futile and immobile. Larwood, after bowling five overs at the day's beginning, did not attack again until ten minutes past one. It would be interesting to have the opinion of Walter Brearley on fast bowling so intermittent as this. Bradman immediately hit Larwood to the square-leg boundary off his legs: this is his most brilliant and drastic stroke: he makes it with his bat cracking sweet in the middle, and the velocity of it cannot be followed by many eyes, naked or bespectacled.

At ten minutes to one* Bradman attained his hundred, and so joined

* Cardus's watch was clearly on Manchester time: Bradman reached his century at seventeen minutes past one, i.e. after ninety-nine minutes' batting.

the immortal company of Victor Trumper and Macartney, the only cricketers who have yet scored centuries in Test Matches before lunch. Bradman's bat hammered perpetually: when he ever did stop scoring for a few balls it was as though he had merely run out of nails momentarily. Richard Tyldesley at one o'clock actually bowled a maiden over to Bradman: from internal and external evidence I concluded that it was one of the cleverest bits of bowling he has achieved in his hard-working career. At lunch Australia were 136 for one, and Bradman's innings was arbitrarily compelled for a while to stay its course.

Woodfull had by this time made 29 in two hours. He was as much a man to be noticed in conjunction with Bradman as Kreisler's conscientious accompanist. I can make no better compliment to Bradman – and give no clearer idea of his cricket – than to say that Woodfull of the two men seemed the more vulnerable and fallible. Yet Woodfull was at his stoutest and most watchful. I imagine the English bowlers were trying to get Woodfull out – leaving Bradman to Providence. Not often is an attack reduced to trying to get the stonewaller out while washing its hands of the brilliant player as a problem insoluble, and apparently everlastingly so. Think of it – a brilliant batsman with no edge to his bat and who never takes a risk. In this respect he is different from any other cricketer I have ever known; Macartney, Trumper and Johnny Tyldesley were always living dangerously on the verge of their resources; Bradman races along on firm feet, with shrewd eyes where he is going. Not once today, in spite of all his crashing thunder and brilliance, did he ever pay anything but respect to the really good ball. The difference between Bradman and the ordinarily good county batsman is that it takes a really good ball to keep Bradman's bat steady. This genius consists of quick feet, a sure eye, colossal confidence and strokes all round the wicket.

At four o'clock Bradman reached 200, after three hours and a half of cricket which for mingled rapidity and security is unparalleled in my experience. But when Bradman achieved his 200 the scoreboard read: Australia 268 for two. Has ever before a Test Match batsman made a proportion of runs so handsome as this? At 194 Woodfull was suddenly bowled, and a Yorkshireman near me said volumes when he cried out, 'Who'd a thowt it?' Woodfull tried to push a stroke to the on. He defended for two hours and fifty minutes; with Bradman he helped to make 192 in two hours and forty minutes; Bradman's share was 142.

Kippax did not look unconquerable when first he came in; Larwood beat him twice in an over. For a while Larwood seemed almost fast – that is, when Bradman was not playing him. In half an hour Kippax got two runs: then he drove Larwood straight for four, which was another taste of that encouragement which must always come to batsmen at the sight of a hard, forward hit from alleged bowling of speed. Richard Tyldesley did not bowl after lunch until a quarter to four: he had meanwhile been trying to perform the duties of an outfield manfully and perspiringly. Larwood also was to be observed during the day in the long field. Chapman did not appear to have any positive plan in mind: Bradman governed the situation entirely. His forcing shots from the back foot became more and more brilliant.

Kippax at last settled down, though with his score 24 he hit a ball perilously into the air near Tate at mid-on. The English fieldsmen wore hereabout a depressed and drooping air; they were men without hope, and Chapman's head hung low. Adversity measures a man and his leadership. It is true that the wicket gave the English bowlers absolutely no help; the trouble was that apart from Tyldesley nobody could present to the Australians problems of flight. The best bowling of Tate, Geary, Larwood and Hammond was an open book to Bradman; he revels in unambiguous speed and the attack direct. England had no 'googly' bowler they could look to for the ball of unexpected venom.

All summer it has been agreed by cricketers of judgement that slow spin was the answer to Bradman. Robins won the Test Match at Trent Bridge with the ball that bowled Bradman. Yet, in this game the Selection Committee have sent an England eleven into the field with less spin bowling in its ranks than we possessed at Lord's and Nottingham. Perhaps now, at long last, the Selection Committee will come to see the stark fact that Australian batsmen, Bradman especially, revel in the vastly overrated fast-medium new-ball bowlers of our credulous epoch. Bradman did not this afternoon pause to consider whether or not a new ball was being used; his only concern about the seam was apparently to flatten it at once.

The notable contribution of Bradman to English cricket this year is an exposure of mediocrity: he has done it by sound but fearless use of orthodox methods. The exposure is all the more complete because Bradman is not a magical Macartney; you can argue nothing from the arts of the inexplicable masters. It has been maintained by some of us for years that the contemporary fraud of the spinless medium-paced bowler would be shown up the first day there was a finely tempered return to batsmanship which played the good ball shrewdly and smote the bad ones with a bat free and with the feet active.

At six o'clock, after slightly under five and a half hours' play, Australia, for the second match in succession, reached the aggregate of 400 for two wickets. Amidst multitudinous cheers Bradman beat the record for the highest innings by any Test Match batsman: it was good that Foster's score had been passed not by a stonewaller hoarding up runs covetously, but by a true son of the game. Bradman arrived at 288 in five hours and a half out of a grand Australian total of 414: no chance to hand had he given and not more than three strokes had he shown which told us that it is human to err. At 423 Kippax's suave innings was ended by a catch of Chapman from a slash cut: the third wicket made 229 in two and three-quarter hours. Just before the close of play and after McCabe had twice cracked strokes to the deep field Bradman's score rounded 300. From the last ball of the day, by a superb drive through the covers, a stroke handsome enough for any batsman who has ever done honour to cricket, he hit his 42nd boundary. That was the royal way to finish a day which Australia will not forget as long as the game is played and loved there.

*

Next day Bradman was caught at the wicket by Duckworth off Tate for 334 after batting for six hours twenty-three minutes (an average of 52 runs an hour) and hitting 46 fours. He received 436 balls.

Cardus found the innings the most remarkable he had ever seen for mingled solidity and brilliance.

> 'Steel, not sensibility, is the stuff of his batsmanship, which really is all substance with little of that volatility of human pulse which no power of reason can perpetually control. The animal spirits in Bradman are never likely to go mad. He is a purist in a hurry: he administers the orthodox in loud and apostolic knocks.'

Four years later the 'animal spirits' did go mad from time to time: at the Oval against England, at Folkestone when he scored 149 not out (at 85 an hour) off Jehangir Khan, M. J. C. Allom, Hammond, Woolley and Freeman, and at Scarborough 132 (at 88 an hour) off M. S. Nichols, K. Farnes, W. E. Bowes, L. F. Townsend and H. Verity.

The 1930 Leeds Test was drawn.

Australia 566 (Tate five for 124); England 391 (Hammond 113; Grimmett five for 135) and 95 for three.

VALE

They vanish, these immortal players, and we suddenly realise with astonishment that years have passed since we heard a passing mention of some of them. At one point they seem as much a part of the permanent scheme of things as the sun which glows upon their familiar faces and attitudes and the grass which makes the background for their portrait; and then, bless us, it is time for even them to go.

Edmund Blunden

Sources

All extracts by Dudley Carew are from *To the Wicket*, Chapman & Hall.

Page

17 Alistair Cooke: Letter from America, BBC, 25 December 1971
19 R. H. Lyttelton; *Giants of the Game*, Ward Lock
21 Frederick Gale: private letter
28 H. S. Altham: *History of Cricket*, Allen & Unwin
34 C. B. Fry: *Wisden* 1901
(Stephen Fry)
36 H. S. Altham: *History of Cricket*, Allen & Unwin
42 R. H. Lyttelton: *Badminton Book of Cricket*, Longmans
47 A. G. Moyes: *Australian Cricket*, Angus and Robertson
48 Ralph Barker: *Ten Great Bowlers*, Chatto & Windus
51 R. G. Barlow: *Forty Seasons of First-Class Cricket*, John Heywood
52 A. G. Moyes: *A Century of Cricketers*, Harrap
55 M. A. Noble: *The Game's the Thing*, Cassell
60 Conan Doyle: *Punch*
(Jonathan Clowes Ltd)
62 C. B. Fry: *Giants of the Game*, Ward Lock
64 Philip Trevor: *Cricket and Cricketers*, Chapman & Hall
67 ed. G. L. Jessop: *Cricket*, C. Arthur Pearson
68 C. B. Fry: *Giants of the Game*, Ward Lock
70 D. L. A. Jephson: *Wisden* 1901
74 A. E. Knight: *The Complete Cricketer*, Methuen
76 Jack Fingleton: *Masters of Cricket*, Heinemann
77 R. C. Robertson-Glasgow: *Crusoe on Cricket*, Alan Ross
80 C. B. Fry, K. S. Ranjitsinhji: *Giants of the Game*, Ward Lock
82 C. B. Fry: *C. B. Fry's Magazine*
(Stephen Fry)
85 Gerald Brodribb: *Hit for Six*, Heinemann
88 Philip Trevor: *The Lighter Side of Cricket*, Methuen
89 A. G. Moyes: *A Century of Cricketers*, Harrap
92 A. A. Thomson: *Cricket My Pleasure*, Museum Press
(Pitman Publishing Ltd)
96 C. B. Fry: *Daily Express*
(Stephen Fry)
101 Based on an advertisement in *Wisden* 1903
103 R. E. Foster: from *Wisden* 1908
106 R. E. Foster: from *Wisden*, 1908
109 Neville Cardus: *Manchester Guardian*
(Miss Margaret Hughes)
113 Bernard Hollowood: *Cricket on the Brain*, Eyre & Spottiswoode
116 Jack Fingleton: *Masters of Cricket*, Heinemann
119 Chris Greyvenstein: *Masters of South African Cricket*, Don Nelson Publisher, Cape Town
127 R. C. Robertson-Glasgow: *Crusoe on Cricket*, Alan Ross
129 Ian Peebles: *Frank Woolley, Pride of Kent*, The Cricketer/Hutchinson
132 Oliver Warner: *Frank Woolley*, Phoenix House
134 R. C. Robertson-Glasgow: *Crusoe on Cricket*, Alan Ross
135 J. M. Kilburn: *In Search of Cricket*, Arthur Barker

Page
139 John Marchant: *The Greatest Test Match*, Faber
149 Neville Cardus: *Manchester Guardian*
(Miss Margaret Hughes)
153 John Arlott: *Portrait of Maurice Tate*, Phoenix House
157 R. C. Robertson-Glasgow: *46 Not Out*, Hollis & Carter
158 Ray Robinson: *Between Wickets*, Collins
161 R. C. Robertson-Glasgow: *46 Not Out*, Hollis & Carter
169 Ray Robinson: *From the Boundary*, Collins
174 Jack Fingleton: *Masters of Cricket*, Heinemann
178 Ray Robinson: *Between Wickets*, Collins
182 R. C. Robertson-Glasgow: *Cricket Prints*, T. Werner Laurie
184 J. M. Kilburn: *Cricket Decade*, Heinemann
186 Ronald Mason: *Walter Hammond*, Hollis & Carter
190 Jack Fingleton: *Cricket Crisis*, Cassell
192 Denzil Batchelor: *The Match I Remember*, T. Werner Laurie
194 Ralph Barker: *Ten Great Bowlers*, Chatto & Windus
197 Ian Peebles: *Talking of Cricket*, Museum Press
(Pitman Publishing Ltd)
200 C. L. R. James: *Beyond a Boundary*, Hutchinson
207 H. S. Altham: *The Heart of Cricket*, The Cricketer/Hutchinson
211 Bill Bowes: *Great Bowlers*, Pelham
213 Jack Fingleton: *Cricket Crisis*, Cassell
216 Jack Fingleton: *Cricket Crisis*, Cassell
218 Denzil Batchelor: *Days without Sunset*, Eyre & Spottiswoode
222 C. L. R. James: *Beyond a Boundary*, Hutchinson, and *Cricket: the Great Ones*, Pelham
226 Jack Fingleton: *Cricket Crisis*, Cassell
233 E. W. Swanton: *Wisden* 1946
238 Alan Ross: *Cape Summer*, Hamish Hamilton
240 Edmund Blunden: *Cricket Country*, Collins
242, 244, 247, Denys Rowbotham: *Manchester Guardian*
250 R. C. Robertson-Glasgow: *Men Only in Sport*, C. Arthur Pearson
(The Hamlyn Publishing Group Ltd)
253 E. W. Swanton: *Denis Compton*, Playfair Books
257 Ray Robinson: *From the Boundary*, Collins
260 R. C. Robertson-Glasgow: *46 Not Out*, Hollis & Carter
261 John Woodcock: *Great Bowlers*, Pelham
263 Jack Fingleton: *The Ashes Crown the Year*, Collins
268 Denys Rowbotham: *Manchester Guardian*
272 John Arlott: *The Echoing Green*, Longmans
274 J. M. Kilburn: *Cricket Decade*, Heinemann
278 Alan Ross: *Cape Summer*, Hamish Hamilton
283 Alistair Cooke: *Manchester Guardian*
287 Frank Tyson: *Great Bowlers*, Pelham
289 Denys Rowbotham: *Manchester Guardian*
291 Alan Ross: 'Watching Benaud Bowl', *Australia 63*, Eyre & Spottiswoode
292 Kenneth Gregory: *Punch*
295 C. L. R. James: *Great Captains*, Pelham
299 Jack Fingleton: *The Greatest Test of All*, Collins
305 Trevor Bailey, *Sir Gary*, Collins
308 C. L. R. James: *The Great All-Rounder*, Pelham
310 E. W. Swanton: *A Sort of Cricket Person*, Collins
312 Henry Blofeld: *Hampshire Handbook 1977*
314 Henry Blofeld: *The Guardian*
316 Kenneth Gregory: BBC Home Service
322 Neville Cardus: *Manchester Guardian*
(Miss Margaret Hughes)
327 Edmund Blunden: *Cricket Country*, Collins

The Editor and publishers wish to thank all those who have given permission to reproduce copyright material. In cases where the copyright owner is other than the author or publisher of a given title, the copyright owner appears in parenthesis on the following line.

While the greatest care has been taken in securing the necessary permission to include extracts from copyright works the publishers offer their apologies in any possible case of accidental infringement.

Index of Authors

General Index

The Masters appear in capitals